PUNISHING A NATION

Human Rights Violations During The Palestinian Uprising December 1987–December 1988

PUNISHING A NATION

Human Rights Violations During
The Palestinian Uprising
December 1987–December 1988

a report prepared by

**Al-Haq
Law in the Service of Man**

South End Press   **Boston, MA**

Dedication

*to Zahi Jaradat, Ghazi Shashtari, Iyad al-Haddad,
Sha'wan Jabarin and 'Abd-al-Karim Kana'an*

our fieldworkers who have been under administrative
detention, without charge or trial, for most of the period
covered by this report.

Without the courage and dedication of human rights monitors
in the field, reports like this cannot be written.

and to Riziq Shuqair

who has been with al-Haq since 1984, in acknowledgement
of his deep commitment to human rights.

First released in December 1988 and printed by South End Press in 1990, this report, like all other al-Haq publications, is a public document. Al-Haq does not claim copyright privileges, and the information herein may be quoted or reproduced, provided the content is not altered in any way. Al-Haq does ask to be properly acknowledged, and to be informed of the intent to reproduce entire chapters.

Cover illustration by Wen-ti Tsen
Text design and production by Sheila Walsh and South End Press
Manufactured in the U.S.A. on recycled, acid-free paper

Library of Congress Cataloging in Publication Data
Punishing a nation.
    Includes bibliographical references.
    1. West Bank--History--Palestinian Uprising, 1987-   . 2. Human rights--West Bank. 3. Gaza Strip--History--Palestinian Uprising, 1987-   . 4. Human rights--Gaza Strip. I. Law in the Service of Man (Organization: Ram Allah)
DS 110.W47P86   1989   323.1'1927405694   89-21986
ISBN 0-89608-379-9
ISBN 0-89608-378-0 (pbk.)

South End Press, 116 Saint Botolph Street, Boston, MA 02115

99 98 97 96 95 94 93 92 91 90   1 2 3 4 5 6 7 8 9 10

CONTENTS

Preface ix
Introduction xi

PART I: USE OF FORCE

Chapter 1: Use of Physical Force by the Israeli Defence Forces   3
  A. Statistics on Deaths and Casualties
  B. The Use of Force in Response to Demonstrations
      1. Live Ammunition
      2. Plastic Bullets
      3. Comment
  C. The Aggressive Use of Force
      1. A Policy of Beating
      2. The Practice of Beatings
      3. Army Brutality: Use of Rubber Bullets
      4. The Use of Tear Gas as a Means of Terrorisation
      5. Harassment and Destruction of Property
      6. Army Raids on Villages and Refugee Camps
      7. Other Forms of Brutality
      8. Death Squads
  D. Investigations
  E. Conclusion
Footnotes to Chapter 1   39
Appendices to Chapter 1   45

Chapter 2: Obstruction of Medical Treatment   59
  A. Introduction
  B. Prior Practice
  C. Legal Issues
      1. Obstruction of Health Care
      2. The Denial of Medical Services
          to Populations Under Prolonged Curfew
      3. Attacks on Medical Personnel in the Field
      4. Military Raids on Hospitals
      5. Medical Treatment in Prisons
          and Detention Centres
      6. The Adoption of Measures which Decrease
          the Quality and Availability of Health Care

    D. Israeli Justification
    E. Conclusion
Footnotes to Chapter 2   77
Appendices to Chapter 2   80

Chapter 3: Settler Provocation and the Use of   98
Excessive Force
    A. Introduction
    B. The Policy of Settlement: 1967 to the Present
        1. Cooperation Between Settlers and Soldiers
        2. The Legal System: Investigation,
           Prosecution, and Sentencing
    C. Settler Provocation and the Use of Excessive Force
        1. Provocation by Settlers
        2. Settlers' Use of Force
    D. Conclusion
Footnotes to Chapter 3   111
Appendices to Chapter 3   115

PART II: ADMINISTRATIVE AND OTHER MEASURES

Chapter 4: Administrative Methods of Punishment   123
    A. Introduction
    B. Deportation
        1. The Israeli Justification
        2. Deportations in International Law
    C. Administrative Detention
        1. The Israeli Justification
        2. Recent Changes in Administrative
           Detention Procedures
        3.The Use of Administrative Detention
           During the Uprising
        4. Administrative Detention in International Law
    D. House Demolition
        1. Past Use of the Measure
        2. House Demolition During the Uprising
        3. Legal Arguments
        4. Conclusion: Demolitions
Footnotes to Chapter 4   140
Appendices to Chapter 4   142

Chapter 5: Curfews and Other Forms of Isolation   154
   A. Curfews
      1. Curfews in International Law
      2. State Practice
      3. Israel's Use of Curfews in
          the Occupied Territories: 1967-1987
      4. The Policy of Curfews Since 9 December 1987
   B. Closures
   C. Other Forms of Isolation
   D. Restrictions on the Press
   E. Harassment of Human Rights Monitors
Footnotes to Chapter 5   183
Appendices to Chapter 5   188

Chapter 6: The Administration of Justice   200
   A. Introduction
   B. The Administration of Justice
      1. Arrest: A Policy of Punishment and Repression
      2. Interrogation
      3. Trial
   C. The Penal System
      1. Estimated Number of Detainees
          During the Uprising
      2. Conventional and Military Centres of Detention
          in the Occupied Territories and Israel
      3. Conditions in Detention Centres
      4. Deaths in Detention and Autopsies
      5. Detention of Palestinian Women
   D. Conclusion
Footnotes to Chapter 6   227
Appendices to Chapter 6   229

PART III: REPRESSION OF PALESTINIAN INFRASTRUCTURE

Chapter 7: Economic Sanctions   241
   A. Historical Background
   B. Economic Measures Against Commerce and Traders
   C. An Economic "War of Attrition":
         Restrictions on Money, Bans on Fuel, Water
         and Electricity, and Destruction of Property
   D. The Forced Payment of Taxes
   E. Punitive Measures Against the Agricultural Sector

Footnotes to Chapter 7 259
Appendices to Chapter 7 261

Chapter 8: Repression of Education **264**
   A. Introduction
   B. Israeli Justifications for Limiting
      Academic Activity
   C. Closure of Educational Institutions
   D. Suppression of Alternative Education
   E. The Effects of the Closure
      of Educational Institutions
   F. Military Raids on Educational Institutions
   G. Military Occupation of Schools
      and Destruction of School Property
   H. Legal Analysis
      1. The Illegality of the Use of Schools
         as Temporary Military Posts
         and of Military Raids on Schools
      2. The Closing of Schools Violates Both
         Local and International Laws
         in Force in the West Bank
   I. Conclusion
Footnotes to Chapter 8 276
Appendices to Chapter 8 279

Chapter 9: Repression of Organisational Activity **283**
   A. Background
   B. Repression of the Labour Movement
   C. Repression of Other Institutions
   D. Banning of Popular Organisations
   E. Rights Violated
Footnotes to Chapter 9 292
Appendices to Chapter 9 293

Conclusion **297**

PREFACE

Punishing A Nation is the result of the collective effort of the al-Haq staff. It began with the documentation of human rights violations, collected by a team of fieldworkers distributed geographically throughout the West Bank. Researchers analysed this information as well as other public sources and documents in the light of international and local law and, aided by al-Haq's support staff, produced this report.

Punishing A Nation is a comprehensive view of the critical status of Palestinian human rights engendered by the Israeli reaction to the uprising that began in December 1987. The report covers the range of human rights violations from December 1987 until December 1988, and focusses on the most widespread and serious of those violations. It does not attempt to be exhaustive in detail; rather, it uses representative examples to illustrate its findings.

Al-Haq does not, to date, have fieldworkers in the Gaza Strip. However, because human rights violations in Gaza are even worse than those in the West Bank, documentation which could be confirmed without actual fieldwork is included in this report. Of course, the applicability of international law to the Israeli occupation of Gaza is the same.

This report is based primarily on our own documentation, which consists of (1) sworn affidavits taken from victims or eye-witnesses, (2) questionnaires on recurring practices like house demolitions, and (3) reports on particular events written by our fieldworkers in those cases where they were unable to obtain sworn statements. In collecting affidavits, al-Haq regards hearsay evidence as inadmissible. Affiants are encouraged to make their names available for publication; they often refuse to do so, however, fearing reprisal.

In documenting human rights violations this past year, al-Haq has faced two very serious handicaps: the dramatic increase in the number and scope of violations, and the administrative detention of four out of our five experienced fieldworkers. Al-Haq had to quickly locate, hire and train additional fieldworkers in our attempt to maintain a level of documentation commensurate with the violations, as well as our usual standards of accuracy.

Any report such as this stands on the documentation provided by field monitors. The documentation of human rights violations is a difficult and sometimes dangerous task. This is why we dedicate *Punishing A Nation* to our fieldworkers in detention. It is al-Haq's view that they are being punished precisely for their dedication to human rights, and it is our hope that this report is worthy of their sacrifice.

INTRODUCTION

This is al-Haq's first annual report which, by force of circumstance, has developed into a report covering the first year of what has come to be known as the Palestinian uprising (Arabic: *intifada*).

The need for an annual report had become increasingly apparent to us after more than 20 years of military occupation of the West Bank and Gaza Strip. The range and severity of Israel's human rights violations in the Occupied Territories necessitated a comprehensive report that documents the predominant patterns of violations in detail, and analyses them in light of both local and international law. The popular uprising which began on 9 December 1987 served to make the need for such a report more urgent.

The nature of the Palestinian uprising, the reasons behind it and the Israeli reaction to it can only be understood in the context of the preceding twenty years of military occupation. As al-Haq and other human rights organisations have tried to show in the past, many of Israel's practices as an occupying power in the West Bank and Gaza constitute clear and flagrant violations of international law, as enshrined in conventions governing belligerent occupations as well as international human rights instruments. In direct contravention of Article 43 of the 1907 Hague Regulations, Israel has endeavoured during the past two decades to alter completely the character of the Territories under its rule.

During the twenty years of occupation, perhaps the most patently illegal and most serious of abuses has been the progressive alienation of Palestinian land and the settling of part of Israel's own civilian population on this land. To facilitate the process of settlement, local laws have been thoroughly altered, as has the administrative structure which the Israeli authorities inherited from their Jordanian and Egyptian predecessors. The settlements are inhabited by Israeli citizens who carry weapons as a matter of course, and have used them against the indigenous population in a large number of documented cases. Legal recourse through the submission of complaints has been severely limited by a lack of proper procedure and the absence of concrete results (e.g. in the High Court), in addition to widespread intimidation and harassment on the part of enforcement agencies such as the police.

The military authorities have also built an elaborate structure of military legislation, amending existing local laws beyond recognition. Over 1,250 military orders are currently in force in the West Bank, and over 900 in Gaza. This new legislation has given sweeping powers to the military, affecting all aspects of the life of the local population, including the economy, culture, and so forth, reaching such detail even as to prohibit the growing of tomatoes or the picking of wild thyme. Permission has to be obtained for a large number of regular, daily activities. For example, the importation, publication, distribution or possession of any printed material is prohibited unless a permit specifying the material has been applied for and received from the Civil Administration. The authority to grant or withhold permits is a powerful tool in the hands of the military, which regularly withholds building permits, family reunification permits, travel documents, drivers' licences and other such documents necessary to the daily life of the population, usually without stating the reasons.

The gradual take-over of the land, in addition to efforts to stifle the Palestinian economy and change the legal and administrative infrastructure, reflect a political agenda that differs widely from Israel's rights and obligations under international law. Palestinians have resisted this transformation, because in addition to being clearly illegal, it negated their basic right to stay and live freely in their own land. Israel's attempt to prejudice the status of the Territories while stifling the lives of the inhabitants—in addition to the inevitable resistance this has elicited— has required a large number of measures designed to keep the population under control.

Al-Haq has documented a gamut of human rights abuses resulting from such measures since it was established in 1979. These include: the expulsion of Palestinian residents of the Territories from their homeland, the demolition and sealing of houses and other collective punishments and reprisals, mass arrests, administrative detention and other restriction orders, censorship, closures of organisations, maltreatment and torture in prisons, and so forth. The totality of these violations have led Palestinians to conclude that the occupation has been anything but the "benevolent" one the Israeli authorities so often make it out to be. (This assertion was made most recently in a report on conditions in "Judea and Samaria" and the Gaza Strip, published by the Israeli Civil Administration on the occasion of the twentieth year of occupation).

Given this situation, coupled with the lack of any means for Palestinians to express themselves without being accused of "security" offences, the popular uprising by the Palestinians in the Occupied Territories should have come as a surprise to no one. The uprising has primarily been an act of collective anger, a reaction to twenty years of expropriation, disenfranchisement, oppression and frustration. In light of the continued failure on the part of the international community to protect the population living under occupation and to safeguard its rights, it also reflects a loss of confidence in the political will and ability of other states to carry out their responsibilities under international law. In that sense, the uprising has also been, in the final analysis, a collective attempt by Palestinians to protect themselves against the predatory behaviour of the Israeli state.

Significantly, the uprising has been, in its predominant characteristics, a popular attempt at disengaging from the administrative structures set up by the occupying power, structures that have served exclusively the occupier's own interests. People from all walks of life have been involved in the uprising, participating in collective acts of civil disobedience, including strikes, a tax revolt and a boycott of Israeli-made products, in addition to the mass demonstrations that have been so widely screened by television networks the world over. Demonstrations have been marked primarily by Palestinians raising flags, burning tires and throwing stones and, recently with increasing frequency, molotov cocktails.

The Israeli response to the uprising can be summarised in a few words: more of the same, but much more. Few of the repressive measures undertaken by the military authorities since December 1987 were without precedent. These include beatings, opening fire at unarmed demonstrators, mass arrests, extra-judicial punishments like deportations, administrative detentions and house demolitions, collective sanctions like prolonged curfews, and other punishments which had been routinely meted out to the occupied population throughout the length of the occupation. A constant feature before and during the uprising has been the sheer disproportionality in the Israeli response to the perceived offence, be it participating in a demonstration, writing a slogan on a wall, or running a trade union. In short, the main patterns prevalent since 1967 have been consistently maintained during the past year.

What has changed, however, is the scale of repression. This has come to involve a larger number of people in more locations in a shorter span of time, and with much greater intensity. This report concentrates on these changes. In addition, one important trend has developed: whereas in the past the authorities were reluctant to admit to abuses, let alone condone them in public, and would at most seek to rationalise them, the exposure given world-wide to Israel's reaction to the uprising has forced the authorities to go on record defending particular policies which even the most casual observer could understand as blatantly illegal. Thus, Minister of Defence Yitzhak Rabin proudly presented a policy of "might, force and beatings" in January, in clear violation of both international *and* Israeli law; and in September he declared that inflicting more casualties was "precisely our aim." Prime Minister Yitzhak Shamir added helpfully, in March 1988, that "the means are insignificant, the main thing is the goal."

This being the case, the task of al-Haq as a human rights organisation has also changed. No longer do we need to document human rights violations in order to prove to our audience that they do in fact take place, as was the case prior to December 1987. The authorities' acknowledgment, and even free endorsement, of some of the more severe practices has rendered the task of evidencing violations redundant. Rather, while we continue to document human rights violations as thoroughly as we have in the past (despite the enormous increase in work and the detention of a number of our field workers), our purpose now, as reflected in this report, has become to indicate the scope of the practices that occur. This should help our audience in assessing the significance and implications of Israel's violations of human rights and international law.

The violations delineated in the following report have been measured in light of both local laws and international laws and conventions relevant to belligerent occupation. The emphasis, however, has been on the presentation of the facts, as documented by al-Haq's fieldwork staff over the course of a year.

This report is divided in three sections, detailing the three principal categories of Israel's response to the Palestinian uprising: the military response, the administrative response and the attack on the Territories' institutional and economic infrastructure. In Part I, the use of physical force is discussed, focusing on the Israeli army's guidelines and practices of beating, opening fire and using tear gas (Chapter 1); obstruction of medical treatment (Chapter 2); and provocations and violence by Israeli settlers (Chapter 3).

In Part II, Israel's administrative response to the uprising is addressed, focusing on extra-judicial punishments such as deportations, administrative detentions and house demolitions (Chapter 4); curfews, blockades and other forms of isolation, as well as measures taken against the press and human rights monitors (Chapter 5); and mass arrests, interrogation, trials and detention (Chapter 6).

Finally, in Part III, we discuss Israel's attack on the Palestinian infrastructure in the Occupied Territories, focusing on punishments of an economic nature (Chapter 7); repression of education (Chapter 8); and repression of various forms of organisational activity, including the closure of institutions (Chapter 9).

Footnotes follow at the end of each chapter. Where necessary, relevant documents (affidavits, case studies, and so forth have been appended at the end of each chapter following the footnotes. Readers should note, however, that invariably more documentation is available on the violations described in the report which has been excluded due to limitations of space only. This documentation is available at al-Haq's offices in Ramallah.

Ramallah, December 1988

Part I
USE OF FORCE

Chapter 1

USE OF PHYSICAL FORCE BY THE ISRAELI DEFENCE FORCES

> Our decision to increase the level of forces in the territories was out of concern over the number of casualties being caused.

These were the words of Israel's Defence Minister Yitzhak Rabin in an interview with the *Jerusalem Post* on 25 December 1987 when the Palestinian uprising had barely entered its third week. Thinking perhaps that there is safety in numbers, Rabin claimed that smaller forces, when caught in a confrontation with demonstrators, were "more prone to react with lethal means" than larger numbers of soldiers.

Not surprisingly, however, Israel's unprecedented troop deployment in the Occupied Territories during the past year has failed to bring greater safety to the population. On the contrary, casualty figures at the end of the first year of the uprising suggest that Israel's massive show of force has multiplied the numbers of wounded and dead. Al-Haq's estimate, based on its own documentation and other public sources, is that slightly over 400 Palestinians were killed in the span of one year, while over 20,000 had been injured.[1] (See Section A below)

When confronted with the high and still-rising casualty figures, Israeli officials have stated that their objective is to crush the uprising while keeping the numbers wounded and killed to a minimum.[2] That they have signally failed to achieve this objective is clear. Twelve months on, the uprising continues and the number of casualties continues to climb.[3] In late September 1988, Rabin no longer showed the "concern over the number of casualties" which he had professed the previous December: "This," he said, in reference to the human toll exacted by the use of plastic bullets, "is precisely our aim."[4]

The official Israeli explanation of the number of casualties needs to be considered from two aspects:

(1) what the Israeli authorities would term "riot control," where the use of force by the Israeli armed forces occurs in the context of and in direct response to demonstrations by Palestinians;

(2) the unprovoked and aggressive use of force in the absence of any immediate confrontation with Palestinians.

An objective analysis of the first aspect requires that "riot control" be seen in its proper context. Active protests by the Palestinian population have formed an integral part of the uprising. Typically, such actions will take the form of a demonstration with a march or procession accompanied by chanting, raising the Palestinian flag, erecting barricades of rocks and overturned municipal dustbins in the middle of the road, burning tires and, once the army arrives on the scene, stone throwing. Many of those involved in such actions are teenagers. Not a single Israeli soldier has been killed in the first year of the uprising during the course of what the authorities refer to as "riot control."

In the second type of incident, violence is carried out by the armed forces in the absence of any active protests by the Palestinian population. Such incidents, including deaths and many casualties documented by al-Haq, have occurred during raids on isolated villages or refugee camps, in schools or in hospitals, or when the victim had already been arrested or was otherwise under the immediate control of the army.

The Israeli authorities have repeatedly stated the importance of adhering to the rule of law, and have stressed that criteria exist for the use of force, criteria which soldiers are obliged to follow at the risk of being disciplined or court-martialled if they fail to do so. Occasions where the Israeli authorities have conceded that excessive force was used are described by them as exceptions to the rule. As recently as 30 November 1988, the Military Commander of the Southern Area (which includes the entire Gaza Strip), Yitzhak Mordechai, was quoted as saying in the *Jerusalem Post* in reference to continued reports of army brutality that the reported incidents "should be seen as aberrations."[5]

The positions taken by the Israeli authorities give rise to a number of questions: (1) What are the Israeli rules on the use of force? (2) Are these rules compatible with international legal provisions on the use of force? (3) Can the claim of "exceptions to the rule" be substantiated in light of the facts?

The purpose of this chapter is to discuss these questions on the basis of the available evidence. In Section A, we present our estimates of the latest casualty figures. Section B uses representative examples of incidents documented by al-Haq to review the use of force by the Israeli army in response to demonstrations. This includes the use of live ammunition and plastic bullets. Attention will be focussed on the legitimacy of the response, that is, whether it was proportional, necessary and in accordance with army guidelines.

In Section C, we address the use of aggressive force by the Israeli army, i.e. violence perpetrated to intimidate and deter the Palestinian population in the absence of any active protest on its part. We particularly examine the actual circumstances in which the incidents occurred. Specifically, the beatings policy will be highlighted in this section, as well as the misuse of rubber bullets and tear gas, army raids and sieges on population centres, and the deployment of special squads which target perceived leaders of demonstrations.

Finally, in Section D, we review the existing complaints procedures in order to determine to what extent, if any, the population in the Occupied Territories can have recourse to the law in the face of abuses perpetrated by Israeli army personnel or settlers.

A. Statistics on Deaths and Casualties

In the West Bank alone al-Haq has documented 204 Palestinians killed between 9 December 1987 and 15 November 1988. This is a conservative figure, reflecting the difficulties al-Haq fieldworkers have faced in covering the range of human rights abuses in the area.[6] Of these deaths, 185 occurred in the course of Israeli army action, while 14 were caused by settlers (see Chapter 3 below). We have no definite information about the identity of those who caused the death of the remaining 5. In addition, we have documentation on another 39 deaths which occurred in the context of the uprising but where the direct causes of death were, for example, a heart attack, or "fear" (the latter being the cause of death written on one death certificate seen by al-Haq). We have excluded this last category from the statistical analysis. From our information, we estimate the total number of Palestinians killed in the West Bank as a result of the uprising to be 269, as of 24 November.

Of the 204 documented deaths, 189 were men and 15 were women; 127 were between the ages of 16 and 25, and 6 were aged 5 or under. The figures for causes of death are as follows:

Live ammunition:	180
Tear gas:	14
Blunt instrument:	4
Beating:	3
Plastic bullets:	1
Sharp instrument:	1
Undefined:	1
Total:	204

For a number of reasons, no reliable figures for the number of wounded exist. Firstly, there are obvious practical difficulties in obtaining statistics from all governmental, private and United Nations Relief and Works Agency for Palestine Refugees (UNRWA) run hospitals and clinics in the West Bank. Secondly, many people are afraid to seek treatment through official channels because of fear of arrest and interrogation, and therefore seek medical care from local doctors or grassroots medical committees. (See Chapter 2 on the "Obstruction of Medical Treatment" for a full discussion of this problem.) Thus comprehensive documentation is impossible. And lastly, it is difficult to obtain accurate information about those who have been taken to hospitals in Israel for "security" or other reasons. This means that even if accurate figures concerning those hospitalised or seeking medical treatment through "official" channels could be obtained, it would undoubtedly be only a fraction of the total figure.

The figures presented by the Israeli authorities on different occasions are clear underestimates and, in addition, often contradict each other. For instance, on 8 October 1988, Defence Minister Rabin stated at a rally in Beersheba that 7,000 Palestinians had been wounded since the start of the uprising.[7] But only six weeks later, the *Jerusalem Post* (28 November) quoted official Israeli sources as claiming that a total of only 3,503 Palestinians had been injured, thereby reducing the earlier figure by a full 50 percent.

Additional attempts, which are independent and therefore more reliable, have been made to provide at least a partial estimate of casualties, from which a total could then be extrapolated. According to a report commissioned by MK Dedi Zucker and written by six Israeli doctors in June 1988, 5,133 people had been hospitalised (as opposed to wounded) from the start of the uprising until the end of April 1988. According to recent figures from a regular summary by the UNRWA, between 9 December 1987 and 30 September 1988, in the Gaza Strip alone a total of 11,041 Palestinians were treated by UNRWA medical staff, referred by the organisation's staff to hospitals, or reported to UNRWA officials by either UNRWA medical staff or regular hospital staff.[8] UNRWA also reported (on 29 November 1988) that in a two-week period in the Gaza Strip this November, 497 Palestinians had required treatment for bullet wounds, beatings and/or tear gas inhalation.[9]

Although al-Haq is not in a position to state precisely the number of wounded, on the basis of the independent reports quoted above, which we accept as reliable, we believe the true toll of casualties sustained by the Palestinian community in the Occupied Territories during the first year of the uprising to be well over 20,000.

In the following sections, the use by the Israeli army of various weapons are highlighted. It is hoped that through extensive testimony from affidavits by victims and eyewitnesses the reader will get a sense not only of the illegality and arbitrariness of Israeli army actions, but also of the human tragedy that lies beneath the cold statistics of injury and death.

B. The Use of Force in Response to Demonstrations

There is a substantial problem in discovering exactly what the Israeli army's guidelines are for the use of force against demonstrators in the Occupied Territories. Such guidelines are not normally made public. Those which have become known (concerning the use of live ammunition, plastic bullets and beatings), have surfaced through the media. These guidelines are considered below. As far as the other main weapons used against the Palestinian population during the uprising are concerned, namely rubber bullets and tear gas, no specific guidelines have been publicised. In addition, it is important to note that the guidelines which have come to light may very well *not* be the ones that are enforced in practice. In other words, from various intimations made by Israeli officials (e.g. during investigations of brutality by soldiers in the Occupied Territories) and independent sources, it appears probable that other informal and unpublicised guidelines exist, which may differ for each army unit.[10]

1. Live Ammunition

Even before the uprising, al-Haq had repeatedly called for the publication of the criteria for opening fire, but received no response to its inquiries from the Israeli authorities.[11] Some information on this subject has however, been published. For example, the 1987 annual report of the West Bank Data Base Project includes an analysis of these guidelines, while *Jerusalem Post* correspondent Joel Greenberg summarised the Israeli army's orders on the opening of fire, in an article on 6 November 1987.[12]

As al-Haq understands the guidelines currently in force, they permit opening fire in three situations, when no alternative means are available. These situations are:

(i) When troops are facing a life-endangering situation, either when being attacked with gunfire or explosives, or during demonstrations when troops are under physical attack, or are being attacked by stones or other "cold" objects. In either case, verbal warnings must be given (in Arabic), and then warning shots are to be fired in the air at an angle of

60 degrees. Only if neither of these steps succeeds in averting the danger may shots be fired directly at a protestor and even then soldiers are to aim only at a demonstrator's legs. Shots should only be fired against a specific attacker who is identified as endangering the life of a human being; extreme caution must be taken, when firing, to ensure that others will not be hit.

(ii) To disperse demonstrators by firing in the air.

(iii) While in the process of making arrests.

Al-Haq takes the position that the use of live ammunition as a method of dispersing demonstrations is absolutely unacceptable. This position is supported by the internationally recognised principles of necessity and proportionality in the use of force. Briefly, these principles mean that force may only be used in circumstances that render it strictly necessary. Further, the force used must be in proportion to the threat. Firearms should only be used in extreme circumstances.

Applying these principles to the facts of the present case, it is clear that the use of live ammunition by the Israeli armed forces in response to demonstrations by Palestinian civilians is entirely disproportionate and unnecessary. Those creating the "disturbance" are armed with no more than hand-held missiles such as stones or, at most, iron bars or molotov cocktails. Thus, with the use of proper equipment such as shields, the lives of Israeli soldiers need never be in jeopardy. Other states have confronted such disturbances with riot shields, and with rifle-propelled tear gas grenades and rubber bullets, both of which have far longer ranges than hand-thrown missiles so that the lives of those confronting the demonstrators are not put in danger. The Israeli army is provided with rubber bullets and tear gas, as well as with other equipment such as water cannon, which are quite adequate to effect the dispersal of a demonstration.[13] Indeed, Israel not only manufactures much of its own riot-control equipment but in fact exports some to other countries such as South Africa. Therefore, since Israel clearly has access to non-lethal weapons and protective equipment, the use of live ammunition is unnecessary.

Furthermore, al-Haq has documented cases where soldiers have opened fire at Palestinians not in possession of missiles of any kind, who could not possibly be conceived of as posing any kind of threat to the soldiers, let alone a danger to their lives. The following incident is an example.

On the morning of 16 April 1988, the affiant, Husna Shihab Muhammad 'Ali Hasanein, a 63-year-old housewife from Jenin Refugee Camp, was in her home when demonstrations erupted in protest at the assassination of Khalil al-Wazir (Abu Jihad) earlier that morning. She heard shooting and shouting, and tear gas began wafting through her house. At around 1:00 p.m., she heard that Bassam al-Hariri, a resident of her neighbourhood, had been killed. She recounts:

> I was there with hundreds of other women for more than half an hour, waiting for the funeral procession to start. Then I went back to the neighbourhood, where I found Umm Ahmad (Sa'dah al-Qar'awi), and together we set off towards the march. A few moments later I heard the sound of gunfire and saw Umm Ahmad lying prostrate on her right side with blood flowing from her mouth, nose and right eye, which was no longer there. Blood flowed and covered her face. I began screaming hysterically. As I tried to find out where she was hurt and what her condition was, I was shot twice in the right leg by what I later found out were rubber bullets. Three young men immediately came, and together we tried to carry the injured woman to safety. While checking her condition, I discovered that her pulse had stopped. She lay perfectly still and unmoving, her body lifeless.[14]

The regulations themselves are open to criticism (whether or not they are adhered to by soldiers) since they permit the shooting of persons fleeing the scene of a demonstration regardless of the circumstances.[15] Mere flight cannot and must not be allowed to justify the infliction of grievous bodily harm. A number of killings documented by al-Haq over the past few years have occurred in precisely such situations and this pattern has continued throughout the uprising.[16] For example, on 16 June 1988, at approximately 6:20 a.m., 34-year-old Intisar Naser Hasan, a housewife from the village of Beit Furik in the Nablus District, heard shouting from her home and went to investigate. She made the following statement under oath in an affidavit taken from her by al-Haq:

> ...when I reached the source of the cries I saw a large number of soldiers in the streets of the village and up on the roofs. When the soldiers saw the crowd of people they started chasing them. A small army vehicle began following me. The vehicle was followed by another one of the same type. The soldiers started shooting with a large automatic machine gun which was mounted on the vehicle. I (and the others who were with me), ran for cover, but the cars chased after us. I looked back and saw some young men fall to the ground wounded. One of them was 20-year-old Naser Mahmoud Jnaini. I saw three soldiers approach him; two of them grabbed him, dragged him along the street and shot him while he was lying there...When I looked in another direction I saw a second young man lying on the ground, bleeding; this was 'Arafat Ahmad Jnaini,

also 20 years old. I saw three soldiers standing around him and heard one of them say: "We warned you not to throw stones." He then kicked him in the stomach.[17]

2. Plastic Bullets

The aggressive use of plastic bullets by the Israeli armed forces in the Occupied Territories, especially in the context of demonstrations, provides a further illustration of the authorities' pursuit of a policy designed to inflict grievous bodily harm indiscriminately, while at the same time asserting a determination to remain within the framework of conventional concepts of "riot control." Defence Minister Rabin claimed that plastic bullets were introduced into the Occupied Territories in August 1988 because rubber bullets and tear gas had been insufficient in deterring stone throwing from distances of more than 30 meters.[18] Rabin later stated: "Our purpose is to increase the number of (wounded) among those who take part in violent activities but not to kill them...I am not worried by the increased number of people who got wounded, as long as they were wounded as a result of being involved actively, by instigating, organizing, and taking part in violent activities."[19]

According to an Army Radio reporter, quoting military sources on 15 August, the authorities maintain that the risk of plastic bullets causing deaths is "minimal." To date, however, the authorities have failed to explain their choice of plastic bullets. Instead of utilizing the flat-nosed "baton-round" plastic bullets seen for instance in Northern Ireland, those fired in the Occupied Territories are small, hard, and sharp-edged. They can and do penetrate the body, and subsequently show up on X-rays.[20] According to al-Haq's information, plastic bullets have already led to at least 13 deaths (12 in the Gaza Strip and 1 in the West Bank).

Guidelines on the use of these bullets were publicised in the *Jerusalem Post* of 5 October 1988 by Chief of General Staff Dan Shomron.[21] Shomron stated that standing orders required that they be fired from a distance of 70 meters or more, and then only by officers or other ranked soldiers who had completed special marksmanship courses. Shomron elaborated that these other ranks may not fire of their own volition, and that orders required that bullets be aimed exclusively at demonstrators' legs.

However, three days *before* this announcement, the military correspondent of the *Jerusalem Post* had already observed that many of the soldiers in the Occupied Territories had been issued plastic bullets "following a short course in which they were trained how to use the bullets." The correspondent continued:

this contradicts the impression created recently by official spokesmen, that plastic bullets were issued only to sharpshooters and officers. This was indeed the case two months ago when the bullets were first introduced but it has been learned that new orders were issued two weeks ago by Defence Minister Rabin.[22]

The explicit aim of increasing injuries has, needless to say, been realised: in the first month after the introduction of plastic bullets, UNRWA reported a six-fold increase in the number of Palestinian casualties in the Gaza Strip.[23]

3. Comment

In the following account, an Israeli army reservist describes his impressions of the extent to which official army guidelines are applied in practice. The account, by Ronit Matalon, was published in *HaAretz* on 11 March 1988.[24]

> On my first day [of service], I heard that during an officers' meeting a question had been put to the commander about what was permitted and what was forbidden. And also, about what would happen to someone who opened fire. The answer to the question was: "I've been here for nine months, hundreds of shots have been fired, tens of people have been wounded, and nobody has been brought to trial."
>
> What actually happens is that every battalion works out its own set of norms, in accordance with its battle experience and the character of its soldiers. Every battalion commander is the sovereign of the area [under his command]. Every company commander is the mukhtar of a village or two, and every soldier manning a roadblock is a little god. He decides what to do: who will be allowed through and who won't be. Try to understand that every person there has considerable leeway when it comes to making decisions...
>
> The best description I can find for what's going on there is total chaos. Our role has remained undefined. There are simply no (rules) governing the implementation of orders, behavioural norms, and methods of punishment. They don't exist.

Statements such as the above, as well as some of the cases documented by al-Haq, demonstrate a recurring failure on the part of Israeli officers and soldiers to conform to internal guidelines. In some cases, the circumstances under which they opened fire were simply not those where the guidelines permitted them to do so. For example, as shown above, soldiers have opened fire directly at people, and not just at their legs, in situations which could not conceivably be considered as life-threatening. In others, even if the circumstances permitted use of live ammunition, proper procedures—prior warning and firing into the air—are not followed.

These are not isolated incidents; the above examples constitute only a tiny proportion of the more than 450 cases documented in sworn statements taken by al-Haq during the uprising, and which themselves represent only a fraction of the total number of such incidents. These incidents have happened throughout the uprising, and continue to happen at the present time. This is, therefore, not just a question of "exceptions to the rule": the cases illustrate consistent illegality by Israeli army personnel in their use of force in response to demonstrations.

In addition, the application of force after the victim is under the control of the army as illustrated above, has been a common practice according to al-Haq's documentation. The deviations from the basic international standards of necessity and proportionality are painfully apparent. Many of the examples illustrate the use of riot-control weapons during disturbances *not* as a means of controlling the demonstration, but as a form of extra-judicial punishment.

C. The Aggressive Use of Force

The right to life and the right to security of the person are the most fundamental and precious human rights. Their protection is required, under international law, in times of war as well as peace. All basic human rights and humanitarian treaties preserve this right. Article 3 of the 1949 Universal Declaration of Human Rights states that:

> Everyone has the right to life, liberty and security of person.[25]

Article 3 of the 1949 Fourth Geneva Convention states:

> ...the following acts shall be prohibited at any time and in any place whatsoever with respect to [protected] persons: (a) violence to life and person, in particular murder of all kinds, mutilation, cruel treatment and torture...[26]

Further, Article 147 of the same Convention includes "wilfully causing great suffering or serious injury to body or health [of protected persons]" as a "grave breach" of the Convention. Under Article 146, each State Party to the Convention is under an obligation "to search for persons alleged to have committed, or to have ordered to be committed, such grave breaches, and shall bring such persons, regardless of their nationality, before its own courts."

The requirement to respect these rights is of particular importance in relation to law enforcement officials, which includes the army as well as the police in the Occupied Territories.[27] The Code of Conduct for Law Enforcement Officials, adopted by the General Assembly of the United Nations on 17 December 1979, permits the use of force by such officials:

> ...only when strictly necessary and to the extent required for the performance of their duty.[28]

The following section reviews the practices of the Israeli armed forces in the absence of any confrontation with the Palestinian population. One of the stated objects of the Israeli response to the uprising has been to instill fear into the Palestinian community in order to intimidate people and deter them from protesting.[29]

1. A Policy of Beatings

On 19 January 1988, having come under increasing international pressure to decrease the use of lethal weapons in the Occupied Territories, the Israeli Minister of Defence, Yitzhak Rabin, announced that riots would be quelled by the use of "force, might and beatings." This amounted to an official sanctioning of a beatings policy that had in fact been in effect since January 4 or 5.[30] These announcements, and the ensuing "epidemic" of brutality by members of the Israeli army against Palestinians caused intense criticism both internationally and within Israel itself.[31]

On 25 January, Mr. Rabin qualified the statement, expressing concern at "indiscriminate" beatings, but continuing to defend the use of force to disperse demonstrators.[32] The policy, he said, had helped to instill fear of the armed forces. He claimed that those cases where "detainees or innocent people" had been beaten were exceptions. The confusion as to exactly what orders had been given was exacerbated by Prime Minister Shamir's denial on 24 January that the armed forces had adopted a policy of deliberate beatings of rioters.[33] Yet, the authorities' objectives were clear: to use force to disperse protest actions and to "instill fear" in the population at large.

The indiscriminate use of force to intimidate the population involves a particularly brutal form of collective punishment, and is patently illegal, both in international and in Israeli law. This position has been adopted by a number of Israeli jurists and other lawyers after the scale of the practice of the beatings became clear. According to Israeli law, "reasonable force" (which is not defined) can only be used to catch a fleeing suspect, to arrest a person, and possibly to disperse illegal demonstrations. If an order to beat is "manifestly illegal," then a soldier has both the right and the duty to disobey it. In this regard, Professor David

Kretzmer of the Hebrew University, who is also a member of the Association for Civil Rights in Israel (ACRI), stated: "If beatings are used as a form of summary punishment, they are manifestly illegal. Anyone who orders such beatings or carries them out is criminally liable."[34]

International outrage reached a peak with the much-publicised brutal beating of four Palestinian youths by Israeli soldiers, filmed by CBS in late February. Domestic pressure mounted as well. On 22 February 1988, a letter was publicised that had been written by the Israeli Attorney General, Yosef Harish, to Defence Minister Rabin, stating that "the number of complaints raised the suspicion that classifying these incidents as exceptions no longer reflects reality."[35] He demanded that the illegality of beating demonstrators be made clear to soldiers.

The next day, 23 February, the Chief of General Staff, Dan Shomron, issued instructions to the army, clarifying the circumstances under which force could be used. In presenting these guidelines Shomron emphasised that the orders were not new and had been in force even before the uprising. It was only because of a very few "aberrations" that he had become convinced of the need to "emphasise and clarify the existing orders." In the letter, Shomron stated:

> I would like to clarify and emphasise that force is to be used for the purpose of fulfilling our task according to law and the orders of the army, from which there should be no deviation. Under no circumstances should force be used as a means of punishment. The use of force is permitted during a violent incident in order to break up a riot, to overcome resistance to legal arrest, and during pursuit after rioters or suspects—all within the confines of the time and place where the incident occurs. Force is not to be used once the objective has been attained—for example, after a riot has been dispersed or after a person is in the hands of our forces and is not resisting. In every instance the use of force must be reasonable...[36]

These last guidelines are entirely reasonable. If it is true that they were in force from the beginning of the uprising, then the events of January-February show a widespread and blatant disregard for army rules. Had these violations of standing orders been followed up conscientiously, or had any degree of seriousness been shown in the application of these rules, a far higher number of soldiers would have been prosecuted.

2. *The Practice of Beatings*

The practice of beating as a method of control is not new in the Occupied Territories. In the months leading up to the uprising al-Haq had become increasingly concerned about more widespread use of beatings and army brutality in refugee camps, villages and towns. In October 1987 al-Haq gave a briefing to the press, expressing its grave concern about army brutality, exemplified by the actions of Border Guards in Balata Refugee Camp earlier that month.[37]

Since 9 December 1987, the use of beating by the Israeli army has been widely publicised. However, al-Haq's documentation shows that it was a repeated occurrence *well before* the January announcement by Rabin discussed above, and that despite less coverage by the media, the practice itself is still widespread and continuing today.[38]

According to al-Haq's documentation, in the first two and a half months of the uprising, the policy of beatings resulted in the following discernible patterns of injuries and circumstances:

(a) Beatings have occurred randomly without any connection to Palestinian protest activity. Typically, victims were arrested from their homes, usually at night. They were then taken to a remote area and beaten severely before being released.

(b) Most beating incidents took place when the person concerned was already in the hands of the army and under circumstances where force was not actually needed to control a situation (for example, *after* the dispersal of a demonstration).

(c) Beatings were administered on the limbs, the joints and on the head with the purpose of causing severe injury to muscle tissue or fracture. Beatings were primarily implemented by the use of clubs, wooden at first, and then, after mid-March when the wooden ones were found to break, plastic or fibreglass truncheons.

(d) Beatings were almost always a group effort with a number of soldiers participating and others observing.

(e) The victims of beatings were also frequently groups rather than individuals.

Al-Haq has documented many cases of beatings illustrating these patterns; the following summary of a sworn statement taken by al-Haq illustrates each of the above points.

Samir "Muhammad Khairi" Salim Khamous, 18, from the village of Hawara in the Nablus District was taken from his home at 10:30 p.m. on 21 January 1988 by soldiers. Twelve people from the village were rounded up, put on a bus, and then driven northwards towards Nablus. Every few hundred meters, 3 detainees and a number of soldiers would get out of the bus, and the bus then drove on. When Samir was told to get out of the bus, along with two other youths, 9 soldiers accompanied them, made them walk into the fields, and then started beating them—3 soldiers to each youth, for about 10-12 minutes. Afterwards, the soldiers took off their handcuffs and left them there. Samir's left leg was broken in two places. No demonstrations had taken place at the time.[39]

The following affidavit by a U.S. citizen, Karen White, about events in Gaza City taken by one of al-Haq's Co-Directors gives a very clear example of the nature and scale of the practice of beatings:

> On Saturday, 30 January 1988, at about 9:45 a.m., I was walking in a side alley running parallel to Omar al-Mukhtar Street in Gaza City. I was with a friend from Scotland, Catriona Drew, and we both noticed a large number of Israeli military troops on Omar al-Mukhtar Street. As we passed through the alley, four Israeli soldiers began to follow us, shouting at us to halt. We stopped, turned and asked what they wanted. They demanded we present some identification, which we did. Catriona and I continued to walk, and as we approached Omar al-Mukhtar Street, observed the following:
>
> At the intersection faced by the Al-Omari mosque, there were about 20 schoolgirls, aged 12-17, standing on the side of the road. I saw two small stones fall into the street, coming from the opposite direction from where the girls stood. At the other end of the block, a youth of 17 or 18 stood alone, facing the opposite direction from the soldiers. I observed a large number of Israeli soldiers running toward him from behind. The soldiers all began to club, kick, slap and punch the boy. I did not see this boy throw any stones, and the two that landed in the intersection had been thrown from the other end of the block, from over the buildings, and not thrown from the street. This was the only boy in sight, and other than the schoolgirls and two elderly women, there were no other people, save the soldiers, on the street.
>
> Two more jeeps came onto the block (making a total of five jeeps there), and several Israeli military troops got out. Four of them appeared to be sharpshooters and they had special guns. The four placed themselves in front of the group of schoolgirls and took aim at the chest and head-level of the group, about ten feet from them. Catriona and I quickly placed ourselves in their line of fire. The soldiers stood about for a moment, got in their jeeps and left, stopping about three blocks away. I emphasize that these girls were not throwing stones, and at no time during this incident were these soldiers' lives at risk.
>
> As Catriona and I turned to leave, we heard terrible screaming behind us. We turned and saw several Israeli soldiers dragging the young man along the ground on his back, kicking him over his

entire body, stamping on his abdomen and genitals, punching him with their fists, and pounding him with wooden truncheons. The boy's head, face and neck were entirely covered with blood, and his nose was obviously broken. He had deep, bleeding gashes on his forearms. The Israeli soldiers pulled him upward and as the boy began to stand, one soldier kicked him twice in the genitals. As the boy doubled over in pain, another soldier kicked him under the chin and the boy fell backward. As he sat on the ground, three soldiers delivered several punches to his face and neck. Then one soldier grabbed his hair and pulled the boy to his feet. He was then pushed and pulled across the street where the soldiers handcuffed him to a door of a closed shop on the street.

While they pushed and pulled him to the opposite side of the street, one Israeli soldier held the boy's arm outward and struck it repeatedly with a wooden truncheon. They then handcuffed him to the door, and one soldier took the boy's head in his two hands and bashed his head as hard as he could repeatedly against the door. The door was covered with the boy's blood. We protested to the Israeli soldiers that we had witnessed that the boy had not thrown any stones and was innocent, that he was not resisting arrest, and that we believed the soldiers' behaviour was unnecessarily excessive. The Israeli soldiers did not respond but continued to beat the boy viciously.

At this point I noticed four soldiers take aim with their rifles at a small girl, aged about 11 or 12 and she fled. The Israeli troops ran after her and I followed them into an alley. All four soldiers raised their truncheons high overhead as the girl cowered against the alley wall, but before they could deliver any blow I had pulled one of them off her. They lowered their truncheons. One of the soldiers had grasped the girl tightly around the upper arm and she whimpered in pain. Another of the four soldiers appeared as if in a frenzy. He shook violently, began screaming, turned and smashed the two headlights and windshield of a car parked in the alley, with the driver inside. This Israeli soldier continued to scream unintelligibly while he pounded the car with his wooden truncheon, even after all the glass had been smashed. I believed, based on the violent behaviour of the soldiers, that had I not intervened, the child might have been seriously injured, as these soldiers appeared to me to be out of control. It seemed to me that the reason they lowered their truncheons was because I was a foreigner and observing them.

The girl ran away and I followed the four Israeli soldiers back into Omar al-Mukhtar Street. I went back to the youth where he was still handcuffed to the door and seven soldiers were still beating him. As I came to him, one Israeli soldier kicked him in his genitals and when the boy bent down, the soldier hit with his fist in the boy's already bloodied face. I asked the boy what his name was. He was screaming with pain and fear and responded loudly several times, "Muhammad Said al-Jamallah." The boy's little sister, who appeared to be about 13 or 14 years old, was standing next to him, screaming. The soldiers began to strike the boy with the butts of their guns in his face, head, chest, stomach, abdomen and knees, simultaneously. Two more jeeps pulled up and Israeli military troops got out. I had asked one of the soldiers who had been present all along who their commanding officer was, and he said it was he, Tommy Logovsky. I took a pen and some paper from my coat pocket to note the name. Another Israeli soldier screamed at me, "why are you writing his name?" I responded that I was writing a report. The same soldier then screamed at me, "for whom?" I replied that it was for a friend in the United States Congress. This Israeli soldier grabbed the paper from my hand and tore it to pieces, using his teeth. Catriona and I turned to watch them drag the boy to one of the jeeps. One soldier promised the boy's sister that the boy would not be beaten any more. Catriona and I approached the jeep before they put the boy in and asked which hospital he would be taken to, and were told a "military hospital." As we approached the jeep, I was punched once in my stomach with a truncheon and once with a fist. Another Israeli soldier behind me hit me several times on my back with the butt of his M-16 rifle.

The Israeli soldiers picked the boy up and threw him over the side of the jeep. We heard his head strike the floor of the jeep. Seven soldiers got into the jeep with the boy and began to pound him very hard with wooden truncheons (one of the truncheons broke, the blow was so forceful), kick him, strike him with their fists, and hit him with their rifle butts, simultaneously.

A physician and two elderly Muslim priests [sic] were trying to get the soldiers to allow them to treat the boy's wounds. These three were struck by wooden truncheons and fists by the Israeli military troops. Only when the soldiers prepared to leave did people other than the schoolgirls and two elderly women appear in the street. Again, I emphasize that *at no time* were the Israeli military troops' lives in danger; there were no riots, demonstrations or other activities in the street that would justify such excessive force. The boy was not resisting arrest, but was pleading for mercy and protesting his innocence all along. In fact, it appeared to me that it was the Israeli military troops who were out of control.[40]

The above affidavit presents a particularly graphic illustration of unprovoked brutality and of the entirely random nature of such acts.

One final example serves to depict the disregard for humanitarian norms which has characterised many of these incidents.

Late in the evening on 19 January 1988, soldiers broke into the house of Mu'in Ahmad Mahmoud Abou-Baker in the town of Ya'bad in the Jenin District, started beating him, and then took him out of the house, continuing to beat him. The beating continued for some time, and he was then tied to an electricity pole, with his hands behind his back. When a woman tried to rescue him, she was hit by the soldiers and fell to the ground. In her own words:

> When I, along with the other women, got to the young man, I saw him lying on the ground, his hands bound behind his back and tied to the electricity pole. I noticed that he was bleeding from the face, his clothes were blood-stained and his hands were bound with a thin metal cord like the one used in construction work. I went closer to him and started untying the cord, when one of the soldiers came up to me and kicked me to the ground and started to shoot bullets at the ground around the young man, not further than 5 or 10 centimeters from the young man's body. But I gathered my strength, with some difficulty, and went back and untied the cord completely; but I discovered that he was also bound with plastic handcuffs that I couldn't take off. And while I was untying the cord, I had to pull it out of his flesh because it was slicing his wrists which were bleeding. I had to retreat for about 10 meters in order to avoid being hit by any of the heavily fired bullets. And when the soldiers saw our determination not to retreat, one of them pelted me with a rock weighing about one kilogram and hit me in my abdomen under my rib-cage; I still suffer from the effects...[41]

Although official sanctioning of the beatings policy was publicly withdrawn in February, in practice the beatings did not stop. Beatings are as common in the Occupied Territories today as they were in February.[42] The main differences seem to be that the policy is less systematic—i.e. there is less emphasis on breaking limbs—and certainly less visible to the international community, partly as a result of restrictions on the media, and partly because the main targets are remote villages and refugee camps, especially in the Gaza Strip.[43]

Al-Haq believes that such deliberate, unprovoked beatings as those described above are grave breaches of the Fourth Geneva Convention as defined under Article 147.

3. Army Brutality: Use of Rubber Bullets

Although the policy of beatings most clearly illustrates the way in which physical force has been used aggressively, the same point can be made much more generally. The following affidavit about the use of rubber bullets, from an American schoolteacher in Ramallah, describes an incident on 7 February 1988 when the affiant was walking along the main street of Ramallah with a group of nine friends. She saw a group of soldiers questioning a girl, and approached, asking if anything was the matter. The soldiers reacted angrily and briefly tried to grab two of the men in the group. As the soldiers left, they threw two tear gas canisters towards the group. In her own words:

> Just as the soldiers were about to drive away, I saw one aim his rifle directly at [me]. I don't remember seeing a face, only the gun through the cloud of the gas. There was a sudden explosion of sound, and I felt myself being hit. I was shot in the throat (to the right of the windpipe), the neck, the right shoulder and the right and left hands. I raised one hand to my throat to see if I was bleeding, as I did not know if I'd been shot by live or rubber ammunition. There was a small amount of blood and no bullet penetration—thus rubber bullets. The soldiers drove away and I...stumbled to a nearby apartment for treatment.[44]

There are many other examples of soldiers shooting at point-blank range at individuals who were in no way posing a threat to their safety, and who were already under the control of the army. The following affidavit was taken by al-Haq on 19 August 1988; the affiant wishes to remain anonymous.

> At approximately 2:00 p.m. on 10 June 1988, while I was on a visit to my family in the 'Ein Beit al-Ma' Refugee Camp, a group of youths erected a number of roadblocks on the street which runs in front of the house. After approximately 10 minutes, 10 soldiers in two army jeeps arrived at the scene and began firing tear gas canisters and rubber bullets in the direction of the youths. This caused them to disperse. The soldiers were able to arrest Iyad Walid Hamdi, whom I know well and is approximately 16 years old. I saw two of the soldiers holding him while the rest of the soldiers continued to chase the youths, and heard one of the soldiers say to Iyad, in Arabic: "We do not want to kill you quickly. We want to kill you slowly." Then, the two soldiers threw Iyad to the ground, and one of them stepped on his chest and aimed the nozzle of his gun within centimeters of his right eye. I saw all this very clearly because I was no farther than 20 meters from the scene. I was in a position where the soldiers could not see me. A few seconds later I heard the sound of a single gunshot, and saw Iyad's eye come out of its socket. The soldiers left and went to join their colleagues. Immediately thereafter I saw a number of youths running towards Iyad. They lifted

him off the ground, put him in a car, and took him away. It later became apparent that the bullet which was fired at Iyad's eye was a rubber one.[45]

Another example involves Nidhal Muhammad Khalil al-'Ataba, 23, from al-Bireh. On 23 April 1988, a group of soldiers in a jeep came to his shop and took his identification card. When he asked for it to be returned, he was told to "come to a place near the al-Bireh municipality." He decided not to go. Half an hour later the soldiers returned and asked him why he had not appeared. He answered: "Had I gone to you, you would have beaten me." They then forced him into the jeep, and drove about 20 km to Mahraqat al-Bireh, near the Israeli settlement of Pisgot. There, his hands tied behind him, he was beaten severely by the soldiers for approximately a quarter of an hour. After releasing him, they told him to run. In his own account, the following then transpired:

> One of the soldiers began to kick me with his foot, chasing me and saying "run, pig." When I was about one hundred meters away from them I heard the motors start and expected that they would follow me. Indeed they did follow me, and one of the soldiers sitting in front ordered me to stand by the side of the road facing him. He aimed his rifle at me and fired several times, hitting most of my body, and I fell to the ground unconscious...It appeared that I was shot with more than fifteen rubber bullets, according to the doctor who told me to stay in the hospital...[46]

4. *The Use of Tear Gas as a Means of Terrorisation*

Tear gas has been widely used internationally to disperse demonstrations. During the past year in the Occupied Territories, Israel has utilised both CS and CN gas, introducing CS gas in January 1988. The effects of CS gas tend to be more serious than those of CN gas.[47] The safe use of such gas depends upon its being deployed in strict accordance with the manufacturers' safety instructions. If tear gas intended for outdoor use only is used in confined areas, for example, serious injury or death can result.

A guide to the use of tear gas published by Federal Laboratories of Saltzburg, Pennsylvania (USA), which has been Israel's main supplier, states that neither CS nor CN gas can be fully classified as non-lethal weapons. The company designated both formulae as "less-than-lethal" when used by properly trained and qualified officers. The manufacturer explicitly cautioned that the product:

> "if not used properly... *can indeed cause death... under no circumstances should grenades cartridges or projectiles designed for use*

in riots be used in confined areas as serious injury may result...do not throw grenades directly at rioters, but on the ground in front of them. [Emphasis in original].[48]

To the best of al-Haq's knowledge, a summary of these instructions is clearly printed on each tear gas canister produced by the company.[49]

Nevertheless, these instructions are regularly ignored by the Israeli armed forces. Al-Haq regularly receives accounts of tear gas being fired into confined spaces, including homes, schools, and hospitals. To give one example, Israeli soldiers fired tear gas canisters into dormitories belonging to the Qalandiya Vocational Training Institute following a demonstration there by students on 10 December 1987. The concentrated exposure to the gas caused several of the students to faint from gas inhalation.[50]

At other times soldiers have targetted individual demonstrators and used tear gas to incapacitate them, either by shooting the canister directly at the person or by throwing a tear gas canister into a shop, home or some other confined space, jeopardising the lives of the persons within.

The following affidavit was taken by al-Haq on 2 May 1988 from an affiant who requested that his identity remain protected:

> At approximately 10:00 a.m. on Tuesday 23 February 1988, several dozen soldiers entered [Nablus] and clashed with its residents. As I was shutting the door of my shop I saw a lot of demonstrators running away and could see the army chasing after them. I saw more than 15 soldiers approaching me. One of them rushed towards me while holding a gas gun. From a distance of about 20 meters, he aimed the gun in my direction and fired; a tear gas canister hit me in the face and I fell to the ground. I was having difficulty breathing, felt nauseous, and my windpipe was dry and burning. My face was bleeding heavily, particularly from my right eye, and was extremely painful. Since then I have not been able to see normally with it as I had been able to before I was hit by the canister.[51]

In another incident, following demonstrations in the village of Beit Fajjar in the Bethlehem District on 22 February 1988, soldiers forced Muhammad Khalil Mousa al-Sheikh into his house, located near the entrance to the town, and shot a tear gas canister inside. An 11-day-old baby, Muhammad Samih, was in the room where the canister landed. Muhammad began having difficulty breathing as the gas spread. His family immediately took him to a local doctor, but were unable to take him to a hospital because the army subsequently imposed a curfew on the town. The baby later died.[52]

Particularly at risk from the effects of tear gas are the elderly, the very young, and those with respiratory problems. Al-Haq has documented a number of cases in which infants died after their exposure to tear gas. A mother of recently-born twins submitted the following sworn statement to al-Haq:

> On 16 November 1987 I gave birth to male twins who were healthy and did not suffer from any illness. On Saturday 16 January 1988 there were demonstrations in the neighbourhood where I live, in Morabiteen Street in the Western Quarter of Qalqiliya. The army started shooting heavily—both bullets and tear gas. A number of tear gas bombs—I do not know how many—fell in the front yard of the house and in the street, and the gas wafted through the rooms of the house. In addition to the tears and coughing from which I suffered, my nursing children immediately began suffering from continuous coughing and a rise in their temperature, which led me to take them to the Health Centre in Qalqiliya directed by Dr. Mahmoud Jarrar. When I arrived at the Health Centre, which is about 500 meters from my house, my son 'Abd-al-Fattah Omar Mahmoud Shreem had already passed away. I immediately took my other son, Mahmoud, to Tulkarem Governmental Hospital where he was given first aid and remained hospitalised for 13 days. I stayed with him the entire time and did not even go to attend my other son's funeral. The burial permit we received from the health department in Qalqiliya did not state the cause of death in writing; they only wrote "Sudden death—cause unknown," although the same physician told me orally that my son had died from the effects of the gas.[53]

Al-Haq has also documented cases where soldiers fired tear gas canisters into homes while no demonstration was taking place. The case of Hassan Ismail Sa'id Saleh, 20, a shopkeeper in Qaddoura Refugee Camp in Ramallah, is illustrative in this respect. On Wednesday, 20 January 1988, at around 1 p.m., soldiers entered the shop of Mr. Saleh and questioned him as to the identities of people who had been involved in stone-throwing and tire-burning in the area. He replied that he did not know, and was then ordered to go inside his shop. The officer who led the group of soldiers then threw a tear gas canister inside the shop, and left, closing the door behind him. Mr. Saleh tried to pour water on the canister, but the gas spread too quickly, and he lost consciousness. Soon after he was rescued by his family and neighbours.[54]

Another example of tear gas being thrown into a home is given by Riyad Bader 'Abdallah Zubeidi, 25, a construction worker from 'Anabta, Tulkarem, who was at home around midday on 11 March 1988 when he heard loud knocking on the door. He went to see who was there and saw four soldiers outside. They ordered him to open the door, but he refused to do so. He inquired why they wanted to come in, but the soldiers did not reply, and one of the soldiers then smashed an outside window, while others tried to break the door down. The affiant took his children to one of the flats upstairs:

> Then I saw one of the soldiers throwing a tear gas bomb into the stairwell of the house. The gas began spreading and going up into rooms.

Approximately 45 people, including 30 children, were living in the buildings, six residential flats. Four children, all under 6 months old, fainted. Others felt dizziness and nausea, and had difficulties breathing.[55]

There has also been considerable concern over the effect of tear gas on pregnant women, although the precise relationship between foetal deaths and sustained exposure to concentrated amounts of tear gas remains unclear. A report issued in May 1988 by the Chief Physician of the Israeli armed forces, Dr. Nimrod Shoshan, stated that 30 women who miscarried at Shifa Hospital in Gaza during the first three months of the uprising had been exposed to tear gas within four hours prior to their miscarriage. Further, in these particular cases (out of a total of 116 who reported exposure to tear gas shortly before miscarrying), he could directly attribute the miscarriage to tear gas exposure. Shoshan noted a 13 percent increase in the number of miscarriages at Shifa Hospital in Gaza from December 1987 to March 1988 as compared with the same period only one year earlier.[56]

A full investigation of the medical consequences of the misuse of tear gas by the Israeli army has been obstructed on more than one occasion by the refusal of the Poison Control Centre in Haifa to disclose the precise components of the gas to doctors requesting such information.[57] Israeli officials explained their refusal on the grounds that the information was classified, although the proper identification of the gas is necessary in order to diagnose the victims of tear gas and provide them with proper treatment.

In June 1988, Amnesty International issued a document expressing its concern about the misuse of tear gas and about the reported deaths of 40 people as a result of tear gas inhalation.[58] The document also expressed the organisation's concern that "by their lack of action, the Israeli military authorities have at the very least been negligent in preventing the misuse of tear-gas as a riot control method and have thereby tolerated if not encouraged its misuse."[59]

In al-Haq's view there is no conceivable justification for throwing tear gas into confined spaces. The instructions on the tear gas canisters which al-Haq has seen are unambiguous and precise. In the above cases and in many other instances, tear gas has been deliberately misused by soldiers in complete disregard for the potentially fatal consequences of their actions. Incidents such as the ones quoted above have occurred with such frequency since the beginning of the uprising that in May 1988 Federal Laboratories refused to deliver any more of the gas to Israel, stating that such shipments would not be continued until the company received "some confirmation that their [the Israelis'] intent [was] not to use it as a weapon."[60]

5. Harassment and Destruction of Property

Wanton destruction of property, including the smashing of objects, the spoiling of foodstuffs, and similar vandalism has occurred repeatedly throughout the uprising, and even before.

The following affidavit was given by Hikmat Muhammad Saleh al-Fahjan, aged 40, from al-'Arroub Refugee Camp in the Hebron District:

> At around 3 p.m. on 22 January 1988, I heard knocking on the front gate to the house. I opened the door, and six soldiers were standing behind the gate. They entered without permission and asked me about "the boys." I told them that there were only little ones. They came into the house and proceeded to smash the glass in the windows and doors, and to smash the colour TV set, the sideboard and a gas stove. Before they came I had prepared for baking and had the dough on the floor and had lit the oven. When they came in, they poured kerosene on the flour and the dough and spilled rice and sugar on the floor. They beat my children Raed and Saed and Mazen, hitting them with clubs on all parts of the body...On that same day they [the soldiers] returned twice to the house looking for any unbroken pane of glass and proceeding to break it. We are still without window panes and the wind is blowing through the house.[61]

A second example concerns an incident in Nablus on 1 November 1988. The affiant, 21-year old Zeid Fawzi Qanaze', stated under oath:

> At about 4.30 p.m....there was a light knocking on our door. I asked who [was there] and [a voice] answered: "Army." I opened the door and four soldiers were standing before me. When I asked them what they wanted, they said: "To enter."...As soon as they entered, they took my ID card and that of my brother Zeidan, who is 17, and ordered us both to stand in front of the East window in our house, and we did...After that, one of the soldiers told us to go into a room in the house, and we did, along with an officer and a soldier with

a wireless...Then the soldier carrying the wireless asked us in Arabic about a third person who had been on the roof, and we answered saying that we did not know, and that we had been sitting with our guests.

The officer [then] started throwing household items out of the window. They included: two electric irons, a vacuum cleaner, an electric heater, two small bags of fruit and a bed cover (quilt). After that he went to the cupboard and emptied it, breaking a glass container filled with butter. Then he came towards me and hit me with his gun butt in the stomach and boxed me several times. The officer then opened the door and called my father into the room, and asked him the same question he had asked us. My father began to scream. He has a heart ailment and high blood pressure. The officer stood on the bed and slammed an electric light bulb with his gun, exploding it in order to terrorise us...

The officer then went to the living room with me, my brother and the soldier. He aimed his gun at the women, and the soldiers shouted at them to stand together in one line. The women were afraid and started screaming. The officer and the soldier then went into the room, taking my brother along, and shut the door. I heard my brother screaming from inside because they were beating him...The women screamed in protest over this assault, and the officer came out with a walking cane used by my father and began to smash the buffet glass and threatened the women with his gun to be silent. He went in once again to the room where my brother and the soldier were, and we heard my brother scream.

My mother, Najwa Qanaze', began to talk to the soldiers in the living room, begging them to let her into the room where her son was being beaten, but one of the soldiers threatened to call the officer to beat her. My father then started screaming and...collapsed onto the floor. I immediately moved to the phone in order to call a doctor, but the officer had come out of the room and prevented me from calling. He went into the room once again. One of the two soldiers remaining with us said: "Call a doctor if you wish," but we couldn't find the telephone directory since the soldiers had made such a mess.

After a while the officer, the soldier and my brother came out of the room and the officer told us: "You are liars. I'm going to destroy the whole house." And he began to smash the buffet with his club, breaking a large number of glass containers, as well as some of the wooden panels of the buffet.

All the soldiers left and went outside. My uncle then called the ambulance and my father was treated. The doctor later arrived and confirmed that my father had had a light stroke.[62]

More recently, soldiers who claimed that they had been stoned in their bus on the Jerusalem-Ramallah road near Qalandiya Refugee Camp, went on a rampage in the camp on Sunday, 20 November 1988, smashing car windows and head lights, puncturing car tires, and overturning one car. According to the *Jerusalem Post* of 22 November 1988, they burst into homes, "breaking doors and windows, vandalizing furniture, and beating occupants."

Seventeen soldiers involved in the incident were sentenced to between 7 and 14 days actual imprisonment shortly thereafter, and four sergeants were given an additional 14 days suspended sentence. Chief of General Staff Dan Shomron said that the soldiers were well aware of army orders for dealing with unrest, but got "carried away." He added that the soldiers, who were paratroopers, were "the best of our youth."[63] On 30 November, the *Jerusalem Post* reported that Minister of Defence Rabin reassured the parents of the soldiers involved that they could still become officers.

6. *Army Raids on Villages and Refugee Camps*

During the uprising, the military has frequently raided villages and refugee camps, often in the most remote areas. During these raids houses are searched, property is destroyed and confiscated, people are beaten, and tear gas is thrown indoors. While the purpose of some raids appears to be the arrest of persons wanted by the authorities, in other cases there seems to be no object aside from terrorising the general population.

For example, at 1:00 a.m. on Saturday 9 July 1988, an IDF unit numbering between 20-30 soldiers went from house to house in the village of 'Aroura in the district of Ramallah, indiscriminately beating unarmed civilians and destroying furniture and other household properties. No one was arrested, no inquiries were made as to the whereabouts of any resident, and in only one case was someone asked for his identification card.[64]

Al-Haq has documentation on a number of other such incidents, involving villages and camps throughout the West Bank.

7. *Other Forms of Brutality*

The following incidents cannot easily be categorised in terms of the type of force used by the Israeli army. They are included because they vividly illustrate the breakdown of "law and order" within the military itself which has been particularly evident since the beginning of the uprising. Two of them also document the use of new "weapons." It remains to be seen whether the use of such weapons has been or will be authorised by the Israeli authorities.

At around 10 a.m. on Sunday, 3 April 1988, Jaber Muhammad Jaber Mamzawi, aged 63, a resident of Askar Refugee Camp near Nablus, was standing in front of his house when he saw his 18-year-old son Khalil being approached by a group of soldiers. He rushed over to his son and heard him being ordered to remove the metal cans and stones (on strings) which were hanging from the electricity wires above. The affiant states that 33,000 volts run through the wires, and that there was a "danger" sign with a skull and cross bones marked on the pylon. When Khalil refused, one of the soldiers told him: "If you do not do that, we will shoot you." According to the affiant:

> At that time a garbage van came to the camp. When my son saw it he called the driver so that he could climb to reach the wires by standing on the top of the van. The driver agreed and my son clambered up, taking with him a wooden stick so that he would be able to clear the wires. When he was on top of the van I saw that my son could not clear the wires with the stick, so he had to use one of his hands. As soon as he touched one of the wires I saw the wires glow bright and saw my son shuddering from the electric shock. I saw him fall on the top of the van and then to the ground.

Khalil Mamzawi, 18, died from electrocution.[65]

The following affidavit describes the throwing of some sort of chemical agent, described by the affiant as a "sort of phosphorous bomb," at Jihad Saleh 'Ali Ibrahim Masa'id, age 20, of Toubas. The incident occurred in October 1988 and is one of several incidents about which al-Haq has recently received reports:

> At around ten in the morning on Wednesday, 26 October 1988, I left my house with my brother Anis, 22, to take our sheep for grazing. We got to the al-Ghor road leading to the village of Tayasir, and were walking on the sidewalk when a medium-sized military vehicle passed by us and slowed down gradually to a total stop about ten meters away from us. I looked into the back of the vehicle and saw two soldiers.
>
> My brother and I were standing side by side when suddenly one of the soldiers threw an object that resembled a tear gas bomb in my direction. When it hit my left shoulder it burst into flames and stuck to my flesh, burning the left side of my face. I grabbed it with both my hands—with my left hand having the better hold—but it stuck to my left hand and I then couldn't get rid of it. It remained in my hand for about a minute until its flame subsided. After that, the

military vehicle departed and no soldier came out of it.

I was then taken to al-Ittihad al-Nisa'i Hospital in Nablus where I received first aid and was under treatment for twelve days. According to the specialists, I had received third-degree burns. The doctors said that the thing that was thrown at me was some sort of a phosphorous bomb. I am still receiving treatment at home. My left hand has been particularly affected by the burns.[66]

In June 1988 al-Haq took an affidavit from a 24-year-old man who prefers to remain anonymous. In it he tells how four soldiers wearing red berets came into his home in the afternoon of 24 June 1988. He was taken into one of the rooms in the house, and the soldiers locked the door. He was questioned about the identity of stone throwers, but when he denied knowing any of them:

> [One of the soldiers] grabbed my hair and pulled me against the wall. Then he opened a briefcase...similar to those usually used by doctors. I looked into it and there was a hatchet with a wooden handle and a syringe about 14 cms long like the one used by doctors. On its nozzle there was a rubber tube connected to a bottle. I couldn't see exactly what was in the bottle, since I didn't have long to look inside his briefcase. I saw other things which I could not distinguish or specify. He placed the case in front of him on the ground. Another soldier pulled my face towards him while the soldier with the briefcase started repeating the same questions. He lifted the axe and passed it across my face for me to see it and placed it behind my left ear and threatened to cut my ear off if I did not provide him with information about the stone throwers. Then he took a piece of white cloth marked with blue lines from the briefcase and covered my eyes. Then two soldiers grabbed me and forced my shoulders into such a position that it became difficult to move. Then one of the soldiers, I think it was the one with the briefcase, took my right hand and punctured my arm [with the syringe], then took the syringe out and started feeling my arm, looking for another place. I felt he was looking for an artery. Then he put the needle into my arm for a few seconds and pulled it out. He took the patch off my eyes and thus I saw the syringe in his hands; he was the soldier with the briefcase, not one of those who had grabbed my shoulders. He gave the syringe to the soldier who was holding my right shoulder. I noticed this time that the syringe was connected to the rubber tube which in turn was connected to a bottle covered with a piece of cloth, making it extremely difficult to see its contents. One of the soldiers held my right hand and another my left while the first soldier started scratching the upper part of my arms with the needle, causing six cuts varying in length

between 5-7 cms. My arm bled.[67]

Several of al-Haq's staff members saw the marks left by the injections and the scratches on his arms. Obviously the incident described above, which is similar to other reports al-Haq has recently received from Gaza, is extremely sinister. Forcibly administering an unidentified substance to a detainee is a very grave matter, with unknown long- and short-term consequences for the victim's health. It also raises questions about medical ethics.

During many of the incidents of the types described above, the soldiers concerned have treated the victims in a humiliating and degrading fashion. Indeed, sometimes humiliation appears to be one of the main aims. The following incident, in October 1988, is illustrative of this attitude:

> At around 5:30 p.m. on Friday, 28 October 1988, while sitting in my house along with members of my family, I heard hard knocking at the door. When I asked who it was, the reply came: "Army." I immediately opened the door. Suddenly, five young soldiers entered the house in a aggressive fashion. I followed them in to see what their intent was. When the soldiers saw my son Hafez, who is 22 years old, they asked him to produce his personal identification, and he did. The soldiers then started cursing us and using foul language, especially at the girls and myself, in Arabic. [The soldiers then began destroying household property, and beating all the members of the family.] On their way out, and when they neared the front door, four of the soldiers turned to face us and opened the zippers of their pants and pulled out their private parts. They held them with their hands and started playing with them before our eyes, laughing and cursing me and my daughters especially.[68]

8. *Death Squads*

The removal of perceived leaders from the Palestinian community through a variety of means, including administrative detention and deportations, has been a regular practice on the part of the Israeli authorities since well before the uprising. (See Chapter 4) At the same time, the targetting of selected individuals appears to have been expanded during the past year to include the kidnapping and outright killing of such persons.

Shortly before the uprising, Minister of Defence Yitzhak Rabin announced the deployment of snipers in all army units. According to reports in the *Jerusalem Post* of 11 December 1987, sniper fire (aimed at the legs only) was intended to be "for selective use" against "ringleaders" only. Then on 25 December 1987, three weeks into the uprising, the

Jerusalem Post reported Rabin as saying: "We are going after the organisers who have come into the schools, their faces masked, and forced pupils, often against their will, to riot."

On 7 July 1988 the *Jerusalem Post* copied a short Reuters item quoting Israeli intelligence sources as saying that an undercover military unit, codenamed "Shimshon" (Hebrew for "Samson"), had been operating in the Gaza Strip in January, using "foreign press" car stickers as a cover. (See also the section on restrictions on the press in Chapter 5 below.) More recently, on 23 October, as quoted in the *Jerusalem Post* the next day, the Reuters news agency reported that:

> security sources said an undercover army unit codenamed "Cherry," deployed in the West Bank to capture Arabs throwing petrol bombs and rocks, had verbal orders to shoot to kill fugitives "with blood on their hands"...security sources stressed that killings were not the unit's *prime* task, although it had shot dead several Palestinians in ambushes and undercover operations. [Emphasis added].

The following day the Israeli armed forces spokesperson issued a statement, which was reprinted in the *Jerusalem Post* on 25 October. It read in part:

> ...There is no unit in the IDF which is authorized to act, or which acts, against the well-known rules for opening fire which are grounded in law.

As the *Post* reporter was quick to note, the official disclaimer "did not deny the existence of undercover units whose job is to arrest throwers of rocks and petrol bombs."

It should in any case also be noted that such squads would presumably consist of units attached to the intelligence services (Shin Bet) rather than the armed forces, although the possibility of coordination between them and the army should not be excluded. One indication of such coordination is that cases known to al-Haq in which activists were shot dead by snipers, such as Ahmad Zeid Salim al-Kilani in the town of Ya'bad on 8 October 1988, the perpetrator was dressed in army fatigues. This was reported by eyewitnesses to al-Haq staff members who visited Ya'bad a few days afterwards. In spite of this, press reports of the incident quoted army sources as stating that Kilani had "apparently" been killed in a "local feud" with other Palestinians in which the army played no role.[69]

Given the authorities' sensitivity to full exposure about undercover death squads eliminating leaders of the uprising in the Occupied Territories (indeed, a number of journalists, including the Reuters correspondent cited above, had their press credentials revoked for suggesting this), it has been and in the forseeable future will probably remain impossible to document the extent of such activities beyond a reasonable doubt. At the same time, al-Haq has been able to thoroughly document cases in which violent crimes (including murder) and kidnappings were perpetrated by armed persons driving civilian vehicles with West Bank licence plates. (Such licence plates are mandated by the military authorities for West Bank Palestinians exclusively.) Their behaviour differs significantly from that which has been observed of the official armed forces. For reasons which are stated below, al-Haq is also of the opinion that those behind these attacks are probably not Jewish settlers.

Reports received by al-Haq indicate that such people have acted with impunity: the persons involved in these summary executions have yet to be charged, and it is not clear that the army is even investigating this category of killings.

In one case documented by al-Haq the affiant, Sultan 'Abd-al-Rahman Husein Abou-Hassan, 21, a resident of Silat al-Harithiya in the Jenin District, was standing with a group of other men near the entrance of the village at 5:30 a.m. on 8 September 1988. A blue Ford with Nablus licence plates drew up near the men, and the affiant could distinguish two men in the front seat wearing civilian clothes and *kaffiyas* (Palestinian scarves). As Sultan Abou-Hassan approached the car, the driver stuck a pistol out of the window, and shot the young man with four bullets in the stomach. Three man then emerged from the car, and one of them shot at one of Mr. Abou-Hassan's companions, Muhammad Ahmad 'Abdallah Abou-Salah. The affiant ran away, but was hit by several other bullets. Both he and Muhammad Abou-Salah fell to the ground. After a few minutes, an Israeli ambulance with the star of David on it appeared, followed by several military cars. The two men were given first aid, and were then taken to the Jenin government hospital. Muhammad Abou-Salah died of his wounds, while Sultan Abou-Hassan made a partial recovery.[70]

The circumstances of the incident—a killing in cold blood, the immediate arrival of an ambulance and army cars on the scene of the incident, the lack of an investigation, and the excising by the military censor of a story about the incident in the Hebrew press a few days later—are enough to raise grave suspicions about the identities of the perpetrators of the attack. Similar events have taken place since then, in other locations in the West Bank, e.g. in Yatta one day later, as was widely reported in the press.

More conventional forms of brutality and intimidation have been practiced by such units as well. In this case the affiant, a housewife in the village of Sa'ir in the Hebron District, recounts how she was at home at approximately 1:30 p.m. on 3 November 1988, looking after her son 'Atif, who had been shot by live ammunition in the knee three weeks previously. Then:

> ...three armed persons in civilian clothes led by a short blond man who was wearing glasses and spoke fluent Arabic entered the house. Then, without anybody's permission, they headed towards my son 'Atif and assaulted him, trampling on his wounded leg. Meanwhile, a group of soldiers, the number of whom I cannot specify, joined them.[71]

The affiant's son was then taken away by the men in civilian attire in a car with blue (West Bank) licence plates.

Al-Haq has also documented cases of street kidnappings, even in broad daylight. For example, on 13 November 1988, at around 10:30 a.m., the affiant was walking with his cousin in the market of the town of Jenin. Suddenly, he was struck from behind on the head, lost his balance, and heard someone order him, in Arabic, to "get in the car." He looked back and saw 8 people in civilian clothes with revolvers, and was then forced into a white Peugeot which he described as "like a hearse, with no windows."

The affiant was bundled onto the floor of the car, which had no seats. Three other people were already there, and then the eight others got in as well. He was blindfolded and his hands and feet were tied. The car drove off, and after about half an hour he heard a sound resembling that of a stone or a bottle hitting the car. He heard the car door open, and shots were fired. He was later transferred into a vehicle which, because he could feel the wind on his face, he assumed to be open to the air. Eventually, he was told to get out. He was unable to do this until they had untied his legs. He was then made to stand for half an hour, until the blindfold was taken off. He realised then that he was in the Jenin military headquarters. After being briefly questioned by a Shin Bet officer named Uri, he was told: "We brought you by mistake," was given his ID card and told to go.[72] This event was corroborated by two other reports received by al-Haq.

Al-Haq bases its contention that such units do not consist of settlers on a number of factors. To date, and despite our continuous investigation of settler activity in the Occupied Territories, we have not documented nor even received reports of a single case in which settlers used civilian Palestinian vehicles to carry out vigilante activities. The immediate arrival of the army, as well as the other details described in the Silat al-Harithiya case, presents additional compelling circumstantial evidence, as does the overt role played by the military authorities in the Jenin kidnapping case. Thus, the existing evidence suggests that these units are either official or, alternatively, consist of civilians so well integrated into the official structure that the distinction is for all intents and purposes meaningless.

The use of such undercover units would be the logical extension of a policy of targeting individuals perceived to play a leading role in organising demonstrations or any other forms of protest. The existence of such units to carry out a more general type of arbitrary violence (as described above) also fits a consistent pattern of Israeli army behaviour, especially during the uprising. If indeed the killing of Palestinians perceived as being leaders in their villages has become an official, albeit concealed practice (as several journalists have suggested on the basis of conversations with unidentified "security sources"), it represents the most serious violation of human rights approved as a matter of policy at the highest levels of the Israeli government yet to be exposed.

D. Investigations

In the face of the high level of casualties among Palestinians in the Occupied Territories caused by the Israeli armed forces since the beginning of the uprising, and given the many charges of army brutality, the evidence of which is supported by affidavits obtained by al-Haq, proper investigations into instances of violence perpetrated by soldiers are an urgent matter. If breaches of standing orders are found to have taken place, charges should be pressed against individual soldiers. On a second level, if orders given to soldiers themselves constitute a violation of the law, those responsible for issuing the orders should be prosecuted.

However, out of 170 files opened in the wake of Israeli actions causing deaths in the Territories from 9 December 1987, until the end of September only 2 had culminated in charges of murder or manslaughter.[73] Throughout the uprising, reports of excessive use of force and failure to follow procedures have been met with the response that these are "exceptions"—aberrations only. To have credibility, such claims need to be backed up by the evidence available from open, independent and impartial investigations. Instead, investigations into army actions are carried out by higher echelons of the Israeli armed forces. Their consistent failure to bring people to trial raises grave doubts about the impartiality of these investigations.

The relatively small number of complaints that are filed is one of the reasons regularly cited by the Israeli military authorities for the comparatively small number of investigations which are initiated. In the 1984 Karp Report on law enforcement in the Occupied Territories the conclusion was drawn that there was "substance to the fear that the pretext of alienation from the authorities...and fear of complaining due to...fear of revenge, do indeed constitute a reason for failure to report...The real situation points to a vicious circle in which occurrences aren't investigated for lack of complaint, while complaints aren't submitted because of lack of proper investigation."[74]

In fact, the police in the Occupied Territories in practice do not receive complaints against the army.[75] It is not simply that there is no real prospect of redress that deters Palestinians from making complaints. Threats and intimidation are commonplace to Palestinians trying to file complaints, and there is also a significant risk of later reprisals. Lawyers themselves are not protected from this—e.g. Mona Rishmawi, a Ramallah lawyer and a member of al-Haq's executive committee, found herself threatened with prosecution on 30 November 1987, four months after she had filed a complaint about the hooding of a prisoner in Ramallah Prison, an event she personally witnessed.[76] Failure to receive complaints is in any case insufficient grounds for failing to investigate incidents such as those which have been occurring so regularly in the past twelve months. The Israeli High Court of Justice itself made this point as far back as 1981.[77]

In the case of deaths caused by the Israeli army, an investigation is automatically carried out, so the question here becomes one of independence and impartiality. All investigations are carried out by the military police. If a preliminary investigation reveals that there may be grounds for pressing charges, the case is referred to the District Military Prosecutor who makes the decision whether to instigate a court martial or a disciplinary trial, or to close the case. If there is evidence that the soldier disregarded orders or the rules of engagement rather than merely misjudging the situation, he may be court-martialled.[78]

Despite the secrecy shrouding the findings of Israeli army investigations, the results are clear in practice. On 27 October Judge Advocate-General Amnon Strashnow stated that only 32 cases had resulted in any sort of disciplinary measure or court hearing at all, according to a report in the *Jerusalem Post* the following day. The highest sentence so far passed has been one year, for manslaughter, for the shooting at point-blank range of a storekeeper (Touqan Nusaba) in Gaza in January.[79] Sentences of four and five months respectively for two of the soldiers involved in the burial incident in Salem near Nablus in February were reduced by half two months later.[80]

In October 1988, four soldiers of the elite Givati Brigade went on trial accused of beating to death Hani Shami from Jabaliya Refugee Camp on 22 August 1988. Their defence was that they had "followed orders"—these orders being "to break the legs of people who violate orders."[81] If such a defence is accepted, the credibility of the Israeli legal system will be seriously dented. It is beyond dispute that "manifestly illegal" orders give rise to a duty to disobey on the part of the soldier receiving them. If he fails to do so, he is liable to be tried for any crimes he commits as a result of following those orders. Of course, for justice to be done, those who issued the orders are also liable under law for any illegalities committed. The Defence Minister, who is in charge of the army, is ultimately responsible for all orders and should therefore be held accountable accordingly. Where orders are oral only, the burden of proving that they actually existed and were issued by a person in a position of responsibility may be more difficult to discharge. However, the culpability of the individual soldier for the actions he committed remains the same.

The announcement by the Israeli authorities of investigations into every fatal incident has considerable influence on the way in which the Israeli state is perceived in public opinion, be it domestic or international. However, a more representative picture only emerges when the results of such investigations become clear: whether or not the findings were ever made public, who conducted the investigation, whether or not the investigation was thorough, and how long it took to be completed. An investigation which is not independent and which fails to take evidence from a variety of sources on both sides of the dispute, and which does not make public its findings, is an abuse of the term. Failure to conduct investigations properly, whether or not complaints are received, involves the complicity of the Israeli authorities at the highest levels. Guidelines for army behaviour are meaningless without proper enforcement of these rules and the knowledge of every soldier that he will be punished for every infringement thereof. The situation described in this chapter shows that this quite clearly is not the case with the Israeli armed forces in the Occupied Territories.

E. Conclusion

One of the Palestinian uprising's most lasting images to outside observers has been that of stone-throwing "shebab" (youths) confronted by armed Israeli soldiers firing lethal weapons. The CBS filming in February 1988 of Palestinian youths being systematically battered with rocks by soldiers in a remote West Bank hillside confirmed, perhaps more so than anything else, the brutal nature of the Israeli repression of the uprising.

While not necessarily the most serious long-term assault on the Palestinian nation—that title being more appropriately accorded to quieter measures of economic and institutional repression (dealt with in Chapters 7, 8 and 9)—the policy of "force, might and beatings" most obviously violates basic individual human rights and the right to life in particular. It is our view that, like attacks on the socio-economic infrastructure of the Occupied Territories, the policy of excessive force has a distinct albeit less sophisticated rationale. The "beatings" policy pursued through the uprising (and briefly articulated in January) points to the continuing goal of repressing the uprising through physical intimidation today with a view to controlling the Palestinian population tomorrow. The suppression of any manifestations of Palestinian resistance has typically been pursued through the physical intimidation of large numbers of people at a time as a form of collective punishment or, alternatively, by pinpointing and either injuring or killing perceived leaders.

This being the Israeli rationale for the violent repression of the uprising, there appears to be a contradiction between the proclaimed restrictions on the use of force and the unspoken policy. With the door open thus far, it is not surprising that army violence frequently exceeds even authorised levels.

In order to establish this, it has been necessary as a preliminary step to answer Israeli justifications of their violent and illegal behaviour. In essence these claim that strict guidelines regulate the use of force by the army; that any deviations from them are merely aberrations; and that in any case there is an effective system of investigating claims concerning illegal behaviour by soldiers.

The evidence documented and presented in this chapter shows the opposite. The Israeli government's claims that its response to the uprising is a lawful one do not fit the facts. The assertion that cases of illegality are mere "exceptions to the rule" cannot stand when seen against a wealth of documented examples showing savage behaviour by the army on a regular basis. The following report in the *Jerusalem Post* of 30 November 1988 summarises this point graphically:

> Figures obtained yesterday from [UNRWA] show that a record number of Palestinian casualties have been reported in the Gaza Strip so far this month—the highest toll in a single month since the start of the uprising. Official reports, on the contrary, show that violent protest in the territories declined sharply in November.

The implications of a sustained popular uprising in the West Bank and Gaza Strip for the long-term status of the Occupied Territories have caused the Israeli authorities to employ whatever means are necessary at whatever cost to eliminate this threat to their status as permanent occupiers.

Finally, if the official Israeli policy of violent repression of rebellion is illegal, it has also been manifestly illogical. Claims that the Palestinian uprising can be crushed through massive force is like dousing a fire with kerosene. The repeated abuse of human rights during the uprising merely serves to remind of the oppression that caused the rebellion to begin with.

FOOTNOTES TO CHAPTER 1

1. It is extremely difficult to give a precise figure for the numbers of casualties. Moreover, official estimates have contradicted themselves openly. See Section A for a discussion of this point and a statistical review of the deaths and casualties.
2. *Jerusalem Post*, 25 December 1987.
3. On 27 September 1988, the *Jerusalem Post* reported UNRWA sources as stating that in the previous two months there had been a six-fold increase in Palestinian casualties after the introduction of plastic bullets.
4. *Jerusalem Post*, 28 September 1988.
5. See also, *Jerusalem Post*, 26 January 1988. "Rabin described the numerous accounts of beating detainees and innocent people as "exceptions." Some soldiers were enthusiastic about the opportunity of beating Arabs but others suffered "distress" he said."
6. Al-Haq believes that this figure represents 90 percent of the total number of Palestinins killed in the West Bank in the period between 9 December 1987 and 15 November 1988.
7. *Jerusalem Post*, 9 October 1988.
8. The report states that "the latter tend to report only those cases of serious injury." These numbers relate to "the casualties directly resulting from the ongoing confrontations between the Palestinian community in the Gaza Strip and the Israeli governing authorities represented by the IDF and the Border Police."

    It should be stressed once more that the difference between the last year and the previous 20 years of occupation is one of scale rather than type. By way of comparison, from the beginning of 1982 until 30 October 1987 al-Haq documented 55 deaths and 239 injuries caused by Israeli army action; 9 people died in 1987 before 9 December 1987.
9. *Jerusalem Post*, 30 November 1988.
10. See Section D of this chapter for reference to the recent trial of four Givati Brigade soldiers for allegedly beating to death Hani Shami from Jabaliya Refugee Camp in August 1988, where orders from the army unit commander to the soldiers were totally inconsistent with the guidelines which have been published.
11. On 19 October 1987, al-Haq published a Briefing Paper in which it requested: (i) publication of the criteria according to which members of the armed forces are allowed to open fire; (ii) a careful review of these standing orders; (iii) thorough and independent inquiry into each use of live ammunition, and (iv) prosecution of those individuals found responsible for the misuse of firearms. (Al-Haq, *Shooting by the Israeli Armed Forces*, October 1987) On other occasions, specific interventions with the military authorities have been made by al-Haq on this point. Full documentation on particular incidents was provided to the authorities, but no reply was received. For example, a letter was sent by al-Haq to Central Area Commander Amram Mitzna on this subject on 25 November 1987.
12. The article stated that shooting at persons is permitted in 3 situations:
    (i) When soldiers' lives are threatened by gunfire or explosives;

(ii) when rioters bodily assault troops or hurl "cold" weapons (rocks, iron-bars, etc.) in a way which poses a "real and present danger to their lives;"

(iii) when stopping a fleeing suspect.

These criteria are virtually identical to those identified in the 1987 West Bank Data Base Project Report, pp. 42-43. This report states that between early 1986 and late 1987 the orders regarding the opening of fire had been widened. Before this time, soldiers were allowed to shoot only when they found themselves in "life-threatening" situations. Under the new orders, soldiers were to include opening fire as part of the procedure of detaining suspects during a "disturbance," with this term being defined as riots, demonstrations, gatherings and roadblocks. If the disturbance was then followed by physical attack or the throwing of rocks or other "cold" objects (e.g. iron bars), then the soldier could open fire after giving a loud warning in Arabic that he intended to do so, and provided there was no alternative means available. If the suspect was not caught or tried to escape, shots could be fired, first at an 80-degree angle in the air, and then, with intent to injure, at the legs.

13. See Appendix 1-A.
14. Al-Haq Affidavit No. 1264. Sa'dah al-Qar'awi died from her injuries.
15. This point was addressed in a letter from the Lawyers Committee for Human Rights to Yitzhak Shamir, on 10 March 1988, in which concern was expressed that this provision was overly broad, and exceeded the "permissible grounds as outlined in the UN Code of Conduct. It would appear to allow shooting at a suspect, regardless of...the reasons for his flight." In a footnote to the Committee's letter (on page 13) it is stated: "IDF regulations define a suspect as a person who can be 'reasonably assumed' to be on his way to perpetrate a terrorist attack or serious crime. A serious crime is defined as murder or attempted murder, illegal possession of weapons, membership or activity in a banned organisation, or hurling stones in a way that endangers lives. Under this definition, virtually any Palestinian fleeing the army is potentially liable to be shot [on] suspicion of membership or activity in the PLO, or stone-throwing. Certainly it would be all but impossible to prove that such an assumption was 'unreasonable' in the circumstances."
16. For example, on 3 April 1987, around 450 Bir Zeit University students were demonstrating in the town of Bir Zeit. A military unit arrived and soldiers opened fire, causing many of the students to run for cover. In a sworn affidavit taken by al-Haq, one of the students, who requested anonymity, described how a friend who was running next to her was injured by army fire. See Al-Haq Affidavit No. 1010.
17. Al-Haq Affidavit No. 1306.
18. According to Israel army radio on 15 August 1988, at 19:30 GMT: "Military sources said tonight that the IDF has recently introduced several new measures against the violence in the territories, including special bullets intended to injure while reducing the risk of killing."
19. *Jerusalem Post*, 28 September 1988.
20. Thus, in contrast to the "baton rounds" used in other countries, such as Northern Ireland, where they are approximately five inches long, about 1.5 inches in diameter, and cannot penetrate the body.
21. *Jerusalem Post*, 5 October 1988.

22. *Jerusalem Post*, 2 October 1988.
23. *Supra*, footnote 3. International condemnation of the use of plastic bullets came swiftly, particularly from the U.S. and U.K. The U.S. State Department spokeswoman Phyllis Oakley stated: "We can see no justification for a policy admittedly designed to cause an increase in casualties." *Jerusalem Post*, 29 September 1988. Vocal criticism from within Israel itself has also been expressed. The Association for Civil Rights in Israel [ACRI], in a letter to Attorney-General Yosef Harish on 29 September 1988, commented: "There is no doubt that opening fire for purposes of deterrence is an illegal act. The matter is reminiscent of the sanction given nine months ago to the use of violence and beatings for purposes of punishment and deterrence." In the same letter ACRI called for legal guidelines to be issued on the use of plastic bullets in the Occupied Territories, commenting that Rabin's statement that the bullets were being used to increase injuries amongst Palestinian rioters was clearly illegal. *Jerusalem Post*, 30 September 1988.
24. Translation from the "Report on the Violations of Human Rights in the Territories during the Uprising, 1988" by the Israeli League for Human and Civil Rights, Tel Aviv, 1988.
25. Universal Declaration of Human Rights, adopted by the UN General Assembly on 10 December 1948.
26. The 1949 Fourth Geneva Convention Relative to the Protection of Civilian Persons in Time of War is the main international law standard applicable to a situation of belligerent occupation. Article 3 is common to all four Geneva Conventions of 1949.
27. Article 3 of the UN Code of Conduct for Law Enforcement Officials.
28. The official commentary to this article states:

    (a) This provision emphasizes that the use of force by law enforcement officials should be exceptional; while it implies that law enforcement officials may be authorized to use force as is reasonably necessary under the circumstances for the prevention of crime or in effecting or assisting in the lawful arrest of offenders or suspected offenders, no force going beyond that may be used.

    (b) National law ordinarily restricts the use of force by law enforcement officials in accordance with a principle of proportionality. It is to be understood that such national principles of proportionality are to be respected in the interpretation of this provision. In no case should this provision be interpreted to authorize the use of force which is disproportionate to the legitimate object to be achieved.

    (c) The use of firearms is considered an extreme measure. Every effort should be made to exclude the use of firearms, especially against children. In general, firearms should not be used except when a suspected offender offers armed resistance or otherwise jeopardizes the lives of others and less extreme measures are not sufficient to restrain or apprehend the suspected offender. In every instance in which a firearm is discharged, a report should be made promptly to the competent authorities.
29. *Jerusalem Post*, 26 January 1988. In the words of Yitzhak Shamir: "The night of the hang-gliders [in Upper Galilee] shattered the barrier of fear of the IDF among the Arabs of Judea, Samaria and Gaza. Our task now is to recreate that barrier and once again put the fear of death into the Arabs of the areas so as to deter them from attacking us any more."

30. *Jerusalem Post*, 20 January 1988. In the same article, Joshua Brilliant comments: "Some soldiers still don't have riot control equipment and are presumably expected to kick Palestinians and hit them with their bare fists. This method is considered more effective than detention. The *Jeruslaem Post* was told a detainee sent to Fara'a Prison will be freed in 18 days unless the authorities have enough evidence to charge him. He may then resume stoning soldiers. But if troops break his hand he won't be able to throw stones for a month and a half." In the *Jerusalem Post* of 26 January 1988, it was stated: "Addressing defence reporters [Rabin] said the policy of beating demonstrators was introduced on January 4 or 5, and announced only last week because reporters had asked him about it. He decided to reveal the facts so as not to create a situation in which one set of directives is transmitted within the army while another picture is presented to the public. The soldiers must feel that they have the backing of the political echelon, he said."
31. See Physicians for Human Rights report of their fact-finding mission to the Occupied Territories on 4-12 February 1988: *Casualties of Conflict: Medical Care and Human Rights in the West Bank and Gaza Strip*, February 1988.
32. *Jerusalem Post*, 26 January 1988.
33. *Jerusalem Post*, 25 January 1988. On 24 January it was reported that the Commander of the Central Area, Amram Mitzna, had ordered commanders to ensure that beatings were only used to break up violent protests and not against persons uninvolved in the "rioting." *Jerusalem Post*, 24 January 1988.
34. *Jerusalem Post*, 25 January 1988: "...there is no right to break someone's arm just because he violated the law...If beatings are used as a form of summary punishment they are manifestly illegal."
35. *Jerusalem Post*, 23 February 1988.
36. *Jerusalem Post*, 24 February 1988.
37. *Army Brutality in the West Bank—A Press Briefing* (Al-Haq, 13 October 1987). The briefing included the following account: "On Friday 17 September 1987 at four o'clock in the morning, the Israeli military authorities imposed a curfew on Balata refugee camp near Nablus, the second curfew in one week. The curfew lasted one day. On September 18, when the atmosphere in the camp was relatively calm, groups of Israeli soldiers went around inside the camp, entering and searching houses, and in some cases arresting camp residents, including children. Some of those who were taken report having been beaten, at times severely, by soldiers. Some were beaten both in front of their families, and later on the roof of a house used by the army as an observation post. All were eventually released; several required hospitalisation."
38. For example, al-Haq documented reports of systematic and widescale beating in Deheisha Refugee Camp in October 1988.
39. Al-Haq Affidavit No. 1153. See also Appendix 1-B for al-Haq Affidavit No. 1151 on the same subject.
40. Al-Haq Affidavit No. 1207.
41. Al-Haq Affidavit No. 1162. See also al-Haq Affidavit No. 1161 in Appendix 1-C. For another example, see Appendix 1-G.
42. See Appendix 1-D for further examples: al-Haq Affidavits Nos. 1447 and 1281.
43. Such events are no longer as widely reported as before, as media interest

in the uprising has declined and those members of the press still covering events are having their work increasingly hampered by Israeli restrictions and harassment. See the section on press harassment in Chapter 5.
44. Al-Haq Affidavit No. 1277.
45. Al-Haq Affidavit No. 1353.
46. Al-Haq Affidavit No. 1255, taken on 24 April 1988; see also al-Haq Affidavit No. 1233 in Appendix 1-E.
47. See Amnesty International, "The Misuse of Tear Gas by Israeli Army Personnel in the Israeli Occupied Territories" (AI INDEX MDE/15/26/88), p. 5. This report also quotes the Federal Laboratories Handbook for comments on the effects of the two types of gas. CS gas, which is stated to have more severe effects than CN gas, is stated to cause "intense irritation of all moist skin areas, mouth, nose and sinuses. Burning sensation causes extreme temporary discomfort."
48. There are also warnings about the contamination of buildings which results when tear gas designed for outdoor use is used in confined spaces: "We must again emphasise that devices intended for external use will carry much greater quantities of chemicals...but if the same volume of chemicals is released within the confines of a building, it can cause injury or death. Moreover it can, and has on many occasions, caused massive contamination that has prevented the use of the buildings for weeks, months and even years." See Federal Laboratories Handbook.
49. See Appendix 1-A.
50. Al-Haq Affidavit No. 1132.
51. Al-Haq Affidavit No. 1263.
52. Al-Haq Affidavit No. 1204.
53. Al-Haq Affidavit No. 1202. Doctors at government hospitals are in practice restricted in what information they can make public, according to hospital officials.
54. Al-Haq Affidavit No. 1227.
55. Al-Haq Affidavit No. 1229.
56. Report of 5 May 1988 in response to press reports and a question in the Knesset from MK Dedi Zucker.
57. *Supra,* footnote 31.
58. Amnesty International, "Misuse" (*Supra,* footnote 47), p. 1: "Local medical personnel have reported that in recent months tear gas appears to have been the cause of or a contributory factor in the deaths of more than 40 Palestinians in the Occupied Territories. Others have been seriously affected and hundreds have required hospital treatment."
59. *Supra,* footnote 47.
60. *Jerusalem Post,* 8 May 1988.
61. Al-Haq Affidavit No. 1183.
62. Al-Haq Affidavit No. 1456.
63. *Jerusalem Post,* 27 November 1988.
64. See Appendix 1-F for a full case sheet.
65. Al-Haq Affidavit No. 1248.
66. Al-Haq Affidavit No. 1459.
67. Al-Haq Affidavit No. 1293.
68. Al-Haq Affidavit No. 1458.
69. *Jerusalem Post,* 9 October 1988.

70. Al-Haq Affidavit No. 1420.
71. Unnumbered affidavit, taken by al-Haq on 4 November 1988.
72. Al-Haq Affidavit No. 1482.
73. Avigdor Feldman in *Hadashot*, 30 September 1988.
74. Report submitted by the Deputy Attorney-General of Israel, Judith Karp, re: Investigation of Suspicions Against Israelis in Judea and Samaria, 25 May 1982; reprinted in the *Palestine Yearbook of International Law*, 1984, Vol. 1, pp. 208-209. Although this report discusses criminal acts by settlers, the conclusions it reaches apply also to the situation concerning investigations into criminal acts by members of the Israeli armed forces.
75. A recent complaint by ACRI to the Legal Advisor of the Civil Administration about this matter prompted a reply in which the Legal Advisor stated that he would instruct police officers to begin to accept complaints, which would then be transferred to him. To date this procedure has not been enforced, as far as al-Haq can ascertain. See Raja Shehadeh, *Occupier's Law: Israel and the West Bank* (Washington, D.C.: Institute for Palestine Studies, second edition 1988), p. 238.
76. Al-Haq Newsletter No. 21.
77. Beit Hadassah case, HCJ 175/81.
78. Amnesty International, "The Use of Live Ammunition by Members of the Israel Defence Forces" (AI INDEX MDE/15/30/88, June 1988). On 27 May 1988, MK Amnon Rubinstein complained about the length of time it was taking for an investigation into an alleged death by beating at the hands of soldiers that had occurred on February 9 to be completed. To date, not even the result of the investigation into the killing of two administrative detainees at the detention facility in the Negev desert on 16 August 1988, Ketsyot/Ansar III, has been made public.
79. *Jerusalem Post*, 6 June 1988. Standards for deciding when to press charges do not appear to be objectively applied. A brigade commander who shot and killed a "Palestinian demonstrator" was found to have exercised "faulty judgement" by IDF Judge-Advocate General Amnon Strashnow, who recommended that he be court-martialled. However, Chief of General Staff Dan Shomrom overruled him on the grounds that the oficer had done "good work" in the past, and should therefore only face a disciplinary hearing. The officer was relieved of his command. *Jerusalem Post*, 17 August 1988.
80. Four Palestinan youths were buried alive in the village of Salem near Nablus when a soldier ordered a military bulldozer to dump earth on the men who had just been beaten by a group of soldiers. *Jerusalem Post*, 15 February 1988.
81. *Jerusalem Post*, 5 October 1988.

Appendix 1-A

WEAPONS USED BY THE ISRAELI ARMED FORCES IN THE OCCUPIED TERRITORIES SINCE 9 DECEMBER 1987 AND THE INJURIES WHICH HAVE RESULTED.

1. Weapons

In the early stages of the uprising, Israeli military sources admitted that they had been taken by surprise by the scale and intensity of the "disturbances" in the Occupied Territories, and had run out of rubber bullets, tear gas and other equipment. This "lack of preparedness" was used to explain at least in part the high numbers of deaths especially in the first weeks.

In late December 1987 attitudes changed. Quantities of basic "riot control" equipment were stockpiled and military sources stated that in future, soldiers would be provided with special training in riot control techniques, and more men would be recruited into the Border Police, the force usually used for "riot control." (*Jerusalem Post*, 29 December 1988) A variety of different weapons and equipment have been introduced since that time, some of which were abandoned once they had proven ineffective. However, neither the equipment nor whatever training may have been instituted for the soldiers have had any noticeable effect in decreasing either deaths or injuries among the Palestinian population of the Occupied Territories. The following paragraphs provide a more technical description of the weapons in use.

(a) Live Ammunition:
Two types of weapons are generally used by the IDF: the M-16 rifle using high-velocity bullets, and the Galil assault rifle. Such high-velocity bullets do great damage to internal organs, significantly more than ordinary bullets. As weapons of riot control they are entirely inappropriate, in particular given the nature of the demonstrations as described above. Ori Nir wrote in *HaAretz* on 3 November 1987 that bullets from "the assault rifles used as personal weapons by IDF soldiers (M-16 and Galil) do great damage because of their muzzle velocity (approx. 990 meters per second), which causes them to spin around inside the victim's body damaging internal organs."

(b) Plastic Bullets:
Plastic bullets are in fairly wide use internationally as a method of "riot control," but not of the type used by Israel in the Occupied Territories. These are approximately the same size and shape as live bullets, made

of an extremely hard type of plastic which shows up on X-rays, capable of penetrating the body and damaging internal organs. Ostensibly non-lethal if fired at a distance of more than 70 meters, the practical difference between these bullets and live ammunition is thus less than might appear by the use of the misnomer "plastic bullets."

(c) Rubber Bullets:
Rubber bullets have been used throughout the uprising; they are short cylinders of hard rubber, with flat ends, 1.8cm in diameter by 1.8cm in length; inside there is a heavy metal core. They do not penetrate the body, but the usual effect is to cause extensive and severe bruising. If shot at close range, or in someone's eye, for example, the injuries can be much more serious. Several cases of shooting by rubber bullets have resulted in people losing an eye.

(d) Tear Gas:
Israel has stated that it has used both CS and CN gas in the Occupied Territories, introducing CS gas in January 1988. At least 39 people have died as a result of inhaling tear gas in this period, and in June a team of Israeli doctors confirmed reports of a substantial increase in miscarriages as a direct result of tear gas inhalation.

Federal Laboratories of Pennsylvania, who supplied Israel with most of its tear gas until May 1988, printed clear instructions as to its proper use on the outside of the teargas canister:

> FOR USE BY TRAINED PERSONNEL ONLY
> WARNING: May Start Fires. Must not be fired directly at persons as death or injury may result.
> FOR OUTDOOR USE ONLY

(e) Other "Riot Control" Equipment:
During the uprising, intermittent use has also been made of gravel-shooters, marble cannons, water cannons, and also helicopters dropping rocks. Most were abandoned once proven ineffective, although gravel-shooters were re-introduced in the West Bank in mid-November. The use of wooden and fibreglass clubs, 60 cm in length, and with a diameter of 5 cm, was introduced in January 1988 as part of the beating policy.

2. Injuries

A report by a team of six Israeli doctors, commissioned by MK Dedi Zucker to look into the medical situation in Gaza concluded that the use of the M-16 rifle is unjustifiable in these circumstances, because of the extensive damage it causes. Further, they stated that its use does not conform to IDF orders which state that only such force as is necessary should be used, and then always with care to cause only minimal injuries.

It appears that a single bullet in most cases causes damage to the body far in excess of the straight trajectory of the bullet. The Boston-based Physicians for Human Rights (PHR), an independent monitoring group which visited the Occupied Territories in early February, reported as follows:

> From gunshot wounds, patients sustained either open comminuted fractures of one or more major bones of the leg, in which the bone is splintered or crushed, with an external wound through which bone may protrude, or complex internal injuries from bullets entering the abdomen or lower back.

(*The Casualties of Conflict: Medical Care and Human Rights in the West Bank and Gaza Strip*—Report of a fact-finding mission by Physicians for Human Rights, 30 March 1988, p. 7)

Later in the report, PHR states that many of the patients they saw who had been shot showed a diffuse pattern of lead fragments. After consulting American ballistics experts, and while acknowledging that further study of the subject is necessary, they concluded that

> ...almost all military weapons, including those used by the Israeli army, fire bullets at such high velocity that even jacketed bullets will fragment inside the body, whether or not they hit bone.

The nature and pattern of injuries suffered shows that approximately 46 percent of gunshot wounds were in the legs, and about 30 percent of the gunshot injuries over one day old seen by the PHR had resulted in long-term or permanent loss of leg function—monoplegics, paraplegics and quadraplegics. (*Casualties of Conflict*, p. 10)

PHR concluded that the extensive nature of the injuries:

> reflect the inappropriateness of high-powered military weapons for civilian crowd control... [T]he wounds that result from bullet fragmentation are extensive, involve damage to many structures, and often cause neurological injury of devastating consequence. (*Casualties of Conflict*, p. 20)

This is not a price that should be paid in preference to investment in proper riot control equipment to put down disturbances in which the weapons used by demonstrators are limited to those they can throw with their hands.

Appendix 1-B

TRANSLATION OF SWORN AFFIDAVIT (#1151) TAKEN BY AL-HAQ

I the undersigned, Shihada 'Abdallah Shihad, aged 27, resident of Hawara in the Nablus District and by nature an ironsmith, having been warned to tell the truth or be subject to criminal liability, hereby state as follows:

At about 10:00 p.m. on Thursday 21 January 1988, I was preparing to go to bed when the son of the chairman of the Howara Village council, Muhammad Jihad Mufdi Al-Hawari, came to inform me that army troops had come to the village wanting to arrest a number of young men and that I was one of them. He informed me that I was to accompany him to the place where the soldiers were assembled at the gas station located at the northern entrance of the village on the road to Nablus. I put on my clothes and accompanied him to the main street where we met his father, the chairman of the village council, who was in his private car. We went together in the car to the place where the soldiers were assembled. There the soldiers ordered me to stand by the wall for about three quarters of an hour, during which time the chairman of the council was bringing the young men wanted by the army. While standing with the other young men I saw large numbers of soldiers (around sixty) and I also saw groups of soldiers gradually arriving from the fields. Each group consisted of about 12 soldiers. I assume that the soldiers had been surrounding the village in case the young men should escape. I also saw a military truck, a bus and two military vehicles parked in the place. I saw a number of officers, amongst whom was officer "Dany" of the military government in Nablus. When all wanted for detention had arrived (about 12 young men), we were ordered by the soldiers to walk towards the bus in groups of three. Near the bus we were searched thoroughly, our hands were tied behind our backs with plastic thongs and we were instructed to get into the red and white bus. We were ordered to sit on the bus floor, in the corridor between the seats. Some of the soldiers sat in the seats, others stood in the front of the bus and at the rear. We were ordered to lower our heads. The soldiers closed all the windows of the bus and the heaters were switched on, causing the temperature to become extremely high. Before the bus started moving, I heard one of the youths, Sa'id Saleh Nimr Oudeh, shouting loudly: "I want water, I want to breathe." Sa'id was placed in the rear and I knew that he has a nervous complaint. I raised my head a little and saw the soldiers beating him with their hands on his face. Then they beat him with the clubs. I heard him say: "Beat me but give me water." At this stage one of the soldiers gagged him with a piece of cloth. The bus moved in the direction of Nablus city. Until that moment I thought that it was heading to Fara'a Detention Camp but I was surprised to see the bus stop at a distance of about 300 meters from the gas station for about ten minutes. I heard people get in and out of the bus. Then the bus moved off and stopped after about 100 meters. Then it moved off again, halting several times until at last it stopped. I was surprised to hear the soldiers ordering me to leave the bus. I realised that the bus was stopping for the youths to be taken into some fields. I was led off by the soldiers together with two young men, Jamal Abdulkadir Soufan and the sick young man Sa'id Saleh Nimer Oudeh. We were taken to the fields neighbouring the main road at a distance of about 100 meters and about one kilometer from the Howara military camp. The soldiers ordered me to sit on the muddy ground. They also ordered the others to do the same, but they were about 5 to 6 meters away from me, one in front of me and one behind. One of the soldiers ordered me in Hebrew, a language which I know, to lie on my back, but I refused to do that. As a result one of the soldiers kicked me hard and I thus fell on the ground. When I tried to get up one of them pressed with his foot on my chest while about eight other soldiers started beating me on my legs with their clubs. The soldiers gagged my mouth tightly with a scarf which I wore round my neck for the cold. While they were beating me I heard one of the young men shouting and crying loudly: "Mother, Mother." I was in great pain. I tried with all my strength to stand and move but the soldier placed his muddy boots over my mouth and pressed on my face and head in order to stop me moving. During the beating I heard one of the soldiers saying in Hebrew, "Maze' Rijlaym Shlouh Afneem?" meaning: "what's this, his feet must be made of stone." I felt extremely weak and unable to move. I was on the point of vomiting. One of the soldiers lifted my hand upwards and let it go, and it dropped to the ground. He repeated this. The soldier who was pressing my face with his boots got hold of me and turned me over on my belly. Then I heard the same soldier who had turned me over (I think it was the officer in charge), say in Hebrew: "Tesnla Maka Biskeen" meaning: "give him a blow with the knife." Immediately I heard one of the soldiers shout loudly but I was motionless. They believed, I think, that I was unable to move, and in spite of this one of the soldiers lifted my face from the mud and played the torch over my face. After that I was left thrown on the ground. Then they brought the young man Sa'id Saleh and told him in Arabic, "You see this friend of yours"—pointing at me—"tell your fellow villagers that they will be beaten like him." The operation of beating continued for about a quarter of an hour. After that the soldiers left the place. When I was sure that they had gone, I tried to stand and saw the blood coming off my leg. I made every effort leaning on the rocks and trees until I got home. I was taken to Rafidia hospital in Nablus where I received first aid. It was found out that I was suffering from the tearing of tissues, wounds, and bruises in both legs and that I could not walk at all. My leg was bleeding very severely and it is still bleeding to this day, 28 January 1988. The deeper wounds were stitched.

Date: 28 January 1988 (Signature)
Name available for publication

Appendix 1-C

TRANSLATION OF SWORN AFFIDAVIT (#1161) TAKEN BY AL-HAQ

I the undersigned, Mouin Ahmad Mahmoud Abu Baker, aged 19, a resident of Ya'bad/Jenin, and a trader, having been warned to tell the truth or be subject to criminal liabiity, hereby declare as follows:

It was about 11.30 a.m. on Tuesday, 19 January 1988, and I was at home in Ya'bad. I was surprised to see about 20 soldiers breaking into our house after breaking the iron door. Upon seeing me, and without asking any questions, they set about me with clubs. They dragged me outside into the street, still beating me with their clubs and with the butts and barrels of their rifles. They threw five empty bottles at me, at all parts of my body. They were attacking me in groups of about fifteen at a time, and I was being beaten from all sides, on my head, face, stomach, back, legs and hands. While they were dragging me bare-foot, through the streets, they found a hosepipe and beat me all over with it. The blood flowed from my head, nose, mouth, face and all parts of my body. They were also verbally abusing me in the worst possible fashion. They continued dragging me in the streets for at least two hours. Then they took me to the eastern part of the village near the gas station where soldiers were gathered and there they tied my hands behind my back with metal wire and a leather belt, and tied me to an electricity pole. My hands were also tied by an iron chain and they started beating me up with their fists, feet, clubs, and the butts of their rifles. My body was covered with blood and I was screaming in pain. It's hard to describe the state that I was in. I fell on the ground, but as I was tied up, I couldn't move. After about an hour and a half, I saw some women coming towards me to untie me from the electricity pole. One elderly woman came forward; a soldier struck her and she fell to the ground. She tried again but the soldiers fired many shots on the ground around me, and they hit the old woman with a stone in her stomach, which caused the women to retreat. Then a local sheikh [Arabic for an old man or religious person] came to untie me; they shot at him, but he kept coming forward, intent on setting me free. The soldiers fell on him with their clubs, and prevented him from getting to me. I remained tied to the electricity pole for about two hours. Then the soldiers tore my clothes and one of them began writing on my back while the others started beating me on the bruises that I had on my back as a result of having been dragged along the ground. After that they left me unconscious, lying on the ground. The youths took me to Jenin Hospital which transfered me to 'Affula Hospital where I was treated. Until this day, I am still unwell. I had stitches on my forehead and nose, due to the deep wounds which I sustained.

Date: 21 January 1988 (Signature)
Name available for publication

Appendix 1-D

TRANSLATION OF SWORN AFFIDAVIT (#1447) TAKEN BY AL-HAQ

I the undersigned, Nader 'Issa Elias Qumsiyyeh, 22 years of age, an olive-wood carver and a resident of Beit Sahour, after being warned to tell the truth or be subject to criminal liability, hereby state as follows:

At around 3:30 p.m. on Sunday 2 October 1988 while I was at my uncle's house, a number of soldiers stormed the house. They beat me inside the house with fists and feet, then took me outside. One soldier pushed me down the stairs and I fell to the ground. They started kicking me. These three soldiers started to club my right hand, causing it to swell up. They stepped on me with their boots. One soldier picked me up and shoved me against the wall so that I fell to the ground. They continued to beat me. They also beat my cousin 'Issa in front of me and one soldier broke a club on his back and they slammed him against the car. They beat us saying all the time that we had thrown stones. They said this and beat us not giving us a chance to speak or defend ourselves. The beating went on for about 20 minutes, then they released us. I couldn't walk, I crawled into my uncle's house, and I could hardly breathe because the beating had concentrated on my lungs and neck. When 'Issa and I returned home, we received first aid.

Date: 5 November 1988   (Signature)
Name available for publication

Appendix 1-E

TRANSLATION OF SWORN AFFIDAVIT (#1281) TAKEN BY AL-HAQ

I, the undersigned Nimir Mohamad Khalil Jfal, 13 years old, a 6th grade student and a resident of Deheisha Camp, Bethlehem, having been warned to tell the truth or be subject to criminal liability, hereby state as follows:

At about 10:30 a.m. Sunday 1 May 1988 I was standing near al-Atrash shop at the entrance of the camp to buy falafel. I heard shooting, so I ran towards our home, but I couldn't get there because of the sudden appearance of the soldiers. When they saw me they started chasing me and got hold of me near the house of Sabri Ali Abdallah. They beat me severely with their clubs and rifle butts injuring my head. I knew that I had been injured because when I put my hand to my head, as it was covered in blood. After that they took me and beat me again by knocking me against the wall of the UNRWA building. One of the soldiers who was about 1.95 meters tall, dark with broad shoulders, beat me with rocks all over my body. I was then led to the permanent military post on the roof of a house situated at the entrance to the camp. I was handed over to two other soldiers who started beating me with their rifle butts and tried to break my feet and hands. I realised that the heavy shooting was because a demonstration was taking place in the camp. The beating continued—one of them caught my right foot and another my left foot whilst I was stretched on the ground the sight of which provoked a large number of residents to crowd around the house on whose roof I was being held. They started shouting at the soldiers in an effort to save me. The soldiers issued threats then and people could not reach the house. The soldiers continued beating me and I fainted. After I came to, a soldier sat on my back and beat my head with stones. He also used a triangular piece of iron to beat my back and head. One of the soldiers burnt my back twice with a cigarette. The beating was taking place in front of a large number of young men. It seems that the people had contacted a medical centre in order to get me off the roof of the house. I realised this when l saw a doctor arguing with the soldiers. The doctor only arrived on the roof after he had been in the hands of the soldiers for two hours. They refused to let him take me, even though I was in bad condition. The doctor continued to argue with the soldiers but again they refused. The man left the site and later came back for the third time. It transpired that he was Dr. Abdul-Hay Sha'wan, Director of Health in the Bethlehem area. After negotiations which continued for half an hour, the soldiers allowed the doctor to transfer me to the hospital. There I was given first aid. After the elapse of twenty minutes in the hospital, muffled young men came and took me to Mount David Hospital in Bethlehem where I received the necessary treatment and where a thorough check-up was performed. It was discovered that I was suffering from bruises in different parts of my body and from two wounds in the head and foot. I left the hospital after three days and was treated at home for about a week. It is important to emphasise the fact that the soldiers used bricks when they beat me when I was on the house roof.

Date: 9 June 1988 (Signature)
Name available for publication

Appendix 1-F

TRANSLATION OF SWORN AFFIDAVIT (#1233) TAKEN BY AL-HAQ

I the undersigned, Ala' Munir Ramzi Maqboul, 18 years old, a student and a resident of Amman Street, Nablus, having been warned to tell the truth or be subject to criminal liability, do declare the following:

On Thursday 17 March 1988, at about 4:00 p.m., I was stepping out of an unfinished building near my house in Amman Street when I saw a medium sized army vehicle coming in my direction. Within seconds I saw three other similar vehicles. I became very frightened and decided to escape to the building and thought of jumping from one of the windows. But the window was too high so I hid inside the house, in a small room at the top. In a few seconds I heard voices inside the house swearing in broken Arabic. I realized that the soldiers had entered the house. Then I saw a soldier looking at me and swearing at me, telling me to come down. At once 6 other soldiers stood with him waiting for me to come down. When I came down, the soldiers surrounded me, forming a circle with me in the centre. One of the soldiers came at a distance of one meter from me, pointing his rifle towards my head. He fired 3 bullets which hit me in my face and mouth, and another three which hit me in my chest and left hand. I realized at once that these were rubber bullets for I hadn't been killed, but I felt very sick and ill and was on the point of collapse. The soldiers started beating me harshly with their clubs and rifles for three minutes and my mouth was bleeding a lot. After that I was ordered to go and get into the army vehicle which I did against my will. They took me to an army centre in Al-Khaldouniyeh school, where they threw me in the school yard for about twenty minutes during which I was in considerble pain bleeding from the mouth and elsewhere. After that a number of soldiers came and began swearing at me and lifted me from the ground and put me in an army vehicle which took me to al-Ittihad al-Nisa'i Hospital where I was treated. A local citizen noticed that I was suffering in the school yard, and so went and informed the hospital. An ambulance was sent too but the army prevented it from getting near. As a result of this attack on me my lower jaw was broken and I lost my teeth; I now can't speak normally. I should also mention that the situation near my house was unstable and there were some demonstrations. That is why I was frightened and hid myself for fear of being attacked by the soldiers.

Date: 9 March 1988 (Signature)
Name available for publication.

Appendix 1-G

CASE STUDY ON 'ARURA

On Saturday 9 July 1988 an IDF unit raided the village of 'Arura in the Ramallah District of the West Bank. For several hours the soldiers, estimated by residents at between 20 and 30, went from house to house indiscriminately beating unarmed civilians and destroying furniture and other household property. During the course of this operation not a single arrest was made or even attempted, the soldiers did not inquire into the whereabouts of any of the residents, and in only one case did they demand to see an identification card.

Al-Haq believes that particular attention needs to be drawn to the case of Hasan 'Abd-al-Rahman Hasa Salih, a 22-year old resident of 'Arura. In a sworn affidavit taken by al-Haq, he stated that he was beaten and buried alive by the IDF during a similar raid on his village on 18 May 1988. His family subsequently filed a complaint with the army, and the incident attracted enough publicity in Israel and internationally for an investigation to be launched, although it was not completed. At one point General Amram Mitzna', the Officer in Charge of the Central Command, visited 'Arura in order to follow the course of the investigation. But on 9 July Hasan Abd-al-Rahman Salih was singled out by soldiers who recognized him from the earlier incident. Hasan Salih was savagely beaten, his head bashed with a rock, requiring brain surgery afterwards at Ramallah Government Hospital.

This case study is based on affidavits, photographs, and other evidence collected by al-Haq staff members who visited 'Arura within 12 hours of the IDF raid.

'Arura (pop. 3000) is a remote village in the Ramallah District of the Israeli-occupied West Bank; it is not near to any of the main access roads in the region. No confrontations with the army nor any unusual activity had been reported there on Friday 8 July 1988.

According to reports from the villagers, the army arrived in one jeep accompanied by two Mercedes sedan taxis bearing the blue licence plates reserved for Palestinian residents of the West Bank. All three vehicles were said to be full, carrying a total of between 20 and 30 men. A number of residents stated in their sworn affidavits that almost immediately after emerging from their vehicles, the soldiers began picking up stones and indiscriminately threw them at the windows of the residents' homes and parked cars. A large amount of glass was shattered, and in Sufian Muhammad Othman's house a rock thrown by soldiers narrowly missed two of his sleeping children.

According to the villagers, the army unit then began going systematically from house to house, beating almost everyone found on the premises and singling out young men for additional abuse. In the process, large quantities of household furniture, appliances, and other goods were also deliberately smashed and destroyed. The villagers interviewed stated that the soldiers spent an average of four to five minutes in every home and then moved on, although in a number of cases they dragged young men outside for further beatings.

Daoud Muhammad Daoud 'Ali Hamdan, 17, a worker from 'Arura, stated the following in a sworn affidavit:

> I woke up in the hands of 12 soldiers dragging me outside the house. In the yard all of them began to beat me with their gun-butts, a wooden table-leg, and their fists, in addition to kicking me. They also knocked my head against the wall about six times, then threw me onto the ground and started pulling me, trampling me underfoot, and beating me on my sexual organs and all over my body with their gun-butts.

Jamil Talib 'Awad Salih, an unemployed 19-year old villager, reported similar brutality:

> [After waking up from the] clamour of soldiers destroying furniture and windows in neighbouring houses....a group of [them] came to our house and immediately began breaking the glass of the windows and destroying and ruining everything they found. One soldier then entered my room and headed directly towards me, grabbed me by the hair, and pulled me like that outside the house for about 10 meters. Ten soldiers beat me with the butts of their guns. All shared in the beating...concentrating on my head so that I fell to the ground. Then the soldiers left me without asking me anything, not even my name...I stood up and moved with difficulty towards my house while bleeding from my head, nose, and mouth.

Jamil Salih required eight stitches. Fatima Ahmad 'Issa, a 32-year-old woman, was beaten in the face until she had a haemorrhage. Sufian 'Othman, the 30-year-old father whose sleeping children narrowly escaped injury from flying glass, was beaten on the face and head, and sustained serious injuries to his tongue. Al-Haq staff members noted that his head was swollen and that he could not speak. His furniture was destroyed as well.

Many of the residents interviewed reported having stones thrown at them by members of the IDF unit. Among those who were stoned by soldiers were Amina Yusif 'Ali, a woman in her fifties, Shehadi Bakr Salih, who stated that he was first severely beaten and then had a large stone thrown at him, and Hasan 'Abd-al-Rahman Hasan Salih, whose case was reviewed above. His was doubtless the most serious:

> They did not search anywhere in the house except my bedroom. After that I told them that I had filed a complaint, and they said to me, "you are Hasan Abd-al-Rahman, this is all we need to know." They dragged me down from the second floor and beat me twice over the head with a rock, and then with clubs and a gun-butt.

The soldiers fractured Hasan's skull and he had to undergo emergency brain surgery in Ramallah hospital. Traces of hair and blood were found on the walls of his house as well as on the rock which was used to crack his skull. After they were finished with Hasan, the soldiers simply left and entered the next house.

It was later discovered that the IDF unit had destroyed his car as well, although it is difficult to tell if the soldiers knew who the car belonged to because a number of other vehicles were damaged as well, including that of Hasan 'Abd-al-Bakr, who was at the time under administrative detention.

Daoud Hamdan (see above) was also the object of special treatment.

According to his signed affidavit:

> They pushed me against a wall and made me face it, and then held my hands behind my back. I was naked above the waist because I had been sleeping that way due to the heat wave. The soldiers lit a cigarette-lighter, which I could tell from the sound it made, and they directed the flames directly at my back, moving the flame back and forth for about five minutes. I was screaming loudly from the pain. After the lighter-fuel ran out (this is what I think happened because we later found an empty lighter), the soldiers began burning me with cigarette-butts for about another four minutes. Then they poured a container full of dirty water from the garden over me. The soldiers again repeatedly knocked my head against the wall, kicked me, and then left.

Daoud also stated that his identification card was taken by the army from his father and not returned. Shahir 'Arouri, a Ramallah-based lawyer who accompanied the al-Haq staff members, stated that he "noticed signs of beating on Daoud's body, noticed obvious big burns on his back, saw his forehead wrapped with bandages, and saw the empty lighter which was found an hour after the reported incident."

During the raid the soldiers confined themselves to a specific part of the village. In all, al-Haq estimates that 15 houses were affected. After the soldiers withdrew, three persons had to be hospitalized, one of them (Hasan Salih) in critical condition. A number of others required stitches and other forms of first-aid treatment.

According to a military spokesperson the army entered the village because a roadblock had been erected and stones were thrown at the soldiers. But the residents deny that this was the case. Furthermore, it is difficult to believe the official version of events because no arrests were made or attempted, and in only one case did the soldiers attempt to identify a person. If the purpose of this military operation was to apprehend those responsible for the alleged incidents, then surely the soldiers would at least have tried to do so. At a time when mass arrests and frequent identification card checks have become the rule in the Israeli-occupied territories, the official account stands in sharp contradiction to the facts.

Appendix 1-H

TRANSLATION OF SWORN AFFIDAVIT (#1245) TAKEN BY AL-HAQ

I the undersigned 'Alam Muhammad Abu Hattab, 23 years old, a resident in Jenin Refugee Camp, and a car mechanic, after having been warned to tell the truth or be subject to criminal liablity, do declare the following:

On Saturday 12 March 1988, at about 4:00 p.m. I returned home and parked my car near one of the houses across the street from al-Zahra Secondary School which is located at the main entrance of the camp. On my way I passed a small uncovered army vehicle in which there were two soldiers. When I had walked about 30 meters, I reached an alley in the middle of which were 5 soldiers. I hesitated between continuing walking, going back or entering a house. Then I heard one of them shouting at me "Stop" in Arabic. I stopped and I saw him coming in my direction with his rifle pointed at me and his finger on the trigger. At a distance of 2 meters from me he shot a complete set of bullets. My face was hit and at once blood began pouring from my head, face and eyes. Blood poured out and covered my shirt, trousers, and the floor. Straight away, this soldier took out plastic handcuffs from his pocket, and tied my hands in front of me. Meanwhile the other soldiers, including the two who were in the jeep, came and began to beat me up with their fists, clubs and the ends of their rifles. They focussed on my head, eyes and ears. I started screaming while trying to cover my eyes with my hands to protect them. They continued beating me for 5 minutes and then I fell to the ground unconscious. When I regained consciousness, I felt my head and eyes and found that they were bandaged, and I was not able to see completely. I heard the voices of my brothers and friends who told me that I had been lying in Rafidya Hospital in Nablus for the past 48 hours. After two days the bandages were taken off my face, and I discovered that I had lost the sight in my right eye. I stayed in the hospital for two whole weeks. I am still suffering great pain in my head and all over my body. Also I am being treated at the Jerusalem Optic Hospital in order to have a glass eye fixed in place of the eye which I lost.

Date: 26 March 1988   (Signature)
Name available for publication

* Please Note: all affidavits contained in the appendices to this chapter end with the following written statement by the affiant: "In accordance with all of the above I hereby sign this statement on this date the [day] of [month and year]." It has been omitted for space considerations.

Chapter 2

OBSTRUCTION OF MEDICAL TREATMENT

A. Introduction

The scale of human rights violations by the Israeli armed forces during the past year, particularly shootings, systematic beatings and the widespread misuse of tear gas, has caused the medical needs of the Palestinians in the Occupied Territories to outstrip the available health services. Since 9 December 1987 the Israeli government has not expanded medical services. To the contrary, the occupation authorities have instituted a number of measures which make it even more difficult to obtain health care.

This chapter demonstrates that even the minimum standards set forth by international humanitarian law governing the treatment of sick and wounded combatants in wartime have been violated by the Israeli authorities in their dealings with unarmed Palestinian civilians. In grave breach of humanitarian law, the Israeli army regularly obstructs ambulances and private cars carrying the sick and wounded, raids hospitals and health clinics, and denies medical teams access to areas under prolonged curfew. Medical care in prisons and military detention centres is at best sub-standard. At worst, prisoners have been denied medical treatment altogether.

Moreover, during the uprising the Israeli government promulgated laws which raised hospitalisation costs and limited the access of Palestinians to Israeli hospitals. These measures have been adopted despite Israel's unambiguous obligation as an occupying power to ensure that the medical needs of the occupied Palestinian population are met.

All these violations are discussed below in the context of international laws protecting the right to health care. Regulations restricting access to medical services issued during the uprisng are considered within this framework, since they have illegitimately circumscribed the right to health care. In this section the debate concerning the effect of the occupation on health standards is not addressed.[1] This topic has been discussed in depth elsewhere and in any case is beyond the scope of this report.[2]

Before providing representative examples of the health-related human rights violations outlined above, this chapter first reviews the pattern of such abuses prior to the uprising and examines the explanations offered by the Israeli government for the conduct of its armed forces.

B. Prior Practice

Recent breaches of medical human rights do not represent a change in practice by the Israeli military. Health-related human rights violations have occurred throughout the 21 years of Israeli occupation of the West Bank and the Gaza Strip. For example, in 1984, al-Haq intervened with the military authorities regarding the obstruction of a private car carrying a critically wounded Bir Zeit University student, Sharaf Khalil Hassan Tibi, to the Ramallah Hospital. Sharaf Tibi was shot by the Israeli army on 21 November 1984 during a demonstration on the university campus.[3] Then, Israeli soldiers delayed the car carrying Mr. Tibi for 25 minutes at an army checkpoint at Jifna, on one of the roads between the university and Ramallah Hospital. The soldiers were aware of the destination of the car, and could see that Mr. Tibi was critically wounded. Mr. Tibi died before reaching the hospital.[4]

On 4 December 1986, the Israeli army again delayed ambulances carrying wounded Bir Zeit University students. Moreover, in what eye-witnesses described as an unprovoked attack, the military fired rubber bullets at students and faculty who were gathered near the entrance of the Ramallah hospital emergency room.[5] During this incident two more people were wounded, one of whom was hit with a rubber bullet at close range.

Also in 1986, the occupying authorities disrupted efforts by doctors with the Gaza Medical Relief Committee to provide free health services to Palestinian residents in Jabaliya Refugee Camp.[6] On 18 July of that year, doctors and health workers from the Committee were treating patients in a private home in Jabaliya. At approximately 10:15 a.m. the Military Governor of Gaza arrived at the house accompanied by a number of soldiers, and ordered the doctors and health personnel to leave the premises.

The following week, the 7 doctors who had participated in the medical relief mission in Jabaliya were arrested and charged with violating the law which governs Gaza charitable societies by having provided basic medical services to the population without first obtaining permission to do so from the Israeli authorities.[7]

Thus, the obstruction of medical care, in all of its various forms, is not new. However, the scope of health-related human rights abuses has dramatically expanded during the current Palestinian uprising. According to al-Haq's documentation, violations of medical human rights have occurred with frightening regularity during the past year in all parts of the Occupied Territories.

C. Legal Issues

International humanitarian law—i.e. the laws of war—sets the minimum standards for treatment of the sick and wounded during armed conflicts. These laws (namely the four Geneva Conventions of 1949 and the 1977 additional Protocols to those conventions) afford special protection to medical facilities and to the sick and wounded. Of this body of law, only the IV Geneva Convention, and to a lesser extent Protocol 1, are referred to in this chapter.

As an occupying power, Israel is legally bound by the IV Geneva Convention. The Israeli government, as mentioned above, takes the position that this Convention is not applicable—*de jure*—to the Occupied Territories. However, the Israeli authorities claim to apply the humanitarian provisions of the Convention, which it has yet to specify, on a *de facto* basis. It is important to note here that the provisions relating to health care are strictly humanitarian in nature and that no assertions to the contrary have ever been made by Israel. These provisions should therefore be adhered to even under Israel's restricted interpretation of the application of the IV Geneva Convention. The Convention provides most of the minimum standards discussed in this chapter.

The following sections present the applicable law and then provide specific instances of its breach by the Israeli authorities. The aim of this review is to illustrate patterns of abuses with selected examples rather than to provide an exhaustive list of violations since 9 December 1987.

1. Obstruction of Health Care

The right of the sick and wounded to receive medical attention is perhaps one of the most basic principles of humanitarian law. Irrespective of the circumstances, the Israeli military is obligated to permit the wounded and sick to be "collected and cared for," and should accord them "particular protection and respect."[8] The right of the injured to humane treatment and to receive health care as expeditiously as possible is inherent in these principles.[9]

To guarantee these rights, the transportation of the wounded to medical facilities must also be granted special "respect and protection."[10] Humanitarian law prohibits attack on vehicles carrying the wounded as well as "interfer[ence] with their running."[11]

Despite these clear regulations, the Israeli armed forces frequently harass, delay and obstruct health workers and local residents attempting to collect the wounded and transport them to hospitals. Moreover, there are numerous examples of physical mistreatment of the wounded. Instances of both these types of abuses are presented below.

a. Delaying the Transportation of the Wounded

The Union of Palestinian Medical Relief Committees, the United Nations Relief and Work Agency (UNRWA), and other humanitarian agencies report regular interference with their efforts to collect and transport the wounded. Shaher Muhammad Mujahed, an ambulance driver with the Red Crescent Society in Hebron, gave al-Haq an affidavit regarding one such incident in mid-December 1987. On 13 December, three separate groups of Israeli soldiers obstructed his attempt to transport a seriously wounded man from Aliya Hospital in Hebron to Hadassah Hospital in West Jerusalem.[12] The ambulance was delayed for a total of at least 50 minutes. Each time he was stopped, he explained he was carrying a critically injured person to Hadassah hospital, yet the soldiers did not grant him free passage.

In a more recent example, on 12 October 1988 in the village of Maythaloun in the Jenin District, the Israeli military for four hours prevented a medical team consisting of four public hospital doctors and the driver of the Jenin municipality ambulance from collecting Palestinians who had been wounded by the army.[13] During this time, the doctors were confined by the military to a house in the village.

Even before the uprising, there was a criticial shortage of ambulances in the Occupied Territories. Within the last year, the Israeli Civil Administration has prevented hospitals and humanitarian organisations from increasing the number of ambulances they operate by systematically denying licences to ambulance drivers. For example, on 4 October 1988 the Israeli authorities rejected an application for licences by ambulance drivers from the Red Crescent Society in Hebron. In a written response to a request by the society no explanation was provided as to why the licence was denied.

However, according to al-Haq's information, in a subsequent meeting between Red Crescent administrators and the Military Governor of Hebron, the latter stated that the licences were denied because "these ambulances may be aiming to participate in the intifada." The Military

Obstruction of Medical Treatment 63

Governor also questioned the administrators as to how they obtained information concerning the location of the wounded and how they were able to arrive so promptly at the scene of a conflict.

At least seven other hospitals and health organisations have reported that their drivers have been refused licences.

Due in part to the shortage of ambulances, the wounded are often forced to depend on private cars for transportation to hospitals. Attempts by non-medical personnel to aid the wounded are also hampered by the Israeli military. For example, on 12 December 1987, Nimer al-Skafi, a shoemaker from the city of Hebron, was shot in the hand by the Israeli army. His cousin, Kamal Muhammad Rashid al-Skafi, reported to al-Haq in a sworn affidavit the soldiers' response when he tried to aid Mr. Nimer al-Skafi:

> I tried to help Nimer, to lift him off the ground, but he [an Israeli soldier] pointed his gun in my direction and said in broken Arabic: "I'll shoot you, get away."[14]

After a delay of approximately 20 minutes the soldiers permitted Mr. al-Skafi to transport his cousin to the hospital.

In addition, local residents who attempt to aid the wounded have been subject to severe physical abuse by Israeli soldiers. A resident of the village of Silwad, near Ramallah, described the following incident:

> On 3 February 1988, at about 10:00 a.m., a large number of Israeli soldiers arrived at the village to stop a demonstration that was taking place that morning. In the confrontation that followed three villagers were wounded: 'Abd-al-Hamid al-Natour, Muhsen Saleh Muhsen, and Wahbi 'Izzat Ahmad Khalil. Villagers rushed to save them. Muhammad Mahmoud 'Abd-al-Rahman Hamed, a 24-year-old man, took one of the wounded in his car, but near the village school soldiers shot several bullets in the direction of the tires of his car. They then pulled the driver and the wounded out of the car. They beat the driver until he fainted, and then dumped both on the sidewalk and left.[15]

The driver never recovered from this beating. On 19 March 1988, he died in Augusta Victoria Hospital in East Jerusalem as a result of internal bleeding.[16]

In the last year there have been several cases in which the obstruction of vehicles carrying the wounded has had fatal consequences. One such case occurred on 16 April 1988: 'Ala al-Din Muhammad Thabet, a 15-year old boy from the village of 'Azmout in the Nablus District, died of gunshot wounds he sustained in the village at approximately 6:30 a.m. on that day. The private car carrying him was delayed at the entrance of the village and then taken over by the Israeli military, which refused to transport him to the hospital and instead took him to a school occupied by the army in Nablus.[17] The following is from an affidavit taken by al-Haq from Murad Muhammad Mahmoud 'Amer, who was holding the injured boy in the back of the car when it was confiscated by the military:

> The car continued until it reached the intersection of Faisal Street and Khillet al-'Amoud [in the city of Nablus]. There, the car veered to the left towards al-'Amiriya School, which was occupied by the military. I immediately knew that they had no intention of aiding the victim, and I began to beg them and shouted at them to save him and take him to the hospital. The car kept going, however, until it drove into the al-'Amiriya School yard and stopped. The two soldiers got out...I sat in the car with the injured boy for another twenty minutes...Then a soldier came and said that I should get him out of the car, making me believe that they were going to take him to the hospital. With great speed, I carried the wounded boy and placed him on a medical stretcher pointed out to me by one of the soldiers. When the injured boy was on the stretcher, one of the soldiers put a blanket on him and did nothing else. I began to scream and accuse the soldiers of deliberately killing him, and demanded once again that they hurry and transport him. I was unable to continue, however, because a soldier approached me, tied my hands and put a blindfold over my eyes and led me to one of the tents in the school...I later learned that 'Ala al-Din Thabet had died.[18]

For further examples of the obstruction of ambulances, see Appendix 2-D.[19]

b. Mistreatment of the Wounded

Al-Haq has received numerous reports of beatings and other forms of mistreatment of the wounded. For example, on 29 May 1988, a 27-year-old Palestinian man shot in the leg by the Israeli military was beaten by soldiers "with the butt of their rifles and kicked" before being transferred to a local health clinic.[20]

A similar incident occurred on 6 June 1988, in Deheisha Refugee Camp in the Bethlehem District: Wajih Khalil Zayed al-Fararja, a boy in his teens, was shot in the leg and then beaten by Israeli soldiers. According to eyewitness accounts, Wajih "remained on the ground for about 40 minutes after being beaten, and the soldiers did not allow his relatives to reach him or get near him."[21] Wajih was not transferred to a hospital until approximately one hour after he was shot.

The cases referred to in both parts of this section are not isolated incidents. Rather, they exemplify the patterns of human rights abuses which have occurred throughout the uprising. It appears from these and many similar instances that little emphasis is placed on giving soldiers instructions to give absolute priority to the right of the wounded to medical treatment. In fact, soldiers regularly cause delays in emergency situations by first seeking the permission of their superior officers before allowing an evidently seriously wounded person to pass a road block to reach a hospital. Surely, such permission should form part of the general instructions given to soldiers, following the absolute requirement under international law that all steps be taken to enable the wounded to receive medical attention.

2. The Denial of Medical Services to Populations Under Prolonged Curfew

Even in times of war, humanitarian law calls upon the parties to a conflict to reach agreements regarding the evacuation of the "wounded, sick, infirm...children and maternity cases...from besieged or encircled areas."[22] In the case under consideration, Israel as an occupying power must ensure adequate food, water, medical supplies and health services for the civilian population under occupation.[23] This obligation does not cease simply because the occupying forces impose a prolonged curfew. On the contrary, medical personnel must in general "be exempted from any measures (such as restrictions on movement, requisitioning of vehicles, supplies or equipment) liable to interfere with the performance of their duty."[24] Thus, medical personnel—as a general rule—should be allowed to enter areas under curfew, and the transportation of the wounded and sick in the course of such measures should not be impeded.[25]

During the uprising, the Israeli army has not adhered to these minimum requirements. Palestinians in areas under curfew have regularly been denied access to medical treatment. For example, according to UNRWA sources, ambulances are generally prevented from entering refugee camps while a curfew is in force. In addition, residents are in many cases not allowed out of their homes to seek medical treatment at UNRWA health clinics, and vehicles carrying food and other basic supplies for refugees have been turned away.

Similarly, individuals requiring hospitalisation due to illness have been denied permission to travel to hospitals in other areas. In one case, 'Aisha Mustafa Muhammad al-Atrash, a 55 year-old woman who resides in Deheisha Refugee Camp in the Bethlehem District, requested permission to go to Augusta Victoria Hospital in East Jerusalem on 29 June 1988 while the camp was under curfew. (According to al-Haq documentation, the curfew lasted from 27 June until 9 July 1988.) Soldiers stationed in the camp refused her request despite the fact that she was suffering from diabetes, high blood pressure and severe stomach pains.[26]

Such practices cannot be justified on any grounds and are in clear violation of Israel's responsibilities as an occupying power.

3. Attacks on Medical Personnel in the Field

Medical personnel "of all categories" must be allowed to carry out their duties and at all times should be "respected and protected."[27] This injunction prohibits physical mistreatment or other forms of reprisal against such persons for providing medical treatment to the population.

Since December 1987 the Israeli authorities have repeatedly violated this law. Doctors, nurses, and in particular ambulance drivers have been beaten and mistreated. For instance, on 11 December 1987, Muhammad Mahmoud Muhammad al-Saqa, an ambulance driver for the Red Crescent Society in Nablus, was pulled out of his ambulance and beaten by Israeli soldiers when he stopped to pick up a woman as he was leaving Balata Refugee Camp. In his sworn statement to al-Haq, Mr. al-Saqa described this incident as follows:

> ...as I was about to leave, I heard a woman shout: "Stop! Stop!" When I stopped the ambulance in order to pick her up, I was surprised by Border Police, who opened the car door. They dragged me out and started beating me with clubs, fists and boots. They threw me to the ground and continued to beat me in the same fashion on my head, my stomach and the rest of my body.[28]

In addition, health personnel have been targetted for arrest and detention. For example, the director of the Gaza Medical Society, Dr. Zaqariya al-Agha, was placed in administrative detention (internment without charge or trial) on 2 April 1988.[29] Dr. 'Abd-al-'Aziz Rantisi, a member of the Gaza Medical Society's Executive Committee, was placed in administrative detention for a six-month period on 6 March 1988; the order was renewed on 5 September 1988 for an additional six months, although upon appeal it was later reduced to four months. The Palestinian Medical Relief Committees report that as of August 1988 five of their members had been detained, three of whom were being held in Ansar III under orders of administrative detention.[30] Dr. Muhammad Jadallah of the Union of Health Care Committees in the West Bank and Gaza was arrested at Ben Gurion Airport upon returning from the U.S. on 20 October 1988, and held in the Moskobiya detention centre in West Jerusalem for two weeks before being released without charges. A member of the same Union, Na'ila 'Ayyash, whose husband Jamal

Zaqqout was recently deported, was placed in administrative detention on 5 October 1988.

Moreover, the Israeli government has closed organisations providing medical care. For example, the offices of the Society of Friends of the Sick in Tulkarem were closed on 28 August 1988. (See the Case Study in Appendix 9-C at the back of Chapter 9) The impact of such measures is particularly devastating at the current time, given the increase in demand for medical services.

4. Military Raids on Hospitals

The Israeli armed forces have a "general obligation to do everything possible to spare hospitals," including the taking of "special precautions" to ensure that hospitals are not adversely affected by confrontations in their vicinity.[31] Deliberate attacks on hospitals are prohibited. Article 18 of the IV Geneva Convention states:

> Civilian hospitals organised to give care to the wounded and sick, the infirm and maternity cases, may in no circumstances be the object of attack, but shall at all times be respected and protected by the parties to the conflict.

This protection is also extended to health clinics and other health facilities where "medical attention is given."[32]

Raids on hospitals cannot be justified by the presence of persons wounded by the Israeli military. According to Article 19 of the IV Geneva Convention, the protection afforded hospitals may only be limited if health facilities are used to "commit acts harmful to the enemy." Providing medical care to the wounded is explicitly excluded from this category.[33]

Moreover, health facilities may in any case never be attacked before "due warning has been given, naming, in all appropriate cases, a reasonable time limit and after such warning has remained unheeded."[34] The warning period "must be long enough to allow...the hospital patients to be removed to a place of safety."[35]

These basic rules of conduct have been ignored by the Israeli military during the past year. Fully armed Israeli soldiers have broken into major Palestinian hospitals such as al-Ittihad al-Nisa'i Hospital in Nablus, 'Aliya Hospital in Hebron, Ramallah Hospital, al-Maqassed Hospital in East Jerusalem, and al-Shifa Hospital in Gaza. Israeli soldiers have beaten people inside hospitals, arrested individuals who were under treatment, and even used tear gas, rubber bullets and live ammunition within hospital precincts.

a. The Use of Force on Hospital Grounds and the Disruption of Health Care

Hospital raids have occurred at all hours of the day and night. (For example, Ramallah Hospital was raided by approximately 200 soldiers at 3:00 a.m. on 19 March 1988). During some of these raids, soldiers search for individuals wounded in confrontations with the army. Others follow demonstrations in the vicinity of medical facilities. Warnings are never given. The following are some documented examples of this practice:

- At 1:00 p.m. on 6 February 1988, two employees of Ramallah Hospital were wounded by Israeli soldiers who surrounded the hospital and fired tear gas and rubber bullets at the out-patient clinic.
- At 4:00 p.m. on 25 February 1988, soldiers surrounded the Ittihad al-Nisa'i Hospital in the city of Nablus, broke into the male and female nurses' quarters and beat up nurses on duty. In addition, all wards of the hospital—the intensive care unit, the children's ward, the emergency room, etc.—were searched and several people visiting hospital patients were beaten. One of the visitors, Bassam Ahmad 'Abd-al-Halim from the village of Mazari' al-Nubani in the Nablus District, was particularly abused. Soldiers broke one of his arms and knocked out several of his teeth. This raid occurred shortly after a molotov cocktail had been thrown at a military vehicle near the hospital.
- At approximately 11:30 p.m. on 21 August 1988, soldiers surrounded al-Maqassed Hospital in East Jerusalem. According to eyewitnesses, "one soldier put his gun to the [hospital] guard's head, while four military tanks and six private cars drove into the hospital."[36] The hospital supervisor on duty that night reported that "we heard soldiers chasing some youngsters inside the hospital, in the cafeteria area. They caught two of them...and severely beat them. One of the soldiers was going to shoot at one of the youths, but 'Abou-Munir' [the Israeli commanding officer] prevented him from doing so."[37]

Military raids seriously impede hospital functioning. In various cases, the Israeli army has prohibited intra-hospital communication, prevented hospital personnel from continuing their work, restricted movement from one area to another, and halted the admission of the sick and wounded. In every case, patients throughout the hospital are disturbed.

In addition, according to al-Haq's documentation, ambulances have regularly been denied permission to enter hospital grounds (for various periods of time) by military checkpoints set up at hospital entrances during such raids.

The disruption of hospital activity is illustrated by the following affidavit taken by al-Haq from a resident doctor in al-Maqassed Hospital, Raghib Akram Raghib al-'Asali, regarding events which took place on 21 August 1988:

> At approximately 11:45 p.m. on Sunday 21 August 1988, while I was at the Maqassed Hospital, I received a call from one of the employees in the [Hospital's] Information Office, who requested that I proceed to the Emergency Ward, located on the bottom floor of the Hospital, because there was a case of heart failure. Immediately, I and four other doctors proceeded to the Emergency Ward to provide the necessary aid. After twenty minutes of treatment, the patient's heart started functioning again. While we were preparing the patient in order to transfer him to the intensive-care unit, I heard a strange sound, and then I saw a soldier rush into the Emergency Ward, while another soldier stood at the door and another by the telephone set. They stopped us from making any telephone calls or leaving the Section, although it was urgently needed to transfer the patient to the intensive-care unit because he needed breathing equipment. I also observed three soldiers and men in civilian clothes. The soldiers stopped any emergency case from being admitted to the section. One of the cases which was barred admittance was a person who had been bitten by a scorpion. The section remained inactive for about 45 minutes. During this time I heard a person screaming loudly and abnormally; it sounded like he was being beaten. After that the soldiers withdrew from the hospital.[38]

In an official report to the Administration of al-Maqassed Hospital, the night supervisor on duty that same night described the following events:

> Every time I asked the soldiers about the reasons behind the raid on the Hospital, they told me to "shut up." They answered me in this manner after I had introduced myself to them as the direct supervisor of the hospital for that night. Then I went up to the first floor after hearing noises coming from the surgery room, the children's ward and the intensive-care room. There I was faced with about twenty [Shin Bet] intelligence men in civilian dress, accompanied by fully-armed soldiers. They raided the intensive-care room, searching in a barbaric way and without any search warrants.
>
> I tried to stop them or even talk to them but they wouldn't listen...After leaving the intensive-care room they raided the children's ward...I became furious and asked the so-called 'Abou-Munir', the commander, to stop these acts and talk to me or show

a search warrant. Every time I tried to stop them from raiding a patient's room they pushed me back. They raided all the wards of the hospital, yelling and shouting...The so-called 'Abou-Munir', accompanied by a soldier, then took me aside, threatened that he would close the Hospital and claimed that there were contacts between some of the administrators of the Hospital and people wanted by the authorities. When I asked him what gave him and his men the right to raid the Hospital, he answered that he had all the right in the world to raid hospitals...[39]

The Ittihad al-Nisa'i Hospital in Nablus was raided by Israeli soldiers on 11 December 1987 while the hospital was swamped with incoming wounded from Balata Refugee Camp following clashes between soldiers and camp residents. A hospital technician assigned to the Blood Bank reported the effects of the raid on his work:

While I was on my way to the Blood Bank Section three soldiers shouted at me and shot volleys of rubber bullets, and therefore I had to return to the operating theatre to ask the doctor to accompany me to the Blood Bank Section in order to bring the needed units. I went back in the company of the doctor to fetch them, but the soldiers who were still shooting rubber bullets stopped us, and then let us go to the section, provided that we would come back by the same route so they could talk to us. It is worth mentioning that the people who entered the hospital to donate blood had to escape the shooting and the tear gas...[40]

The regular use of force by the army within hospital premises demonstrates the failure of the Israeli government to adhere to its obligation to respect and protect medical establishments. For a commanding officer to assert an unconditional right to raid hospitals is entirely unacceptable and indicates an urgent need for clear guidelines where none apparently exist and for compliance with such guidelines in accordance with international law.

b. Forced Removal of the Wounded from Hospitals

Some raids on hospitals are carried out specifically in order to arrest persons wounded in clashes with the Israeli army. The army obtains information regarding such persons from all hospitals and clinics pursuant to regulations issued by the Civil Administration on 20 December 1987.[41] These regulations oblige hospitals in the Occupied Territories to report any person requiring treatment "for wounds or injuries resulting from clashes with the Israeli Defence Forces" to the Civil Administration within 24 hours of the person's arrival at the hospital.[42] Such reports should include the "complete name, identification number, sex, age or

Obstruction of Medical Treatment 71

date of birth, address of the wounded person, the time the person arrived at the hospital, and who accompanied the wounded person."[43]

This data is used by the Israeli military to further its policy of arresting those they have wounded. For example, Dr. Otto Walter (a Jerusalem resident who is the Director of the International Lutheran Federation and affiliated with the Augusta Victoria Hospital in East Jerusalem), reported to al-Haq that two hours after he reported 4 young men wounded in clashes with the military, Augusta Victoria Hospital was raided and the four patients were arrested.[44]

Most of those arrested and removed from hospitals are transferred directly to prisons, where they are often denied needed medical services. For example, Muhid Salameh Shahin, a 22-year-old man, was removed from al-Maqassed Hospital on 19 November 1988 although, according to a medical report issued by his doctor, his "general condition is still unstable [and] he needs intensive care for his eyes and wounds on both hands."[45] Mr. Shahin was transferred to al-Moskobiya Detention Centre (commonly known as the Russian Compound) in West Jerusalem.

Some prisoners are transferred to Israeli hospitals. While in general, facilities in Israeli hospitals are better, other aspects of the treatment accorded Palestinians transferred to those hospitals by the military are far from preferable. Such persons are kept hand- or footcuffed to hospital beds under armed guard, and are usually denied visits even by immediate family members or their personal doctor.

For instance, Dr. Otto Walter (of the International Lutheran Federation) described his experiences when he attempted to visit four of his patients who had been forcibly removed from Augusta Victoria Hospital on 25 August 1988, as follows:

> On the morning of 26 August 1988, I went to Hadassah Hospital on Mount Scopus to pay a visit [to] the injured. After an hour of waiting, I was told that [they] had been transferred at 3:00 a.m. to "Shaare Zedek" Hospital in [West] Jerusalem. I immediately headed to the hospital. I talked to the man in charge. An hour later, they told me that they had transferred the injured to Hadassah. I went back to Hadassah Hospital where the army was present. The soldier on guard told me no visitors were allowed. I also saw three soldiers inside the intensive-care room which was next to that of the injured. I expressed my protest and asked to see the officer in charge. I was told that I had to wait half an hour. Then, a soldier told me that visits were prohibited and I could not see the officer. I banged my hand on the table and said that nobody has the right to stop a doctor from seeing his patients. So, I kept on waiting once again until I was allowed at 12:30 p.m. to see my patients. They were lying on an

unfit stretcher and were cuffed with iron cuffs [on] their legs.[46]

The practice of forcibly removing patients from hospitals is an outrageous violation of medical human rights. It is important to understand that these persons are not charged with any crime. They have simply been the victims of the shooting and beating policies of the Israeli authorities. And anyone injured or wounded by the armed forces can be subject to such arrest. Thus, the reporting requirement coupled with raids on hospitals to remove the wounded have effectively served to discourage many Palestinians from seeking health care at hospitals or health clinics.

5. Medical Treatment in Prisons and Detention Centres

Article 76 of the IV Geneva Convention grants prisoners the right to medical attention. The relevant clause of the article states that:

> They [detainees] shall receive the medical treatment required by their state of health.

In a clear breach of this law, prisoners and administrative detainees are often denied medical care. Those services which are available are grossly inadequate.

For instance, in the Dhahriya Detention Centre near al-Khalil (Hebron) there is only one health officer although approximately 650 detainees are held there.[47] It is therefore difficult for prisoners to gain access to this doctor unless they have a serious health problem. The treatment they are provided with—regardless of their complaint—generally consists of two "Acamol" pills (a non-aspirin analgesic).

Skin diseases and lice are the most common medical problems encountered by detainees at Dhahriya (largely due to insufficient bathing facilities and unsanitary conditions). One detainee with a skin disease described his experience when he sought medical treatment as follows:

> On 29 December 1987, I felt a rather strong itch all over my thighs, so I asked the captain to permit me to visit the doctor. When they granted me permission, I was taken into another room where there was a person in civilian clothes, who, instead of examining me, accused me of throwing stones and threatened that if I did not confess to him that this was so, I would be sentenced to a long period in jail.[48]

The detainee did not receive medicine for his skin disease while in Dhahriya.

In addition, there have been documented reports of serious

breaches of medical ethics at Dhahriya. According to al-Haq's documentation, the medical officer carries a club with which he hits detainees, particularly during the initial examination which occurs when individuals arrive at the centre.[49]

Moreover, at least one detainee was beaten by soldiers while receiving medical attention in Dhahriya's clinic. On 4 April 1988, a Palestinian man was brought to the centre. Before being detained he had been badly beaten, particularly on his head, by soldiers. He was bleeding heavily when he arrived. Soldiers brought the detainee to the clinic and, while he was being treated, began to beat him once again, this time in the presence of the medical officer.[50]

Health services are also inadequate at Ketsyot, popularly known as Ansar III.[51] There is only one medical officer for over 2,500 Palestinians detained there. Thus, the detainees, like those at Dhahriya, find it difficult to gain access to the medical officer. Treatment, when obtained, consists of water, aspirin or a tranquilliser. Detainees with serious health problems are transferred to the hospital in Beersheba, although even there they often do not obtain the necessary medical treatment.

The case of Mr. 'Iz-al-Din al-'Ariyan is just one example. Mr. al-'Ariyan, a 50-year-old pharmacist from Ramallah who was under administrative detention in Ansar III, suffered from back pains that he developed while in prison. He spent his time in Ansar III lying on his mattress unable to move. He reported to al-Haq that he started feeling the pain after the military forced him and other prisoners in his section to sit for more than 3 hours under the heat of the sun on 17 May 1988. Detainees were forbidden to move while the army was carrying out an extensive search in the tents. He says that "this imposed some pressure on the lowest part of the vertebrae. When we were asked to stand up, I could not."[52]

When lawyers from al-Haq visited Ansar III on 30 May 1988, Mr. al-'Ariyan was not brought from his tent because he was unable to walk. When the lawyers asked to see him in his tent, their request was refused.

Al-Haq intervened immediately with the International Committee of the Red Cross (ICRC) regarding Mr. al-'Ariyan's condition. A doctor from the ICRC visited him two days later and asked for Mr. al-'Ariyan's back to be X-rayed to determine the cause of the problem. Some days later, Mr. al-'Ariyan was taken to Beersheba hospital for the X-ray, but although he was examined by a doctor there, no X-ray was ever taken. The cause of his back problems was never diagnosed while he was in Ansar III.

Mr. al-'Ariyan's reports about the medical treatment that he received in Ansar III are not unique. Other detainees suffering from heart problems, skin diseases, ulcers and kidney problems, eye problems, diabetes, and other medical problems, who were either having treatment before their arrest—e.g. those forcibly removed from hospitals—or who developed medical problems during their detention, have reported to al-Haq that they have not been allowed to receive medication at Ansar III.

6. *The Adoption of Measures Which Decrease the Quality and Availability of Health Care*

As an occupying power, Israel has an obligation to maintain health services in the West Bank and Gaza Strip. This requirement is set forth in Article 56 of the IV Geneva Convention:

> [To] the fullest extent of the means available to it, the Occupying Power has the duty of ensuring and maintaining, with the co-operation of national and local authorities, the medical and hospital establishments and services, public health and hygiene in the Occupied Territory, with particular reference to the adoption and application of the prophylactic and preventative measures necessary to combat the spread of contagious diseases and epidemics.

Yet, instead of "ensuring" and "maintaining" medical establishments, the Israeli authorities have adopted policies in the past year which undermine the infrastructure of public health services in the Occupied Territories.

Prior to the uprising, Palestinian patients requiring sophisticated health services were routinely referred to Israeli hospitals.[53] During the uprising, increasing numbers of patients have needed specialised care not available in public hospitals in the West Bank or the Gaza Strip. In this context, the Israeli military authorities have promulgated regulations which restrict the access of Palestinians to Israeli hospitals. According to a recent military decision, West Bank residents who are members of the national health plan may no longer be referred to Israeli hospitals. In addition, national health insurance fees were increased by 70 percent.

These measures were accompanied by a series of steps, taken during June and July of 1988, which limit both the capacity of public health facilities to provide health services and of the local population to afford hospitalisation costs. These steps include:

- a 50 percent cut in the budget of public hospitals in the West Bank;
- the dismissal of 25 percent of public health employees, including 100 physicians[54];
- a 50 percent increase in the cost of treatment at public hospitals, both in the Occupied Territories and within Israel, bringing the cost

of staying in hospital to $150.00 per night.[55]

Moreover, according to the Union of Medical Relief Committees, during the summer of 1988 the Israeli authorities informed hospital administrators "not to treat injured people—even in case[s] of severe emergency—before they pay the cost of treatment."[56]

These measures have undermined the medical care infrastructure at a time when health facilities are most needed by Palestinians living under Israeli occupation. In al-Haq's opinion the collective implementation of these steps demonstrates a total disregard for the civilian population's right to health care.

D. Israeli Justification

Reports of health-related human rights abuses have elicited responses from the Israeli authorities which range from straightforward denials to a general security rationale which claims that such actions are inevitable given the exigencies created by the current Palestinian uprising. This argument is relied upon particularly as a justification for military raids on hospitals. According to Israeli officials,

> ...force has had to be used to remove rioters from hospital premises. However, it is more appropriate to place the responsibility for these events on the rioters than on security personnel who are trying to assure the hospitals' continued functioning.[57]

On 20 December 1987, a senior Israeli military spokesman offered another explanation for the army's practice of removing the wounded from hospitals when he stated "[w]e forcibly entered [Gaza's] al-Shifa' Hospital and took out patients, because the treatment they can expect in Ashkelon or at [Beersheba's] Soroka Hospital is better."[58]

In al-Haq's opinion, the response of the Israeli government when confronted with evidence of gross violations of medical human rights committed by its armed forces undermines any hope that the government will attempt to limit such abuses. As is shown in the preceding sections, its claims are not borne out by the facts; moreover, they fail as legal justifications. The rules of conduct examined above are designed to satisfy security concerns which arise during wartime and belligerent occupation; therefore, their breach cannot be justified on the basis of the exigencies of the current uprising.

E. Conclusion

The Palestinian inhabitants of the Occupied Territories are "protected persons" who should receive the benefits of the minimum standards set forth by the IV Geneva Convention. Those standards were developed with the understanding that civilian populations under belligerent occupation have historically been at the mercy of the occupier.

Few if any provisions of international law are more widely endorsed by the community of states than those in the IV Geneva Convention relating to health care. There is no question as to their humanitarian nature. As stated above, the Israeli government claims to observe the humanitarian provisions of these conventions. The facts shown in this chapter, however, directly contradict this claim.

Instead of granting "respect and protection" to those injured and to the hospitals and private humanitarian agencies which provide them with relief, the Israeli government has used its armed forces to attack these individuals and institutions. Comparable practices in armed conflicts such as the Iran-Iraq war, the Salvadoran civil war or the civil war in Afghanistan have been condemned as war crimes by the international community. As shown above, wounded combatants may not be denied medical care. Medical personnel and institutions aiding such combatants may not be subject to attack. Not only is the Palestinian uprising not an armed conflict, but the civilian residents of the Occupied Territories cannot possibly be considered combatants under international law. At the very least, they should be afforded the rights extended soldiers in time of war.

FOOTNOTES TO CHAPTER 2

1. The two sides to this debate were summarised in a recent publication by the Union of Palestinian Medical Relief Committees as follows:

   As the debate stands now, on the one hand, we find the Israeli military attempting to use certain indices for proving health status improvement—such as the reduction in overall infant mortality during the past twenty years—to justify unacceptable health conditions. On the other hand, reactions to the Israeli military position have at times been of the variety that emphasizes that health status and services have deteriorated since 1967. Such a position is problematic too in that it tends to omit examining the questions in an objective and impartial way, and thus represents an unsuccessful attempt to respond...The picture that is presented in this type of debate however, is incomplete. What appears to be also necessary is to add to the formula the possible impact of certain external factors—such as funding that trickles into the Occupied Territories from outside and feeds into health services—on the overall situation. A comprehensive review requires an examination of the parts within the context of the whole, based on the foundations of a combination of theory and practical knowledge of the conditions in the area.

   Quoted from: The Union of Palestinian Medical Relief Committees, West Bank and Gaza, *An Overview of Health Conditions and Services in the Israeli-Occupied Territories*, August 1987, pp. 5-6.
2. Ibid.
3. The killing of Sharaf Tibi was reported by both the Israeli press and international press services such as the Associated Press. See: Associated Press dispatch, 21 November 1984. For a detailed account of the incident see: *No Mercy, A Report on Army Actions at Birzeit University on November 21, 1984*, Birzeit Public Relations Office, December 1984.
4. Subsequently, the Israeli government conducted an investigation, the results of which were never made public. To the best of al-Haq's knowledge, this was the last investigation into this type of case carried out by the Israeli authorities.
5. For a detailed review of these incidents see: Birzeit University Public Relations Office, *Students Under Fire, A Preliminary Report On Army Actions At Birzeit University On December 4, 1986*, December 1986.
6. Gaza Medical Relief Committee, *Press Release, Gaza Medical Relief Committee Under Fire*, 23 July 1986. See also: Gaza Medical Relief Committee, *Renewed Repression of Gaza Medical Relief Committee*, 31 July 1986.
7. Ibid.
8. Article 16, IV Geneva Convention 1949. The rights and duties articulated by Article 16 (Part II) are applicable to the Occupied Territories. According to Jean Pictet, a leading commentator on international law and the principal authority on the Geneva Conventions, "The mere fact of persons residing in a territory belonging to or occupied by a party to the conflict, is sufficient to make Part II of the Convention applicable to him." Pictet, Jean (ed.), *Commentary: IV Geneva Convention Relative to the Protection of Civilian Persons in Time of War* (International Committee of the Red Cross, 1958),

pp. 118-119. (Hereinafter: *Commentary*)
9. These principles are explicitly stated in other humanitarian instruments. Article 10(2) of Protocol I provides:
   In all circumstances they [the wounded and sick] shall be treated humanely and shall receive, to the fullest extent practicable and with the least possible delay, the medical care required by their condition. [Emphasis added]
   Israel is not a state party to this Protocol.
10. Article 21, IV Geneva Convention of 1949.
11. Pictet, *Commentary*, p. 171. According to Pictet, "To respect medical convoys means, in the first place, not to attack them, not to harm them in any way, which also means not to interfere with their running." Pictet, p. 171.
12. Al-Haq Affidavit No. 1137. See Appendix 2-A for a full text of the affidavit.
13. Al-Haq documentation. Al-Haq investigated this case in October 1988.
14. Al-Haq Affidavit No. 1129. This affidavit is reprinted in full in Appendix 2-B.
15. Al-Haq documentation. This case was documented by al-Haq in February 1988.
16. *Ibid.*
17. Al-Haq Affidavit No. 1291. See Appendix 2-C for the text of this affidavit.
18. *Ibid.*
19. See Appendix 2-D, which contains the following affidavits with additional information: Affidavits Nos. 1136, 1144 and 1179.
20. Al-Haq Affidavit No. 1284. This affidavit is reproduced in full in Appendix 2-E.
21. Al-Haq Affidavit No. 1282. The full text of this affidavit appears in Appendix 2-F.
22. Article 17, IV Geneva Convention 1949.
23. Article 55, IV Geneva Convention 1949.
24. Pictet, *Commentary*, p. 314.
25. Articles 63, 56, 55, IV Geneva Convention of 1949.
26. Al-Haq Affidavit No. 1303.
27. Article 56, IV Geneva Convention 1949, Article 20 (which provides protection specifically to full and part-time hospital employees) and Article 63 (which grants similar protection to those with humanitarian agencies such as the International Committee of the Red Cross, the Red Crescent and other relief societies).
28. Al-Haq Affidavit No. 1135. See Appendix 2-G for full text of the affidavit.
29. *Al-Fajr Jerusalem Palestinian Weekly*, 8 May 1988.
30. The detained doctors are Dr. Muhammad Abboushi, Dr. Hanna Rishmawi, Dr. Jamil Qumsiya and Dr. Sa'id Darras, and the nurse is Hanan Bannoura.
31. Pictet, *Commentary*, pp. 147-8.
32. *Ibid.*, p. 145.
33. Article 19, IV Geneva Convention 1949.
34. *Ibid.*
35. Pictet, *Commentary*, p. 155.
36. Witness interviewed by al-Haq on 23 August 1988.
37. Intra-hospital communique from the Night Supervisor of al-Maqassed Hospital to the Administrator of the hospital, 21 August 1988, p. 2. See Appendix 2-H for an English translation.

38. Al-Haq Affidavit No. 1290.
39. Intra-hospital communique, *supra*, note 37.
40. Al-Haq Affidavit No. 1138.
41. Civil Administration in Judea and Samaria, Medical Services, Department of Hospital Managements, *Circular,* 20 December 1987. See Appendix 2-I for the full text of this circular.
42. *Ibid.*
43. *Ibid.*, point 4.
44. Al-Haq Affidavit No. 1408. The text of the affidavit appears in Appendix 2-J.
45. Report prepared by Dr. Atallah, Orthopaedic Resident, al-Maqassed Hospital, regarding Muhid Shahin, 21 November 1988.
46. Al-Haq Affidavit No. 1408. (*Supra,* note 44).
47. Over 3,000 Palestinians have been imprisoned at Dhahriya since its establishment as a detention centre in December 1987. For a detailed examination of conditions there, see: al-Haq, *Dahriyyeh: Centre for Punishment,* May 1988.
48. *Ibid.*, p. 11.
49. *Ibid.*, p. 2.
50. *Ibid.*, p. 10.
51. Most detainees at Ansar III are held under orders of administrative detention. For a more detailed discussion of conditions there, see: al-Haq, *Ansar 3: A Case for Closure,* August 1988.
52. *Ibid.*, p. 18.
53. Union of Palestinian Medical Relief Committees, *Overview,* pp. 34-35. For a detailed discussion of health conditions and the structure of medical services in the West Bank and Gaza, see same.
54. The Union of Palestinian Medical Relief Committees, *The Uprising: Consequences for Health and Palestinian Response,* August 1988, p. 4.
55. *Ibid.* The Medical Relief Committees note that U.S. $150.00 represents approximately one-half of the average monthly income of residents in the West Bank and Gaza Strip.
56. *Ibid.*, p. 5.
57. *Response of the Government of Israel to "the Casualties of Conflict, Medical Care and Human Rights in the West Bank and Gaza,"* issued on 24 May 1988, p. 6. (The report referred to by the authorities was published by Physicians for Human Rights on 30 March 1988).
58. *Al-Awdah* (English Weekly), 28 December 1987.

Appendix 2-A

TRANSLATION OF SWORN AFFIDAVIT (#1137) TAKEN BY AL-HAQ

I the undersigned, Shaher Muhammad Hamed Mujahed, 38 years of age, an ambulance driver for the Red Crescent Society in Hebron and resident of the City of Hebron, having been warned to tell the truth or be subject to criminal liability, hereby state as follows:

I work as an ambulance driver for the Red Crescent Society in Hebron. On 13 December 1987, the person in charge of the Society informed me that there was an injured person at Hebron University who needed help. I immediately went to the university campus and had no problems with soldiers on the way. I found that the injured person had been taken in a civilian vehicle to 'Alia Hospital in Hebron, so I went to the hospital. It was about 10:30 in the morning. The injured person's companions told me that they wanted to take him to Jerusalem. I waited in front of the hospital, and after about half an hour, the patient was brought out of the hospital and I put him in the ambulance along with a male nurse from the hospital and two other persons.

I started to drive but an officer came and ordered me to wait. I heard the nurse say to the officer that the injured man was in no condition to wait, but he [the officer] insisted that we stay. The ambulance stayed there with the injured person inside bleeding for at least fifteen minutes. An Israeli policeman then came—he had been inside the hospital—and ordered me to move. The officer's excuse for holding me up was to try to get a military vehicle to accompany me to Jerusalem.

When I reached Ras al-Joura, which is about three kilometers from the hospital, a military vehicle (a Border Police jeep) stopped me and asked where I was heading. I said that I was going to Hadassah Hospital/ Ein Karem in Jerusalem. He questioned me for about five minutes.

I drove on to Hadassah hospital, but when I reached the military government building in Bethlehem, a group of soldiers motioned me to stop. I was held up there another half an hour. A military jeep accompanied me from Bethlehem to the hospital.

On 19 December 1988, at approximately 11:30 a.m., I drove the ambulance to the University after having heard that a female student had fainted from the effects of tear gas fired by soldiers. When I reached the main entrance of the University, I left the ambulance and went inside to get the injured girl. One of the soldiers in the University shot a tear gas canister at me to prevent me from moving her. After inhaling the gas I was unable to breathe or move, and felt like I was suffocating. I was unable to drive the ambulance for about a quarter of an hour.

I later took the injured girl and drove towards the hospital. When I passed by soldiers, one of them stopped me and asked about the patient. He opened the ambulance door and saw her unconcious, and he did not hold me up.

In accordance with all of the above, I hereby sign this statement on the date of 20 December 1987.

(Signature)

Name available for publication.

Appendix 2-B

TRANSLATION OF SWORN AFFIDAVIT (#1129) TAKEN BY AL-HAQ

I the undersigned, Kamal Muhammad Rashid al-Skafi, 28 years of age, shoemaker, resident of the city of Hebron, having been warned to tell the truth or be subject to criminal liability, hereby state as follows:

I work in a shoe-making shop in al-Sheikh neighbourhood in the city of Hebron. The shop is about one kilometer away from the city centre. My injured cousin Nimer al-Skafi works in a shoe store in the same neighbourhood approximately 20 meters away from mine.

The story began when I heard my cousin Nimer shouting and saying "My hand, my hand, help me..." I came out of the shop and saw Nimer on the ground screaming with blood flowing out of his hand. I was surprised to see a soldier standing near Nimer, no more than one half a meter away and pointing his gun at Nimer's head. I tried to help Nimer, to lift him off the ground, but he pointed his gun in my direction and said, in broken Arabic: "I'll shoot you, get away." The soldier was of a fair complexion, tall, thin, dressed in light-colored military khakis, wearing a brown beret, and his gun had a metal butt which folds. Nimer was on the ground screaming and the soldier was threatening me and other workers who had appeared to see what was going on, and preventing us from helping Nimer and aiding him. Approximately five minutes later, around five soldiers came. I then went and started my car which was parked in front of the shop in order to help Nimer, but the same soldier made me get out of the car. At this time a group of neighbourhood women came and started to scream and try to help Nimer. The soldiers let me take Nimer to the hospital, but only after taking our identification cards and the license plate number, which took about fifteen minutes. I then insisted on taking him to the hospital and helped by other workers, put him in the car.

While on the way to the hospital, which is about 2 kilometers from where the incident took place, I encountered a group of soldiers who stopped me and asked for my identification. I told them that there was an injured man in the car and that I did not have my ID. After about three minutes they let me go and I finally got to the hospital. There a military officer immediately came with an Israeli policeman. They looked at Nimer's injury and left. Another soldier came (a Druse, I believe) and asked me about my relationship to the injured man and why I aided him, and left.

In accordance with all the above, I hereby sign this statement on this date, the 12 December 1987.
(Signature):
Name available for publication.

Appendix 2-C

TRANSLATION OF SWORN AFFIDAVIT (#1291) TAKEN BY AL-HAQ

I the undersigned, Murad Muhammad Mahmoud 'Amer, 25 years of age, a labourer and resident of 'Azmout village, Nablus, having been warned to tell the truth or be subject to criminal liability, hereby state as follows:

At around 6:30 a.m. on Monday 16 April 1988, after the call to prayer, and while returning home after a visit to the cemetery, I heard some shooting and immediately rushed towards the source of the sound. I arrived at the entrance to the village where I saw a young man lying on the ground in a pool of blood.

I also saw Saleh Thabet standing by the injured youth who was his brother, 'Ala al-Din Muhammad Thabet, fifteen years of age. I picked the injured youth up and put him in a Fiat owned by Tareq 'Alawneh, a resident of the village. I sat in the car, pressing on the injured boy's neck where he had been shot. The car moved off, driven by Tareq 'Alawneh and the wounded youth's brother, Saleh Thabet. When the car arrived at a stone barricade, we stopped and Saleh and Tareq got out—and were joined by two other young men—to remove the barricade in order for the car to pass. As soon as the young men began to clear the road, shots were fired at them. I looked towards the source of the shooting and saw soldiers on the roof of a house, firing at the men and at the car.

The two other youths, Shaker Rasmi 'Affaneh, aged 19, and Maher 'Alawneh, aged 22, were slightly injured. They ran away towards the village, while Saleh and Tareq continued to clear the road block. I saw a number of soldiers approach Saleh and Tareq and ask them what had happened in the village. Saleh said that there was a wounded person in the car, and that he was wounded by soldiers' fire. They answered, laughing, that they did not fire their guns, and said that Saleh and Tareq were to clear the road up properly before they would allow the car to move.

By then, the road had already been cleared enough for the car to get through. But the soldiers insisted that they clear the road completely in spite of Saleh's insistent demand that the wounded youth be allowed through. At this time a military vehicle was blocking the road in front of us, so Saleh and Tareq were forced to clear the entire street. When they were almost finished, two soldiers approached the car, and one of them sat down behind the steering wheel and the other next to him. He started the car and drove very fast after the military car moved out of the way. He did not stop to pick up the driver nor the injured boy's brother.

He kept driving until we reached the 'Azmout/al-Hatab intersection. There we stopped for about three minutes, and the soldier who was driving got out and spoke with one of the officers. He was behaving very calmly. I started screaming at the soldiers and begging them to hurry and transport the injured boy but my shouting was met with silence. After three minutes, the soldier returned and started driving on the Elon Moreh—'Askar road, which was far from the City of Nablus. The soldier could have taken a shorter route. The car drove very slowly, and I asked the soldiers for a bottle of water which was in the car, so as to sprinkle the injured boy's face, but the soldiers did not even answer me. On the way on Amman Street, the soldiers stopped the car for three more minutes while the driver went to a military vehicle parked on the opposite side of the street and chatted with the soldiers there.

The car continued until it reached the intersection of Faisal Street and Khillet al-'Amoud. There, the car veered to the left towards al-'Amiriya school, which was occupied by the army. I knew immediately that they had no intention of aiding the victim, and I began to beg them and shouted at them to save him and take him to hospital. The car kept going, however, until it drove into al-'Amiriya School yard and stopped. The two soldiers got out. I had not stopped demanding that the victim be aided, but it was of no use.

I sat in the car with the injured boy for another twenty minutes, during which I kept demanding and insisting. Then a soldier came and said that I should get him out of the car, making me believe that they were going to take him to hospital. With great speed, I carried the wounded and placed him on a medical stretcher pointed out to me by one of the soldiers. When the injured boy was on the stretcher, one of the soldiers put a blanket on him and did nothing else. I began to scream and accused the soldiers of deliberately killing him, and demanding once again that they hurry and transport him. I was unable to continue, however, because a soldier approached me, tied my hands and put a blindfold on my eyes and led me to one of the tents in the school. I was there for about fifteen minutes, after which an officer came and untied me. I immediately asked after the victim and he said that the army had taken him to the hospital and that he was alright. I asked to be taken to the hospital but the officer said it was none of my business and that I should go home.

They released me and I arrived back at the village where I later learned that 'Ala al-Din Thabet had died, and that he had not been taken to hospital except for an autopsy. This is what happened.

In accordance with all of the above, I hereby sign this statement on the date of 19 June 1988.

(Signature)

Name available for publication.

Appendix 2-D.1

ADDITIONAL AFFIDAVITS CONCERNING OBSTRUCTION OF AMBULANCES AND PRIVATE CARS CARRYING THE WOUNDED

TRANSLATION OF SWORN AFFIDAVIT (#1136) TAKEN BY AL HAQ

I the undersigned, _____, 23 years of age, a nurse in the _____ hospital and a resident of_____, having been warned to tell the truth or be subject to criminal liability, hereby state as follows:

At approximately 1:30 p.m. on Friday 11 December 1987, reports reached the _____ hospital in _____ that someone had been shot in Balata camp. I went with a doctor and a nurse from the hospital to Balata camp in an ambulance belonging to the Red Crescent Society of Nablus. At the main entrance to Balata camp, soldiers ordered us to stop. There I saw a Civil Administration officer, Charlie, along with a number of other soldiers. They asked us where we were going and we informed them that we wanted to aid the wounded. They permitted us to pass but only on the condition that we return by the same route, through the main entrance to the camp. As we entered the camp, soldiers ordered us to halt and asked: "Who gave you permission to enter?" We answered: "Charlie." They then held us until they checked, searching the ambulance for wounded. We had to stop around ten times, giving the same explanation. As we returned to the entrance of the camp, the soldiers stopped us and held us there for about an hour and a half. Along with us, three other ambulances belonging to the Red Crescent and Rafidiya Hospital were also being held. We were held in order to go eventually to receive the bodies of the dead from their families, since the families refused to hand them over to the army. Soldiers accompanied the ambulances to the homes of those who had been killed and the corpses were taken. When the loaded ambulances gathered again at the entrance, the soldiers ordered us to go to military headquarters in Nablus, where the ambulances were held for four hours. I had to leave the ambulance along with three other nurses and return to the hospital, while the ambulances remained, with the corpses, at the military headquarters. I later learned that the ambulances had transported the bodies to the autopsy centre in Abu Kbir and returned them around 2:00 a.m. when the dead were eventually buried.

In accordance with all of the above I hereby sign this statement on this date, the 17 of December 1987.

(Signature)
Name withheld from publication

Appendix 2-D.2

TRANSLATION OF SWORN AFFIDAVIT (#1144) TAKEN BY AL-HAQ

I the undersigned, Husam Mahmoud Abdel-Rahman Khader, age 26, an employee at the vegetable oil company in Nablus, and a resident of Balata Refugee camp, having been warned to tell the truth or be subject to criminal liability, hereby state as follows:

On Friday 11 December 1987, at about 12:00 p.m., after prayer was over and while people were leaving the mosque, around 12 border guards who were standing a few meters away from the main door of the mosque overlooking the market street started separating the young men from the old who were leaving the mosque. This angered them because they considered it as a violation of religious feelings and of the sacred mosque. This action encouraged the people to protest, and they started chanting "Allahu Akbar, Allahu Akbar."

At that time I was inside the mosque and I heard the chantings of the people. I then went outside to see what was happening; while I was leaving I heard the shooting of live bullets. At the entrance of the mosque, I saw the people chanting and I saw between 20-30 soldiers standing at about 30 meters distance from the people; they were shooting in all directions. I saw soldiers shooting in the air, while others crouched in a combat position, pointing their guns towards the people. A few moments later, I was shot suddenly in my right thigh. I touched the place of the wound which was bleeding heavily. A number of people ran towards me. While the intensive shooting was still going on in all directions, they carried me through the alleys of the camp for about 100 meters. Then I was put into a private car and I think two women accompanied me.

On our way to the hospital, the border guards, who were gathering on the southern entrance to the camp, stopped the car and asked about me, my injury, my name and my identification card. This lasted for five minutes which made one of the women who were accompanying me shout at the soldiers because my health condition was deteriorating due to the heavy bleeding. They then allowed the car to pass. When we arrived at al-Ittihad al-Nisa'i Hospital I saw dozens of soldiers at the entrance of the hospital and on the main road. I also saw a military ambulance; the soldiers were forbidding anyone from entering the hospital.

The people accompanying me were afraid that the soldiers would arrest me so they took me to the Anglican Hospital where I was given first aid and then went back to al-Ittihad al-Nisa'i Hospital. When I arrived there I didn't see any soldiers but saw a large number of people gathering at the entrance of the hospital. Before I went to the operating room, a police officer and an officer from the military government came and questioned me about my injury but I refused to give them any information because of my poor health, as well as my psychological condition after I heard that tens of people from the camp were killed and injured. The police officer Jamal Ghanem threatened me by saying "you will regret that."

At this point, i.e. around 1:30 p.m., I saw from my hospital room, which overlooks the entrance of the hospital, tens of soldiers, and officers and security men preventing the people from entering the hospital. I saw them shooting live and rubber bullets, then I was taken to the operating room where I was given medical treatment. I left the operating room and while I was transferred to the patients' room, the nurses told me that I was given a new life because two bullets had been shot inside the room where I had been waiting to go to the operating room. During the time I spent at the hospital, which lasted for 6 days, I lived with the other injured people in a bad psychological atmosphere due to the fear of being arrested.

This actually happened with a large number of youths, who were injured on the previous days such as _____*, who was arrested on his third day in the hospital from al-Ittihad al-Nisa'i Hospital and _____*, who was arrested from the camp at night right after he was injured, and also _____*, who was injured on 23 November 1987 and was arrested from the hospital while he was in poor health. They are still in al-Fara'a prison. It is worth mentioning that on my third day in the hospital an officer, Jamal Ghanem, accompanied by two other policemen, came to the hospital and wrote down my name, and my identification card number and the place where the bullet had entered my body.

In accordance with all of the above, I hereby sign this statement on this date, the 27 December, 1987.

(Signature)

Name available for publication

* Names have been withheld to protect the identity of the individuals involved.

Appendix 2-D.3

TRANSLATION OF SWORN AFFIDAVIT (#1179) TAKEN BY AL-HAQ

I the undersigned, Ya'coub 'Ata Abdallah 'Ataya, 26 years of age, a driver by occupation, and a resident of Kufer Na'ma, having been warned to tell the truth or be subject to criminal liability, hereby state as follows:

At around 3:30 p.m. on 13 January 1988, there was tension in the village: the young men began to gather around the main roads into the village, placing stone barricades and burning tires in protest at the conditions in the West Bank and Gaza and at the occupation authorities' inhuman measures in the territories. After about half an hour, a large Israeli army force arrived, approximately 30 soldiers. They spread out in groups, firing live ammunition at the demonstrators. They also shot tear gas near the houses. While the soldiers continued shooting, women and children began to gather, chanting nationalist and anti-Israeli slogans. At this time, I noticed Hassan fighting the soldiers who had surrounded the women. I saw with my own eyes one of the soldiers, who was hiding behind an olive tree, pointing his gun at Hassan and firing, hitting Hassan's chest and hand.

When Hassan fell to the ground, we tried to save him. I was one of those who carried him and I noticed that his face had turned dark. We put him in a private car owned by a village resident. We went towards Ramallah and on the way a soldiers' checkpoint stopped us. Even though we told them that we are carrying a wounded man and that we had to hurry because his injury was serious, they would not allow us to continue, and demanded that we get out of the car. One of the soldiers shot a tear gas canister near the car. After approximately ten minutes, we were allowed to continue. I noticed then that Hassan was still moving his legs and his hands. When we reached Ramallah Government Hospital, Hassan was admitted to the operating room, but some of the employees told us that he had died. The doctor on duty asked us to go home and said that they—the hospital—would send the body after completing the necessary procedures. We returned to the village but Hassan's body did not come.

At eight in the evening, I went with the village mukhtar to the hospital. There we saw a police car and one of the policemen asked us to accompany him to the Civil Administration in Ramallah to receive the body. Half an hour after our arrival at the office of the Civil Administration, the officer started asking me about my work, and said why are you on strike, using threatening language and tone. While we were in his office, he contacted the Commander of the Central Region, Amram Mitzna'—I knew this because I know Hebrew. After waiting for about an hour, the officer told the mukhtar that the body would be buried under strict guard, and with only four close relatives present, but the mukhtar refused those conditions. Then the officer said that he would hand over the body, but only after we signed a guarantee to keep order.

At about 2:00 a.m., three military vehicles came and we were given the body which was placed in a hearse belonging to the municipality of Ramallah. We proceeded with a military vehicle in front and two behind.

The cars drove slowly and every once in a while, the soldiers would stop the cars and spread out on high alert as though something had attacked them. When we reached the Kufer Na'ma intersection, the soldiers put three road blocks at the three entrances to the village, and asked us to go into town and proceed with the burial with only 15 people present. They threatened us saying that if any disturbances happened, they would take the body away, and they also demanded that the burial should take one hour only. Everything went off peacefully. I should mention that the body did not undergo an autopsy at Abu Kbir because the Ramallah mayor intervened against it. Now the soldiers come to the village daily and goad the residents by taking their IDs and forcing them to stand with their arms held high.

In accordance with all of the above, I hereby sign this statement on the date, 19 January 1988.

(Signature)

Name available for publication.

Appendix 2-E

TRANSLATION OF SWORN AFFIDAVIT (#1284) TAKEN BY AL-HAQ

I the undersigned, _____ , 27 years of age, a resident of Jab'a, having been warned to tell the truth or be subject to criminal liability, hereby state as follows:

At 5:00 p.m. Monday 29 May 1988, I arrived at my village Jab'a after returning from work in Israel and saw a great number of soldiers in the village. I immediately made my way to my home and after about half an hour I was told by someone that the army had withdrawn from the village. I and other young men went out to the street searching for casualties in the village. When we arrived at the main square in the village we were surprised to see two soldiers emerge from a narrow road and start shooting at us with an automatic weapon. I was injured in my right leg but in spite of being wounded I ran for a distance of about 50 meters until I fell on the ground. Moments later I saw the two soldiers approaching me. When they arrived they beat me with the butt of their rifles and kicked me. I asked them to stop beating me and to take me to a hospital and one of them told me that they would transfer me later on.

I lay bleeding for five minutes and then the two soldiers took me to the doctor's clinic in the village. He stopped the bleeding and summoned a civilian car to take me and him to the hospital. It is worth noting that the soldier who shot me gave the doctor a piece of paper permitting me to leave the village. But when the car which was taking me to the hospital reached a military checkpoint near the Jab'a olive press, the soldiers stopped us and refused to let us pass even though the doctor presented the permit. We stayed there for about 1/4 of an hour. We were then allowed to proceed out of the village to the hospital.

In accordance with all of the above, I hereby sign this statement on the date of 29 May 1988.
(Signature)
Name withheld.

Appendix 2-F

TRANSLATION OF SWORN AFFIDAVIT (#1282) TAKEN BY AL HAQ

I the undersigned, Kamal Sidki Sadik Khamis, 14 years of age, a student, and a resident of Deheisha camp near Bethlehem, having been warned to tell the truth or be subject to criminal liability, hereby state as follows:

While I and my colleague Wajih Khalil Zayed al-Fararja were walking last Monday, 6 June 1988 at about 6.20 p.m. in the direction of our house, a third young man named 'Amer Mahmoud al-Ma'adi joined us. After three minutes, while we were still walking in the direction of our house, I saw two soldiers who ordered us to stop. We did. One of them searched us and the other guarded us. One of the soldiers slapped me on the face. After two minutes, I observed the other soldier who was guarding the site walking a distance of about 5 meters and opening fire. I did not realise then that my colleague was injured. The soldier who was standing by us beat my head against the head of my colleague Wajih; we both fell down on the ground.

When I looked at Wajih, I observed blood stains on his trousers and specifically on his leg. I then realised that he was injured. The soldier who had fired came nearer and both soldiers beat Wajih and attacked him. I shouted loudly and a number of residents crowded near me and near my colleague Wajih and the other youth. The two soldiers communicated with their brigade and a number of soldiers then arrived on the scene. The father of the injured person, Wajih, was there but he could not reach his son. Wajih remained on the ground for about 40 minutes and the soldiers did not allow his relatives to reach him or get near him. Wajih's face was badly wounded and he needed hospitalisation.

Ten minutes later, another soldier arrived and started looking at Wajih's leg. He tore the trousers' leg and it was apparent Wajih's leg was very swollen. The soldier tied the leg with a piece of cloth next to the wound, apparently to stop the bleeding. In about five minutes, an Israeli ambulance and an Arab ambulance arrived but the soldiers refused to put Wajih in the Arab ambulance, claiming that it was not equipped with a doctor. The Israeli ambulance took him to the Beit Jala Government Hospital in Beit Jala. There, his leg was operated on and it was discovered that he had been hit in the left leg with a dumdum bullet.

In accordance with all of the above, I hereby sign this statement on this date, 13 June 1988.
(Signature)
Name available for publication.

Appendix 2-G

TRANSLATION OF SWORN AFFIDAVIT (#1135) TAKEN BY AL-HAQ

I the undersigned, Muhammad Mahmoud Muhammad al-Saqa, 25 years of age, an ambulance driver for the Red Crescent Society and a resident of Nablus, having been warned to tell the truth or be subject to criminal liability, hereby state as follows:

At around 12:30 p.m. on Friday 11 December 1987, the Red Crescent Society headquarters in Nablus received a telephone call saying that there were injuries in Balata Camp. I and nurse Ibrahim Lutfi Jamil Elias set off in the ambulance to Balata camp in order to aid and transport the injured. At the entrance to the camp, Border Police ordered me to stop and took our identification cards, and one of the officers told me to bring all the wounded to the camp entrance where the soldiers were gathered. This discussion went on for about five minutes after which we entered the camp, going in the direction of the UNRWA schools. There we were stopped by four soldiers and they asked who had given us permission to enter. We told them it was the soldiers at the entrance. They ordered us to remove the stone barricades in the road on the pretext of facilitating the ambulance's passage. This took another five minutes, after which we continued on towards the schools.

We drove around looking for injured but found none and turned back. At the camp entrance the same officer who had allowed us in asked about the wounded and we informed him that we had found none. But he said: "Drive around the camp again and if you find any bring them here." We went back in and drove around but found no wounded or injured. We returned to the camp entrance and when we told the officer that we had found no wounded, he ordered us to stand aside.

Around ten minutes later, a Hinschel model car drove by with three wounded. I followed it and took them into the ambulance. The child was already dead but the two women were wounded. I took all three to al-Ittihad al-Nisai Hospital.

I returned to Balata camp once again. I entered the camp, but not through the main street. I drove around the camp for about half an hour then went to the main Nablus-Jerusalem thoroughfare. A military vehicle with two soldiers pulled up next to me. They ordered me not to drive around the camp saying: "When injuries occur we'll send for you." I went to the main entrance to the camp, however, and there I saw two ambulances, one belonging to Rafidia Hospital and the other to the Red Crescent Society. When we tried to enter the camp, soldiers prevented us and ordered us to return to our place of work. The two other cars departed, and as I was about to leave, I heard a woman shout: "Stop! Stop!" When I stopped the ambulance in order to pick her up, I was surprised by Border Police, who opened the car door. They dragged me out and started beating me with clubs, fists and boots. They threw me to the ground and continued to beat me in the same fashion on my head, my stomach and the rest of my body. My head was cut and started bleeding. Later I drove away in the ambulance.

While driving by Bir Ya'coub [Jacob's Well] near the camp, I picked up a wounded person and took him to al-Ittihad al-Nisai Hospital. My head wound was still bleeding then and my colleague gave me first aid while I was driving. From al-Ittihad al-Nisai I took two male and two female nurses and returned to Balata Camp, heading towards the mosque where we had heard there were people wounded. Soldiers stopped me and one of them grabbed me by the ear, pulling it several times, and hitting my head against the car. My right ear bled after being cut by the soldier's finger nails.

By then I was no longer able to drive the ambulance. One of the nurses drove instead and we returned to al-Ittihad al-Nisai where I received first aid. Someone else took charge of the ambulance.

In accordance with all of the above, I hereby sign this statement on the date of 17 December 1987.

(Signature)

Name available for publication.

Appendix 2-H

INTRA-HOSPITAL COMMUNIQUE TRANSLATED BY AL-HAQ

Al-Maqased Islamic Charitable Hospital, Jerusalem.

From:	Night Supervisor	Topic:	Raid of the hospital by the military authorities.
To:	Administrator of Hospital.		
Via:	Chief Nurse		
		Date:	21/8/1988.

On Sunday 21 August 1988, at 11:30 p.m., I was called by the beeper to the emergency room to help care for a patient who was in critical condition. At 12:00 midnight one of the nurses told me that a military force consisting of four cars, two police mini-buses and two military jeeps were parked in front of and all around the hospital. The hospital was surrounded with a big military force and there were soldiers inside the hospital as well. At once I left the patient to be attended by one of the nurses.

As I rushed outside the emergency room, I came face to face with an armed soldier standing at the inner door of the room preventing anyone from entering or leaving and also barring anyone from using the telephone. Another soldier was standing at the outer door of the emergency room, two were in the hall, one was at the entrance of the X-Ray room, and another was near the laboratory. I was startled by their presence since they had not given any warning. The soldier at the inner door of the emergency room stopped me from calling the intensive-care unit in order to give instructions to complete admitting the patient. Another soldier prevented one of the nurses from entering the laboratory in order to make the tests regarding the percentage of gas that was inside the patient's body. These tests are very important to save the patient's life. After 10 minutes of bitter argument between me and the soldier, during which he threatened to hit me, he allowed the nurse to go in.

It should be mentioned here that the patient could have lost his life during these few minutes because the tests that the nurse wanted to make were important for the doctor in order to provide the patient with the right treatment. After that I went upstairs. I saw a fully armed soldier standing in the administration offices. Every time I asked the soldiers about the reasons behind the raid on the hospital, they told me to "shut up." They answered me in this manner after I had introduced myself to them as the direct supervisor of the hospital that night.

Then I went up to the first floor after hearing noises coming from the surgery room, the children's ward and the intensive-care room. There I was faced with about twenty [Shin Bet] Intelligence men in civilian dress, accompanied by fully-armed soldiers. They raided the intensive-care room, searching in a barbaric way and without any search warrants. I tried to stop them or even talk to them but they wouldn't listen. I therefore called Dr. Rustom al-Nammari and Chief Nurse Miss Hulwa Qassis. After leaving the intensive-care room they raided the children's ward thereby spreading fear in the hearts of the children. I became furious and asked the so-called "Abu-Munir," the commander, to stop these acts and talk to me or show a search warrant.

Every time I tried to stop them from raiding a patient's room they pushed me back. They raided all the wards of the hospital, yelling and shouting all around the place. Then the so-called "Abu-Munir" accompanied by a soldier took me aside, threatened that he would close the hospital and claimed that there were contacts between some of the administrators of the hospital and people wanted by the authorities. When I asked him what gave him and his men the right to raid the hospital, he answered me that he had all the right in the world to raid hospitals. While we were arguing we heard soldiers chasing some youngsters inside the hospital, specifically in the cafeteria area. They caught two of them and beat them severely. One of the soldiers was going to shoot at one of the youths but "Abu-Munir" prevented him from doing so. The raid lasted for 45 minutes after which they left, taking with them about four youngsters.

Appendix 2-I

CIVIL ADMINISTRATION IN JUDEA AND SAMARIA

Medical Services
Department of Hospital Management
P.O. Box 413
Tel: 1657, 3392, 3393-5

Circular

Date: 20 December 1987
Number: 23/1/3455

Manager of al-Ittihad al-Nisa'i Hospital, Nablus

Subject: Reports regarding those who are treated in one of the hospitals in the area from wounds or injuries resulting from clashes with the IDF.

On 13 December 1988, I received a letter (ref. 549/87) from the Manager of the Medical Services to the following effect:

1. The Health Officer must receive a report on every person wounded in clashes with the IDF, whether he is treated in a government or private hospital.

2. The initial report must be directly delivered by phone to the Health Officer's office or home, and must include the following:
   (a) Complete name
   (b) Sex
   (c) I.D. card number
   (d) Type of injury (in details)
   (e) Location of the incident

3. Initial reports in writing should be sent to the following:
   (a) Hospital Management Department
   (b) Health Officer
   (c) Area Administrative Governor

4. The final detailed report should be sent in writing by the hospital management to the Health Officer no later than 24 hours after the incident took place. The report must include the following:
   (a) Complete name
   (b) I.D card number
   (c) Sex
   (d) Age or date of birth
   (e) Address of the wounded

(f) Date and time of the incident
(g) Time the wounded arrived at the hospital
(h) Who accompanied the wounded
(i) Location of the incident, and, if possible, other details
(j) Details on the type of injury and type of treatment
(k) Additional treatment to be given to the wounded

5. If the condition of the wounded is critical, an oral daily report should be delivered to the Health Officer and another report in writing from the manager of the hospital should be sent to the Department of Hospital Management.

You are kindly requested to act accordingly.

Dr. Muhammad Sa'id Kamal
Director of the West Bank Hospital Department

cc: Medical Services Director

Health Officer telephone numbers:
02-976253
02-976252
02-976251
02-976530
02-976080
02-976857

Appendix 2-J

TRANSLATION OF SWORN AFFIDAVIT (#1408) TAKEN BY AL-HAQ

I the undersigned, Dr. Otto Walter, 71 years old, a German citizen and a resident of Jerusalem, and the Director of the International Lutheran Federation, having been warned to tell the truth or be subject to criminal liability, hereby state as follows:

On Thursday August 25, 1988 at 2:00 p.m. three injured people from al-Am'ari camp in Ramallah and one from Balata camp in Nablus arrived at Augusta Victoria Hospital. All four were wounded in their legs. Between the hours six to eight in the evening a military official called me from Jerusalem to check about the condition of the injured and to get their names. I immediately called Dr. Majaj, the medical director of the hospital, and informed him about the call I received. We reached a decision that there was no way we could conceal the names of the injured. So I left my office which overlooks the hospital and headed towards the hospital in order to get the names. When the military official called once more I gave him the names. Then I left for home.

At 10:00 p.m., one of the hospital staff called me saying that the hospital had been raided by the army. So I went to the hospital and saw them at the entrance. I saw six military vehicles and an ambulance in the hospital yard. Soldiers were carrying the injured on wheelchairs. A medical chief in his military uniform was present. I asked what this was all about and was told that they had orders to arrest the injured young men. They showed me the orders. He also informed me that they wanted to transfer them to Hadassah Hospital [in West Jerusalem].

On the morning of 26 August 1988, I went to Hadassah Hospital at Mount Scopus to pay a visit to the injured. After an hour of waiting, I was told by the information office that the injured had been transfered at 3:00 a.m. to "Sha'are Zedek" hospital in [West] Jerusalem. I immediately headed for that hospital. I talked to the man in charge. An hour later they told me that they had transferred the injured to Hadassah. I went back to Hadassah Hospital where I saw that the army was present. The soldier on guard told me that no visitors were allowed. I also saw three soldiers inside the intensive-care room which was next to that of the injured. I expressed my protest and asked to see the officer-in-charge. I was told that I had to wait half an hour. Then a soldier told me that visits were prohibited and I could not see the officer. I banged my hand on the table and said that nobody has the right to stop a doctor from seeing his patients. I then waited once more until at 12:30 p.m. I was finally allowed to see my patients.

They were lying on an unfit stretcher and were shackled with leg irons. Then I went home. At about 7:00 p.m. I learned that the injured were taken back to Augusta Victoria Hospital and I then visited them once more.

In accordance with all of the above, I hereby sign this statement on 19 September 1988.

(Signature)
Name available for publication

Chapter 3

SETTLER PROVOCATION AND THE USE OF EXCESSIVE FORCE

A. Introduction

Echoing dozens of similar official and unofficial statements of the past 21 years, Israeli Prime Minister Yitzhak Shamir declared on 21 December 1987 that:

> There is no force in the world, neither rioters, terrorists, nor international pressure which will prevent settlement by the people of Israel in all parts of the Land of Israel.[1]

The policy of settlement has not changed as a result of the current Palestinian uprising. Rather, Israeli politicians and others continue to articulate the importance of settlement of the Occupied Territories for strategic and biblical/historical reasons.[2] Israel's occupation of the West Bank and Gaza Strip has been given a distinctly permanent feel by the process of settlement; indeed it is questionable whether Israel's presence in the West Bank and Gaza Strip can any longer be called an "occupation" in a conventional, legal sense of the word. The transfer of 70,000 Israeli citizens into the West Bank and Gaza Strip (illegally) and the acquisition (mostly illegally) of over 50 percent of the land is simply not reconcilable with "occupation": it is perhaps better described as a form of colonisation.

Nor has the incidence of Palestinian suffering caused directly by settlers diminished during the uprising. On the contrary, recorded cases of Palestinian deaths have increased from a yearly average of 6 in the period 1980-1984 to at least 15 this year.[3] Settlers continue to justify the shooting of fleeing stone throwers as self-defence (two charges of manslaughter are currently being defended in the courts in these terms, and a further one is pending). This makes little logical sense; no settler has been killed by stones during the current uprising, let alone by fleeing stone throwers. The five who have died in a total of two incidents were killed in entirely different circumstances. The notion that settlers shoot Palestinians in self-defence then can only refer to a different concept altogether: namely, that settlers see themselves as entitled to shoot Palestinians in defence of the land which they view as part of "Eretz (Greater) Israel." The very presence of a non-Jewish population on this land clearly poses a threat to the realisation of their vision.

The following brief survey of incidents during the uprising analyses the policy of settlement and its most ardent supporters, the settlers themselves, in the following stages:

a) *The policy of settlement* as exemplified in government support for the settlers; cooperation between army and settlers in carrying out acts of violence; and lack of accountability of settlers in the law courts.

b) *Settler violence,* including acts of provocation and the excessive use of force in the name of self-defence or retaliation (see Appendix 3-B for a list of incidents recorded by al-Haq fieldworkers).[4]

B. The Policy of Settlement: 1967 to the Present

The government of Israel has never made a secret of its basic political position (and indeed the position held by most Israelis) that it regards the establishment of settlements in the Occupied Territories as an overriding goal.[5] Thus the Allon Plan, presented to the Israeli cabinet in draft form as early as July 1967 aimed to establish settlements in strategic areas, particularly the Jordan Valley, in order to maximise Israel's security while minimising the geographic expansion of Israel's Arab minority and preventing Arab development in those areas.[6] This commitment to particular areas of strategic importance continues to be reflected in the statements of Israeli officials. As recently as 6 October 1988, for example, Police Minister Haim Bar-Lev proposed withdrawing troops from the Occupied Territories as part of a temporary measure to reduce friction, but stated at the same time that Israel would want to keep its settlements along the border between Jordan and the West Bank and that the 70,000 Jews in 131 settlements in the Territories should have the right to stay, even if the territory reverted to Arab control.[7]

Early on in the occupation an elaborate system of bodies revolving around an 'Inter-Ministerial Settlement Committee' was set up with a view to planning and implementing the settlement process. Large sums of money from both the Israeli government and groups such as the World Zionist Organisation have been invested in settlements. Between 1968 and 1986 capital investment reached a total of $2 billion.[8] Given that settlements are the result of declared government policy, it is not surprising that separate administrative and legal systems have been created and justified on the grounds of both security and improvement of the well-being of the "local" inhabitants, i.e. Israeli settlers.

So far as administration is concerned a system of local and regional councils was established which enjoy greater autonomy than their

Palestinian equivalents. The former elect their own leaders and impose taxes; they also receive state services as part of the Israeli government budget. Palestinian municipalities, on the other hand, have not been permitted to hold their own elections since 1976 and require permission from the military authorities in order to borrow money or even accept a financial gift.

In addition, a dual legal system has been created in the Occupied Territories (described in greater detail in chapter 6 below): separate Israeli courts now have jurisdiction over a wide range of matters affecting both Palestinians and Jews. The result is that Jewish settlers are not accountable in local courts for their actions. Consequently the administrative separation of Jew and Arab stands reinforced.

Israel justifies its changes in the laws that were in force in 1967 (i.e. Jordanian law in the West Bank) either in terms of security requirements or as being in the interests of the local inhabitants. The first argument generally appears in the context of the process of settlement itself, i.e. that settlements serve as centres for preserving order in times of peace and as lines of defence in times of war. As will be seen later, it is the adoption of settlers as a law-enforcement body that has resulted in many violations of human rights.

The second argument—that measures serving settlers (such as separate road networks and electricity grids) are for the benefit of the "local population"—appears disingenuous. Even if made in good faith, such arguments have serious implications since provisions in the relevant international law designed to protect the interests of the population subjected to occupation are being used to benefit the citizens of the occupying power.

1. Cooperation Between Settlers and Soldiers

The role of settlers is to preserve order in the environs of their settlements. Such is the express view of the Israeli government.[9] This view was also implicit in a statement by Amram Mitzna, the Military Commander of the Central Area (which includes the entire West Bank), who said, following the shooting of two soldiers by a settler on 31 August 1988, that "lessons would have to be learned regarding the army's operations, use of guns by civilians and *coordination between the IDF and settlers.*" (Emphasis added)[10]

Although such views have provoked some criticism from members of the police forces, they do not seriously alter the basic commitment to the idea of settlers as law enforcement agencies.[11] Thus on the day of the Israeli elections, 1 November 1988, residents of the settlement of

Kiryat Arba near al-Khalil (Hebron) were reported to have operated a system of checking the identification cards of local Palestinians:

> [a] settler on security patrol in a white jeep, a German shepherd dog beside him, called over the Arab occupants of a car that had stopped for petrol at the service-station. He checked their identification cards and ordered them out.[12]

In order to facilitate this role settlers are permitted to perform their military reserve duty locally. In addition to this, the access to weapons and other military equipment gained through military service anywhere in Israel or the Occupied Territories provides settlers with firepower throughout the year.[13]

Al-Haq has documented several examples of the policy of cooperation between the army and settlers in action, both before and during the current uprising.[14] In June 1987, for example, al-Haq wrote an intervention to the Legal Advisor of the Military Government after approximately 200 settlers (including at least one dressed in khaki) arrived at the Deheisha Refugee Camp near Bethlehem in buses, firing guns and tear gas grenades at homes in the camp. None of the settlers was restrained by the soldiers stationed near the camp, who were watching and in one case seen to be helping the settlers.

During the uprising this pattern has continued. For example, on 22 February 1988, Rawda Muhammad Lutfi Najib Hassan, a 14-year-old girl, was shot by rifle fire coming from four civilian cars and a *military vehicle* that had arrived outside her brother's house. The girl's brother, 'Adnan Muhammad Lutfi Najib Hassan, a 40-year-old farmer, has described under oath (in al-Haq Affidavit No. 1203) the events of that winter evening:

> At around 5:00 p.m. on the evening of Monday 22 February 1988, I and my 14-year-old sister Rawda Muhammad Lutfi Najib Hassan went to the house of my younger brother 'Ayed Muhammad Lutfi Najib who is 35 years old. The house is located on the main street between Baqa al-Sharqiya and Jenin. At around 7:30 that same evening, we saw car headlights approaching the house which is approximately 80 meters from the street. When my sister Rawda saw the headlights, she immediately went down from the second floor to the entrance thinking that her brother's wife and her other brother Jasser were arriving, along with a number of relatives who had gone to Nazareth that morning to purchase supplies for her brother Jasser's wedding. I was surprised to hear the sounds of gun shots. When I opened a second-story window to inquire, several shots were suddenly fired at me, breaking the glass on the sun veranda. At that moment I saw a medium-sized military vehicle and

two civilian cars parked in the yard of the house. I also saw two other civilian cars stopped on the main street.

It was then that I saw my sister running towards me in the room saying, "They shot me." I embraced her and carried her down to the yard to take her to the hospital because she was bleeding. As I arrived at the front door to the house, I saw the three vehicles about to leave, and was surprised by gun shots aimed at me and fired from the two cars parked on the street. I hid from the bullets inside my truck which was parked in front of the house, and while hiding I heard the bullets pierce the body of the truck. My sister was still in my lap, bleeding. The entire incident lasted about five minutes, after which all the vehicles left. I heard more shooting as they headed East on the Baqa al-Sharqiya–Jenin road.

I took my sister to Dr. Yousef Hourani, a resident of the village. He said it was necessary to take her immediately to the hospital because of the seriousness of her condition; she was then unable to speak or move. I took her immediately in the car of a friend of mine who also went with me to Olga Hospital in al-Khdeira. This friend is Husni Younes, also a resident of the village. She was admitted to the Emergency Ward, but an hour later, that is, around 9 o'clock, the doctors informed me that my sister had died.

On 28 February 1988, at 9:30 p.m., settlers from the Halamesh settlement attacked 'Aboud village near Ramallah, accompanied by Israeli troops. Soldiers illuminated the area while settlers opened fire on villagers, killing two: Ra'id Mahmoud 'Awad al-Barghouti, 17, and Ahmad Ibrahim al-Barghouti, 20. A curfew was then imposed on the village.

Another clear example of cooperation between soldiers and settlers occurred at Bab al-Zawiya in the city of Hebron on 30 September 1988. At around 10 a.m., while troops were clearing the centre of Hebron to allow settler-leader Rabbi Moshe Levinger free passage, Levinger himself, accompanied by two other settlers, started firing a pistol in the direction of a group of youths. A man, Kayed Hassan Salah, 42, was shot dead and another wounded. Soldiers who were standing approximately 3 meters from Rabbi Levinger watched the events and did nothing to prevent the incident. Troops later arrived at the scene and dispersed the youths. Despite the fact that the police found that Levinger was indeed responsible for the death of a Palestinian civilian and recommended that he be prosecuted, he was not detained in custody. On 30 November 1988, the Jerusalem Post reported:

The State Attorney's Office yesterday rejected a police recommendation that Hebron activist Rabbi Moshe Levinger be charged with shooting to death a Palestinian during a stone-throwing incident in the West Bank town two months ago. Claiming there was insufficient evidence, the State Attorney declined to prosecute.

In other cases, settlers have carried out arbitrary arrests for the military even where the need for an immediate arrest is not evident. For example, on 3 February 1988, settlers looking for a youth who they said had thrown stones entered Khawla Bint al-Azwar School in al-Bireh and, despite the fact that they said it was a boy they were looking for, arrested 2 schoolgirls aged 10 and 15, drove the girls to the entrance of al-Am'ari Refugee Camp, and handed them over to soldiers.

2. *The Legal System: Investigation, Prosecution, and Sentencing*

Settlers have taken advantage of certain features of the legal system in the Occupied Territories, radically altered from the form in which the Israeli government was in many respects legally bound to keep it, to achieve a position in which they are virtually unaccountable for their actions. In particular, settlers have benefited from a dual system of law in the Occupied Territories under which Palestinian courts are prevented from dealing with cases concerning Israelis, but Palestinians accused of criminal offences are tried either in a military court or a local court depending on the view of the military authorities; if tried in a military court, there is no appeal from the decision.[15]

The division of functions between the police and the military police has in the past been insufficiently clear. In February 1984 the Karp Commission, investigating suspicions against settlers in the West Bank, reported that lack of cooperation arose "in the matter of the splitting of cases in Military Police investigations which require the Military Police to get help from the police."[16] The Commission made a number of findings which illustrate the problems that have beset Palestinians seeking redress from the authorities:

(a) Of the 70 cases that were reported to the inquiry team, 53 had been closed by the police without results.

(b) The inquiry team's analysis of those cases that were investigated showed that in at least one case there was cooperation between soldiers and settlers while the latter committed acts of violence.

(c) In cases where no complaint was lodged, no investigation was carried out.

(d) The number of cases ending in closure exceeded the number acceptable in other spheres; there was a correlation between this and the lack of speed in investigation.

(e) In general, police investigations of incidents involving settlers showed a reluctance to treat the suspects as offenders in the usual sense; and even when they were so treated, police investigation teams were subject to external interference from military government personnel concerning the opening of investigations.

During the Palestinian uprising the treatment of settlers by the law courts has followed the general pattern of accommodation and support reflected in the behaviour of government ministers and army. On 30 July 1988 the police recommended prosecution of settlers responsible for only 3 out of 13 deaths caused by settlers up until then, namely those of Rabeh Husein Ghanem, 17, of Beitin, allegedly shot to death by Pinhas Wallerstein, the head of the Binyamin Regional Council; 'Abd-al-Baset Mahmoud 'Abdallah, 27, of Qaddoum, shot by a settler called Shimon; and Jouda Muhammad 'Awad, 28, a shepherd from Turmus 'Ayya, shot by Yisrael Ze'ev.[17] All face charges of manslaughter and are basing their defences on self-defence. The trial of Yisrael Ze'ev began on 9 October 1988; that of Pinhas Wallerstein began on 11 October 1988.

Of the other deaths caused by settlers, the police files on 'Abd-al-Baset Mahmoud 'Abdallah (killed on 8 February 1988) and Rawda Muhammad Hassan (killed on 22 February 1988) were still with the District Attorney-General when inquiries were made in August. Others, listed in Appendix 3-B, fall into a category of cases in which the file has been closed or the police state that they have no knowledge of the incident, or the family of the victim have requested that there be no investigation.

The Karp Commission's findings, summarised above, included the following reflections on possible reasons for a lack of complaint in the wake of settler acts of violence:

> The potential reasons for this absence of complaints may [include]...drawing conclusions from a lack of results in previous complaints to the police or from police refusal to handle complaints.

This conclusion, dating from 1984, remains valid in 1988. Moreover, the record of investigating and prosecuting settlers for causing unjustifiable death in the last twelve months alone (especially in clear-cut situations such as the Levinger case above) appears to confirm that the Israeli legal system is an indispensible prop of the policy of settlement.[18]

While settlers have been well-treated by the legal system, Palestinians have not. The often exaggerated response of the authorities to incidents in which Israelis are hurt or injured (whether or not there has been any kind of investigation of the facts) is best understood as a pretext for carrying out the policy of continued settlement. For example, following the well-publicised events in the village of Beita near Nablus on 6 April 1988, the government and the Israeli legal system combined in taking exceptionally severe measures against those whom Israeli officials and the public at large presumed to be guilty.[19] The army carried out a range of punitive measures against the villagers of Beita which is unequalled in recent years. The area was sealed off from 6 April until 30 April 1988; a total of 14 houses were demolished, and a number of others were damaged; scores of olive and almond trees belonging to the village were uprooted; some 60 villagers were arrested and all other males rounded up in the village school, supposedly for questioning, where they were to remain for the next five days; a number of villagers were prosecuted (including the sister of one of the Palestinians killed, Munira Da'oud Saleh, who was convicted and sentenced to a term of imprisonment); and finally, six villagers were deported to Lebanon.[20] These measures were carried out despite the fact that many of the details of the incident were unclear.

Such measures constitute nothing more than the necessary conditions for settlement of the area. Thus the Minister of Religion, Zevulun Hammer, announced immediately after the incident in Beita on 6 April: "Beita does not exist on the map of Israel. A settlement should be built there and named Tirza Porat" (the name of the settler-girl who died in the incident). During the curfew on the village, soldiers in fact allowed settlers to enter and declare the establishment of a new settlement.

Again on 7 November 1988, events followed a similar pattern following the stabbing to death of an IDF soldier, David Danieli, in the settlement of Mesu'a in the Jordan Valley by a Palestinian named Ahmad Husein 'Abdallah Bisharat from the village of Tammoun, who was then himself shot dead by another soldier. The IDF response was to bulldoze scores of makeshift homes of Palestinian migrant shepherds and labourers in the Jiftlik area (where Bisharat was living) in the Jordan Valley, displacing more than 100 families in the process. In addition all cars and tractors in Tammoun were taken by the IDF and placed in the courtyard of the local mosque. All these measures occurred after Bisharat had been summarily executed.[21]

Not only was the response of the IDF a clear example of (illegal) collective punishment, but in al-Haq's view the unlikely step of confiscating tractors and cars in response to a stabbing can only be fully understood in the context of the strategic importance attached by Israel to the Jordan Rift valley since 1967: depriving the local inhabitants of the means of cultivating the land is a logical first step towards the goal of removing them altogether.

C. Settler Provocation and the Use of Excessive Force

In a report issued by the Palestine Human Rights Campaign in 1985 incidents of settler violence in the years 1980-1984 were collected and categorised. The report found that the level of settler violence had risen over the period studied (only settlers wearing civilian clothes were included). The number Palestinians reported killed by settlers in 1980 was 1; in 1981, 2; in 1982, 7; in 1983, 9; and in 1984, 4. The number of Palestinians reported injured by settlers in 1980 was 11; in 1981, 35; in 1982, 40; in 1983, 83; and in 1984, 22.[22] These figures are a representative sample of settler incidents (not including the hundreds of harassments that occur annually involving property destruction, provocation, etc.) over a 5-year period and are intended to give an idea of the background to the present discussion of events during the uprising.

The following discussion of incidents aims to analyse some of the more typical incidents involving settlers; a fuller list of incidents, including the names of those killed by settlers since December 1987, can be found in Appendix 3-B.

1. Provocation by Settlers

Many examples exist of settlers asserting their presence in an openly provocative manner during the uprising. The following extract from one of al-Haq's fieldwork reports describes one typical example which occurred in the neighbouring villages of Sa'ir and Shuyoukh near al-Khalil (Hebron) on 3 June 1988:

> At about 10:30 a.m. a group of settlers entered the village of Sa'ir. The group consisted of youths carrying guns and rifles. They were wearing yarmulkas (skull caps). They entered by the Ras al-'Aroud road, i.e. from the direction of the Kiryat Arba settlement which lies between al-Khalil and Sa'ir. While they were walking down the street, they started asking people where the al-'Ali mosque was. Rumour spread that their target was the mosque. In response, hundreds of residents gathered inside the mosque, on its roof and in the alleyways. The youths of the village climbed onto the roofs of houses to confront the settlers, especially after their presence had been announced through the mosque loudspeaker. The settlers were walking along the main road that looks down on the mosque and the village (as the road is high-up and Sa'ir lies in a valley). Some children began to throw stones at the settlers to stop

them. The settlers started shooting and changed direction towards the village of Shuyoukh, which lies on one of the mountains overlooking Sa'ir. They reached some of the houses on the outskirts of Shuyoukh and began smashing panes of glass by throwing stones, and threatened people by pointing their weapons at them. It should be noted that at this point nobody in Shuyukh had obstructed their path nor done anything against them. However, when the residents became certain that the settlers were intent on destruction inside the village, they gathered in the village centre and on the roofs, and confronted them. The settlers began shooting; one who had sighting equipment on his gun took aim and fired, hitting Khaled 'Azmi 'Abd-al-Rahman al-Lahaliya, 17, in his left arm. The villagers started throwing stones to drive the settlers out of the village. On the eastern edge of the village, the same person who had wounded Khaled took aim at another youth and hit him with three bullets, two in the stomach and the other in the chest near the heart. The youth, Mustafa Ahmad 'Abd-al-Mohsen, 19, was taken to the 'Aliya government hospital in al-Khalil, which is about 8 km away from Shuyoukh, where he died. After his body was brought back to Shuyoukh at 1:30 p.m. and buried, two military jeeps, a helicopter and a reconnaisance aircraft came, but they weren't able to land in the village. After that, ten military cars were called, among them a jeep, a troop-carrier, a bulldozer, a vehicle emitting gas, and Shin Bet cars. The plane also landed a number of soldiers in Ras al-'Aroud, one of the neighbourhoods of the village of Sa'ir. They broke into Shuyoukh claiming they wanted details of the incidents, or so they told one of the mukhtars (the heads of the village) who accompanied them. At about 5 o'clock they left the area. [Date of report: 4 June 1988]

In another example, on 23 July 1988, at around 12:15 p.m., a group of supporters of the racist Kach movement tried to enter the old city of Jerusalem through the Damascus Gate. When the police stopped them, they began overturning stalls, threatening their owners and throwing stones and cola cans at passers-by. Israeli Border Guards began to throw tear gas canisters at the Palestinians who were present in the area, arresting three of them, two of whom were detained without charge, for periods of 10 and 25 days respectively.[23]

Other incidents of provocation involve the act of settlement itself, usually by "pioneer" groups of settlers with or without the initial approval of the Israeli government. Following the October 1973 war, groups emerged such as the Golan Settlement Committee and *Gush Emunim* ("Bloc of the Faithful") which were intent on accelerating the process of settlement. Both these groups continued the tactic of setting up *de facto* communities in order to create facts on the ground which could later be legitimised by the government.

For example, on 24 September 1988, members of the "Eitan" settlement group set up a makeshift settlement at Karantal, north-west of Jericho, bringing tents and equipment. They were evicted by troops on 26 September. Other settlements of a similar nature were reportedly planned for the area near Kufel Haris in the Nablus area, in the area between the settlement of Ariel and the village of Lubban al-Sharqiya north of Ramallah, and near Rafah in the Gaza Strip.[24]

On 4 October 1988, the *Jerusalem Post* reported that a group of settlers "wearing prayer shawls and carrying rifles celebrated Simhat Tora by dancing through the streets [of Hebron], surrounded by a security ring of soldiers." On 20 October, the *Jerusalem Post* reported a tour of the Gaza Strip by settlers in a caravan of 50 buses. The *Post* reported that "an elderly woman got off one bus, did a mock Arab dance and shouted, 'Let's drive them crazy.'"

2. Settlers' Use of Force

> My mother opened the car; I saw that stones were being thrown towards the balcony of our house. I heard screaming from inside our home and a stone was thrown at my mother. I carried my daughter as they threw stones at us and crawled out of the car. Stones were thrown at the car and the back window was smashed.

The event described in this statement took place on 5 October 1988. The victims, a 29-year-old housewife and her mother and daughter, residents of Beit Sahour near Bethlehem, were the Palestinian objects of an attack by 30 armed Israeli settlers. A very similar attack happened in the same area a few days later.[25]

During the present uprising many of the worst excesses of settler violence have occurred in response to alleged stone throwing, as a punishment and as an opportunity to kill under the guise of self-defence. Guidelines on the use of weapons, issued from time to time by various official and unofficial groups, should not be permitted to distract attention from what is evidently a situation in which settlers shoot to kill when and as they wish.

Towards the beginning of the uprising the settlers of Kiryat Arba and Hebron passed a resolution containing guidelines concerning what they referred to as "legitimate self-defence": if attacked with stones or petrol bombs, settlers were to try and catch the stone throwers, throw stones back themselves, fire in the air or shoot at the stone throwers if the person felt that his life was in danger.[26] However, more recently on 12 November

Settler Provocation and Use of Excessive Force 109

1988, the "Council of Settlements in Judea, Samaria and Gaza" adopted a resolution which more accurately reflected settler practice, namely that settlers should fire at stone throwers even when their life is not endangered.[27]

On 2 September 1988 Amram Mitzna, the Central Area Commander, stated that "a civilian should use his gun solely for self-defence, to extricate himself from a life-threatening situation, when there is no alternative to using his weapon. He is not there to solve the problem, punish someone, or take deterrent action."[28] It is apparent to al-Haq that such announcements have no effect on settler perceptions of what is or is not legitimate action. The following examples illustrate settler interpretations of "legitimate self-defence."

On 11 January 1988, in the village of Beittin near Ramallah, two Gush Emunim settlers got out of their car when their road was blocked. They chased two youths whom they suspected of throwing stones, and one of the two settlers, Pinhas Wallerstein, opened fire. Ziyad 'Abd-al-'Aziz, 22, a labourer, was shot and wounded, while his friend, Rabeh Husein Muhammad Ghanem, 18, was killed.

On 4 February 1988, Kamel 'Abed Jaradat, an 18-year-old labourer from the village of Sa'ir near Hebron, was standing on the veranda of his uncle's flat in the village. The road beneath was blocked by rocks and burning tires. Settlers passing in a jeep stopped when confronted with the road block. One of the settlers emerged from the vehicle and started firing his gun towards the children and youths gathered in the street. Some of the children ran into the house from which the affiant was watching the events. The affiant was shot twice in the left thigh, while another boy, Hamed Sa'adi, was injured.[29]

Najeh Jamil Hassan Hijaz, an 18-year old student from the village of Turmus 'Ayya near Ramallah, took part in a demonstration on 9 March 1988 at the junction of the road to his village with the main Nablus/Jerusalem road. According to witnesses, a bus carrying settlers drew close and, as it passed, one shot was fired from the bus, killing Najeh instantly. The bus then continued on its way. Soldiers came to the village four days later, sealing off the road to the village with large boulders. Even a week later neither soldiers nor police had visited Najeh's family to try to establish the circumstances of death or to locate the killer.[30]

It was only in late August 1988, after a settler opened fire at soldiers (thinking they were Palestinians), that the authorities began to show some concern about settler use of weapons (see Amram Mitzna's statement above). The army's investigation into the case showed that there was no direct threat to the life of the settler.[31]

It is clear from the incidents documented by al-Haq that most instances of settlers using their weapons in "self-defence" are precisely for the purposes of punishment and retaliation for instances of stone throwing. Although regulations concerning self-defence are frequently vague and inexact, it would seem plain sense that where a stone has already been thrown and the attacker has fled, use of a firearm could not legitimately be called self-defence. The problems facing the victims of settler reprisals are not merely evidential but relate fundamentally to the fact that settlers are regarded as a form of "people's army," virtually unchecked by the usual law enforcement agencies and representing a powerful ideological commitment from the highest levels of authority in the State of Israel.

D. Conclusion

The Israeli Labour Party politician Abba Eban recently concluded, while addressing the Knesset Foreign Affairs and Defence Committee, that the IDF were on a "'mission impossible' since the juxtaposition of 2 peoples on the same soil of pre-1948 Eretz Yisrael was a 100 percent recipe for violence."[32] While Eban's sense of history is not one with which Palestinians would agree, his conclusions are undoubtedly correct.

It is clear that the balance between the political aim of territorial aggrandisement in the name of "external" security and biblical-historical right on the one hand, and the cost both financially and in terms of "policing" the settlements and their environs on the other is weighted heavily in favour of the former. In the past minor differences of approach towards settlements were detectable in the policy statements of Labour and Likud, but neither party fundamentally questioned the existence of settlements in the Occupied Territories. Indeed in a recent speech delivered during the opening of a new settlement near Ramallah, Prime Minister Yitzhak Shamir announced:

> Those who would divide the Land of Israel, divide the people of Israel...Some things are above politics, and settlement is one of those things.[33]

(Shamir was appointed to head the new Israeli government on 14 November 1988).

During the uprising political, military and judicial support for the settlers has continued as before; no attempt appears to have been made by Israel as an Occupier to adhere to any notion of the rule of law as regards its expansionist ambitions as a state or as the party responsible for the actions of its nationals in the Occuped Territories.[34] While the level of some violations, particularly numbers killed by settlers, have worsened, the nature of these violations has remained all too familiar.

FOOTNOTES TO CHAPTER 3

1. *Jerusalem Post,* 23 December 1987.
2. Settlements are generally justified in two ways: biblical-historical right and strategic necessity. Since settlements began to be established in the Occupied Territories in 1967, acquisition of land in the West Bank and Gaza Strip for settlement by Jews has been justified in terms of historical right stemming from the Jewish presence there over 2000 years ago. This position was clearly stated in the "Manifesto of the Land of Israel Movement" (August 1967). According to the Manifesto, no government should be permitted to give up the "Land of Israel"; any government that was perceived as weak in this respect was subject to violent protest by settlers, as demonstrated in the early 1980s. (See the Palestine Human Rights Campaign report *Israeli Settler Violence in the Occupied Territories 1980-1984* (1985), pp. 1-13.)

    Under the Labour government the argument that settlements also served a 'security' function formed part of unofficial government policy into the mid-1970s, although in many cases where settlers 'established facts' by creating *de facto* communities, such as in the centre of Hebron, the security argument was more a thinly veiled excuse for accomodating the settlers' demands than it was an actual reason.

    In 1974, then Prime Minister Yitzhak Rabin stated that Israel's policy of settlement in the Occupied Territories "was based on a series of priorities, on security and political considerations, on settlement requirements and on the existing possibilities and restrictions." Again in 1976 Yigal Allon, the former Foreign Minister, said "...if you sum up the empirical behaviour of the Government of Israel in determining the points of settlement, you'll find that they add up to a concept: that is, settlements are placed in strategically important areas likely to become borderlines in the future." See the National Lawyers Guild report *Treatment of Palestinians in the Israeli-Occupied West Bank and Gaza* (1977), p. 8.

    In order to encourage settlement the Israeli government has made extensive efforts to attract Israelis from the densely-populated areas of Jerusalem and Tel Aviv to move to the Occupied Territories and commute to work. This has found a response particularly among middle-class families seeking their 'suburban' dream and poor families unable to protect themselves against spiralling housing prices in high-demand areas. The government has made a conscious effort to raise standards of education and health provision, water and electricity supply, and to subsidise the price of housing in the West Bank and Gaza Strip in order to stimulate the flow of non-religious as well as religious settlers into what is conceived of as a sort of metropolitan hinterland. (See Annette Hochstein, *Metropolitan Links between Israel and the West Bank.* West Bank Data Base Project [WBDP], 1983.) For example, per capita expenditure on state-provided services in Jewish settlements in the West Bank was 88.5 percent higher than in comparable Israeli municipalities; spending on regional councils in the West Bank was 43 percent higher than in Israel. (See also Aaron Dehter, *How Expensive Are West Bank Settlements?* (WBDP, 1987), p. II.)
3. See the report by the Palestine Human Rights Campaign, *Israeli Settler*

Violence, p. 15.
4. Sources of information include: newspapers, which are most reliable in assessing numbers killed by settlers and least reliable as a gauge of the range of more minor incidents that in some sense are perhaps the most important; affidavits taken by al-Haq fieldworkers; and reports by al-Haq and other organisations. Throughout, care has been taken to select only those cases where it is reasonably certain that those involved are indeed settlers and not Shin Bet or other agents dressed in civilian clothes.
5. In the case of *Suleiman Tawfik Ayoub et. al. v. The Minister of Defence* the government argued in its affidavit that:

> 16(a) [the] establishment of the settlement in the area of the Beit El [military] camp not only does not conflict with the military requirement but actually serves it, in that it is part of the security conception of the government which bases the security system *inter alia* on Jewish settlements. In accordance with this concept all Israeli settlements in the territories occupied by the IDF constitute part of the IDF's regional defence system...In times of calm these settlements mainly serve the purpose of presence and control of vital areas, maintaining observation, and the like. The importance of these settlements is enhanced in particular in times of war when the regular army forces are shifted, in the main, from their bases for purposes of operational activity and the said settlements constitute the principal component of presence and security control in the areas in which they are located.

6. See William Harris, *Taking Root: Israeli Settlement in the West Bank, the Golan and Gaza-Sinai, 1967-1980,* (Research Studies Press, 1980), p. 38.
7. *Jerusalem Post,* 6 October 1988.
8. See Dehter, p. 1.
9. See *supra,* note 5.
10. *Jerusalem Post,* 2 September 1988.
11. From Israel's point of view the process of settling the Occupied Territories has, of course, not been without cost. Financially alone it is estimated that the settlements cost around $2 billion per annum (see *supra,* note 8). There is also a cost in terms of the internal violence and disorder that characterises the relationship between settlers and the local Palestinian population. Indeed there are several examples of statements from the more high-ranking members of the Israeli police and armed forces testifying to the role of settlers in causing and provoking acts of violence.

    Concern about the possibility of increased settler violence was voiced by security officials following an increase in incidents between settlers and Palestinians in early February 1988. See *Jerusalem Post,* 5 February 1988.

    On 4 May 1988, following the well-publicised Beita incident in April, the Israeli Chief of Staff Dan Shomron stated to the Knesset Foreign Affairs and Defence Committee that settlers were a source of tension in the Occupied Territories. He said that stone throwers should be reported to the IDF and the IDF alone should deal with the matter. Settler leaders expressed outrage at the criticism. Shomron also stated that the legal system seemed to grind at a slower pace for Jews than for Arabs.

    Following the shooting of 2 soldiers by a settler after a petrol bomb attack on the latter's car, the Military Commander of the Central Area, Amram Mitzna, said (as reported in the *Jerusalem Post* of 1 September 1988) that

Settler Provocation and Use of Excessive Force 113

there had been several incidents in which soldiers' lives had been endangered by settlers firing their guns.
12. *Jerusalem Post*, 2 November 1988.
13. See PHRC, *Settler Violence*, p. 16.
14. See for example the collection of al-Haq's affidavits *In Their Own Words* (World Council of Churches, 1983).
15. See Raja Shehadeh, *Occupier's Law: Israel and the West Bank* (Washington, DC: Institute for Palestine Studies, second edition 1988), pp. 76-103.
16. The "Karp Report," reprinted in *Palestine Yearbook of International Law*, Vol. 1, 1984.
17. *Jerusalem Post*, 31 July 1988.
18. The "Karp Report," *op. cit.* p. 208. Information concerning police investigations into deaths caused by settlers during the uprising was kindly made available to al-Haq by Professor Stan Cohen of the Hebrew University who is currently engaged in a study of settler violence with the Palestine Human Rights Information Centre.
19. The facts of the Beita incident were as follows: on 6 April 1988, a group of 16 settlers from the Elon Moreh settlement, accompanied by two armed escorts, went on a hiking trip in the vicinity of the village of Beita. Following a confrontation with villagers, two Palestinians (see Appendix 3-B) and an Israeli girl were shot dead by Roman Aldubi, one of the armed escorts. Initially, it was assumed by politicians and media that the girl was killed by Palestinians. This presumption, which was later proven to be without foundation, led to the unparallelled measures described in the text. Following the incident, Israeli Justice Minister Avraham Sharir called upon the government "to raze the village of Beita and expel all rioters from the territories." Other senior ministers united in condemning the "murderers" and "terrorists" responsible. The Minister of Religious Affairs, Zevulun Hammer, declaimed: "Beita does not exist on the map of Israel. A settlement should be built there and named Tirza Porat" (after the settler killed by her companion during the incident). (See PHRIC Report on Beita, 25 April 1988). Defence Minister Yitzhak Rabin, attending the funeral of Tirza Porat, referred in a passionate speech to "Arab murderers" and called for the vengeance of God on those who had killed the girl.
20. The residents deported from Beita on 18 April 1988 are:
    1. 'Omar Muhammad Da'oud
    2. Najeh Jamil Dweikat
    3. Mahmoud 'Abed Beni-Shamsa
    4. Mustafa Mahmoud Hamayel
    5. Sari Hilal Hamayel
    6. Ibrahim Khader 'Ali
21. *Jerusalem Post*, 9 November 1988.
22. PHRC, *Settler Violence*, p. 15.
23. Al-Haq documentation.
24. *Jerusalem Post*, 27 September 1988.
25. Al-Haq Affidavit No. 1451.
26. *Jerusalem Post*, 5 February 1988.
27. *Jerusalem Post*, 13 November 1988.
28. *Jerusalem Post*, 2 September 1988.
29. Al-Haq Affidavit No. 1195.

30. Al-Haq documentation.
31. *Jerusalem Post,* 1 and 2 September 1988. The facts as reported were that a petrol bomb was thrown at the settler's car, who stopped some 60 meters later, got out of his car, and shot the two soldiers.
32. *Jerusalem Post,* 9 November 1988.
33. *Jerusalem Post,* 27 October 1988.
34. Article 49 of the IV Geneva Convention prohibits absolutely the transfer of citizens of the occupying power into the occupied territory. In his analysis of Article 49, Jean S. Pictet, a leading commentator on international law and the principal authority on the Fourth Geneva Convention, observes that:

    It is intended to prevent a practice adopted during the Second World War by certain Powers which transferred portions of their own population to occupied territory for political or racial reasons or in order, as they claimed, to colonize those territories. [Jean S. Pictet (ed.), *Commentary: IV Geneva Convention Relative to the Protection of Civilian Persons in Time of War* (International Committee of the Red Cross, 1958), p. 283.]

Appendix 3-A

LEGAL ASPECTS OF SETTLEMENT IN THE OCCUPIED TERRITORIES

Both the IV Hague Convention (1907) and the IV Geneva Convention (1949) contain provisions relevant to the practice of settlement of an Occupied Territory.

1. Israeli Settlements in General

Under the IV Geneva Convention the practice of establishing settlements is expressly forbidden. Article 49(6) states that:

> The Occupying Power shall not deport or transfer parts of its own population into the territory it occupies.

2. Dual Legal System

The Israeli government has set up a dual legal system under which Israelis living in the Territories are not subject to the local courts. This is prohibited under international law. Article 23 of the Hague Convention Regulations states:

> It is especially forbidden...to declare abolished, suspended, or inadmissible in a court of law the rights and actions of the nationals of the hostile party.

More generally under Article 43 of the Hague Regulations the Occupier is bound, unless absolutely prevented, to respect the laws in force in the occupied territory.

3. Responsibility of the Israeli Government for the Actions of Israeli Individuals in the Territory

The Israeli government is responsible for the actions of its citizens in the Occupied Territories. This is provided for in Article 29 of the IV Geneva Convention which states:

> The Party to the conflict in whose hands protected persons may be is responsible for the treatment accorded to them by its agents, irrespective of any individual responsibility that may be incurred.

The prohibition against violence applies to "any...measure of brutality whether applied by civilian or military agents."

4. Protection of the Individual

The inhabitants of occupied territory are well protected under international law. Article 27 of the IV Geneva Convention provides that:

> Protected persons (indigenous civilians) are entitled, in all circumstances, to respect for their persons...and shall be protected especially against all acts of violence or threats thereof...

Under Article 33 of the IV Geneva Convention:

> All measures of intimidation or of terrorism are prohibited.

Appendix 3-B

SOME INCIDENTS OF SETTLER VIOLENCE BETWEEN 9 DECEMBER 1987 AND 31 OCTOBER 1988 DOCUMENTED BY AL-HAQ

Caveat: The following list makes no attempt to be comprehensive. Each incident that has been listed has been investigated and documented by al-Haq fieldworkers, and every effort has been made to ensure as far as possible that those described as settlers are not in fact Shin Bet or other Israeli agents dressed in civilian clothes.

Please Note: Dates are written as follows: Day/Month/Year.

FATAL INJURIES, West Bank
11/1/88: Beitin, Ramallah. Settlers shot and killed Rabeh Hussein Ghanem, 18, a 12-grade student.
8/2/88: Kufer Qaddoum. Settlers shot and killed 'Abd-al-Baset Mahmoud 'Abdallah, 25. He was shot in the neck and head by live ammunition.
21/2/88: Deir 'Ammar. Settlers shot and killed Kamel Darwish with live ammunition.
22/2/88: Baqa al-Sharqiya (Tulkarem). Settlers shot and killed Rawda Muhammad Lutfi Najib Hassan, 14. She was shot in the chest with a live bullet.
27/2/88: 'Aboud (Ramallah). Settlers shot and killed Ra'id Mahmoud 'Awad al-Barghouti, 17. He was shot in the head with live ammunition.
27/2/88: 'Aboud (Ramallah). Settlers shot and killed Ahmad Ibrahim Mustafa al-Barghouti, 20. He was shot in the intestine with live ammunition.
8/3/88: Mazra'a al-Sharqiya (Ramallah). Settlers shot and killed Khadra Muhammad Ihmeda, 35.
9/3/88: Turmus 'Ayya (Ramallah). Settlers shot and killed Najeh Jamil Hassan Hijaz, 18. He was shot in the chest with live ammunition.
6/4/88: Beita (Nablus). Settlers shot and killed Hatem Fayez Ahmad al-Jaber, 22.
6/4/88: Beita (Nablus). Settlers shot and killed Mousa Saleh Beni-Shamsa, 20.
28/4/88: Kufer Malek (Ramallah). Settlers came to the village around noon and opened fire. They returned later the same day accompanied by a large

number of soldiers and chased a number of villagers into the surrounding hills, shooting as they ran. One young Palestinian male was killed and three were injured including a child (Nabil Muhammad Suleiman). (*NB:* Because of some controversy over whether this death was caused by a settler or a soldier, it has not been included in al-Haq's total estimate of deaths caused by settlers during the uprising as documented by us, which is 14 in the West Bank and 1 in the Gaza Strip.)

5/5/88: Turmus 'Ayya. A settler shot and killed Jouda 'Awad. He was shot in the head with live ammunition.

3/6/88: Shuyoukh (Hebron). Settlers shot and killed Mustafa Ahmad al-Halayqa, 19, a 12-grade student. He was shot twice in the stomach and once in the chest near the heart with live ammunition.

9/7/88: East Jerusalem. Settlers shot and killed Nidal Fou'ad al-Rabadi, 16. He was shot in the right leg and left side of his head with two live bullets.

30/9/88: Hebron. Settler leader Rabbi Moshe Levinger shot and killed Kayed Hassan Salah, 42. He was shot with a live bullet.

FATAL INJURIES, Gaza Strip

28/7/88: Gaza. Hani 'Adel al-Turq, 37, was shot and killed by settlers. He was shot in the thigh and stomach.

NON-FATAL INJURIES

11/1/88: Beitin (Ramallah). A settler shot Zayed 'Abd-al-Hamed in the thigh.

2/2/88: Deheisha Refugee Camp (Bethlehem). Army and settlers broke into the camp and shot Tawfiq Ahmad 'Abed and beat everyone in his family.

3/2/88: Bir Zeit (Ramallah). At 10 a.m. settlers kidnapped two schoolgirls, beat them and then dumped them on the sidewalk of the main road to Ramallah.

4/2/88: Sa'ir (Hebron). Settlers shot Kamel Jaradat in the thigh with 2 bullets.

7/2/88: Sinjel (Ramallah). Settlers shot Hatem Jaber Karakra, 26, in the right hand.

8/2/88: Jalazon Refugee Camp (Ramallah). Settlers took 'Abd-al-Hakim Ghanam, 22, from inside the camp, then shot live ammunition towards some of the residents. Ghanam was found later near the settlement of Beit El, unconscious from beatings.

8/2/88: Kufer Qaddoum (Tulkarem). Settlers shot Ahmad 'Abdallah Shamlawi, 19, in the left thigh with a live bullet.

20/2/88: Toubas (Jenin). Settlers shot Falah Mahmoud Abou-Arra, 22, in the back with a live bullet.

20/2/88: Toubas (Jenin). Settlers shot Mahmoud Faleh Daraghma, 15, in his right hand with a bullet.

20/2/88: Toubas (Jenin). Settlers shot Ilham 'Iqab Sawafta, 20, in the right side of her waist with a live bullet.

20/2/88: Toubas (Jenin). Settlers shot Dalal Yousef Sawafta, 25, in the chest with a live bullet.

4/3/88: Mazra'a al-Gharbiya (Ramallah). Settlers shot Saleh 'Abd-al-Rahman Hassan, 30, in his stomach with 2 bullets.

4/3/88: Burqa (Nablus). Settlers shot 'Imad 'Abd-al-Majed Daghlas, 16, in his left shoulder with a live bullet.

6/3/88: Bidiya (Tulkarem). Settlers shot Husein Muhammad Salama, 24, in the left thigh with a live bullet.

6/3/88: Bidiya (Tulkarem). Settlers shot Hamad Jamil Abou-Safiya in the left leg

with a live bullet.
7/3/88: Idhna (Hebron). Settlers shot 'Ayed Ibrahim Jayadi, 30, in the right leg.
8/3/88: Balata Refugee Camp (Nablus). Settlers shot Fida' Muhammad al-Wadi, 17, in her right ear with a live bullet.
8/3/88: Balata Refugee Camp (Nablus). Settlers shot Murad 'Abd-al-Jabbar Dweikat, 21, in the testes with a live bullet.
9/3/88: Hebron. Settlers shot Rashid 'Oweida Misk, 22, in the thighs with two live bullets.
9/3/88: Masha (Nablus). Settlers shot Latif 'Abd-al-Qader Muhammad 'Amer, 19, in his left leg.
10/3/88: Hebron. Settlers shot Neifouth 'Abd-alHamid Abou-'Aisha, 27, in her right shoulder with a live bullet.
13/3/88: 'Ajja (Jenin). Settlers shot Hikmat Sa'id Ma'ali, 16, in his right thigh with two live bullets.
13/3/88: Balata Refugee Camp (Nablus). Settlers shot Ahmad 'Abdallah Mousa Shamlawi, 22, in the left thigh.
16/3/88: 'Awarta (Nablus). Settlers shot Ghassan Husein 'Awad, 23, in his left arm with a live bullet.
25/3/88: Yasouf (Nablus). Settlers shot 'Abdallah Ahmad I'biya, 23, in his left leg with a live bullet.
25/3/88: Yasouf (Nablus). Settlers shot 'Aisha 'Abdallah I'biya, 70, in her stomach with a live bullet.
4/4/88: Mazra'a al-Gharbiya (Ramallah). At 4 p.m., 15 settlers entered the village and started shooting at villagers. Saleh 'Abd-al-Rahman Hassan was wounded in his stomach.
6/4/88: Beita (Nablus). Settlers shot Taysir Saleh Khader, 29, in his stomach with a live bullet.
6/4/88: Beita (Nablus). Settlers shot Falah Muhammad Beni-Shamsa, 19, in his stomach with a live bullet.
4/5/88: Toura (Jenin). Settlers from the settlement of Reihan near Ya'bad attacked the village and shot at a number of children, injuring Munir Kabha, 13, in the foot.
21/5/88: Funduqumiya (Jenin). Settlers shot Umaya Qarari, 16, in her left forearm with a live bullet.
3/6/88: Shuyoukh (Hebron). Settlers shot Khaled 'Azmi al-Haliya, 15, in his left forearm with a live bullet.
12/6/88: Deheisha Refugee Camp (Bethlehem). Settlers shot 'Abdallah al-Ja'fari, 26, in his right foot with a live bullet using a pistol.
13/6/88: Jenin. Settlers shot 'Omar Ahmad Kheil, 19, in the chest with a live bullet.
21/6/88: Nablus. Settlers shot Ahmad Ibrahim al-Ghandour, 10, in his right knee joint with a live bullet.
24/6/88: Nablus. Settlers shot Yahya Subhi Ghazal, 20, in his right leg with a live bullet.
24/6/88: Nablus. Settlers shot Yousef Misbah Jaber, 18, in his right shoulder with a live bullet.
30/6/88: Silat al-Harethiya (Jenin). Settlers shot Suleiman Mousa Tahina, 13, in the right thigh and knee with live bullets.
30/9/88: Hebron. Settler (Rabbi Moshe Levinger) shot and wounded 1 Palestinian.

Settler Provocation and Use of Excessive Force 119

OTHER TYPES OF SETTLER HARASSMENT

12/12/87: 'Anabta (Tulkarem). At about midnight, 50 settlers attacked the village, smashing windows and a car and threatening the villagers.

5/1/88: 'Anabta, Tulkarem. Settlers entered the village in their cars, threatening the villagers that they would open fire if stones were thrown again at Israeli cars.

12/1/88: Ras Karkar (Ramallah). Settlers vandalised a cucumber field belonging to the village.

1/2/88: 'Anabta (Tulkarem). Settlers came at night and smashed cars belonging to 'Abd-al-Rahim Jarallah, Luqman Zayed and Samir 'Ali Riziq, as well as some windows during a curfew imposed by the army.

1/2/88: Al-Jedira (Ramallah). Settlers from the settlement of Givat Ze'ev attacked the village at night, smashing windows, as well as the cars of 'Ali Muhanna Qasem, Ibrahim Qasem and Muhammad Subhi.

2/2/88: 'Ein Yabroud (Ramallah). Ten settlers from the settlement of Ofra entered the village, firing at the windows of the mosque and of four houses.

5/2/88: Qalandiya Refugee Camp (Ramallah). Between 20-30 settlers tried to break into the camp as the residents of the camp were going to prayers. The residents confronted them and the settlers withdrew. Later about 100 soldiers arrived, firing live ammunition, aluminium discs and tear gas, breaking into houses and beating up a number of the residents.

6/2/88: Ya'bad (Jenin). Settlers clashed with residents, injuring 22, and damaging 30 cars.

7/2/88: Old City of East Jerusalem. Settlers threw tear gas canisters.

7/2/88: Balata Refugee Camp (Nablus). Settlers attempted to kidnap Hammad Ahmad Suleiman, 9, but were stopped by local residents of the camp.

8/2/88: Qalqiliya. Settlers entered the town shooting rubber bullets and smashing a car and house windows.

8/2/88: Silwad (Ramallah). Settlers attacked the village, keeping Samer Sharif 'Abd-al-Rahman and Yousef Idris 'Ayad as hostages.

8/2/88: 'Atara (Ramallah). Settlers kidnapped Ayman Husein Mahmoud, 14, from the village of Jaljoya and released him in the village of 'Atara.

8/2/88: Al-'Izariya (Jerusalem). Settlers smashed the windows of cars and houses.

13/2/88: Yurin (Nablus). Settlers attacked the village, sawing down a telegraph pole.

15/2/88: 'Awarta (Nablus). Settlers uprooted a number of olive trees.

24/2/88: 'Anabta (Tulkarem). At night settlers smashed the windows and doors of houses and of the gas station of the village.

29/2/88: Yurin (Nablus). Settlers attacked the village opening fire on a water container belonging to Samir Tadros, pouring oil into the village water well, and damaging the village clinic and a telegraph pole.

1/3/88: Kufel Hares (Nablus). Settlers from the settlement of Ariel attacked the house of Salim Abou-Yaqoub.

2/3/88: Beit Ummar (Hebron). Settlers burned a car belonging to 'Asri 'Issa Saleh 'Adi.

8/3/88: Kufel Hares (Nablus). Between 8-10 settlers from the settlement of Ariel attacked a house belonging to Salim Suleiman Ya'coub which is situated on the main road between Salfit and Kufel Hares. The settlers threw stones at the house breaking glass, and then a "smoke bomb." They threw a petrol bomb at his Volkswagen and smashed its headlights.

10/3/88 and the next two days: Hebron. Settlers smashed the windows of 45 cars, and burned another two.

11/3/88: Turmus 'Ayya (Ramallah). Settlers came to the village at night on horses, trampling crops and plants in the village fields.

14/3/88: Hebron. Settlers damaged 15 cars.

16/3/88: Beit 'Our al-Tahta (Ramallah). Settlers attacked the village and destroyed furniture belonging to Muhammad Da'oud.

17/3/88: Sinjel (Ramallah). At 10 p.m. settlers from the settlement of Shilo came into the village and fired their guns, apparently to scare residents.

25/3/88: Al-Bireh. Settlers from the settlement of Pizgot attacked the town, smashing cars and writing slogans on walls.

25/3/88: 'Asakra (Bethlehem). About 30 settlers destroyed the roots of about 15 olive trees near the main road.

18/4/88: Halhoul (Hebron). Settlers opened fire from 3 cars in the al-Kanb area.

21/4/88: Sa'ir (Hebron). Two settlers in cars came from the direction of Kiryat Arba settlement, opened fire in the direction of houses in Ras al-Aroud, breaking the window panes of 2 of them, and then left.

29/4/88-2/5/88: Hebron. Settlers wandered around the city accompanied by soldiers, provoking local inhabitants. On 29/4/88 they smashed the windows of three cars.

5/6/88: Ya'bad (Jenin). A settler entered a local boys' secondary school, pointed his gun at 3 students and after a struggle with one of them took his satchel.

23/7/88: Old City of East Jerusalem. Kach supporters overturned stalls and threatened their owners in the Damascus Gate area.

30/7/88: Hebron. A settler opened fire in the area of Bab al-Zawiya, causing commercial life to stop for some 10 minutes. Soldiers then came and closed off the area, and arrested a number of youths.

24/9/88: Hebron. Settlers from Kiryat Arba settlement gathered in the Haram Araha area near the settlement and smashed the windows of Palestinian-owned cars that passed on the road.

5/11/88: Beit Sahour (Bethlehem). Settlers threw stones at Iman Rishmawi, her mother and daughter, and smashed the back window screen of her car.

19/10/88: Beit Sahour (Bethlehem). Settlers threw stones at the house of Khalil Attalah Danoun smashing a window.

27/10/88: Deheisha Refugee Camp (Bethlehem). Settlers opened fire towards the refugee camp. No one was hurt.

Part II
ADMINISTRATIVE AND OTHER MEASURES

Chapter 4

ADMINISTRATIVE METHODS OF PUNISHMENT

A. Introduction

Since the beginning of the Israeli occupation of the West Bank and Gaza Strip in 1967, the military government has consistently employed various methods of administrative punishment in order to control the indigenous Palestinian population. These measures include town arrest, the demolition of homes, deportation, and administrative detention. One element these practices have in common is that their implementation is almost entirely devoid of due process; they are imposed by administrative order and there is no appeals procedure based upon the facts of the case.

While none of the measures discussed in this chapter are new, there has been a drastic increase in their use by the Israeli authorities since the beginning of the uprising. The use of administrative detention, for example, has increased by more than 4,000 percent in the first year of the uprising as compared to the 12-month period before it. There have also been several changes in the method and criteria by which some of these measures are implemented.

This chapter examines the administrative practices of deportation, administrative detention, and house demolition during the first year of the uprising. It also addresses the previous use of these measures by the Israeli authorities and their validity in the context of international law.[1]

B. Deportation

Although the level of deportations during the uprising has not reached the peak established in the late 1960's and early 1970's, when hundreds of residents of the Occupied Territories were deported each year, the last 12 months did bring a doubling of the number of Palestinians expelled from their homeland in comparison with the previous two-and-a-half years. In addition, the authorities set a new record in 1988 for the number of Palestinians served with deportation orders on a single day when an unprecedented 25 such orders were issued on 17 August.[2]

Under successive Labour Party governments between 1967 and 1977, at least 1,156 Palestinians were deported by the military authorities from the Occupied Territories.[3] During the next eight years, deportation by administrative decree was used much more sparingly by the military authorities: one Palestinian was deported in 1979, three in 1980, and one in February 1985. When the Labour Party again assumed the Ministry of Defence with Yitzhak Rabin filling the portfolio in 1985, however, deportations, along with other administrative punishments, increased as part of the "Iron Fist" policy in the Occupied Territories, declared by Rabin that August. Between August 1985 and December 1987, 42 Palestinians were deported and orders against three others, which were not carried out until April 1988, were issued.

During the past year, the military authorities have deported 32 Palestinians and served administrative expulsion orders against an additional 27. At the time of writing the latter group was still in the process of appealing its orders. The first four deportations took place on 13 January 1988 despite the explicit and unanimous condemnation of the practise by the United Nations Security Council. All fifteen of its members, including the United States, voted for Resolution 607 (6 January 1988) condemning Israel's deportations policy. Despite this clear consensus by the world community, 25 more Palestinians were deported between the date of the U.N. resolution and 17 August. No new expulsion orders were served between late August and the end of November; this was apparently related to the strong rebuke, delivered with an explicit threat of damage to bilateral relations, which was issued by the US to Israel in response to the 25 orders served and four deportations carried out on 17 August.[4] The 25 orders were issued at a time of growing popular support inside Israel for a "transfer", or mass expulsion, of Palestinians from the Occupied Territories to neighbouring Arab states.[5]

It is clear from past experience that the Israeli authorities resort to deportations at times when they are under pressure from the Israeli right wing, and especially the settler movement, to take punitive action against the Palestinian residents of the West Bank and Gaza Strip. It was in this context that the "Iron Fist" policy was launched by the Israeli government in August 1985. Similarly, following the incident in the village of Beita on 6 April 1988, in which an Israeli settler killed two Palestinians in addition to a girl in his own entourage, the authorities immediately ordered the expulsion of six Beita residents who were *allegedly* involved in the incident. The expulsions came on the heels of demands by Israel's right wing, including even the Justice Minister, Avraham Sharir (whom one would expect to defend adherence to the

Administrative Methods of Punishment 125

rule of law), "to raze the village of Beita and expel all rioters from the territories."[6]

In addition to being clearly punitive actions following demands by the settler lobby for tough sanctions, deportations have also constituted an attempt by the military government to prevent the emergence of an indigenous Palestinian leadership in the Territories. It can generally be concluded from an analysis of the register of Palestinians deported since the beginning of the occupation that, if there is any consistency to the policy at all, the authorities have preferred to target Palestinians who through their activities in local organisations and movements are perceived by the authorities as having gained leadership positions in their communities. Municipal elections having been banned and other forms of political organisation having been similarly outlawed, Palestinians have sought to maintain the structure of their society since 1967 by setting up a number of service-oriented associations and grassroots organisations. (For further details see the introduction to chapter 9). Over a period of time, these organisations have produced their own cadres which, in a society denied a political leadership, have to the extent possible played a political role. By removing this group through selective deportations, the Israeli authorities continue their policy of keeping Palestinians leaderless and hence easier to control.

The popular uprising in the Occupied Territories has brought to the fore a new generation of Palestinians capable of giving direction to grassroots activity. In this context, the military government has carried out its policy of deportations consistently with its previous practice: it acted when pressured to do so by the right wing, especially the settler community, by deporting Palestinians at random (e.g. Beita) but also aggressively targetted community leaders such as trade unionists, journalists, lawyers, student activists and others. These individuals have not been accused of, or charged with, any illegal conduct. To illustrate this point, 6 of those ordered deported during the uprising have been trade-union leaders. Of these, the three who received expulsion orders on 17 August while in administrative detention in Ansar III, were—along with 22 others—accused *retroactively* of membership in popular committees, which were not outlawed until *18* August, the following day. The trade unionists were not formally charged with membership in popular committees; informal association was apparently deemed sufficient to justify the orders to the public. (Case studies on two deportees are appended to this chapter.)

1. The Israeli Justification

Deportation orders are issued by an Area Commander, who relies on powers contained in the British Defence (Emergency) Regulations of 1945 (or, in cases of those alleged to have entered the Occupied Territories illegally, military orders). The expulsion orders are based on an administrative decision. No formal charges are brought against the deportee and no trial is held. While the prospective deportee does have the right to appeal the order to a military objections committee and, as a final resort, to the Israeli High Court of Justice, only general allegations need to be made in these forums by the authorities against the deportee. Evidence, if it in fact exists at all, is submitted in secret by the military government, and both the defendant and his or her lawyer are routinely denied access to it, thus making its refutation an impossible task.

In addition, the powers of both the objections committee and the High Court are severely circumscribed. The committee is empowered to make only non-binding recommendations to the Military Commander, who is the same person who issued the order, appointed the committee, and the superior officer of its members. It is therefore doubtful that a junior officer would, even if he wanted to, contradict the decision of his superior. This has happened only once since 1985, in the case of Khalil Abou-Ziyad who was nevertheless deported (although for a limited period of three years) on 28 August 1985.

Appeals to the High Court present similar constraints. The High Court reviews the order issued by the Military Commander solely on procedural as opposed to substantive grounds. The Court merely seeks to ascertain whether the Commander has stayed within the limits of the powers granted him by law (in this case the Defence (Emergency) Regulations as well as international law of belligerent occupation), and that he has acted in good faith. At no point does the Court publicly inquire into the substance of the allegations. So far, the Court has not overturned a single deportation order; it has in fact come out fully in support of the actions of the Military Commander. This was re-affirmed in 1988 when the Court ruled that Article 49 of the Fourth Geneva Convention of 1949 Relative to the Protection of Civilian Persons in Time of War does not apply to the deportations carried out by Israel. Contrary to the express wording of the article and its interpretation by impartial legal scholars (including the International Committee of the Red Cross, which is the guardian of the Geneva Conventions), the Court argued that the article refers solely to mass transfers, and not to individual deportations.

The majority of Palestinians deported or ordered deported during the uprising have been accused of incitement or membership in an organisation banned by the authorities, i.e. a faction of the PLO or the local United National Leadership of the Uprising. If in fact evidence exists that the deportee belongs to an outlawed movement, there is nothing which prevents the authorities from formally charging the person in question and proving their case in a court of law. This would also give deportees the right to defend themselves against the military government's accusations in a fair trial.

2. Deportations in International Law

The Israeli argument that deportations are legal because they are issued under the Defence (Emergency) Regulations of 1945 is invalid because these Regulations were revoked by the British government on the eve of their departure in 1948, and could therefore not have been inherited by the Israeli authorities when they seized the West Bank and Gaza Strip from Jordan and Egypt, respectively, in 1967.[7] There is, in short, no legal basis in local law which allows for the deportation of a resident of the Territories to another country. The Jordanian Constitution of 1952, in fact, explicitly prohibits deportations.

In addition, deportations constitute a clear violation of international law. The Fourth Geneva Convention, the main instrument governing the conduct of occupying powers, expressly bans deportations of any kind. The relevant paragraph of Article 49 of this Convention states:

> Individual or mass forcible transfers, as well as deportations of protected persons from occupied territory to the territory of the Occupying Power or to that of any other country, occupied or not, are prohibited, regardless of their motive.

Deportations are also banned by the Charter of the Nuremberg Military Tribunal (1945), which, in Article 6 (A and B) defined the practice as a "war crime" and a "crime against humanity."

Finally, the administrative procedures used by the Israeli military government to deport Palestinians entails a number of violations of the right to due process; deportees are not charged and are denied the right to defend themselves in a fair trial. Deportations are also a transgression of the principles of natural justice, since deportees are not informed of any charges against them and thus cannot possibly make a case in their own defence.[8]

Permanent exile, which constitutes a complete uprooting from one's homeland, is one of the most inhumane forms of punishment. Deportees are exiled to foreign countries where they have no recognised rights and are at the mercy of those who offer them shelter as refugees. In addition, cultural and familial ties are severed, forcing the deportee's spouse and children to make the painful decision between reuniting the family in exile or remaining separated in the land of their birth.

C. Administrative Detention

Of the 18,000 Palestinians whom the Israeli authorities acknowledge having arrested during the uprising, 3-4,000 have been placed under administrative detention. By definition, these individuals have been imprisoned without charge or trial, in most cases for a period of at least six months. The majority of these detainees have been held in the Ketsyot Military Detention Centre, commonly known as Ansar III, which is located in the inhospitable climate of the Negev desert.[9] In November 1988, the Israeli authorities claimed that there were 1,590 people under administrative detention.[10]

Administrative detention, also known as preventive detention or internment, entails the imprisonment of individuals by the executive without charge or trial using administrative procedures. Under the military regime in force in the West Bank and Gaza, executive power is vested in the armed forces and it is thus they who issue such orders. According to current Israeli military legislation, the duration of such detentions may initially be up to six months but the order is renewable indefinitely.

During the first 13 years of the occupation, the Israeli authorities consistently resorted to the administrative detention of Palestinian residents of the West Bank and Gaza Strip in lieu of providing them with formal charges and fair trials. Then in 1980, apparently due to international and domestic pressure, the measure was gradually phased out. It was resumed, however, on 4 August 1985 with the implementation of the Israeli cabinet's self-proclaimed "Iron Fist" policy for the Occupied Territories.

Between August 1985 and 9 December 1987, at least 316 Palestinians from the Occupied Territories were administratively detained; of these, 74 were still interned when the uprising began.

1. The Israeli Justification

The Israeli authorities have repeatedly attempted to justify their use of administrative detention. In a public statement from the Attorney General's office on 26 January 1986, for example, the following assertions were made:

[A]n administrative detention order can be issued only for reasons of state or public security...

It should be emphasized that administrative detention is not intended as punishment for violations committed, but rather to prevent the perpetration of illegal acts by the individual concerned...

This measure is resorted to only in those circumstances where normal judicial procedures cannot be followed because of the danger to the lives of witnesses or because secret sources of information cannot be revealed in open court. Typically, such orders are issued against leaders or members of terrorist organizations...

It is submitted that in the light of the history of the use of administrative detention in democratic nations, and taking into account Israel's special and difficult security situation, *the limited and careful use of administrative detention in Israel and the administered areas, subject to judicial review as it is, is reasonable and in compliance with local and international law.* [Emphasis added]

2. Recent Changes in Administrative Detention Procedures

As massive numbers of arrests have been carried out in the past year, Israel has amended its own military legislation to allow for a more flexible use of administrative detention orders. According to al-Haq's estimates, between 9 December 1987 and 5 June 1988 alone (the latter date marking the 21st commemoration of the Israeli occupation), more than 2,500 Palestinians from the West Bank and Gaza Strip were placed under administrative detention. In addition, whereas before the uprising such individuals were normally held in special sections of conventional prisons, the authorities have since opened the Ansar III Military Detention Centre to accommodate the unprecedented number of new internees.[11]

Military Order #378 ("Order Concerning Security Regulations"), issued in the West Bank in May 1970 and subsequently amended by Military Orders 815 and 876 of 1980, and similar unnumbered orders issued at about the same times in the Gaza Strip, constitute the military legislation governing administrative detention in the Occupied Territories. During the uprising, these provisions have been amended further in order to relax the procedures required for interning Palestinians.

In the wake of the 1979 Camp David Accords between Egypt, Israel, and the United States, various amendments were made to Military Order #378. Detainees were given the right to judicial review before a military judge within 96 hours of the issuance of their administrative detention order. At the same time, it was also stipulated that such orders could only be revoked if it could be proved that the order was not issued for objective reasons of security or public safety, was issued in bad faith, or for irrelevant considerations; in other words, reversing the burden of proof and placing the onus on the detainee to show that his or her detention is unjustified. The amendments to Military Order #378, enacted in 1980, also provided for procedures to appeal the judge's decision to the President of the military courts (Article 87 Section E), and, in Article 87 (C) made detention orders subject to a periodic review at least once every 3 months by a judge.

Yet, even before the recent re-amendment of these regulations, the limited means of recourse outlined above proved to be ineffective. This was largely because in the initial hearing and subsequent periodic reviews to determine the legality of the detention, the military government's alleged evidence against detainees was submitted in secret and both the detainee and his/her lawyer were denied access to it. This relaxation of the normal rules of evidence was permitted by Article 87 (D) of Military Order #378, provided that the judge was convinced that such a deviation would be useful for the purposes of revealing the truth and the achievement of justice. What was codified as an exceptional measure, however, rapidly became the common standard in cases of detention without trial. In practice, this meant that a person was guilty until proven innocent and that the burden of presumed guilt had to be overcome without the benefit of facts to refute. Additionally, the vague character of allegations made by the military authorities often made them impossible to disprove.

On 17 March 1988 the provisions governing administrative detention were amended once again. The new regulations grant *any military commander* in the Israeli armed forces the authority to issue an administrative detention order whereas previously this could only be done by an Area Commander (of which there is one each for the West Bank and Gaza).

The limited, quasi-judicial review process was also cancelled in March. In its place, the administrative detainee is given only the option, which he/she must initiate (as opposed to it being an automatic procedure as previously), of appealing the order. The appeal itself is heard by a panel of officers, the "military appeals commitee."

According to press reports which summarised the official position on this matter, the new regulations were implemented in order to "ease the heavy burden on the military courts and military prosecutor resulting from the large number of the administrative detention orders issued the last three months."[12]

The military appeals committee mentioned above convenes in the prison itself. Formerly consisting of three judges, now only one attends the hearing.[13] Evidence is still submitted in secret, the permissibility of this practice having been established in the Israeli High Court itself. Appeals, therefore, take an average of approximately 10 minutes each.

Often, the prosecutor will come to a hearing unprepared and, with only a copy of the detention order in hand, simply state that the "secret evidence" will be examined by the judge at the Defence Ministry in Tel Aviv. No date for a subsequent hearing is set, the proceedings are brought to a close, and the prosecutor leaves the room. In cases where the prosecutor does not even have the necessary documentation in his possession, the hearing is postponed to a future date, which is often left unannounced.

Even in cases where specific accusations or evidence brought by the prosecutor is proven to be fictitious, the proceedings manage to carry on with their set agenda. In the case of al-Haq fieldworker Sha'wan Jabarin, for example, the prosecutor accused him of participating in an attack on a bus in the village of Sa'ir. Sha'wan's lawyers quickly pointed out that the attack took place on 25 March 1988, a full nine days after their client had been interned. Nevertheless, on 2 June 1988, the administrative detention order in question was upheld, and on 8 September it was renewed for an additional six months quoting the same charge.

3. *The Use of Administrative Detention During the Uprising*

As stated above, 3-4,000 people have been placed under administrative detention since the beginning of the uprising. Among them are journalists, editors, trade unionists, student activists, community leaders, doctors, lawyers, and human rights monitors, including 5 of al-Haq's employees. The status of one more al-Haq employee in detention is still unknown at press time. The detainees also include 13 women, the first to be interned since the re-introduction of the measure in August 1985.

According to the *Jerusalem Post*, Israeli Knesset member Dedi Zucker, in a letter to the Israel Bar Association and the heads of the country's law faculties on 18 May 1988, stated that the scale of administrative detention practised by Israel "calls into question [its] claim to be a state that respects the basic freedoms of man [sic]," and shows "that the political echelon has clearly lost control over the situation [in the Occupied Territories]."[14] Using the conservative figure of 1,900 administrative detainees, Zucker also noted that "one out of every 200 men over the age of 18" from the Occupied Territories were imprisoned without charge or trial (while 7,600 were incarcerated by other means).[15]

> Zucker's report concludes with a "profile" based on 330 cases of [administrative detention] of which he has full details. Of these, 15 percent are aged between 16 and 21; 58 between 21 and 30; the rest are over 30.
>
> Twenty-five percent were enrolled in tertiary educational institutions; 4 percent have six years or less of schooling; 53 percent have had between seven and 11 years; 6 percent have had 12 years; and 10 percent hold university degrees.
>
> The failure of the legal community to take a firm stand on the issue, Zucker says, is tantamount to complicity and support for the system. Pleading security considerations, without probing exactly what these mean and what the limits are, will leave those who seek to evade the issue in the position of having to justify the arrests, Zucker warns.[16]

4. *Administrative Detention in International Law*

Imprisonment without charge or trial constitutes a serious infringement of the individual's rights to protection from arbitrary arrest and due process. Both Article 9 of the Universal Declaration of Human Rights (UDHR) and Article 9 (1) of the International Covenant on Civil and Political Rights (ICCPR) state that "No one shall be subjected to arbitrary arrest or detention."

On the right to due process, Article 10 of the UDHR states that

> Every one is entitled in full equality to a fair and public hearing by an independent and impartial tribunal, in the determination of his rights and obligations and of any criminal charge against him.

The provisions for administrative detention as laid down in Military Order 378 (as amended) are clearly in violation of both these articles, and therefore fail to conform to the minimum standards required by the rule of law.

Article 78 of the Fourth Geneva Convention (1949) does permit the occupying power to use internment "for imperative reasons of security." However, it is highly questionable whether "imperative reasons of security" demand that thousands of persons be detained without charge, trial, or the right to have their imprisonment reviewed by an impartial body. The Attorney General's statement of 26 January 1986 goes to great lengths to emphasise the exceptional nature of administrative detention. However, with so many Palestinians having been administratively detained during the past 12 months and with at least 1,590 currently interned, it does not appear that the Attorney General's claims in any way reflect actual practice in the Occupied Territories. The widespread and apparently indiscriminate use of this measure simply belies the Israeli authorities' claim that the measure is only used in special circumstances.

D. House Demolition

The Israeli military authorities have used house demolitions and sealings to punish the families of Palestinians suspected of "security offences" throughout the 21 years of the occupation. During the past year, the use of such measures has increased dramatically; at least 145 houses have been razed to the ground or welded shut by administrative decree since 9 December 1987 in the West Bank alone. Furthermore, the military government has demolished a large number of homes for reasons which in the past would only have elicited such a harsh measure in isolated cases.

At the same time, the Israeli authorities have also demolished hundreds of homes because they were allegedly built without proper permits. While not directly related to "security considerations," the crackdown on "illegal structures" has in fact been linked by Israeli officials to their continuing effort to control the uprising.[17] Such cases, however, although they are greater in number, will not be addressed in this report and only demolitions and sealings relating to alleged security offences will be considered.[18]

1. Past Use of the Measure

The demolition of homes in retribution for security-related offences by the Israeli military government is, to the best of al-Haq's knowledge, a unique international phenomenon. No other government practises this form of collective punishment.

While al-Haq itself has not been able to do a comprehensive study of house demolitions by the Israeli authorities during the first 15 years of occupation, authoritative sources make it possible to distinguish several stages in the policy's development since 1967:

i.)1967 – mid 1970's: While al-Haq has no detailed records of house demolitions during the early years of the occupation, their use is known to have been widespread during this time. In the first year of Israeli rule, several villages in the Occupied Territories were either completely or partially destroyed, leaving thousands of people homeless. In addition, at least 1,000 houses were demolished as a form of punishment during the first decade of the occupation.

ii.) late 1970's – 1985: According to al-Haq's information, house demolitions and sealings in this period appear to have been largely confined to cases in which Israeli soldiers or settlers had been killed or wounded in armed attacks by Palestinians. The available documentation indicates that, in the West Bank (including East Jerusalem), no more than 20 houses were demolished or destroyed per annum between the late 1970's and 1985.

iii.) May 1985 – 9 December 1987: Shortly before their announcement of an "Iron Fist" policy toward the Occupied Territories in August of 1985, the Israeli military authorities began to increase the use of these punitive measures. Of the 55 cases documented by al-Haq in the West Bank between May and December of 1985 (a rather sharp increase), 24 (43.6 percent) were demolished, a further 24 (43.6 percent) were completely sealed, and the other 7 (12.8 percent) were partially sealed.

Apparently in response to the widespread international criticism of their destruction of homes in the Occupied Territories, the Israeli authorities shifted the emphasis of their policy from demolition and complete sealing to partial sealing. Countering accusations that the policy was one of collective punishment, the authorities claimed that the adjusted policy singled out only the room of the person involved in alleged security offences. According to al-Haq's documentation for 1986 there was a significant proportional shift in the policy; of a total of 48 houses affected, 12 (25 percent) were demolished, 10 (22 percent) were completely sealed, while 25 (53 percent) were partially sealed, representing an almost complete reversal of the previous year's statistics. A similar pattern was observed between January and December of 1987, during which, of a total of 37 houses issued with demolition or sealing orders in the West Bank, 5 (13 percent) were demolished, 15 (40 percent) entirely sealed, and 18 (47 percent) partially sealed.

2. *House Demolition During the Uprising*

According to al-Haq's documentation the military government, in a reversal of the trend it pursued in the months prior to the uprising: increased the proportion of demolitions to sealings (and especially partial sealings); has been increasingly predisposed toward the demolition or sealing of a home even when no firearms were used or no injuries were reported; and has damaged greater numbers of adjacent houses in the process of carrying out demolitions.

The authorities have increased the proportion of demolitions to sealings. Since 9 December 1987, the authorities have used the harshest form of this measure available to them, reversing the more recent trends described above. According to al-Haq's documentation, 64 percent (93 houses) of all houses affected have been entirely demolished, as opposed to only 13 percent in 1987. There has been a corresponding decrease in the use of partial sealing orders. Only 3 houses have been partially sealed since December 1987 (2 percent), whereas partial sealings accounted for 47 percent of all cases in 1987.

The military government has never publicly stated the criteria which govern its house-demolition policy in the Occupied Territories. It appears from our documentation, however, that in the past the authorities weighed a number of factors before deciding to take action against the home of a suspect and whether to demolish or seal, in total or in part, the residence in question. These factors included the severity of the offence, the location of the house in question (i.e. whether it was in a camp, village, or city), the standing of the family in the community, and the number of family members affected by the demolition or sealing order. Al-Haq has been unable to detect any such considerations on the authorities' part since the beginning of the uprising.

The authorities have been more easily prepared to demolish or seal houses even when no firearms were used or no injuries were reported. Most house-demolition cases during the uprising have involved a Palestinian being accused of throwing a firebomb which did not cause death or injury. In some cases houses have even been demolished because molotov cocktails were thrown from their vicinity, and in other cases because the suspect threw such a device at a municipal building, even though it failed to explode. While this is not an entirely new development on the part of the Israeli authorities, it was in the past confined to isolated cases whereas it has now become a pervasive practice.

Houses have also been demolished because one of their occupants was charged with "incitement" by the military government. Al-Haq has documented at least 16 such cases in the villages of Bidya, Beita, and Silat al-Harethiya. Al-Haq has no record of "incitement" being used as a justification for demolitions in the past.

Since December 1988, houses have even been demolished in cases where the owners had absolutely no relation to the alleged offence. In the villages of Beit Ommar and Idhna, for example, houses were demolished on the pretext that firebombs had been thrown at military vehicles *from their general vicinity.* On 15 June 1988, in the village of Beit Ommar, the uninhabited house of Na'imi and Na'ima 'Abd-al-'Aziz Salih, aged 50 and 35 respectively, was demolished for this reason. Similarly, the house of Mahmoud Ahmad Gharabla in the village of Idhna was demolished in June 1988 after the Israeli authorities charged that a molotov cocktail had been thrown at an army jeep from nearby, causing injuries. The house had been uninhabited for some time, and the owners, who lived elsewhere, were absent at the time of the demolition.

The authorities have damaged greater numbers of adjacent houses in the process of carrying out demolitions. Adjacent houses have been damaged on an unprecedented scale in the course of demolitions during the uprising. In the villages of Beita and Bidya, and in the Jenin Refugee Camp, and most recently (on 28 November) in Jalazon Refugee Camp, for example, al-Haq documented substantial damage to neighbouring houses as a result of demolitions. Not only the greater scale of demolitions, but also the increasing recklessness of soldiers carrying out the orders appear to be responsible for this trend.

Some patterns prevalent before December 1987 continued throughout the uprising. In all except two cases documented by al-Haq, the house demolition order was executed before the individual in question was brought to trial. In a number of these instances the measure was implemented before there was even a charge sheet, and in six cases the army destroyed a house before the accused had been arrested. When the army did manage to arrest the accused, the demolition or sealing of his/her family's home often took place within a few hours. While such occurrences are by no means unprecedented, they have been increasingly frequent since December 1987.

On 31 October 1988, the military authorities arrested Yunis Takruri, a resident of Jericho, on the suspicion that he had participated in a firebomb attack the previous night which left four Israelis dead. Almost immediately afterwards, and under pressure from an angry electorate preparing to go to the polls, the armed forces announced that Takruri had confessed to his role in the attack and that the home of his grandmother (where he had been living), along with those of six other suspects, had been demolished as a "minimum punishment."[19] Then, after a week-long interrogation, the military decided that there were no grounds for prosecution against Takruri after all and released him. To date, not one person has been charged in the incident. In al-Haq's view, the summary demolition of 7 homes in the Jericho case gives an accurate description of the dangers and violations inherent in an administrative measure whose executive procedures systematically violate the right to due process.

Families have not been given enough time to remove their possessions before their house is demolished. This has also been a serious problem in the past. In some cases a family is given no time at all to remove their belongings and the home is demolished along with all its contents. This happened, for example, to two families in the village of Biddou in the Ramallah area. In other cases documented by al-Haq, soldiers either destroyed furniture while removing it from homes about to be demolished, or else placed household goods so close to the house that they were destroyed during the demolition.

3. Legal Arguments

House demolition and sealing not directly necessitated by military operations, as well as collective punishment in general, is expressly forbidden by the Fourth Geneva Convention of 1949, which is the basic legal instrument governing the conduct of occupying powers and to which Israel is a signatory. The policy of demolitions and sealings is also in clear violation of basic principles of human rights. As an illegal, extra-judicial measure of collective punishment with unacceptable humanitarian consequences, it has been widely condemned both locally and internationally.

The Israeli authorities maintain that local laws permit the demolition and sealing of homes, citing Article 119 (A) of the British Defence (Emergency) Regulations of 1945. These Regulations, however, were cancelled by the British in 1948 before the Mandate came to an end and were never applied to the West Bank by Jordan, which succeeded the British. Thus, no valid local law allows for the authorities to engage in the demolition of homes.[20]

The Israeli authorities further claim that house demolition is permitted under Article 53 of the Fourth Geneva Convention of 1949. The Article states, however, that destruction of "personal property belonging individually or collectively to private persons" is prohibited "except where such destruction is rendered absolutely necessary by military operations." In its interpretation of the clause, the International Committee of the Red Cross, which is the guardian of the Geneva Conventions, stated that:

> Destruction of property as mentioned in Article 53 cannot be justified under the terms of that article unless such destruction is absolutely necessary—i.e. materially indispensable—for the armed forces to engage in action, such as making way for them. This exception to the prohibition cannot justify destruction as a punishment or deterrent, since to preclude this type of destruction is an essential aim of the article.[21]

Despite this, the Israeli High Court of Justice on 24 March 1986 ruled that demolitions are justified as a deterrent.

In al-Haq's view, house demolitions are a clear form of collective punishment since people who are not accused of any offence are punished. Article 33 of the Fourth Geneva Convention states that no resident of an occupied territory "may be punished for an offence he or she has not personally committed," and furthermore explicitly forbids collective punishment. Additionally, the demolition of homes as it is practised by the Israeli authorities in the Occupied Territories constitutes extra-judicial punishment, which is expressly prohibited by the Universal Declaration of Human Rights (UDHR).

House demolitions are often executed without any prior notification of the residents, and in any case families can only appeal the measure to a military objections committee, whose mandate is of a strictly advisory nature, within a 48-hour period. The UDHR clearly states than no individual or group of persons may be punished without due process and a fair trial. Another reason the Israeli legal system has offered no meaningful recourse to opponents of the practice is the Israeli judiciary's traditional reluctance to confront the policies of the military government in the Occupied Territories.

The question of the lack of an appeals procedure or judicial review in house demolitions was raised by the Association for Civil Rights in Israel (ACRI) in a case which was still pending in the High Court of Justice as this report went to press. On 11 April 1988, in response to a petition filed by ACRI, the High Court ordered the armed forces not to destroy any more homes in the village of Beita without first giving their occupants 48 hours notice. This ruling, however, was expressly restricted to Beita, where 14 homes were destroyed following the well-publicised events there in April 1988.[22]

In August, ACRI filed a second petition asking that the decision be extended to cover all of the West Bank and Gaza. The military responded by stating that it would allow a hearing before demolition except in "exceptional cases," which it defined as those resulting in death or injury, or in which the military commander deemed that a "speedy act of deterrence" was required.[23] Petrol bomb attacks, even those not causing injury, were asserted to constitute circumstances requiring immediate retribution.[24] As can be seen, these "exceptions" are so broad that they could be offered in justification of virtually every case of demolition which has so far occurred.

In 1987 al-Haq released a comprehensive report on house demolitions which explains in detail how such measures violate basic human rights principles and why the legal justifications offered by the Israeli authorities are not valid under international law.[25]

4. Conclusion: Demolitions

The new dimensions of the house-demolition policy, particularly the increasing number of houses being demolished rather than sealed and the use of this measure in instances where it has not been applied in the past, is a cause of great concern to al-Haq, which considers such actions a form of collective punishment standing in direct violation of both international law and basic human rights.

While the increase in the number of demolitions itself could, perhaps, be explained by the authorities as having been precipitated by the increase in the number of "security offences," the change in criteria for the use of this measure, as well as the severity of its application, in fact brings into further question previous claims by the authorities that their use of demolition and sealing is confined to only "the most serious cases."

It appears to al-Haq that the changes in the use of this measure largely reflect both political criteria and the continued frustration of the authorities at their failure to end the uprising. Jewish settlers living in the Occupied Territories have repeatedly called for the destruction of houses, and indeed entire villages, in which people who have thrown molotov cocktails reside. The Military Commander of the Central Area (which includes the entire West Bank), General Amram Mitzna, stated that demolitions were being used because they were "a powerful deterrent action to signal and clarify that we will do everything and take all measures to stop this phenomenon of petrol bombs."[26] In an apparent reflection of this zeal on the part of decision-makers in the military government, the armed forces demolished 16 houses in "petrol-bomb related" incidents in a single 24-hour period on 19 June 1988.[27]

Three case studies of house demolitions which were documented by al-Haq are appended to this chapter.

FOOTNOTES TO CHAPTER 4

1. The documentation for this chapter consists primarily of the extensive records al-Haq has been keeping on deportation, administrative detention, and house demolition for a number of years. To the extent possible, these records have been continually updated during the uprising, although due to the unprecedented scope of the violations, our methods have had to be adapted. For instance, whereas before the uprising al-Haq kept detailed information on every administrative detainee, the thousands of such cases in the past year have made this task simply impossible.

   Al-Haq's documentation relies primarily on sworn affidavits taken by a staff of experienced fieldworkers who have been trained to apply internationally accepted standard rules of evidence. Additionally, fieldworker reports written after rigorous on-scene interviews are also used. References to international law are not footnoted. Press reports, which are footnotes, were used primarily to refer to official statements and confirmed incidents.

   Readers interested in a more detailed discussion of the issues presented should consult the three studies prepared by al-Haq on these subjects. These publications are: Joost R. Hiltermann, *Israel's Deportation Policy in the Occupied West Bank and Gaza Strip*, (Ramallah; al-Haq Occasional Paper No. 2 *Second Edition*, 1988), also reprinted in part in the *Palestine Yearbook of International Law* (vol. III; 1986), pp. 154-187; Emma Playfair, *Administrative Detention in the Occupied West Bank*, (Ramallah; al-Haq Occasional Paper No. 1, 1986); and, Emma Playfair, *Demolition and Sealing of Houses as a Punitive Measure in the Israeli-Occupied West Bank*, (Ramallah, al-Haq Occasional Paper No. 5, 1987).
2. *al-Fajr, al-Quds, al-Sha'b,* and the *Jerusalem Post,* 18 August 1988.
3. "Deportation" is used in this section to refer to the act by which Palestinian residents of the Occupied Territories are issued expulsion or banishment orders under Articles 108 and 112 of the British Defence (Emergency) Regulations 1945, or Military Order 329 (West Bank), or Military Order 290 (Gaza Strip), and deported from their homeland. It does not include the far greater number of Palestinians who, due to other administrative measures, are either prevented from remaining in or returning to their homeland, nor does it include those Palestinians who, while in detention for "security offences", make a deal with the authorities whereby they are released in exchange for their departure from the Territories. For a full analysis of Israel's use of deportations, see Hiltermann, *Israel's Deportation Policy.*
4. *Jerusalem Post,* 24 August 1988.
5. A new Israeli political party, *Moledet* ("Homeland"), bases its programme on precisely this platform. Its two representatives in the Knesset (Israel's parliament) were elected on 1 November 1988. One of them, Ya'ir Sprinzak, became the Acting Speaker of the Knesset in November due to his seniority. Otherwise, the idea of "transfer" is discussed in public by adherents of several, mostly right-wing, Israeli political parties.
6. See the report on the Beita events by the Jerusalem-based Palestine Human Rights Campaign (PHRIC) dated 25 April 1988. The report is also available from the PHRIC's Chicago affiliate, the Database Project on Palestinian

Rights.
7. See the forthcoming al-Haq publication on the validity of the Defence Regulations. Additionally, in response to its inquiries, al-Haq has received written statements from both the British Foreign Office and the Jordanian Ministry of Defence attesting to the revocation and consequent inapplicability of the Defence (Emergency) Regulations to the West Bank after 15 May 1948.
8. For a more detailed argument on the illegality of deportations, see Hiltermann, *Israel's Deportation Policy.*
9. For a detailed summary of prison conditions, particularly those at Ansar III, see Chapter 6.
10. *Jerusalem Post*, 28 November 1988. See Chapter 6 for additional details on the number of detainees.
11. Both Ansar III and several other prison facilities are located outside the territories occupied by Israel in 1967, and the detention of prisoners in these locations is a direct contravention of international law. See the discussion on this point in Chapter 6.
12. *Ha'aretz*, 20 March 1988.
13. The judge, often a soldier doing reserve-duty in the Occupied Territories, is required to have at least some legal background.
14. *Jerusalem Post*, 19 May 1988. Zucker belongs to the Citizens Rights Movement (RATZ).
15. *Ibid.*
16. *Ibid.*
17. See for instance the *Jerusalem Post*, 21 October 1988.
18. The PHRIC recently completed an in-depth study on the demolition of homes in the Occupied Territories for permit reasons, which found a clear correlation between this practice and the political priorities of the military government. The report is from the PHRIC's Chicago office (see footnote 6).
19. *Jerusalem Post*, 1 November 1988. The statement was attributed to the Military Commander of the Central Area, General Amram Mitza.
20. See also footnote 7 above.
21. From an interpretation by the ICRC of Article 53 of the Fourth Geneva Convention of 12 August 1949, with particular reference to the expression "military operations," dated 25 November 1981, signed by Jacques Moreillon and approved by Jean S. Pictet.
22. For further details to the events in Beita see Chapter 3.
23. *Jerusalem Post*, 8 August 1988.
24. *Ibid.*
25. See Emma Playfair, *Demolition and Sealing of Houses as a Punitive Measure in the Israeli-Occupied West Bank*, (Al-Haq/LSM 1987).
26. *Jerusalem Post*, 20 June 1988.
27. *Ibid.*

Appendix 4-A

LIST A: PALESTINIANS ORDERED EXPELLED FROM THE OCCUPIED TERRITORIES SINCE THE BEGINNING OF THE UPRISING, 9 DECEMBER 1987*

NO.	NAME	TOWN	ORDER	APP	DEP DATE
01	Jibril Mahmoud Muhammad al-Rujoub	Doura	FP/DR	Y/N	13/01/88
02	Jamal 'Abdallah Shaker Jabbara	Qalqiliya	FP/DR	Y/N	13/01/88
03	Husam Mahmoud Khader	Balata C.	DefRg	Y/N	13/01/88
04	Bashir Ahmad al-Kheiri	Ramallah	DefRg	Y/N	13/01/88
05	Muhammad Abou Samra	Gaza	DefRg	Y/N	11/04/88
06	Khalil al-Qouqa	Gaza	DefRg	Y/N	11/04/88
07	Fereij Ahmad al-Kheiri	Gaza	DefRg	Y/N	11/04/88
08	Hasan Ghanem Abou Shaqra	Khan Younes	DefRg	Y/N	11/04/88
09	Bashir Mahmoud Nafe' Ahmad Hamad	Qalandiya Camp	DefRg	Y/N	11/04/88
10	'Umar Muhammed Sa'id Da'oud	Beita	DefRg	Y/N	19/04/88
11	Najeh Jamil Sa'ada Dweikat	Beita	DefRg	Y/N	19/04/88
12	Mahmoud 'Abed Ibrahim Beni Shemsin	Beita	DefRg	Y/N	19/04/88
13	Mustafa Mahmoud Hamdan Hamayel	Beita	DefRg	Y/N	19/04/88
14	Sari Hilal Taher Hamayel	Beita	DefRg	Y/N	19/04/88
15	Ibrahim Khader 'Ali	Beita	DefRg	Y/N	19/04/88
16	Ghassan 'Ali al-Masri	Ramallah	DefRg	Y/N	19/04/88
17	Ahmad Fawzi Khaled al-Dik	Kufer al-Dik	DefRg	Y/N	19/04/88
18	'Adnan Dagher	Al-Bira	DefRg	Y/N	01/08/88
19	Ahmad Muhammad Jaber Suleiman	Turmous Aya	DefRg	Y/N	01/08/88
20	Ziyad Husni Nakhal	Gaza	DefRg	Y/N	01/08/88
21	Jamal 'Awad Zaqout	Gaza	DefRg	Y/N	01/08/88
22	Lu'ay Nafi' 'Ali 'Abdou	Nablus	DefRg	Y/N	01/08/88
23	Mursi 'Abd-al-Hadi Abou-Ghawayla	Qalandiya	DefRg	Y/N	01/08/88
24	Samir Mahmoud Sebeihat	Al-Bira	DefRg	Y/N	01/08/88

Administrative Methods of Punishment 143

NO.	NAME	TOWN	ORDER	APP	DEP DATE
25	Jamal Dhiyab Abou-Latifa	Qalandiya	DefRg	Y/N	01/08/88
26	Yusri Darwish al-Hamas	Rafah	DefRg	Y/N	17/08/88
27	Fathi Muhammad Ashqaqi	Rafah	DefRg	Y/N	17/08/88
28	Ahmad Mustafa Abou-Mu'aylaq	Gaza	DefRg	Y/N	17/08/88
29	Muhammad 'Abdallah Sabri Gharabla	Gaza	DefRg	Y/N	17/08/88
30	Muhammad 'Abdallah al-Labadi	Abou Dis	DefRg	Y	08/07/88
31	Radwan Muhammad Ziyada	Hebron	DefRg	Y	08/07/88
32	Taysir Ghareb 'Arouri	Al-Bira	DefRg	Y	17/08/88
33	Majed 'Abdallah al-Labadi	Abou Dis	DefRg	Y	17/08/88
34	Muhammad al-Matour	Al-Bira	DefRg	Y	17/08/88
35	Mas'oud Zu'aytar	Nablus	DefRg	Y	17/08/88
36	Bilal Shakhshir	Nablus	DefRg	Y	17/08/88
37	Hani Haloub	Toulkarem	DefRg	Y	17/08/88
38	Taysir Salah Naserallah	Balata C.	DefRg	Y	17/08/88
39	'Abd-al-Hamid al-Baba	Al-'Amari	DefRg	Y	17/08/88
40	'Oda Yousef Ma'ala	Kufer Na'ma	DefRg	Y	17/08/88
41	'Akef Wahid al-Hamdallah	'Anabta	DefRg	Y	17/08/88
42	Uthman Da'oud	Qalqiliya	DefRg	Y	17/08/88
43	Yousef 'Oda	Balata C.	DefRg	Y	17/08/88
44	'Issam Amin 'Abd-al-Fatah Daba'i	Nablus	DefRg	Y	17/08/88
45	Sarhan Dweikat	Balata C.	DefRg	Y	17/08/88
46	Jamal Faraj	Deheisha	DefRg	Y	17/08/88
47	Sa'id Baraka	Beni Suheila	DefRg	Y	17/08/88
48	Nabil Tamous	Gaza	DefRg	Y	17/08/88
49	Fathi Hajaj	Bureij C.	DefRg	Y	17/08/88
50	Riyad Wajih 'Ajour	Gaza	DefRg	Y	17/08/88
51	'Abdallah Abou-Samhadanna	Gaza	DefRg	Y	17/08/88
52	'Ayish Abou-Sa'da	Jabaliya	DefRg	Y	17/08/88
53	Rizeq Biyarghou	Gaza	DefRg	Y	17/08/88
54	Muhammad Madoukh	Gaza	DefRg	Y	17/08/88
55	Mun'em Abou-'Ataya	Gaza	DefRg	Y	17/08/88
56	'Atta Abou-Kersh	Shate' C.	DefRg	Y	17/08/88

LIST B: PALESTINIANS ORDERED EXPELLED FROM THE OCCUPIED TERRITORIES IN 1984 - 1987*

NO.	NAME	TOWN	ORDER	APP	DEP DATE
01	'Abd-al-'Aziz 'Ali Shahin	Rafah	MilOr	YES	17/02/85
02	Khalil Abou-Ziyad	'Izariya	DefRg	Y/N	28/08/85
03	Muhammad Hasan Gharir	Deheisha	FP/MO	NO	15/09/85
04	Walid Muhammad Kasrawi	Jenin	FP/MO	YES	15/09/85
05	Salem Ahmad Breiwesh	Hebron	FP/MO	YES	15/09/85
06	Khaled Mahmoud Daloul	Nablus	FP/MO	YES	15/09/85
07	'Issa Muhammad Shahin	Bethlehem	FP/MO	YES	15/09/85
08	Bader Darwish al-Qawasmi	Hebron	FP/MO	YES	15/09/85
09	Mahmoud 'Abdallah Hamdan	Bethlehem	FP/MO	YES	15/09/85
10	Jum'a 'Awad Abou-Hamed	Qalqilya	FP/MO	YES	15/09/85
11	Muhammad Hamdan Abou-'Asaba	Tulkarem	FP/MO	YES	15/09/85
12	'Abd-al-Qader Muhammad al-Wahesh	Bethlehem	FP/MO	YES	15/09/85
13	'Abd-al-Ghaffar Ahmad Abou-'Asaba	Tulkarem	FP/MO	YES	15/09/85
14	Muhammad Merawweh Hanini	Beit Dajan	FP/MO	YES	15/09/85
15	'Idallah al-'Awni	Nablus	FP/MO	NO	15/09/85
16	'Adnan Muhammad Baladi	Tulkarem	FP/MO	NO	15/09/85
17	Nathmi Husein Hamdan	Beit Iba	FP/MO	NO	15/09/85
18	Saleh Khader Abou-Murtada	Beit Dajan	FP/MO	NO	15/09/85
19	Khalil 'Abd-al-Hamid Salami	Gaza	FP/MO	NO	15/09/85
20	Muhammad Ahmad Beirouti	Hebron	FP/MO	NO	15/09/85
21	Walid Ahmad Nazzal	Qabatiya	DefRg	YES	01/10/85
22	Amin Ramzi Maqboul	Nablus	DefRg	YES	01/10/85
23	Bahjat Mustafa al-Jayousi	Jayous	DefRg	YES	01/10/85
24	Khamis Husein Naserallah	Beit Furiq	FP/MO	YES	27/11/85
25	Younis Salem al-Rujoub	Doura	FP/DR	NO	09/12/85
26	Mahmoud 'Abdallah De'is	Beni Na'im	DefRg	NO	09/12/85
27	Khaled Muhammad Tantash	Jerusalem	FP/MO	Y/N	17/12/85
28	'Azmi Salah al-Shu'aibi	Al-Bira	DefRg	Y/N	31/01/86
29	'Ali 'Abdallah Abou-Hilal	Abou Dis	DefRg	Y/N	31/01/86
30	Hasan Mahmoud 'Abd-al-Jawad Fararja	Deheisha	DefRg	Y/N	31/01/86
31	Mahmoud Fa'noun	Nahalin	DefRg	NO	05/02/86
32	Hasan Muhammad al-Amoudi	Bureij	FP/DR	Y/N	05/02/86

Administrative Methods of Punishment 145

NO.	NAME	TOWN	ORDER	APP	DEP DATE
33	JalalHafeth'Aziza	Bureij	FP/DR	Y/N	05/02/86
34	'Adnan Mansour Ghanem	Tulkarem	FP/DR	NO	10/02/86
35	Ahmad 'Abd-al-Majed Radad	Tulkarem	FP/MO	YES	12/02/86
36	Zaki Abou Steiti	Jabaliya	FP/DR	Y/N	28/04/86
37	Akram 'Abd-al-Salam Haniya	Ramallah	DefRg	Y/N	28/12/86
38	Muhammad Yousef Dahlan	Khan Younes	DefRg	Y/N	26/01/87
39	Khalil Ibrahim 'Ashour	Nablus	DefRg	Y/N	14/05/87
40	Marwan Huseib al-Barghouthi	Kubar	DefRg	Y/N	14/05/87
41	Ahmad 'Abd-al-Fatah Naser	Khan Younes	FP/DR	NO	31/05/87
42	Jihad 'Abdallah al-Museimi	Balata C.	FP/DR	NO	04/06/87
43	Zaqariya Hamed al-Nahhas	Al-Bira	MilOr	Y/N	05/10/87
44	'Abd-al-Naser Muhammad 'Abd-al-'Aziz	Jenin	DefRg	YES	11/04/88
45	'Abd-al-'Aziz 'Abd-al-Rahman 'Uda Rafi'	Gaza	DefRg	YES	11/04/88
46	Jamal Shati Younes al-Hindi	Jenin Camp	DefRg	YES	11/04/88

* NOTE

PLEASE NOTE: These are lists of Palestinians *ordered* expelled. This explains why three Palestinians (B44, B45, B46), although deported in 1988 after the beginning of the uprising, are included in the pre-uprising list, List B.

These lists do not include those Palestinians who have been deported following the expiry of their prison term, or those who at the time of their conviction supposedly agreed to be deported in order to receive a reduced term in jail, nor Palestinian residents of the Occupied Territories who were not allowed to re-enter the area following a stay abroad.

ABBREVIATIONS:
FP = Palestinians freed during the prisoner exchange on 20 May 1985.
MO or MilOr = Deported by virtue of military order, i.e. M.O. 329 for the West Bank, and M.O. 290 for Gaza.
DR or DefRg = Deported by virtue of the British Defence (Emergency) Regulations of 1945.

Updated as of: 15 November 1988
Source: Al-Haq

Appendix 4-B

DEPORTATION CASE STUDY #1: 'ADNAN DAGHER

'Adnan 'Abd-al-Fattah Dagher, 35, a resident of al-Bireh in the Israeli-Occupied West Bank, was served with a deportation order on 11 April 1988. It was issued by the Military Commander of the Central Area, General Amram Mitzna, on the basis of the Defence (Emergency) Regulations of 1945. Eleven other residents of the Occupied Territories were served with similar orders on the same day. Eight of these have already been expelled, and deportation proceedings against an additional 10 Palestinians were begun on 10 July. In all, 20 inhabitants of the West Bank and the Israeli-occupied Gaza Strip have been expelled since the beginning of the year, and 14 others are currently in prison pending the execution of their deportation orders.

'Adnan's deportation order was processed without charge or trial. The only allegations against him of which his lawyers have any knowledge are purported membership in the Palestine Communist Party and in the United National Leadership of the Uprising. 'Adnan has never been charged with or convicted of any offence, violent or otherwise.

A father of three, 'Adnan is an active and committed trade unionist. Since 1969 he has been a member of the Ramallah General Institutions and Construction Workers' Union (RGICWU). His early work in the union included leading a union membership drive, working in its cultural committee, and, in his spare time, playing on its soccer team. 'Adnan was arrested in 1974 and subsequently placed under 4 consecutive six-month terms of administrative detention (renewable periods of detention without charge or trial). After his release in 1976, he became a writer for *al-Fajr* newspaper, and later, in February 1978, a reporter for *al-Tali'a*, a Palestinian weekly. He also returned to his work with the RGICWU, and in 1980 was elected to its executive committee. Among 'Adnan's projects in the union was a drive to secure health insurance for its members and the formation of a union cooperative through which workers could buy work clothes, as well as school supplies and clothes for their children at reduced cost. He was elected president of the union in 1983. After finishing his term in office, he chaired the union's cultural committee where he was in charge of editing workers' poetry and short stories for the union newsletter, and gave lectures on cultural issues and worker safety and health.

'Adnan is described by friends and colleagues as a serious person who is intensely dedicated to the realisation of the rights of Palestinian workers. His knowledge of the situation of Palestinian labourers in the Occupied Territories and inside Israel, as well as his knowledge of both Israeli and Jordanian labour law have made him an important resource for labour organising. Before his recent arrest, 'Adnan could usually be found in the union's office in al-Bireh, where a steady stream of workers would pass by to ask for his help and for advice on their legal rights. He was also instrumental in bringing public attention to the special problems of Palestinian workers inside Israel. 'Adnan frequently met with delegations of trade unionists from abroad who were visiting the Occupied Territories.

'Adnan was arrested on 18 March 1988, and issued a six-month administrative detention order the next day. Less than one month later, however, he was served with a deportation order. During this period his wife and children were not allowed to visit him. They have since been allowed a weekly visit. On 1 June, his lawyers, Ibrahim al-Barghouthi and Felicia Langer, were notified that the order had been upheld by a military objections committee. 'Adnan then took his case to the Israeli High Court of Justice but withdrew the appeal when his lawyers were denied access to evidence which had been submitted in secret. 'Adnan can now be deported at any time the military authorities find convenient.

'Adnan's lawyers believe that he is being deported for political reasons. They base this view on the fact that 'Adnan's change in status from administrative detention to deportation occurred only 4 days after the Beita Incident (6 April 1988), in which a settler-girl was shot to death by an armed escort. The incident led to calls for the mass deportation of Palestinian villagers by the politically powerful settler movement. Furthermore, the harsher measure issued against 'Adnan seems to lack a corresponding change in the allegations against him. On 12 May 1988, 'Adnan's lawyers submitted a written request to the military authorities to find out whether there had in fact been a change in the accusations against 'Adnan that might justify the change from administrative detention to deportation. To date, no response has been received to this request.

UPDATE: 'Adnan Dagher was deported to Lebanon, along with seven other Palestinians, on 1 August 1988. According to the *Jerusalem Post* of 2 August, "he is accused of distributing subversive literature and organizing strikes and disturbances."

SOURCE: Al-Haq Fact Sheet #1: Deportations from the Israeli-Occupied Territories

Appendix 4-C

DEPORTATION CASE STUDY #2: MURSI ABOU-GHAWAYLA

Mursi 'Abd-al-Hadi Hasan Abou-Ghawayla, 21, a resident of Qalandiya Refugee Camp in the Israeli-occupied West Bank, was served with a deportation order on 8 July 1988. It was issued by the Military Commander of the Central Area, General Amram Mitzna, on the basis of the Defence (Emergency) Regulations of 1945. Five other residents of the West Bank as well as four persons from the Israeli-occupied Gaza Strip were issued with similar orders on the same day. If the deportations proceed as scheduled, Mursi Abou-Ghawayla will be one of the youngest persons to have been deported by the Israeli authorities since the occupation began in 1967.

Mursi Abou-Ghawayla is the eldest in a family of 8 boys and 5 girls. Between 1983 and 1986 he was detained for interrogation a total of five times and spent between 11 and 57 days in custody during each arrest. In 1984 he was imprisoned for two months for throwing stones, and in 1985 sentenced to four additional months in prison on charges of demonstrating, incitement, stone-throwing, and writing nationalist slogans on walls. On 11 April 1987, he was served with a three-month administrative detention order (internment without charge or trial).

His most recent arrest came on 28 December 1987. At approximately 1:30 a.m. a group of about 30 soldiers, including a number of high-ranking officers, broke into his house, handcuffed and blindfolded him, and took him to 'Atlit detention centre near Haifa. 'Atlit lies outside the territories occupied by Israel in 1967 and thus the transfer was a clear violation of Article 76 of the Fourth Geneva Convention of 1949, to which Israel is a signatory. According to his parents, Mursi was severely beaten at 'Atlit and then taken to Jnaid Prison in Nablus, where he was served with a six-month administrative detention order, which was renewed for one month on 28 June 1988. On 7 July the deportation order was issued. Mursi's family was not informed by the authorities and learned of the action through the media. The authorities are alleging that Mursi is a leader in the Shabiba, a grassroots youth movement in the Occupied Territories which was declared illegal on 19 March 1988, almost three months after the date of his arrest.

Mursi's lawyer, Jawad Boulos, appealed the deportation order to a military objections committee on 10 July. Because the defence was denied access to evidence which had been submitted by the authorities in secret, however, the appeal was withdrawn on the same day.

Mursi has not been able to complete his secondary education because of arrests in 1983 which prevented him from taking his final exams. He later enrolled in a United Nations vocational training centre in Qalandiya where he completed his studies. His family had been impatiently waiting for him to graduate and start working in order to support them, because, according to his parents, his father has not been able to work due to heart disease, diabetes, a severe ulcer, and poor eyesight. But Mursi's repeated arrests and related deteriorating health have prevented him from seeking employment.

Mursi Abou-Ghawayla's deportation will seriously affect the fortunes of his family, which have already been declining in the last several years with the incapacitation of his father. A younger brother is currently also serving a prison sentence in Jenin prison. The deportation will leave the Abou-Ghawayla family without a bread-winner and make the raising and education of his 12 brothers and sisters much more difficult than it already is. Because the appeal was withdrawn, Mursi can now be deported at any time the military government finds convenient.

UPDATE: Mursi Abou-Ghawayla was deported to Lebanon, along with 7 other Palestinians, on 1 August 1988. According to the *Jerusalem Post* of 2 August, he is "accused of leading disturbances" and "considered a Shabiba leader."

SOURCE: Al-Haq Fact Sheet #1: Deportation From The Israeli-Occupied Territories

Appendix 4-D

HOUSE DEMOLITIONS CASE STUDY #1: JENIN REFUGEE CAMP

The two-story, 12-room house of Ibrahim 'Id al-'Amer in the Jenin Refugee Camp was demolished by the IDF on 16 June 1988. According to an army spokesperson, the action was taken because Ibrahim's son Ziyad, who was arrested on 24 May, is accused of throwing a molotov cocktail at a military vehicle. The camp had been under curfew for four days at the time of the demolition.

According to al-Haq's information, the family was told by the soldiers that they had ten minutes to remove all of their possessions before they would demolish the house. The soldiers said that they were demolishing the house because of their son Ziyad. When the family tried to persuade them that the house did not belong to Ziyad, they started to throw the furniture out of the house.

Al-Haq's fieldworker in the area reported that in the process of demolishing the al-'Amer house the military caused substantial damage to 15 other homes. Additionally, at least one neighbour was injured by flying debris.

Another house in Jenin Camp, that of Muhammad Salih Abou-Ghalyoun, was also demolished. The house had two floors consisting of 12 rooms. According to an army spokesperson, it was demolished because Muhammad's brother Nidal was accused of throwing a molotov cocktail. The military authorities did not claim that the molotov caused any casualties.

A total of 4 rooms were demolished in neighbouring houses as a result of the Abou-Ghalyoun demolition. According to a sworn affidavit taken by al-Haq from one of the neighbours, one wall of their house measuring 10 meters long by 1.7 high, a gate 2 x 3 meters, 22 concrete steps, and another wall 5 x 1.7 meters were also destroyed. In addition, all the glass in the windows and doors of the house was shattered. The explosion also destroyed a dish cupboard and its contents, two video recorders, two television sets, and other items including chairs, a camera, and a closet.

SOURCE: Al-Haq Fact Sheet #2: House Demolitions in the Occupied Territories (forthcoming)

Appendix 4-E

HOUSE DEMOLITION CASE STUDY #2: JALAZON REFUGEE CAMP

On 3 August 1988, the IDF demolished the home of the al-Ramahi family in Jalazon Refugee Camp. Nine other homes, including three others in Jalazon were demolished on the same day.

The al-Ramahis had moved into the house only two months earlier. On 4 March, the military authorities sealed the families' former residence following the arrest of Mahmoud Mustafa 'Abdallah al-Ramahi, 45-years old and a journalist with *al-Fajr* newspaper. Mahmoud had been arrested on 7 November 1986 and accused by the military authorities of leading an armed cell. He was sentenced to five years in prison and a house-sealing order was issued against the al-Ramahi home. His 40-year-old wife and six children (ages 5-20) were only allowed use of the veranda. The armed cell had not been found responsible for any killings.

The al-Ramahi family, which was then living on the veranda, sought and obtained a permit from the United Nations Relief and Works Agency (UNRWA), which owns the land in Jalazon, to build living quarters on top of their sealed house. However, on 21 July 1987, the military government demanded that construction cease and charged Ayman al-Ramahi, the eldest of the children, with violating the sealing order. He has not yet been brought to trial.

The al-Ramahi family was in urgent need of decent housing because the health of Samah, the youngest of the children, who was only five years old, had begun to deteriorate the day the house was sealed and she had developed a serious medical condition. Samah was diagnosed as suffering from kidney failure and is forced to remain on kidney dialysis. In order to perform this procedure, minimal living conditions are needed, which include proper housing, running water and electricity and other sanitary needs, in order to obtain sterilisation.

Jonathan Kuttab, co-director of al-Haq, wrote to Dr. Ephraim Sneh, then head of the military government in the West Bank and himself a physician, asking that the sealing order be rescinded. The letter stated that it is crucial for the girl's health that she have at least minimal living conditions, and made an "urgent appeal to [Dr. Sneh] to authorize the unsealing of at least one room in the house of the Ramahi family [along with the bathroom and kitchen]...on humanitarian grounds in order to protect this 5-year-old girl from further unnecessary suffering." The letter was not answered until 13 weeks later (October 29), and contained only a brief statement that the request had been denied.

By this time the al-Ramahi family had succeeded in obtaining a new home in Jalazon Camp and Samah's minimum medical requirements were being attended to. However, in late June 1988, an 18-year-old son of the al-Ramahis, Ma'moun, was arrested on suspicion of throwing a molotov cocktail and was incarcerated in Dhahriya prison. Although he has not yet been charged and the authorities are not claiming that the molotov caused any casualties, the military government on August 3 ordered that the new al-Ramahi home be demolished.

During the demolition a scuffle broke out between the soldiers and the family. According to al-Haq's information all of the al-Ramahis were beaten and tear-gassed, including 5-year-old and ailing Samah, who was sprayed in the face with a hand-held canister. Mrs. al-Ramahi's identification papers were confiscated and then the house was demolished.

Mrs. al-Ramahi has since been to both the police station and the Civil Administration to retrieve her ID, but on both occasions was forcibly ejected from the building and told that people from Jalazon have no business coming to the government offices. The family is now again living in the veranda of their previous home, with all the risks to Samah's health and other discomfort that this entails.

SOURCE: Al-Haq Fact Sheet #2: House Demolitions in the Occupied Territories (forthcoming).

Appendix 4-F

HOUSE DEMOLITIONS CASE STUDY #3: JAMMALA VILLAGE

The two-story, eight-room house of Sabri 'Abdallah Abou-Kamesh, a 47-year old villager from Jammala in the Ramallah area, was dynamited by the Israeli armed forces on August 3, 1988. The residence, which had running water and electricity, was inhabited by 18 people: Sabri Abou-Kamesh, his wife, their 15 children, one of whom was born only hours before the demolition, and his 85-year old mother. According to the Israeli military authorities, the home was demolished because Sabri's son Ramadan, 21, is accused of throwing a molotov cocktail. It was not claimed that any injuries were caused. Additionally, Ramadan had not yet been charged or put on trial at the time of the demolition, and the Abou-Kamesh family was not notified of the demolition order until one hour before its execution.

In a sworn affidavit given at the al-Haq offices in Ramallah, Sabri Abou-Kamesh stated that a group of soldiers arrived at 1:00 a.m. while the village was under curfew and notified the family that they had 30 minutes to remove their possessions because the army intended to demolish the house. Only three neighbours were allowed to assist them. The soldiers left to first seal a different house and returned approximately one hour later. During this interval the family and neighbours were still unable to remove all their possessions from the home, including a storage cupboard, a refrigerator, various furniture, and kitchen appliances. In addition, many of the goods which were removed were placed at a short distance from the house to facilitate the rescue operation.

In the ensuing explosion the house and its remaining contents, along with a number of goods placed within the vicinity, were destroyed or irreparably damaged. Among the irretrievable items were 20 of 40 18-kilogram barrels of olive oil estimated at 25 Jordanian Dinars each (total worth approximately US$ 1,500.00), and 5 of 10 tons of wheat. These products were a main source of livelihood for the 18-member Abou-Kamesh family. The IDF left the family, including the 1-day old child and 85-year old grandmother, on the street to fend for themselves. They were eventually supplied with three tents by the International Committee of the Red Cross, but these will be sorely inadequate to protect the Abou-Kamesh family from the winter climate.

SOURCE: Al-Haq Fact Sheet #2: House Demolitions in the Occupied Territories.

Chapter 5

CURFEWS AND OTHER FORMS OF ISOLATION

One way in which the Israeli military authorities have attempted to control the current uprising in the Occupied Territories has been through the enforced isolation of population centres. Although the armed forces have claimed that measures such as curfews, closures, and sealings are necessary "to restore order" and for other unspecified "security reasons," al-Haq believes that the pattern of Israeli behaviour lends itself to a different interpretation altogether. Rather, as indicated by the unprecedented scope of these actions, the consistent use of violence and intimidation during their course, and the widescale interference with humanitarian relief which has maximised their deleterious effect, the main thrust behind the isolation policy has been to collectively punish the civilian population in order to wear down its opposition to the military government.

The purpose of this chapter is to discuss the various means employed by the Israeli authorities to isolate the civilian population of the Occupied Territories, and to examine the validity of these measures in the context of international law. Throughout, the aim is to give a general assessment supplied with illustrative examples rather than a comprehensive account. Additionally, violations of human rights often associated with isolation, such as beatings, arrests, house demolitions, economic sanctions, and medical care will not be investigated in any detail if they are discussed elsewhere in this report.[1]

A. Curfews

In the period between 9 December 1987 and 9 December 1988, the military government in the Occupied Territories imposed a minimum of 1,600 curfews on various locations in the West Bank and Gaza Strip.[2] Of these, an estimated minimum of 400 were prolonged curfews which were in force 24 hours a day and lasted from 3 to 40 days.[3] (All curfews referred to in this section are round-the-clock unless otherwise stated). The scope of the measure has meant that almost every one of the estimated 1.7 million Palestinian residents of these regions has been forcibly confined to their home on at least one occasion during the past year, and also that a clear majority have been subjected to prolonged curfew as well, in many cases repeatedly so. The effect has been not only a complete disruption of daily life and near-catastrophic economic losses, but also widespread hunger and medical emergency.

While it is perhaps not unusual for military regimes to resort to extreme measures of a collective nature and curfews in particular during periods of rebellion, its use by the armed forces in the Occupied Territories during the Palestinian uprising far surpasses anything that has been witnessed in similar situations in recent years. With few exceptions, on any given day at least 25,000 Palestinians have been involuntarily confined to their homes, and this figure has reached into the hundreds of thousands with persistent regularity. On several occasions, most notably during the period surrounding the 19th session of the Palestine National Council in Algiers and the proclamation of an independent Palestinian state (12-15 November 1988), in excess of one million people, including the entire population of the Gaza Strip, were under curfew.

This section examines the use of curfews by the military government in the Occupied Territories as it evolved from a disproportionate military response to demonstrations and stone throwing into an officially enunciated policy of collective punishment. First, however, the legal context and customary state practice is discussed in order to provide the proper criteria for an evaluation of Israel's use of this measure.

1. Curfews in International Law

While neither of the main instruments of international law pertaining to the conduct of occupying powers (the 1907 Hague Regulations and the Fourth Geneva Convention of 1949) mention curfews as such, there are clear provisions in these treaties as to what purposes enforced confinement may and may not serve. The general criterion, as with other practices not explicitly permitted or prohibited, is that the occupying power, irrespective of the legality of its presence, has a right to ensure the security of its own forces but also an obligation to respect the interests of the civilian population. In other words, as suggested by Article 43 of the Hague Regulations, the occupying power's actions must be balanced by these two paramount considerations and not determined by one to the exclusion of the other, lest they lose their validity under international law. To give an example, international law recognises the right of occupation forces to apprehend persons involved in armed resistance.

Thus, while a curfew imposed on a residential quarter immediately subsequent to a guerilla attack in order to facilitate arrests may be justified, it can not be extended for other purposes. To prolong a curfew in order to deter others from contemplating similar acts and punish an uncooperative civilian population, for instance, would be a clear disruption of the balance between security interests and the rights of the civilian population.

There are, however, also explicit formulations in international law relevant to this discussion. The most important of these relate to collective punishment. Article 50 of the Hague Regulations states that:

> No general penalty, pecuniary or otherwise, shall be inflicted upon the population on account of the acts of individuals for which they cannot be regarded as jointly and severally responsible.

This prohibition is expanded and clarified in the Fourth Geneva Convention. Article 33, which embodies the general principle with regard to such measures, is unambiguous and absolute:

> ...Collective penalties and likewise all measures of intimidation or of terrorism are prohibited. Pillage is prohibited. Reprisals against protected persons and their property are prohibited.[4]

The Convention goes on, with equally precise language, to detail a number of specific practices which may not under any circumstances be employed by the occupying authorities. As such, they have a direct bearing on the evaluation of the Israeli armed forces' conduct in enforcing curfews.

One set of articles (#'s 55-57, 59-63) concerns the mandatory provision of basic necessities to the general population, and to children and the medically infirm in particular. In effect, the authorities are bound by three sets of obligations:

(1) to ensure the normal supply and to facilitate the distribution of foodstuffs, medical supplies, and other essential items, and to ensure the normal functioning of medical personnel, services, and institutions;

(2) to supplement the provision and distribution of the above goods and services, and the maintenance of the above institutions, if they are inadequate; and,

(3) to unconditionally refrain from interference in any of the above, especially with respect to relief consignments.

In addition, the occupying authorities are also bound, except under extraordinary circumstances, to maintain the orderly functioning of the Red Cross/Red Crescent and other relief societies (Article 63); to "permit ministers of religion to give spiritual assistance to the members of their religious communities" (Article 58); and to refrain from "any destruction of real or personal property belonging individually or collectively to private persons...or to social or cooperative organizations" (Article 53).[5]

The point that while all civilians have a right of immunity from the actions of occupying powers some groups should be accorded special consideration, is in fact repeatedly made:

> The Occupying Power shall, with the cooperation of the national and local authorities, facilitate the proper working of all institutions devoted to the care and education of children...
>
> The Occupying Power shall not hinder the application of any preferential measures in regard to food, medical care and protection against the effects of war, which may have been adopted prior to the occupation in favour of children under fifteen years, expectant mothers, and mothers of children under seven years. (Article 50)

And finally, international law is replete with references which prohibit humiliation and other degrading treatment of civilians by soldiers.

Thus, curfews are from the outset subject to strict limitations from the point of view of international law. First and foremost, collective punishment is not a valid rationale, and in fact a flagrantly illegitimate one, for their imposition. Secondly, any valid security considerations that exist for forcibly confining civilian populations to their homes are explicitly limited by the occupation authorities' duty to ensure the maintenance of normal public life. Their use is therefore to be kept to a minimum both in terms of frequency and duration. And finally, curfews may never be used as a pretext to deny civilians the right to essential goods and services. As expressed by Jean Pictet, a leading commentator on international law and the principal authority on the Geneva Conventions:

> It must be emphasized that under no circumstances may the occupation authorities invoke reasons of security to justify the general suspension of all humanitarian activities in an occupied territory.[6]

2. *State Practice*

While curfews have been employed by governments throughout the world for a variety of reasons, they have virtually without exception been accorded the status of an extraordinary and temporary measure. As such, they most frequently occur during times of violent political upheaval, such as coups d'etat and other imminent threats to the survival of a regime, or during a state of emergency characterised by civil strife, looting, and vandalism.

Most frequently, a government will officially announce that it has issued an order forbidding people from leaving their homes during specified hours, such as dusk-to-dawn, warn people that they risk arrest or being shot if they venture outdoors, and call upon the armed forces to enforce the order. At the appointed hour, however, the curfew is lifted and public life is permitted to resume its normal course. While such conditions may be imposed for the most unjustifiable of reasons and create medical emergencies if no procedure is established to deal with them, they rarely persist for more than a few days and thus do not create unusual hardship for the general population.

In more extreme cases governments have issued 24-hour curfew orders, and at times renewed these for a limited number of days as well. Standard practice with round-the-clock curfews, however, is to provide a reprieve, usually of two hours, once a day. Additionally, because of the inherent difficulties posed by such conditions, efforts are often made, even by the most repressive of governments, to ensure the proper distribution of food, medicine, and other essential items, and to facilitate the activities of health personnel. The denial of basic utilities such as water and electricity during a curfew is rarely, if ever, even contemplated.

A review of contemporary state practice with regard to curfews clearly indicates that it is seen as a measure so extraordinary that it often follows the official announcement of a state of emergency by the head of state.[7] Furthermore, in a decade characterised by violent political upheaval, armed conflict and popular rebellion, there is no parallel to its use by the Israeli military authorities in the Occupied Territories. This becomes all the more revealing when one considers that the uprising has not been an armed conflict and that the military government has an almost complete monopoly on the use of armed force.

3. Israel's Use of Curfews in the Occupied Territories: 1967-1987

> ...On the second day [of the curfew], Saturday the 12th, which is a day of rest for labourers when they buy provisions for their household, some labourers tried to go to the stores to buy bread, kerosene, and milk, but the soldiers prevented them and ordered them to stay indoors. Anyone leaving the house had his identity card confiscated regardless of the motive for which he was leaving his house. The confiscation of the cards was also accompanied by attacks by the soldiers on the people by assaulting them, cursing and ridiculing them. This continued to be the case all day Saturday...[8]

One of the first acts taken by the Israeli armed forces command after the conquest of the West Bank in June 1967 was to place it under an indefinite 24-hour curfew which was only gradually lifted.[9] Over the years, enforced confinement has been routinely employed by the military authorities in their attempts to control the local population, and is in fact "one of the most common methods of collective punishment resorted to in the occupied territories."[10] The use of curfews has become particularly widespread since the late 1970's. Furthermore, throughout the occupation, no Jewish settlement has ever been placed under curfew. Whenever violence between the Palestinian and Jewish settler communities occurs, it has been standard practice to place the Arab locality involved under curfew, irrespective of the nature or place of the incident. Additionally, Jewish settlers have generally been permitted free access to roads leading through Palestinian population centres under curfew, while Palestinians are routinely denied this right.[11]

According to Chapter 6 (Article 89) of the "Order Concerning Security Regulations" (Military Order #378) of 1 May 1970, the authority to declare a curfew is vested in local military commanders. The penalty for violating curfews, as stipulated in Article 92 of the order (which has since been updated) consists of heavy fines, five years imprisonment, or both. Practically speaking, however, such penalties are never imposed. Although curfew violators have been prosecuted by the military authorities, they are more commonly subjected to arbitrary fines or beatings.

More seriously, throughout the first 20 years of occupation the armed forces failed to establish procedures to deal with emergencies which might occur during a curfew. In the context of a situation in which curfews have been used not as an extraordinary measure but rather as a policy instrument, and given that, as elsewhere, soldiers have the authority to shoot curfew violators, this has resulted in numerous avoidable casualties. Al-Haq considers this practice to constitute an extra-judicial form of punishment as well.

Whereas the Israeli authorities have maintained that curfews are imposed for "security reasons," "the pursuit of terrorists," and "the restoration of public order," there has in fact been a consistent pattern of extending curfews well beyond any period which could legitimately be justified as security related. Furthermore, the armed forces have taken measures against the captive population which clearly exceed their security interests. The following case, which concerns a 5-day curfew imposed on the twin cities of al-Bireh and Ramallah in April 1985 after a Jewish settler was shot dead in the central marketplace, was monitored by al-Haq:

Initially, the military authorities announced that the [total] curfew [imposed on 31 March] would be lifted on Wednesday 3 April, but it was then continued until further notice. The [approximately 40,000] inhabitants were allowed out of their homes for one hour on the third day and about two hours on the fifth day to enable them to do essential shopping...

[Al-Haq believes] that although there may have been a legitimate security reason for the imposition of the curfew and its maintenance until Monday 1 April, its continuance beyond this date served no security purpose but was a measure imposed in collective punishment of the population...

This conclusion was reached for the following reasons:

(1) Areas that had been tightly cordoned off were not then searched in detail, and from Monday 1 April there was no apparent attempt to further an investigation by systematic search or other use of the curfew.

(2) Access to and from substantial parts of the town was not effectively controlled and some individuals had been able to enter and leave without difficulty. The cordoning was thus not preventing either the escape of suspects or the entry of [Jewish vigilantes]...

On Thursday afternoon the curfew was officially lifted in the outer parts of the two cities, but it was still continued in the central "Manara" business area...

[At 4:00 p.m. on Sunday 7 April the curfew was finally lifted,] which just enabled the Christian population to celebrate part of Easter.

On lifting the curfew however the authorities issued 2-month closure orders against more than 20 shops in al-Bireh and Ramallah, the reason being that the shopowners had failed to assist them in identifying [suspects]. This justification is not convincing however, since from the information gathered by [al-Haq] most of the shopowners were not even questioned by the soldiers.[12]

After a 3-day curfew on the Ein Beit-al-Ma' Refugee Camp near Nablus in August of the same year following a bomb attack, al-Haq documented the following violations:

1: Random gunfire, beatings and insults against camp residents. Some soldiers even threw stones at residents.

2: All males over 14 were taken to the mosque courtyard and kept there the entire night; some were made to stand for hours with their hands raised while others were made to lie on the ground; cigarettes were taken from the men by the soldiers, torn up and thrown away; the men were forbidden to go to the toilet and were generally abused. The men's ID's were confiscated and many arrests were made.

3: While the men were being detained soldiers raided many houses, breaking windows and doors, terrorising the women and children, and insulting the dignity of the women.

4: When the men were finally released soldiers shot in the air in their direction, alarming both the men and their families who were waiting for them.[13]

While routine violations such as those described above may be viewed as coincidental to the imposition of a curfew because they result from the deliberate acts of the armed forces, prolonged curfews by their very nature incur irretrievable social and economic losses to the confined population. Children cannot attend school, wage-earners and shop-owners cannot travel to their workplaces, and agricultural workers are prevented from planting, harvesting, and otherwise tending to their fields and livestock. In addition, basic social services largely cease to function, and where larger towns and cities are involved, the outlying regions are often affected as well.

Between January and April of 1983, for instance, the town of Dhahriya lost 50 days worth of income and schooling as a result of various curfews.[14] In the West Bank during March of 1983 alone, more than two years prior to the introduction of the self-proclaimed "iron fist" policy, prolonged curfews of 10 days or more were imposed on 7 refugee camps and 2 towns, a combined population of at least 60,000. Furthermore, the Old City of Nablus was intermittently under curfew for a total of 14 days during that month.[15]

In addition to the above, the Israeli military has on many occasions magnified the effects of prolonged curfews by shutting off utilities and interfering with relief supplies.[16] This has had detrimental effects not only on infants and others requiring special care, but also on the nutrition and hygiene of the general population.

Thus, even before the beginning of the current uprising, a clear pattern could be discerned in which the military government imposed curfews, extended them, and took measures during them as a measure of collective punishment unrelated to any legitimate security concerns.

4. *The Policy of Curfews Since 9 December 1987*

With the entire Gaza Strip still under curfew [for the fourth successive day] at least one million Palestinians [in the Occupied Territories] were confined to their homes yesterday.[17]

When the uprising erupted in the Gaza Strip's Jabaliya Refugee Camp on 9 December 1987, it was immediately placed under a total curfew which was maintained for 8 consecutive days. By 13 January 1988, the date on which all eight Gaza refugee camps were simultaneously put under a 10-day curfew, the 64,000 residents of Jabaliya had already spent 22 days under enforced confinement. The 13,000 inhabitants of Balata Refugee Camp near Nablus, where the uprising began in the West Bank, were under curfew for 26 out of these 35 days.[18]

By the end of the first month of the uprising over half a million residents of the Occupied Territories in approximately 20 separate locations had been under prolonged curfew. Tens if not hundreds of thousands of others had been subjected to shorter periods of enforced confinement. Throughout the next 11 months the use of curfews, and particularly protracted ones, not only persisted, but became continually more widespread as the uprising came to involve every segment of Palestinian society. The Jalazon Refugee Camp near Ramallah, for example, spent 100 of the first 170 days of the uprising under curfew.

Enforced mass confinement for extensive periods of time has become so routine in the Occupied Territories that on 7 November 1988, in what constituted an advance notification of five days, the Israeli newspaper *HaAretz* reported that the military government intended to place all Gaza refugee camps and possibly Gaza City as well under curfew from 12-15 November.[19] In fact, as Palestinians had widely been anticipating, the entire Gaza Strip, with an estimated population of 700,000, was placed under a total curfew "until further notice" on the night of 11 November. It was not lifted until the morning of the 17th, making it the longest blanket curfew on the Gaza Strip since the beginning of the occupation. At the same time, as of 9 December 1988, all residents of the Gaza Strip have spent 262 consecutive nights under curfew. The measure was introduced on 14 March and was in effect from 10:00 p.m. to 3:00 a.m. With the revocation of Daylight Savings Time on 3 September, however, it has been in effect as of 9:00 p.m.

A daily register of prolonged curfews alone during the past year, compiled by researchers at al-Haq, found the following:

- 4 of the 8 refugee camps in the Gaza Strip (Bureij, Jabaliya, Nusseirat, and Shatti'), or approximately 150,000 people, spent a combined total of at least 520 days under prolonged curfew during the past year. This figure excludes, among others, most general strike days (now usually 1-2 days a week in the Gaza Strip) on which all eight camps are often curfewed by the armed forces.
- The entire Gaza Strip has been placed under a total curfew on 4

occasions during the first year of the uprising, for a total of 16 days.[20] In all, more than 60 percent of the the population of the Occupied Territories (almost 1,000,000 people), including the entire population of the Gaza Strip (700,000), Nablus and its surrounding refugee camps (125,000), Qalqiliya, the Tulkarem Refugee Camp, 'Anabta, and a number of other refugee camps and villages, have been under prolonged curfew at least 5 times. A number of these locations have been under prolonged curfew more than 10 times.

- Nablus, the largest city in the West Bank with a population of at least 100,000, spent more than 65, or approximately 1 out of every 5 days under total curfew during the first year of the uprising. Prolonged curfews were imposed for periods of 10, 7 (twice), 6, 5, and 4 (twice) days.
- The nearby Balata Refugee Camp was under prolonged curfew for a total of more than 130 days during the same period. If one adds the shorter curfews it is likely that this camp has been under curfew more often than not during the past year. Al-Haq estimates that the same is true for at least 3 other locations.
- Al-Haq recorded 118 continuous curfews of between 5 and 9 days, 48 of between 10 and 14 days, 13 of between 15 and 19 days, 7 of between 20 and 24 days, 4 of between 25 and 29 days, and 1 of 40 days. This comes to a total of between 1,545 and 2,305 total prolonged curfew days which only includes incidents exceeding 5 days. Expressed differently, the residents involved were subjected to a total of between 37,080 and 55,320 curfew hours, or between 4.2 and 6.3 years under curfew in the last annum.[21]
- At the upper ranges, more prolonged curfews were recorded between July and December 1988 than from December 1987 to June 1988.
- In the West Bank alone, more than 80 locations have been put under prolonged curfew during the past year. (As noted above, so has every location in the Gaza Strip.) On 16 January, 17 locations in the Occupied Territories were simultaneously under prolonged curfew. Between 17 and 24 April, 24 locations were simultaneously under prolonged curfew. As noted in the introduction, on 15 November, the day that Palestinian statehood was proclaimed, the entire Gaza Strip, all West Bank refugee camps, all major towns and cities except for al-Bireh/Ramallah, al-Khalil (Hebron), and East Jerusalem, in addition to a number of villages were under curfew.

There have also been numerous flagrant violations of international law and basic humanitarian standards by the Israeli armed forces during

curfews. Among those which have been the most common are the following:
- Indiscriminate opening of fire at residents found outside of their homes during curfew hours, resulting in death and injury. An al-Haq field worker stated that this practice should be viewed with special concern because there is no established emergency procedure which residents can utilise apart from making direct contact with an army patrol. Thus, if there is a situation requiring urgent action, such as a heart attack in the family, one is faced with a severe dilemma: to risk the death of a loved one for lack of treatment or one's own death by venturing outdoors to obtain assistance. In one 48-hour period (28-29 August) during a curfew in Nablus, the following 4 persons were shot and wounded for defying the curfew:

1. Bilal Shu'aibi, 42, "left his house to wait for an ambulance, after calling the vehicle to evacuate his 10-year old son who had tonsillitis and a fever…soldiers standing behind a metal door 120 meters away fired at him, though there were no clashes in the area."[22]

2. Jamal Qalbouna, 17, was shot "when he left his home to pick figs near his home."[23]

3. Marrah Kandilo, 9, "was shot in the leg when she rushed out of her home on Friday [the 28th] after mistaking an army announcement extending the curfew for a cancellation of the ban."[24]

4. "a 23-year old man was shot in the leg for violating the curfew."[25]

"'There is no shooting at curfew-breakers,' an IDF spokeswoman said [in reaction to the above incidents]."[26]
- Severe beatings and other forms of physical abuse inflicted on residents defying curfews.[27]
- Arbitrarily breaking into houses, smashing windows, destroying furniture and food, assaulting residents and causing serious bodily harm with clubs, gun-butts, fists, and boots, and carrying out mass arrests. By 24 January 1988, a mere 5 days after Defence Minister Yitzhak Rabin announced that his army was using a policy of "force, might, and beatings," 200 cases of broken limbs requiring casts had been reported in the Jabaliya Refugee Camp alone, which at the time was under curfew for the 12th day running.[28] In a rare public statement issued on 21 February 1988, Maurice Aubert, the Vice-President of the International Committee of the Red Cross in Geneva, protested that "hundreds of people have been subject to physical violence…particularly during curfews."[29]
- Mass roundups, which often include physical abuse, humiliating

and degrading treatment, and the confiscation of identity cards. Residents—usually males between the ages of 14 and 60—have been made to stand outdoors for most or all of the night, during which they are ordered to assume uncomfortable body-positions, physically harassed and beaten, and deprived of bathroom facilities, cigarettes, or warm clothing. Residents have also been ordered to chant slogans and sing songs in praise of the Israeli state, its army, and various elite units; curse Palestine, the Uprising, and various leaders of the national movement; and to physically assault and humiliate each other. Humiliation has also taken place inside homes. In one case documented by al-Haq in Deheisha Refugee Camp near Bethlehem on 27 June 1988, "soldiers ordered a child to spit on his mother or else they would run wild through the house."[30]

- Forbidding residents to open their windows or even the outside metal shutters. Despite such orders, soldiers have thrown toxic tear-gas canisters into homes. While medical facilities are inadequate to conclusively prove that the sustained inhalation of tear-gas in enclosed spaces by infants has resulted in their death, it is generally accepted that this has indeed been the case.[31]
- Refusing access to medical personnel. Obstructing the free passage of ambulances picking up or carrying casualties. Physically assaulting doctors and nurses. Interdicting medical supplies.[32]
- Preventing the delivery of food and other essential items, confiscating and/or destroying food or, alternatively, forcing residents to destroy it themselves. Preventing relief agencies from leaving emergency supplies at entrances so that they can be distributed by the armed forces.[33]
- Preventing women from going to neighbourhood ovens to bake bread, and spoiling their dough.[34]
- Cutting off the water and/or electricity supplies, severing telephone links, and interdicting fuel supplies. (It should be noted that most residents of the Occupied Territories use kerosene heaters and gas stoves.) The severing of electricity for extended periods of time has also caused refrigerated foods to spoil.[35]
- Denial of regular reprieves for residents to stock up on foodstuffs and other essential supplies. In a number of cases curfews have been in force an entire week or longer before being lifted for one or two hours. Since the summer of 1988, prolonged curfews are generally only lifted one to two hours a week. Even this, however, is not guaranteed. Often, the army announce such reprieves at unusual hours, only to reimpose the curfew at the slightest hint of a demon-

stration, shooting violators. Often, if curfews last less than a week, they are not interrupted at all.[36]
- Preventing sanitation work such as garbage collection, resulting in dangerous threats to the health and hygiene of a concentrated population already suffering from poor waste disposal facilities.
- Preventing residents from tending to their crops and livestock, even during reprieves, for the duration of the curfew.[37]
- Preventing domestic economic activity, such as the pressing of olives, by force.[38]
- Throwing tear-gas into chicken coops and other enclosed spaces holding domestic animals, resulting in their asphyxiation.[39]
- Shooting to pieces or smashing with clubs solar heating-panels and water tanks located on rooftops. Urinating and/or defacating into water tanks. Such incidents have been documented in, among other places, Nablus and its surrounding refugee camps, and the camps of al-Am'ari and Jalazon near Ramallah. According to a report filed by an al-Haq field worker, soldiers in the village of Beit 'Our-al-Tahta near Ramallah went so far as to throw tear-gas canisters into drinking water wells, and filled others with sand and mud.
- Confiscating cars and other private property.[40]
- The use of public buildings, particularly schools, as military barracks, prisons, and punishment centres, which often entails serious damage.[41]
- Sealing streets and entrances with cement-filled barrels or large earthen mounds. Erecting concrete walls or fences around refugee camps. These structures are either permanent or maintained for many months after the lifting of the curfew. During a curfew on Qalqiliya on 11 August 1988, 26 streets and alleys were blocked off by concrete barrels. In the al-Am'ari Refugee Camp near Ramallah 10 days later, the armed forces used the opportunity of a curfew to complete the sealing with cement barrels of every entrance to the camp, so that cars could no longer enter. At the Nur Shams Camp outside Tulkarem, soldiers erected a 6-meter high and 400-foot long metal fence, because the previous one had been repeatedly destroyed by the residents out of protest. It has since had to be re-erected as well.[42]
- Extending curfews until a community 'delivers' suspects to the armed forces or pays taxes and fines.[43]
- Unnecessary delays, or complete denials in the obtaining of permission to enter or leave a location under curfew irrespective of the humanitarian considerations.[44]

- The use of profane language by soldiers announcing curfews through loudspeakers: among the common insults directed at local residents have been "dogs," "sons of dogs," "sons of whores," and others which residents were too ashamed to repeat. Al-Haq field workers add that the Arabic word *manyac* ("butt-fucker") has become a standard term for soldiers when addressing the local population.
- The maintenance of an atmosphere of terror through random gunfire and the broadcast of shrieks, threats, sirens and profanities through loudspeakers, especially late at night.
- A ban on the presence of journalists and human-rights monitors, which gives the armed forces the freedom to pursue the above violations.[45]

In addition to the above, curfews have also resulted in ruined crops, depleted livestock, lost wages, and irredeemable missed schooldays. In the case of agriculture, crops have failed because farmers are prevented from planting, irrigating, or harvesting them within the required seasonal limits. Livestock has suffered similarly. Industrial and service workers who are employed outside the Occupied Territories have been prevented from travelling to their jobs. Shop owners have been hard hit by prolonged curfews because they already operate on reduced strike hours. Given the generally depressed economic state of the Occupied Territories during the uprising, these losses should be viewed with special concern.

The severity with which the Israeli armed forces have enforced these measures is indicated by the following affidavit, taken in November 1988 from 'Atallah Kuttab, a professor of Civil Engineering at Bir Zeit University:

> At approximately 12:00 noon on Tuesday 16 November 1988 a colleague of mine and I went to the 'Arroub Refugee Camp near al-Khalil (Hebron) in the Israeli-occupied West Bank to inspect a sewage project. When I arrived at 'Arroub there was no army checkpoint at the entrance or any other visible military presence in the camp, and I was surprised to note that the streets of the camp, which are usually very busy, were deserted. When I got approximately halfway into the camp, I suddenly noticed a group of soldiers who were at an observation point on top of a building yelling at me and motioning that I should leave. I asked them to come down because I couldn't understand anything they were saying. While I was involved in this exchange with the soldiers, my colleague, who was in a separate car, pulled up next to me. As he was waiting, a young man opened a window to what appeared to

be a small shop and began pleading with us to save him. He told us that he had to go to the Augusta Victoria Hospital in Jerusalem for medical tests, showed us an official form to this effect, and stated that he had been imprisoned in the shop, a bread-bakery, for three days, and that the camp was under curfew. At this point the soldiers arrived and began threatening the young man. I intervened and asked the soldiers what the problem was. The officer in charge said that the camp was under curfew and that the young man had broken the law, but refused to be more specific, telling me I should ask the young man for further details. I did, and he told me that three days ago, during the curfew, he had been caught by the soldiers selling bread to the residents of the camp in violation of specific orders to the contrary, and that he had therefore been severely beaten, instructed to lock himself in the store and not attempt to sell anything again, and then beaten again on several other occasions. My colleague, who is an American, turned to the soldiers and said: "You did this to him for selling bread," to which the officer in charge responded, "That's a good way to put it." After this I expressed my intention to take the young man to the hospital, pointing out that he was not only sick, showing them the form from the hospital, but that he had been severely beaten as well. The officer in charge told me that he would arrange for a local doctor to treat him, even though the form stated that his tests should be performed at a hospital. At the suggestion of being returned to the custody of the soldiers the young man became hysterical, stating that he refused to be left at their mercy and preferred to be sent directly to prison. The officer in charge gave his personal assurances that there would be no further beatings, but the young man was unconvinced and continued to insist that if he could not come with us he should be sent to prison immediately. At this point an UNRWA vehicle arrived at the scene and we were able to convince the soldiers to allow it to take the young man to the hospital. We made certain, however, that the UNRWA car actually got past the entrance of the camp. Once we were outside 'Arroub, the young man asked us for our telephone numbers in case the army came to get him that night.[46]

The scope with which the military government has pursued its curfews policy can leave no doubt as to the deliberate use of this measure as an instrument of collective punishment. This is all the more so if one considers that during such times, food, medicine, water, electricity, and the economic livelihood of hundreds of thousands of residents have intentionally been wielded by the Israeli authorities as a weapon with which to combat the civilian population. Clearly, any regime which consciously withholds supplies of milk from infants, prevents the sick from going to hospitals, and determines that the elderly should spend weeks in the bitter cold for lack of kerosene is guilty of a most calculated form of cruelty. For it is not that these supplies are not available and the Israelis are being asked to fulfill their obligations under international law and supply them; to the contrary, they have been arriving in plentiful supplies wherever curfews are being imposed, only to be turned back or destroyed at army checkpoints.

International relief organisations have in fact repeatedly protested to the Israeli authorities about the obstruction of their mission both by the curfews themselves and additional measures taken by the armed forces. On 20 January, for example, UNRWA spokesperson Maher Nasser stated that "curfew is the primary obstacle" facing his organisation's food, medical, and child nutrition relief programmes, and reported "an acute food shortage" in the refugee camps of the Gaza Strip.[47] As he was speaking, all eight camps in Gaza were under a simultaneous total curfew for the ninth successive day while one of them, Khan Yunis, had been sealed for two weeks. Furthermore, that same day the armed forces interdicted four trucks carrying food relief intended for the estimated 250,000 residents of the camps.[48] Rejecting persistent reports of severe food and water shortages and blanket power cuts, Defence Minister Rabin simply stated that "there are ample supplies of whatever is needed by the population" and that it was in any case "contradictory" for Palestinians to complain about shortages while continuing commercial strikes (which by definition do not occur in locations under curfew).[49] On 17 April, during the 32nd day of a 40-day curfew on the Jalazon Refugee Camp near Ramallah, an UNRWA convoy was turned back by the army on the pretext that the food "could trigger further unrest." During this curfew, the longest thus far reported in the Occupied Territories, electricity supplies were cut, medical personnel were harassed before being allowed to enter the camp, and residents reported to al-Haq staff members that they had to burn their own furniture because of fuel shortages created by army interdictions.

During January, when the armed forces were still often allowing residents under curfew a reprieve of one hour every day or two, UNRWA was already encountering serious difficulties. As Maher Nasser stated:

> The lifting of the curfews for one hour every 24 hours is not enough for people to buy food [or obtain other necessities]. In some camps only women are allowed to leave the camps. In others no one is allowed to go out of the camp during this hour. Take Jabaliya Refugee Camp as an example. There are 52,000 refugees living there. No one could believe it possible that in one hour all these people could buy what they need.[50]

Since then, however, the situation has become much worse, and it is currently a general rule that curfews are at best only lifted for one to two hours every 3 days, but often less frequently. After a 28-day curfew on the Tulkarem Refugee Camp and the adjacent village of Dhannaba from 2 to 30 September, for instance, an al-Haq field worker report stated that the curfew had only been lifted twice for a period of two hours each during the entire period.

The Israeli authorities have repeatedly expressed their intention to use curfews as an instrument of pacification. As early as 13 January, the date on which all eight Gaza camps were simultaneously curfewed, the Israeli cabinet, according to the *Jerusalem Post*, "approved IDF proposals...[which included] the expanded use of curfews...It is understood that the IDF has found that curfews are highly effective in quelling disturbances, especially in refugee camps."[51] Several days later, Minister of Defence Rabin stated that "I would rather see photos of curfew than photos of shootings, burning tires, and Molotov cocktails." On 25 January Rabin elaborated further:

> The combination of curfew, of taking the initiative, and of the use of physical force...have brought about calm and left the impression that we wanted: a renewal of fear from the power of the IDF.[52]

By 8 February, Police Minister Haim Bar-Lev was publicly advocating what had in fact already become government policy:

> One way [to control the population] is to close the areas for two, three, four days or more if need be and see if afterwards the people will feel like doing these things.[53]

Also in January, the power to declare curfews, previously invested in military commanders, was devolved to the senior officer present.[54]

Some Israelis have claimed that curfews are in fact a humanitarian measure because they remove the 'necessity' for more severe actions. For instance, on 4 November 1988, during a lecture at the Kings College Faculty of Law in London University, Yoram Dinstein, the dean of Tel Aviv Law School and the editor of the "Israeli Yearbook of Human Rights" stated that he had personally suggested the expanded use of curfews in order to avoid further violations of international law and human rights. Such assertions, however, provoke serious doubts, given both the scope of the measure and the veritable plethora of gross transgressions which have occurred during curfews.[55]

The Israeli government has clearly been using curfews as a policy and an instrument of collective punishment. In the course of its application, clear and repeated breaches of international law and humanitarian standards have been the rule rather than the exception, to the point that al-Haq can only conclude that these violations are themselves an integral component of the policy. This is all the more serious in view of the fact that the Israeli authorities have made a common practice out of what is intended to be an extraordinary measure. As the uprising enters its second year there is every indication and every reason to believe that the situation will deteriorate yet further.

B. Closures

According to Chapter 6 (Article 90) of the "Order Concerning Security Regulations" (Military Order #378) proclaimed by the military government in the Israeli-occupied West Bank on 1 May 1970:

> (A) A military commander may by order declare any area or place to be a closed area for the purposes of this order. Any person who, during any period in which any such order is enforced in relation to any area or place, enters that area or place or leaves the same without a permit in writing issued by or on behalf of a military commander or by means of a permit issued on the basis of a false declaration shall be guilty of an offence under this order.
>
> (B) Any person who enters an area or place closed in accordance with sub-paragraph (A) without a permit in writing issued by or on behalf of a military commander or pursuant to a permit issued on the basis of a false declaration, or remains in the area or place at the expiration of the validity of such permit or in contravention of its conditions may be removed from such area or place by any soldier.

Furthermore, Article 94 ("Burden of Proof") states that

> It shall be upon any person charged in connection with an offence under the security regulations to prove that his case comes within any exemption, allowance or right which he pleads or that he is in possession of any licence, permit, consent or authorisation.

As with curfews, the authority to declare closed military areas was devolved in January to the senior officer present.

Due to the frequency with which closures have been imposed, their exact number is impossible to determine. Al-Haq estimates, however, that they reach into the thousands, for the following reasons:

- Observations by staff members, field workers, and journalists that closed military areas are declared more frequently than curfews, and press reports indicating the same.

- The tendency to declare any area where demonstrations, army raids, or visible violations of international law and human rights are occurring a closed military area. (This has especially been the case since the decision in January to restrict press coverage of the uprising.)
- The outfitting of soldiers with ready-to-use closed military area forms.

During the uprising, closures (the majority of which have been of relatively short duration) have become part of the standard working conditions for journalists. And on several occasions the Occupied Territories in their entirety have been sealed from the outside world by military order, as was most recently the case from 31 October to 2 November and 11-17 November 1988. The military order closing the Occupied Territories stated no reason. On other occasions, the military authorities have justified this violation of press freedom on the grounds that the media has incited residents to demonstrate against the occupation. Yet, to the best of al-Haq's knowledge, during the first year of the uprising, no television crew was present to film the killing of a Palestinian by the army, indicating their general absence at the scenes of the most violent confrontations. (See also section D on restrictions on the press below.)

Palestinians have, however, been killed when closed military areas were in effect, a fact which substantiates al-Haq's concern that such conditions present the armed forces with clear opportunities to conceal their practices against the civilian population, especially if a curfew is simultaneously declared. This is especially the case with prolonged closed military zones, which have no security rationale whatsoever.

During prolonged closures, at least as many of which have been informal (referred to as "sieges" by the local population), the army erects checkpoints or physical barriers at the entrances to the location, and although residents are permitted to venture outdoors within the area affected (subject to arbitrary restrictions), the army usually prevents the entry of foodstuffs and other essential items and prohibits workers, farmers, and others from leaving, even if only to attend to their fields. Violations which occur during closures are similar to those during curfews, although there is a larger emphasis on arrests, mass roundups, and economic punishments. And while protracted closures are probably less frequent than prolonged curfews, they tend to be longer in duration. Some examples:
- Qabatiya (Jenin District): was sealed ("under siege") from 24 February to 3 April 1988 (41 days). During the closure, water and electricity

was cut, all telephones were disconnected, nothing was allowed in or out, and the armed forces repeatedly raided homes, brutalising residents, vandalising property, and destroying food supplies. In addition, over 120 people were arrested, and the town was intermittently placed under curfew. "The scene," stated one commentator, "cannot escape comparison with that of U.S. General Philip Sheridan ordering his troops to starve out the native Americans and 'attack their commissaries.'"[56]

- Silat al-Harithiya (Jenin District): 8 March to 12 April (36 days).
- Yamoun (Jenin District): 9 March to 12 April (37 days).
- Qalqiliya (Tulkarem District): 16 March to 10 April (26 days). Qalqiliya was also subjected to several other prolonged closures.

C. Other Forms of Isolation

a. Sealings:

Throughout the Occupied Territories, the armed forces have sealed streets, alleyways, and entrances to refugee camps and villages. In most refugee camps, all but one entrance has been sealed by concrete-filled barrels, and in many cases a large fence or concrete wall has been erected as well. In 'Askar Refugee Camp near Nablus, for example, twelve out of thirteen entrances have been sealed. Between 1 March and 19 May 1988, a much-reduced staff of al-Haq field workers recorded more than 70 incidents of sealing in the West Bank alone. The practice has had a real effect on the civilian population concerned, which must often make long and cumbersome detours for even the most menial errand. More seriously, in a number of locations, it now takes much longer to transport patients to hospitals than before because ambulances must take roundabout roads. On 10 March 1988, the day after Najih Jamil Hijaz was shot to death by Jewish settlers in the village of Turmus 'Ayya near Ramallah, the army sealed the main access road to the village with large boulders. After this action, the residents were left with only one road, which leads straight past the neighbouring Jewish settlement, from which to enter and leave the village.

b. Disconnection of water and electricity supplies:

Often, such actions are so unmistakably taken to collectively punish the civilian population that no justifications are even offered. On other occasions, the Israeli authorities have stated that they disconnect water and electricity supplies only because residents have not been paying their bills. However, as in other countries, Palestinians subscribe to their water and electricity supply on an individual rather than communal basis. Thus, to shut off these utilities in a collective manner without the normal procedure of individual notification, and then to disconnect people without arrears as well, raises serious questions about the actual motivations underlying the armed forces' actions. Additionally, on other occasions the military government has ordered privately-owned companies to disconnect clients from their electricity grid. This was the case, for instance, in the village of Sa'ir near Hebron (March 1988), which has its own generator. Similarly, the Jerusalem District Electricity Company, a private, Palestinian-owned company, has on many occasions been ordered to disconnect subscribers both within Jerusalem (*e.g.* Jabel Mukabber on 7 February 1988) and in the Ramallah District, which it also serves (eg. the villages of Deir Abou-Mish'al and Deir al-Sudan, both near Ramallah, in April). On other occasions, as for example during the convention of the 19th session of the Palestine National Council in Algiers from 12-15 November 1988, the electricity was disconnected in the entire Gaza Strip and large areas of the West Bank. Such cutoffs have also been prolonged, as in the town of Qabatiya near Jenin which was left without electricity for 4 months after residents killed a collaborator on 24 February. By any legal or humanitarian standard, the disconnection of essential utilities is a clearly unacceptable practice which no justification can rationalise.

c. Severing of telecommunications:

Since 16 March 1988 all international telecommunications to and from the Occupied Territories have been cut. Local telecommunications have been cut for prolonged periods of time in selected locations as well, and all communications links in the West Bank and Gaza Strip have been severed on a number of occasions, most recently from 11-17 November.

In reaction to the disconnection of international telecommunications in March al-Haq issued the following press release:

> The decision by the Israeli government to sever all [international] telephone links to the West Bank and Gaza except on Israeli settlements as of March 16, 1988 is bound to increase the incidence of human rights violations and delay the quick and effective intervention by international human rights organizations. This action is viewed by al-Haq as yet another attempt at closing the area and preventing the dissemination of information about what is occurring here.
>
> The official justification for this action given by the authorities was to prevent coordination between the PLO [Palestine Liberation Organisation] outside and the Palestinian leadership within the Occupied Territories. Al-Haq does not accept this justification since

such communication can continue through Jerusalem and Israel.

Al-Haq is already suffering from this restriction. Before March 16, the organisation made regular telephone contacts with several international human rights organisations amongst which were Amnesty International and the International Commission of Jurists in Geneva. This is no longer possible.

To the extent that quick communication of imminent violations is the most effective means at our disposal to stop such violations, the organisation has been deprived of this tool. In the past, outside knowledge of what is happening here and interventions of international human rights organisations have been, in our opinion, of extreme significance.

The cutting of telephone links is also affecting a large portion of the population with family members outside, who, because of the current situation need to be in contact with their relatives to assure them about their safety and well-being. A society which has been divided in 1948 and 1967 and where applications for family reunion are rarely granted has a large proportion of its members scattered around the globe.

This latest measure is viewed by al-Haq as another attempt at making life for Palestinians living in the [Occupied Territories] yet more intolerable.

On 2 October 1988, the military government extended the disconnection of international telecommunications until 9 April 1989. The Israeli authorities have stated that persons who want their international telephone lines reconnected can apply for a permit to this effect from the military government. The offer, however, has met with little or no response. As with the rest of the permit system in the Occupied Territories, their availability has been completely politicised by the authorities, and Palestinians have refused to grant the armed forces yet another carrot and stick with which to control their lives. And furthermore, while perhaps not a right in the strict sense of the term, access to an existing communications network intended for public use should certainly not be treated as a select privilege.

D. Restrictions on the Press

In addition to the above methods of isolating communities, either as a punishment or to bar access to outsiders, including the press and human-rights monitors, the Israeli military authorities have taken steps against the local and foreign media to obstruct the free flow of information. The most salient of these steps include:

(1) the detention, usually administrative, or deportation of Palestinian journalists and correspondents, especially those who work for or transmit information to foreign journalists and press agencies;

(2) the temporary or permanent closure of Palestinian press agencies who transmit information from the various localities in the Territories to foreign journalists;

(3) censorship of articles in the local press and the banning of the publication or distribution of daily papers for defined periods of time;

(4) harassment, including beating and withdrawing of press credentials, of journalists, and closing areas to the media;

(5) using journalism as a cover to enter localities and make arrests, thereby raising doubts among Palestinians about the integrity of journalists, who consequently are hampered in their important work.

Common throughout the twenty-one years of military occupation, the detention of journalists without charges or trial has increased drastically during the uprising. During the first year of the uprising, at least twenty Palestinian journalists and correspondents from the Territories were placed in administrative detention.[57] The detainees included Radwan Abou-'Ayyash, the head of the Arab Journalists Association in East Jerusalem; Salah al-Zuhayka, the editor of the daily *al-Sha'ab*; Ahmad Abou-Lashin, who runs the Gaza Press Service; editors and journalists with the various newspapers and magazines, like Mutawakkel Taha, the literary editor at *al-Awda* magazine; correspondents working for foreign press agencies, like Sam'an Khouri, who is employed by Agence France Press; and correspondents for *al-Sha'ab*, *al-Fajr*, *al-Quds* and other dailies, weeklies and press agencies in Nablus, Tulkarem, Jenin, Hebron and other towns and villages, like Na'im Tubassi, the Ramallah correspondent of *al-Sha'ab*.

Several journalists have been ordered deported: Ghassan al-Masri, a reporter for *al-Awda* magazine; Bashir Nafe', a reporter for *al-Fajr* daily; Jibril al-Rujoub, an editor with *Abir* magazine and Samir Sbeihat, an editor of *al-Fajr* daily. In addition, a number of journalists have been banned from travelling since the beginning of the uprising.

Since the beginning of the uprising, the authorities have also closed down a number of Palestinian press agencies. The largest of the press agencies, the Palestine Press Service (PPS) in East Jerusalem, was closed down for a period of 6 months on 31 March 1988 by order of the Military Commander of the Central Area. The order was renewed for a year on 30 September. The PPS, which is owned by Raymonda Tawil and Ibrahim Kara'in, had been one of the foreign press's key sources of information about events in the Territories. Its work consisted of processing information from a wide variety of sources, including its own correspondents, and transmitting this information quickly to subscribers. Foreign journalists in particular valued this resource, and indeed it enabled on-the-spot coverage of events which otherwise would not have been exposed until much later.

Other press offices that have been closed during the uprising include: the Gaza Press Office (owner: Ahmad Abou-Lashin), closed for 6 months on 26 January; the Office of Press Services in Gaza (owner: Hassan al-Wahidi, closed for 1 year on 26 January; the Bethlehem Press Office (owner: Jawdat Mana'), closed for 3 months on 14 March; and the al-Haya information and publishing office of Nabil al-Julani, closed on 28 August for 1 year. In addition, the Israeli *Derekh HaNitzotz/Tariq al-Sharara* Hebrew and Arabic weekly in West Jerusalem was closed down by the authorities on 18 February; its Israeli Jewish editors currently face charges for allegedly offering services to a banned organisation, while its Palestinian editor, Ribhi Arouri, spent six months in administrative detention.

In addition, the military authorities have continued their practice of censorship, rampant long before the beginning of the uprising, and the banning of the publication or distribution of daily newspapers and periodicals.[58] To give only a few examples: the daily *al-Fajr* was banned from distribution for 10 days on 11 December 1987, for 14 days on 17 April 1988, and for 45 days on 16 September; the daily *al-Sha'ab* was banned from publication for 7 days on 15 February; the daily *al-Quds* was banned from distribution for 1 month on 23 December 1987, and again for 45 days on 22 January 1988.

All the above measures are effected on the basis of the obsolete British Defence (Emergency) Regulations 1945 (see the forthcoming report on this issue by al-Haq) or, in the case of administrative detention, of Military Order 378 (which has incorporated and replaces the relevant section in the Defence Regulations).

Administrative detention is detention without charges or trial for renewable periods of six months. Although detainees have the right to appeal to a military appeals committee, the authorities routinely deny them and their lawyers access to the evidence that the authorities claim exists against them. In the absence of open evidence presented in an open trial, the burden is shifted onto the detainee to prove that he is innocent; however, in the absence of clear charges, the detainee is effectively denied the chance to defend himself.

The standard justification used by the authorities to detain journalists or close press agencies is that these journalists are members of banned organisations and that the press offices are fronts for such organisations. However, because the authorities resort to administrative procedures, they do not have to provide evidence for these allegations, and in fact never do.

At other times, the authorities have banned journalists from filming particular incidents, or have confiscated film, notebooks and equipment,[59] or have restricted journalists' access to locations by producing a military closure order[60] In one particular example, in Rafah in the Gaza Strip, television crews were reportedly barred from filming an apparent beating by soldiers of a boy who had been arrested.[61] The *Jerusalem Post* reported about its own correspondents in the Territories on 1 January 1988:

> This paper's defence reporter, Joshua Brilliant, asked to join soldiers on patrol, and was twice refused. When he tried to speak informally with soldiers at a roadblock in Kalkilya, a lieutenant ran up and cut the conversation short. Soldiers have placed hands in front of television cameras, and reporters have been barred from zones of IDF operation. It is as if the army which had no hesitation about reporters accompanying it to Beirut has something to hide about its behaviour in the territories.

In addition, on at least two occasions during the past year the Israeli authorities have suspended the press credentials of foreign journalists who failed to submit their stories to the military censor. On 26 April, the authorities suspended the credentials of Glenn Frankel, the correspondent of *The Washington Post*, and Martin Fletcher, the NBC correspondent in Israel and the Territories, for not submitting their stories on the assassination of Khalil al-Wazir (Abou-Jihad) by Israeli commandos to the military censor. On 25 October, the government suspended the press credentials of Paul Taylor and Steve Weizman of Reuters and Andrew Whitley, the correspondent of *The Financial Times*, for not submitting stories about the existence of Israeli "death squads" eliminating Palestinian leaders in the Occupied Territories to the military censor.[62]

Occasionally, journalists have been beaten by soldiers,[63] and in one case, an American journalist, Neal Kassidy, was injured by a soldier's bullet in Nablus on 18 October. On 14 June, the Foreign Press Association in Israel and the Occupied Territories issued a strong protest against army and police beatings and harassment of journalists, and its chairperson, Robert Slater of *Time* magazine, stated that he had received reports of between 100 and 150 incidents of harassment and beating of foreign journalists since the beginning of the uprising. In the words of Slater:

Israel is not the only country in the world where the foreign press is under attack. But it is shocking to imagine that this country in particular, because of an atmosphere produced and nurtured by public and military officials, has seen fit to turn against us physically and verbally.[64]

Finally, al-Haq has received reports that Israeli intelligence agents have posed as journalists in order to penetrate camps and villages and make arrests. ABC News, for example, claimed that Shin Bet agents had impersonated ABC News personnel to make an arrest in the village of Salfit at the end of June.[65] The authorities have denied that the incident happened, or that this was official policy.[66] Although it is difficult to determine conclusively that the Shin Bet has in fact used the cover of journalism to effect arrests, the frequency of reported incidents strongly suggests that this may indeed be the case. Regardless, the phenomenon has been reported so widely that it has raised suspicions among the population about journalists, especially foreign and Israeli journalists, blocking the latter's access to villages and camps in the Territories, and hence diminishing their role in monitoring human rights abuses.

The obstruction of the out-going flow of information hints at a motive on the part of the authorities of wanting to prevent public knowledge of violations of human rights in the Territories. On more than one occasion, the authorities have expressed dismay at Israel's poor image in world opinion due to the actions of the Israeli army in the West Bank and Gaza.[67] On more than one occasion, the media have been blamed for abetting the uprising.[68] Rather than dealing with the violations directly, the authorities appear to have attempted, increasingly after February 1988, to cover up their occurrence, by detaining journalists and closing press offices, and by deterring foreign journalists from visiting areas in the Territories.

As for the obstruction of incoming information, it appears that the authorities have tried to minimise the impact of events relevant to the Palestine question occurring outside the Occupied Territories, such as the assassination of Khalil al-Wazir (Abou-Jihad) in April and the declaration of an independent Palestinian state on 15 November. However, because practices like censorship and the banning of papers do not effectively block the flow of information, since Palestinians can tune in to foreign radio stations and since underground forms of communication have thrived throughout the uprising, censorship and banning orders seem to be designed more as a way of asserting control than as a method of interdicting the flow of information. As such, these practices constitute a form of punishment not otherwise justifiable on security grounds.

E. Harassment of Human Rights Monitors

On 27 November 1988 the *Jerusalem Post* reported that

> UN officials sought permission to visit the territories [the West Bank and Gaza Strip] on November 10, but to date they have not received a reply to their request.[69]

Another United Nations body, the Special Committee to Investigate Israeli Practices Affecting the Human Rights of the Population of the Occupied Territories, has been denied permission to enter the West Bank and Gaza Strip since it was first established.

While such forms of obstruction of human rights monitors by the Israeli authorities are common, there have been more serious violations as well. During the past year, a number have been imprisoned without charge or trial, including 6 members of al-Haq's staff; 2 field workers from the Jerusalem-based Palestine Human Rights Information Center (PHRIC), 'Adli Yazuri and Ya'coub 'Odeh; aGaza defence lawyer with a well-established record in defence of political prisoners, Raji Sourani; and the Vice-President of the Gaza Bar Association, Yunis Ahmad al-Jarrou. Among the other forms of harassment, the PHRIC, for example, reported the confiscation of three of its field workers' ID cards for extended periods of time, during which the individuals could not effectively go about their work and had to report to the authorities on a daily basis, at which time they were subjected to physical and other forms of abuse. Additionally, PHRIC field workers have been taken into custody for interrogation and singled out at army checkpoints.

The harassment of al-Haq began during the first 10 days of the uprising when, on 18 December 1987, Ghazi 'Afif Muhammad Shashtari, a field worker for the Nablus District who has been with the organisation since 1983, was taken from his home by Israeli soldiers and intelligence agents at 2:00a.m. After spending a week in Nablus prison, during which the authorities denied having him in their custody and refused to give al-Haq, his lawyers or family any information of his whereabouts, Shashtari was moved to the al-Fara'a detention centre, where he was kept for an additional 18 days before being served with a six-month administrative detention order on 6 January 1988. When the military government opened the Ansar III military detention centre, Shashtari was transferred to it and there served out his administrative detention order. On 20 June 1988, the order was renewed for an additional six months. An appeal against the order was filed on 22 June but not acted upon until 23 August, when the case was heard without prior notification of Shashtari's lawyers, who could therefore not be present, and the appeal was subsequently rejected. On 20 December 1988, by which time Ghazi Shashtari will have spent more than one year in custody without charge or trial, his administrative detention order will come up for renewal a second time. Al-Haq has received no indication whatsoever as to how the military government will proceed in this matter.

In March 1988, 3 additional al-Haq field workers, 'Abd-al-Karim Ahmad Kana'an, Sha'wan Ratib 'Abdallah Jabarin, and Zahi 'Abd-al-Hadi Jaradat were arrested, served with six-month administrative detention orders, and taken to Ansar III. Kana'an and Jaradat were beaten during their apprehension by Israeli soldiers, and Kana'an could not be located by his lawyers until two weeks after his arrest. Similarly, when al-Haq staff members went to Ansar III in May to locate Jabarin, the prison authorities denied that he was there:

> On our first attempt to visit Sha'wan Jabarin, the prison authorities denied that he was in the prison at all. He was eventually brought to us on our second visit, when we refused to leave the prison until we saw him. The explanation was that we had failed to give his prisoner number; his full name, identity card number and date of detention were insufficient to identify him in Ansar III, where he is simply prisoner No. 3506.[70]

On 8 September Jabarin and Jaradat's detentions were extended for an additional six months until 8 March 1989. Eleven days later, on 19 September, Kana'an was released. Then, on 18 October, Iyad 'Ali Muhammad al-Haddad, a part-time al-Haq field observer for the Ramallah area, was arrested and taken to the Dhahriya detention centre near Hebron. Although by press time neither al-Haq nor his family and lawyer have been able to find out the exact status of his imprisonment, his current detention in Ansar III strongly suggests that he has been served with an administrative detention order.

Most recently, at 1:00 a.m. on 19 November, a group of approximately 10 soldiers entered the apartment of al-Haq researcher Riziq Shuqeir in al-Bireh and arrested him. When he demanded that he be told what he was being taken in for, according to his wife, he was informed that he had been served with an order of administrative detention. It so happened that al-Haq field worker 'Abd-al-Karim Kana'an, who had been released exactly two months earlier, was spending the night at Shuqeir's house because he did not want to drive home to Tulkarem late at night after attending a wedding in East Jerusalem. When the soldiers became aware of his presence in the apartment, and even though they did not know who he was and carried no warrant for his arrest, they apprehended him as well. Two days later he was served with another six-month administrative detention order. As for Shuqeir, it was only on 27 November, after a special request was made to the International Committee of the Red Cross, that he was located in the Dhahriya detention centre near Hebron. At press time, nothing had yet been revealed by the authorities about his status.

The al-Haq employees detained by the military regime have neither been charged with any offence against the law nor put on trial. Instead, the authorities have made vague accusations against them and refused to substantiate any of their allegations in a court of law. Furthermore, as pressure on the Israeli government has increased world-wide in this affair, accusations have been made against al-Haq itself. For instance, in response to an inquiry by United States Senator Mark O. Hatfield, Israel's ambassador to the United States Moshe Arad, in a letter dated 11 July 1988, intimated that the organisation is a PLO front masquerading as an affiliate of the International Commission of Jurists and stated that "most of its members are supporters of 'Fatah' and other factions of the PLO terrorist organization." He then went on to accuse the field workers in question of being activists in the Popular Front for the Liberation of Palestine (PFLP) and Democratic Front for the Liberation of Palestine (DFLP). In lieu of the sentencing and convictions which do not exist, the Ambassador also attempted to indict the individuals in question by presenting their previous prison records as incontrovertible proof of their wrong-doing. However, not only did much of his evidence itself consist of previous administrative detentions and other forms of imprisonment without charge or trial, but the implication that individuals should serve two separate sentences for the same offence is unacceptable.

From the outset, al-Haq has stated that its employees were imprisoned for their human rights activities unless the contrary is proven in a court of law. In the absence of any charge, public evidence, or fair trial, it continues to demand their immediate and unconditional release. A growing international consensus stands behind this contention, and both Ghazi Shashtari and Zahi Jaradat have been adopted as "Prisoners of Conscience" by Amnesty International. In May, Shashtari was also designated Amnesty International's "Prisoner of the Month," and the cases of al-Haq's human rights defenders are addressed in forthcoming reports by Human Rights Watch and the Lawyers Committee for Human Rights, both in New York.

FOOTNOTES TO CHAPTER 5

1. The documentation for this chapter consists of affidavits taken by al-Haq field workers in accordance with internationally accepted standard rules of evidence, written field worker reports submitted after rigorous on-scene interviews with residents involved, material collected by al-Haq staff members, published academic and professional texts, and, lastly, press reports.
2. This and subsequent figures are derived from a daily register of prolonged curfews in force in the Israeli-occupied West Bank and Gaza Strip since the beginning of the uprising on 9 December 1988. The list, PROLONGED CURFEWS IMPOSED BY THE ISRAELI ARMED FORCES DURING THE FIRST YEAR OF THE UPRISING, was compiled by al-Haq researchers and relies on information supplied to al-Haq's database by field workers and on cross-referenced press and media reports. Because al-Haq's work is not oriented toward being comprehensive or compiling lists, and because four of its field workers have been in administrative detention for most of the uprising, in the majority of cases the documentation was obtained from press reports. The newspapers surveyed include the daily *al-Fajr, al-Quds, al-Sha'ab*, and the *Jerusalem Post*, and the weekly *al-Bayader al-Siyasi, al-Fajr* Weekly (English), and *al-Tali'a*. Sometimes official statements broadcast on radio or television were also used for verification.

    The figures supplied are best seen as conservatively accurate. Because the sheer volume of curfews imposed has made it impossible to arrive at figures entirely beyond reproach, every precaution was taken not to record a curfew unless it was mentioned in at least two newspapers, preferably with references to official armed forces spokespersons. This means, for instance, that a number of curfews which could not be verified in this manner were simply not recorded, while others may have been noted as ending earlier than they actually did. Moreover, after the uprising engulfed the West Bank, curfews in the Gaza Strip were reported less regularly, and their documentation is thus clearly deficient. Additionally, after the register was completed a number of cases were discovered in which a curfew's duration was properly noted but the beginning and end dates were off by one or two days. Thus, while the register used for this chapter may contain additional inaccuracies, al-Haq is convinced that exact figures would not only reinforce its findings but also show them to be understated.

    The total figure of 1,600 curfews, short and prolonged, while not actually recorded, was arrived at by multiplying the number of prolonged curfews (400) by 4. Given that the number of night curfews (262 in the Gaza Strip alone) itself exceeds prolonged curfews, and considering the number of shorter curfews (estimated from press reports), al-Haq believes this ratio to be accurate and quite likely conservative as well.
3. While in the context of Israel's curfew policy during the past year the case could be made that 2-day curfews are prolonged as well, al-Haq has decided on 72 hours as the cutoff point. The 40-day curfew, the longest so far, was recorded from 16 March to 25 April in the Jalazon Refugee Camp near Ramallah.
4. All citations of the Fourth Geneva Convention are from *The Geneva Con-*

ventions of August 12, 1949 published by the International Committee of the Red Cross in Geneva, Switzerland.
5. Violations resulting from "extraordinary circumstances," which in other articles are viewed as legitimate only if directly related to unavoidable military hostilities in progress, are clearly prohibited if their intent is punitive or otherwise malicious.
6. Pictet, Jean S. (ed.), *Commentary: IV Geneva Conventions Relative to the Protection of Civilian Persons in Time of War* (Geneva; International Committee of the Red Cross, 1958), p.333. This is the official commentary to the Convention.
7. This was the case, for example, during the rebellion in Algeria in October 1988.
8. Excerpt from affidavit #310 taken by al-Haq in 1983 from 'Adnan Abu-Jibne, a 28-year old resident of Qalandiya Refugee Camp, describing conditions under curfew. The curfew lasted 24 days, and according to the *Jerusalem Post* of 1 April 1983: "Military sources confirmed that during this period three adults in the camp died of 'purely natural causes,' while local Arab sources claim that at least two infants also died because of inadequate medical care."

A full version of this detailed and lengthy affidavit can be found in Shehadeh, Raja, *Occupier's Law: Israel and the West Bank* (Washington, DC: Institute for Palestine Studies, 1985); pp. 136-141.
9. The total curfew was imposed by force of Military Proclamation #1 (7 June 1967).
10. International Center for Peace in the Middle East (ICPME), *Research on Human Rights in the Occupied Territories, 1979-1983* (Tel Aviv: Interim Report, November 1983); pp. 60-61.
11. The clear discrimination in Israel's curfew policy has also been taken to extremes. According to *al-Fajr Jerusalem Palestinian Weekly* (26 April 1985), "[the] Israeli authorities clamped a curfew on 20 Palestinian villages in the West Bank [on 25 April] as hundreds of Gush Emunim [an organisation of ultra-nationalist Jewish settlers] staged a march from Salfit to Qalqilya."
12. *Al-Haq Newsletter #7 (March/April 1985)*, pp. 1-3.
13. For the full account see *Al-Haq Newsletter #9 (July-October 1985)*, pp. 7-8. The newsletter also contains details of an intervention sent by al-Haq to the military government in response to this incident, asking "whether any steps would be taken to bring those guilty of this behaviour to justice, and, since such behaviour during curfews is a common phenomenon and is often reported, whether punitive measures had been taken against similar offenders in the past." No reply was ever received.
14. ICPME, *Research on Human Rights in the Occupied Territories*, p. 62.
15. See Shehadeh, *Occupier's Law*, p. 205 (fn. #44) for full references.
16. This was the case, for example, in a number of refugee camps during March of 1983. In a press release issued on the 28th of that month, al-Haq stated that

...Since the 8[th of March], the [Jalazon] camp was under continuous siege with no one permitted in or out and no supplies, rations, or services allowed in. On March 14, the military authorities threatened the population that their water and electricity supplies would be cut if they violated the curfew, and the camp was in fact deprived of water during all that day.

...Schools and clinics [in the camps under curfew] are closed, residents are not allowed to go to their places of employment, and access to food and medicine is restricted, even to households with infant, infirmed, aged, or pregnant members.

...Shortages of food, medicine and kerosene were reported during the curfews. All health (UNRWA) facilities were closed.

17. *Jerusalem Post*, 16 November 1988.
18. The population figures for Jabaliya and Balata exceed those provided by the United Nations Relief and Works Agency for Palestine Refugees (UNRWA) because they include the residents of Jabaliya village (pop. 12,000) and Balata village (pop. 1000), respectively. Located almost within limits of the camps which took their names, they are placed under curfew whenever the camps are. It should also be noted that exact or even accurate population figures for the Occupied Territories are impossible to obtain because the last official census was in September 1967 and the military government has failed to take one since. Thus, a variety of credible estimates, such as UNRWA or the West Bank Data Base Project, were used instead.
19. Cited in *al-Sha'ab*, 8 November 1988.
20. This figure excludes the widely-anticipated total curfew during the anniversary of the uprising on 9 December, which had not yet taken place at press time.
21. In the calculation of these figures the first day of a curfew was not counted to compensate for the difficulty of establishing the precise time of its imposition and lifting. Additionally, al-Haq received reports of a number of other prolonged curfews which could not be verified because, for instance, it was impossible to discriminate between a curfew and a closed military area. Thus, the actual figures may be significantly higher than recorded.
22. *Jerusalem Post*, 30 August 1988.
23. *Ibid*.
24. *Ibid*.
25. *Ibid*.
26. *Ibid*. The army statement contradicts other statements to the contrary and in any case there was no mention of subsequent judicial proceedings against the soldiers involved.
27. See Appendix 5-D and the affidavit in the text below.
28. *Jerusalem Post*, 25 January 1988.
29. *Jerusalem Post*, 22 February 1988. For examples of raids on houses see Appendices 5-A, 5-B, 5-D, 5-E, and 5-F.
30. See Appendix 5-F. More explicit examples can be found in *Report on the Violations of Human Rights in the Territories During the Uprising, 1988*, by the Israeli League for Civil and Human Rights, Part IV (Tel Aviv, 1988).
31. See Appendices 5-C and 5-F. See Chapter 1 for a discussion of the medical evidence available.
32. See Appendices 5-C, 5-F and 5-G, and also chapter 2 on the obstruction of medical treatment.
33. For obvious reasons, this has been a particularly acute problem during the longest curfews. See Appendices 5-E and 5-F.
34. See Appendix 5-F.
35. See Appendices 5-D, 5-E, 5-F, and 5-G, and other examples given in this

section.
36. See Appendices 5-A, 5-B, 5-E, 5-F, and other examples given below.
37. See Appendix 5-A and Chapter 7 on economic sanctions.
38. See Chapter 7.
39. See Appendix 5-F.
40. See Appendix 5-E. In another incident in July of 1988, al-Haq intervened after soldiers, during a curfew imposed on the town of Beit Sahour, confiscated dozens of cars and broke into homes and took jewelry and money from residents as punishment for their non-payment of taxes. (See Appendix 7-A at the end of Chapter 7).
41. See Appendix 5-E.
42. See Appendices 5-E and 5-G, and the relevant section below.
43. See Appendix 5-E.
44. See Appendices 5-C, 5-F and Chapter 2 on the obstruction of medical treatment.
45. See Appendix 5-F.
46. Al-Haq affidavit #1471.
47. *Al-Fajr English Jerusalem Palestinian Weekly*, 24 January 1988.
48. *Jerusalem Post*, 20 January 1988.
49. *Ibid.* Note that this was the same day the Minister of Defence officially proclaimed the policy of "force, might, and beatings."
50. *Al-Fajr Weekly*, 24 January 1988.
51. *Jerusalem Post*, 14 January 1988. This is despite the fact that the Legal Advisor of the military government, David Yahav, in a letter to al-Haq (see Appendix 7-B for full text) describes curfews as a "drastic measure."
52. *Yediot Ahronot*, 25 January 1988. Cited in *HaAretz* four days later, Rabin made the following statement: "According to my estimation what is happening [the uprising] is being carried out within a clear political tendency behind which stand Iran, Iraq, Syria and, foremostly, the PLO."
53. *Jerusalem Post*, 9 February 1988.
54. Carmen Shalev, "The Price of Insurgency: Civil Rights in the Occupied Territories," (published under the auspices of the West Bank Database Project; Tel Aviv, 1988), p. 35.
55. The lecture was attended by an al-Haq staff member. Ten months and more than 1,000 curfews after the fact, Professor Dinstein did not express any regret about his advice and, on this particular occasion, declined to discuss any of the abuses that had been perpetrated in the interim.
56. Joseph Schechla, "*Intifadah* in Palestine," *Without Prejudice: The EAFORD International Review of Racial Discrimination*, Vol. I, #2, p. 91.
57. This number does not include journalists placed in "investigative" or "preventive" detention, which usually lasts between a few hours to a number of days or sometimes even weeks. This practice is widespread, especially at times preceding periods of possible tension, as on the days immediately previous to the Israeli elections on 1 November 1988. The Committee to Protect Journalists reported on 7 October that from the beginning of the uprising until October, at least 39 Palestinian journalists had been detained for two days or longer. (Letter to Yitzhak Rabin, 7 October 1988).
58. See, for example, the report published by the Committee to Protect Journalists and Article 19, *Journalism Under Occupation: Israel's Regulation of*

the *Palestinian Press*, October 1988. See also, Meron Benvenisti, *Israeli Censorship of Arab Publications*, West Bank Data Base Project, 1983; and Virgil Falloon, *Excessive Secrecy, Lack of Guidelines: A Report on Military Censorship in the West Bank*, al-Haq/Law in the Service of Man, 1985.

59. For example, *Jerusalem Post*, 5 April 1988.
60. For example, at the end of March, the entire West Bank was closed for three days to journalists.
61. *Jerusalem Post*, 16 December 1987.
62. *Jerusalem Post*, 27 April 1988 and 26 October 1988.
63. For example, in Beni Suheila, as reported in the *Jerusalem Post*, 10 January 1988, or in East Jerusalem, *Jerusalem Post*, 17 January 1988, or in Ramallah, *Jerusalem Post*, 25 September 1988.
64. *Jerusalem Post*, 15 June 1988.
65. *Jerusalem Post*, 7 July 1988.
66. *Jerusalem Post*, 13 July 1988.
67. For example, Prime Minister Shamir, quoted in the *Jerusalem Post* of 16 December 1987, stated: "Every photo or TV film of a riot does Israel damage."
68. For example, by Ariel Sharon, quoted in the *Jerusalem Post*, 10 February 1988.
69. *Jerusalem Post*, 27 November 1988. In Israeli lexicon, the West Bank and Gaza Strip are never referred to as "the Occupied Territories," and only seldom as the West Bank and Gaza Strip. Instead, they are referred to as "the territories," "Judea, Samaria, and Gaza," "the administered areas," or simply "the areas" or "regions." As the quotation indicates, this semantic confusion also exists in the pages of the *Jerusalem Post*, a paper generally identified with the Israeli Labour Party.
70. Al-Haq/Law in the Service of Man, *Ansar 3: The Case for Closure* (Ramallah, 1988), p. 4. The report contains many additional details of the detention of al-Haq's field workers.

Appendix 5-A

TRANSLATION OF SWORN AFFIDAVIT (#1468) TAKEN BY AL-HAQ

I, the undersigned Mahmoud Ahmad Salih Khalluf, 70 years of age, a resident of the village of Burqin [near Jenin] and a farmer, having been warned to state the truth or be subject to criminal liability, hereby state as follows:

At approximately 5:00 a.m. on 21 October 1988, while I was inside my house in the village of Burqin, I heard loudspeakers announcing the imposition of a curfew. I went to the balcony of my house, from where I could see dozens of soldiers, a bus, and many military vehicles. I also could see the military force going through the alleys and streets of the village, and the army vehicle which was announcing the curfew on the authority of the military governor of the Jenin District. The streets were empty at this time. At approximately 1:00 p.m. four members of the Burqin village council came to my house and asked me to accompany them to a meeting which was to be held the next day with representatives of the military governor at the Burqin Girls' Preparatory School. This I did. When I arrived at the school it was teeming with dozens of soldiers and army vehicles and [Israeli] yellow-plated civilian cars. I sat down, and approximately half an hour later, shortly after 11:30 a.m., I, the other village notables, and the members of the village council were summoned to a meeting with a military officer. Immediately after the meeting began the officer told us: "I order you to deliver 70 persons from your village to the military government." He then said: "I want 25 persons, or else I will maintain the curfew for as long as I can." I told the officer that it was not our job to do what he had asked and that we could do nothing, and that the authorities could act as they pleased. The officer replied: "The mosques will remain closed and there will be no prayers until the persons are handed over." The meeting ended and I returned to my house. After approximately one week a group of soldiers raided my house and searched it a number of times. We were only allowed outdoors to buy essential items for two hours every three days throughout the curfew, which lasted until 3:30 p.m. on 11 November 1988. It should be noted that the curfew had a negative effect on the olive harvest, and especially for me because I own 50 dunums which yield no less than 1,840 kilos of olive oil. The losses I incurred were doubled, firstly because curfew delayed the harvesting for 22 days, and secondly because 50 large sacks I had prepared to be pressed before the curfew rotted.

In accordance with all of the above I hereby sign this statement on this date, the 12th of November 1988.

(Signature)

Name available for publication.

Appendix 5-B

TRANSLATION OF SWORN AFFIDAVIT (#1445) TAKEN BY AL-HAQ

I, the undersigned Nawal Jiryis Ya'qoub Qumsiyya, 38 years of age, a resident of Beit Sahour and a housewife, having been warned to state the truth or be subject to criminal liability, hereby state as follows:

At approximately 3:30 p.m. on 30 October 1988, while I was at home in the Wad Abu Sa'd neighbourhood of Beit Sahour, which was then under curfew, our house was surrounded by a detachment of soldiers. A number of other soldiers went up on the roof of our house and seven of them broke into the house. My eldest son, 19-year old 'Issa Jiryis Qumsiyya, and the son of my neighbour, Nadir 'Issa Elias Qumsiyya, were in the house at the time. My son 'Issa, who could not see the soldiers, asked who was there. Upon hearing him a soldier ran directly at him and, inside the house, began kicking him in the back and hitting him across the face. The soldiers then dragged him outside, where, while still beating him, they demanded to see his ID card. 'Issa came back inside to get his ID card. At the same time, other soldiers were searching the house and they saw Nadir, who was in the kitchen drinking coffee. They began beating him as well, and dragged him outside in the process. 'Issa, who had found his ID, went back outside. I began to yell at the soldiers, who cursed me and began beating the boys again with clubs, hands, and boots. They also stepped all over them. They even attacked me when I went outside. A soldier pushed me, stepped on my foot, and ordered me to return home. They continued beating the boys for about 20 minutes, and then they released them. They had bruises all over their bodies and 'Issa lost consciousness after he returned. While I was treating their wounds, I heard the soldiers shouting and cursing. I looked out the window and saw them beating my younger son Ra'id Jiryis Qumsiyya, who is 15 years old, and his friend Ziad 'Abdallah al-Hourani. They were beating them with their hands, their legs, and clubs. When I told the soldiers that Ra'id and Ziad are too young to be beaten, a soldier ordered me to go back inside the house or else he would shoot me. He threatened that if we threw stones at them they would demolish our house. I was in a very bad state and crying. The soldiers told my son 'Issa that if anybody threw stones at them from any other house they would come back and shoot him. Another soldier said to me: "You want *intifada?* I'll teach you how to make *intifada!*" When I screamed and said that this is my son he told me, "I want to shoot him so you people can have another hero."

In accordance with all of the above I hereby sign this statement on this date the 11th of November 1988.
(Signature)
Name available for publication.

Appendix 5-C

TRANSLATION OF SWORN AFFIDAVIT (#1340) TAKEN BY AL-HAQ

I, the undersigned Rabi'a Deeb 'Abdallah Shawish, 24 years of age, a resident of Deheisha Refugee Camp in the Bethlehem District and a nurse by occupation, having been warned to state the truth or be subject to criminal liability, hereby state as follows:

At approximately 7:30 p.m. on Sunday 31 July 1988, while I was sitting at home with my family, I heard the sounds of tear-gas canisters being fired. I noticed one such canister which fell behind the window of the room in which we were seated. The window is situated in an enclosed area and the smoke permeated the room in a very concentrated way. At the same time, we could not open the door to the house because of the shooting. We suffered a lot from the gas, but there were no visible side effects that day. The next day my father, who is 65, my sister Nabila, 17, my brother Tha'ir, 8, my brother Muhammad and I all suffered from diarrhea, vomiting, and high temperatures. That morning the military had imposed a curfew on the camp and the soldiers would not allow us to leave our home. It was not until Tuesday 2 August, by which time my temperature had risen to 40 degrees centigrade, that we were allowed outdoors. I was taken to the hospital after permission had been obtained by the soldiers from their superiors, a process which took two hours. I came back to the camp at 11:00 p.m. because I have no health insurance. That same day an ambulance came to take my father to the hospital but the soldiers refused to let him leave the camp. Finally, on Wednesday 3

August, after the curfew was lifted, my father and my sister Nabila were taken to the Augusta Victoria Hospital, where they remained for two days.

(Signature)
Name available for publication.

Appendix 5-D

TRANSLATION OF SWORN AFFIDAVIT (#1478) TAKEN BY AL-HAQ

I the undersigned, Fatima Nishmash Muhammad 'Ali Abu-Ahmad, 47 years of age, a resident of Jenin Refugee Camp and a housewife, having been warned to state the truth or be subject to criminal liability hereby state as follows:

At approximately 7:00 p.m. on 16 November 1988 I was preparing supper for my family. Some of my children were on the roof of the house, which is located on the west hill of the Jenin Refugee Camp, and the others were inside the house. I heard the sound of women ululating in the refugee camp and children setting off fireworks in celebration of the proclamation of Palestinian Statehood by the Palestine National Council in Algiers. At this time the camp had been under curfew since 1:30 a.m. of the 15th of November 1988. In addition to the curfew, at approximately 5:45 p.m. on the 16th, the electricity was cut in the camp and the city of Jenin. In order to light the house during the electricity cut we had lit a kerosene lamp. While I was preparing supper I heard a strange noise coming from near the house. I ran towards the living room and was surprised to encounter a large number of soldiers, some of whom I bumped into at the entrance of my home. I was momentarily shocked, and asked one of them what they wanted. "Shut up!," he immediately responded, and they broke into the rooms of the house. I saw them fanning out through the house. Some of them started to smash the glass panels to the dining room cabinet with their gun-butts. I saw two of them grab my husband, Muhammad 'Ali Nishmash (Abu-'Atif) who is 50 years old. They held him by his shoulders and began hitting him with their gun-butts. I saw another one of them beating my husband with a club. They also hit him across the face and kicked him. During this, I also saw some of them breaking the metal grates to the balcony, and heard the sound of breaking glass in two different rooms inside the house. They were speaking in Hebrew, and some of them were saying, "where are the kids, we want the kids." A few minutes later, I saw two of them dragging my husband, and one of them was ordering him to tell them where the stairwell is. This took place in front of the house. Then I saw them dragging and beating him again, until they got to the roof of the house. All this time the other soldiers were still searching inside the house, indiscriminately scattering everything they handled. I saw one of them breaking flower-vases, which were located in the living room. After approximately 10 minutes the soldiers left my house, and I counted 8 of them. They waited for a short period around the house, and approximately 2 minutes later I saw 2 soldiers, who had been dragging my husband, come down off the roof. When they joined the rest of their group I saw them leave the area. My husband stayed in bed until the curfew was lifted the next day. At that point he went to see a doctor for first-aid treatment. Until this day he still suffers from severe pain and bruises in many parts of his body. He still cannot move unaided. I would also like to mention that although the curfew was lifted at approximately 1:30 a.m. on the 16th of November, the electricity remained cut for about 4 1/2 hours thereafter.

In accordance with all of the above I hereby sign this statement on this date, the 19th of November 1988.
(Signature)
Name available for publication

Appendix 5-E

The following report was compiled by an al-Haq field worker after a 14-day curfew (26 August - 9 September) on the village of Beni Na'im near Hebron. It presents a representative illustration of the effects of protracted curfews:

At approximately 2:00 p.m. the army announced the imposition of a curfew through loudspeakers mounted on military jeeps. Soldiers fanned throughout the village and carried out an arrest campaign. Among those arrested were the following:
1. 'Adnan Suleiman Mansour, age 25.
2. Tariq Isma'il Manasra, age 22.
3. 'Abd-al-Nasir Isma'il Manasra, age 18.
4. Muhammad Abu-Hussein Manasra, age 28.
5. 'Abd-al-Karim Muhammad Mahmoud Manasra, age 22.

What affected the people the most were the continuous raids on their homes. Three days after the curfew food shortages were becoming apparent, especially with regard to milk for infants. Because the people had to feed them goat milk instead, many children suffered from diarrhea and dehydration. Among the children who are known to have been ill are the following:

1. Maythalun Bahjat Manasra, 4 months.
2. Khalid 'Ali Hussein Mwasi, 3 months
3. Nida' Mahmud Manasra, 1 1/2 years.
4. Mu'tassim Fayiz al-Khadur, 5 months.
5. Ala' Hussein Mansour, 6 months.

The water and electricity supplies to the village were also cut. Some time afterwards the International Committee of the Red Cross distributed buckets of water to the residents. The soldiers, however, knocked the buckets off the heads of the women who were carrying them, causing them to spill on the ground. The army took all the cars to the secondary school yard and forced their owners to go to the tax office and obtain certificates of payment, and imposed taxes and fines on a number of cars even though they are privately owned and not required to pay the fees demanded. The vehicles of those who refused to pay remained in the possession of the army after the curfew was lifted. The southern, eastern, and northern entrances to the village were sealed by earthen mounds and large boulders, and a checkpoint was erected at the main entrance. The curfew was lifted for two hours every three days so that people could purchase needed supplies from the stores, but the problem was that the stores were running out of food. During these two hours residents were also subjected to harassments by the soldiers. Before the imposition of the curfew many villagers had left their grapes to dry in the fields to make raisins. The length of the curfew and the heat caused these grapes to rot, which was a big loss to the farmers. Any male violating the curfew was taken to the school, where the soldiers established their headquarters, and was subjected to severe clubbings. But if a woman violated the curfew, the victim would be her husband, as happened with Halima 'Issa Manasra. When she violated the curfew the soldiers took her husband Muhammad Mahmoud Manasra, 45, to the school, beat him severely, and then transferred him to the headquarters of the military government in al-Khalil (Hebron), from where he was released.

Appendix 5-F

A REPORT ON THE EVENTS IN JALAZON CAMP FROM 5 TO 25 MARCH 1988

Note: The following report was compiled by residents of the Jalazon Refugee Camp near Ramallah during the curfews which were imposed on the camp on 5 March and from 16 March to 25 April. Al-Haq has verified the details presented below.

At 5:00 a.m. on Saturday 5 March 1988, a large number of soldiers laid siege to Jalazon Camp. They were ferried in by helicopters and dropped around the camp to ensure that it was completely surrounded and sealed off. Then, using loudspeakers, the army imposed a curfew on Jalazon. The rest of the force, which consisted of approximately 2,000 soldiers, entered the camp and began breaking into houses in the most violent way, ransacking homes, smashing wooden doors and windows, and strewing around clothes and mattresses. Among the houses known to have been searched were those of Mustafa 'Uthman 'Orabi, the house of the camp services director, and the house of Jum'a Hasan Nakhleh. Many youths were taken and summarily beaten, denied even the time to put on their shoes or get dressed. Many were almost naked and barefoot. They were taken to the schoolyard, blindfolded and with their hands tied behind their backs, and kept there for the entire day. Some clashes erupted between soldiers and the parents of the youths during the raids on the houses. The soldiers attacked and beat the fathers, mothers, and sisters of those who were arrested. Among the people who are known to have been beaten are the following:

Jum'a Hasan Nakhleh, his wife, and his daughters.
Tawfiq Muhammad Daoud and his mother.
Jamil 'Uthman Safi and his wife.
Ma'zuza Tayyim.

The arrests continued until 2:00 p.m. A number of those arrested were taken to the Jnaid Prison [near Nablus] and put into administrative detention without charge or trial. The others were taken to the Dhahriya Military Detention Center near al-Khalil (Hebron). Those arrested were:

1 Ahmad Mas'oud Khalid, camp services director, 56 (administrative detention).
2 Hasan Mustafa Dhib Sharaka, 31 (administrative detention).
3 Nasir Sa'd-al-Din Qattai, 22 (administrative detention).
4 Usama Rasim al-Tursha, 25 (administrative detention).
5 Muhammad 'Abd-al-Raziq D'ous, 25 (administrative detention).
6 Mustafa 'Uthman 'Orabi, 25 (administrative detention).

7 Subhi Hammuda 'Abd-al-Latif, 30 (administrative detention).
8 Fadl 'Issa al-Khalidi, 21 (administrative detention).
9 Muhammad 'Ali al-Faqih, 35 (administrative detention).
10 Ashraf Ahmad al-Bayyid, 15
11 Ra'id Yusif al-Ghalith, 17
12 Nadir Ahmad al-Ghalith, 18
13 Fayiq Sha'ban Ghazzawi, 18
14 'Abd-al-Nasir Khalil al-Basfi
15 Muhammad Khalil al-Basfi
16 Rafiq Muhammad Daoud
17 Muhammad Sha'ban al-Ghazzawi
18 Mahdi Wajih al-Ramahi
19 Khalid 'Abd-al-Fattah al-Kanash
20 Munthir 'Abd-al-Khaliq al-Barghouthi
21 Mahmoud 'Abd-al-'Aziz Salih
22 Khalid 'Issa Salama
23 Yusif Musa Nakhleh
24 Zaki Khalil al-Masri
25 Munthir Ibrahim Rashid
26 Ramadan Ibrahim Rashid
27 Fu'ad Ibrahim al-Hodali
28 Ya'ish Ibrahim Nakhleh
29 Subhi Naif
30 Muhannad 'Abd-al-Rahim Abu-Shamma
31 Safi Ahmad Tayyim
32 Muhammad Jum'a Hasan Nakhleh
33 Hafiz Yasin Farraj
34 Khalid Yasin Farraj
35 Hamdi Muhammad Hajir
36 Nasir Faris al-Sayid
37 Ziad Ya'qoub Rashid
38 'Abd-al-Hakim 'Orabi
39 Ibrahim 'Abd-al-Latif Hammouda
40 Jamal Dhib Ibrahim
41 Ziad 'Abd-al-Ra'ouf Bayyud
42 Majid 'Abd-al-Razaq Dhuwa'i
43 Sami 'Abd-al-Fattah Abu-Sabri
44 Jihad Jamil 'Uthman
45 'Uthman Jamil 'Uthman
46 Suleiman Mas'oud al-Zuq

An announcement was made to the residents which, in the name of the military governor, urged the inhabitants of the camp not to cooperate with the "riotous minority in its midst which has just been arrested." The residents were told that otherwise their own and their children's security could not be guaranteed. The residents were also told that engaging in protest would only increase the arrests, beatings and destruction. The curfew was lifted at 6:00 p.m. on that same day [5 March 1988].

[The 40-day curfew on Jalazon, the longest thus far, was imposed on the night of 16 March after demonstrations in which thousands participated led to renewed clashes with the armed forces. The following document was written on 26 March, after which it was smuggled out of the camp.]

After the curfew was imposed the army raided homes throughout the night, ordered residents outdoors, beat them, and forced them to clean the streets. During the curfew the army took the following measures:

- The electricity supply to the camp was disconnected.
- No food was allowed into the camp.
- Any food being carried by residents was destroyed by soldiers.
- Soldiers spoiled dough by stepping on it and prevented women from going to neighbourhood ovens to bake their bread.
- There was a shortage of flour, vegetables, and milk for infants.
- There was a shortage of fuel, gas, and kerosene, which caused the residents to spend cold and dark nights.

After the curfew had been in effect for 5 days the residents were allowed to leave their homes for one hour. By this time, however, all refrigerated foodstuffs, such as meat, fish and dairy products had spoiled because of the electricity cut. A delegation from "Peace Now" came to the camp and lodged a protest with the authorities about the ill-treatment of the residents of the camp. When the delegation arrived the army immediately changed its behaviour. They allowed the inhabitants of the camp to leave their homes and permitted an UNRWA truck to deliver bread to the residents. As soon as the delegation left, however, the soldiers quickly and violently forced the residents back into their homes, destroyed foodstuffs, chased women with their jeeps, and prevented the distribution of the bread which had been delivered by UNRWA.

[The last report covers the period from 26 March until 3 April 1988]

The curfew on the Jalazon camp is still in force, and it is now also a closed military area which journalists cannot enter. Local and foreign journalists are prevented by the armed forces from getting near the camp. The people are subjected to the army's violence and brutality on a daily basis, which includes the firing of tear-gas canisters into homes. This practice has caused medical complications for young children and the elderly. Furthermore, the army is prohibiting the transportation of the wounded to hospitals. Because the electricity supply continues to be disconnected by the military authorities, the women of the camp have been baking bread on an open flame instead of in an oven. Whenever soldiers see women baking bread, they fire tear-gas at them. The starvation policy has reached a point where the army is destroying chickens, rabbits, pigeons, and goats by asphyxiating them with tear-gas. Since the beginning of the curfew, no food or other items necessary for subsistence have been allowed into the camp, and the stores are completely empty. Essential items such as flour, vegetables, meat, milk, and fuel have been completely depleted. The residents of the camp are only allowed out of their homes one hour every two days, but there is absolutely nothing to buy. For this reason we appeal to world public opinion and international organisations to intervene in order to lift the siege and allow at least supplies necessary for the care of our children to enter the camp.

[The report goes on to describe the various ways in which the residents of the camps are persevering, and gives details of demonstrations which were organised in defiance of the curfew and the army's violent reaction to them. It was the last document received by al-Haq during the curfew, which lasted until 25 April.]

After the curfew was lifted, al-Haq was able to confirm from other sources that the following measures had also taken place:

- In an interview conducted by al-Haq with Israeli reserve soldiers, one soldier involved in enforcing the 40-day curfew on Jalazon stated that he had shot a pregnant woman in the stomach with a round of rubber bullets because she refused to enter her home. He also stated that he belonged to an elite unit whose responsibility it was to intimidate and harass the population, for example by jumping up and down on people's roofs and banging on windows with clubs so that residents would keep them closed. Asked if he felt he was violating army regulations, the soldier stated that it was his impression that units could do whatever they felt was necessary to enforce the curfew, and that furthermore no member of his unit had been charged with any offence.
- Nawal Hasan Mustafa Sharafa, 7 months pregnant, miscarried after being exposed to intense concentrations of tear gas.
- A tear gas canister was thrown into the house of Safia 'Ala al-Din, a 55-year old blind woman.
- Wooden structures located on top of the houses of 'Omar Maqdadi, Musa Ramahi, Abu-Isma'il Badouri, and al-'Abd 'Omar were demolished.
- On more than one occasion, soldiers fired randomly into the air and throw tear-gas canisters into homes before lifting the curfew for one hour. Tear-gas was also fired into the central market during the reprieve.
- Wajeeh Rabadi, a 45-year old baker, and his 18-year old son Nasir

were beaten by soldiers after they refused to "cooperate" with the army. They were told that collaboration would result in the bakery being re-opened.
- If the soldiers could see smoke from burning wood, which was used to bake bread, they would tear-gas the house in question.
- People who required hospitalisation but were prevented from leaving the camp sometimes tried to smuggle themselves out through the hills at one end of the camp. If soldiers saw them they would be shot at, forced to return, and beaten.
- All telephone lines were cut throughout the curfew, and the water supply was severed in certain parts of the camp as well. The electricity was not reconnected until 25 April.
- A number of stores along with their contents were demolished by the army, as was a gas station.

Appendix 5-G

TEXT OF INTERVENTION SENT BY AL-HAQ ON 30 JUNE 1988

Ref: 2637
Re: Military curfews and closure of Palestinian areas

Al-Haq is concerned about the situation of hundreds of Palestinian residents* of four areas which have been placed under curfew by the Israeli military authorities for prolonged periods of time. At least two of these areas have currently been under curfew for over 21 days. While there is some legitimacy to imposing curfews for security purposes no justification, however, warrants the excessive duration of many of these measures, some of the most serious of which are listed below. Prolonged curfews are acts of collective punishment against the civilian population and as such are in violation of Article 37 of the Fourth Geneva Convention of 1949.** Those places known by al-Haq to be under lengthy curfew are:

1. Tulkarm town and Tulkarm camp: have been under curfew since June 6 (24 days). Additionally, approximately 19 roads in Tulkarm have been closed by cement blocks and all telephone lines have been cut.

2. Beit Furik (Nablus District): has been under curfew since June 18 (12 days).

3. Kharbatha Bani Harith (Ramallah District): has been under curfew

since June 25.

4. Dhannaba (Tulkarm District): has been under curfew since June 6 (24 days).

5. 'Anabta (Tulkarm District): Has been under curfew since June 11 (19 days).

While we have not been able to obtain first-hand information as to the situation of those inside the areas under curfew, Israeli radio has received reports of shortages of food and medical supplies. Past experience has shown that such curfews cause severe hardship especially to those with medical problems, or living in overcrowded conditions or without adequate food and fuel supplies.

We ask for your immediate intervention with the Israeli military authorities to lift the curfews from the areas currently under siege and to desist from this practice in the future.

* Actually, the affected population was closer to 50,000 people. Tulkarm alone has an estimated 30,000 residents.

** This should read "Article 33."

Chapter 6

THE ADMINISTRATION OF JUSTICE

A. Introduction

It has always been a central aspect of al-Haq's work to monitor the system by which "law and order" is maintained in the Occupied Territories. In this we include executive functions of arrest, interrogation and detention as well as the judicial functions of interpretation and application of the law. It is our view that the role of the judiciary during an occupation should be the application of local law as amended by emergency military orders but only in so far as it is in accordance with international law. This includes the punishment of individuals where required by domestic law and in so far as is permitted by international law. The relevant international law applicable in the Occupied Territories comprises—at the very least—the IV Geneva Convention Relative to the Protection of Civilian Persons in Time of War of 1949 (hereafter the "Fourth Geneva Convention"), the IV Hague Convention Regulations of 1907 (hereafter the "Hague Regulations") and certain principles of customary human rights law.[1]

The role of the executive, i.e. the Military Government (which also acts as a legislature), is the maintenance of "public order and civil life"; this includes the arrest and interrogation of suspected law breakers and the maintenance of centres of detention.

It has been apparent from our documentation of this theoretical system of preserving "public order" in the West Bank and Gaza Strip that, rather than embodying principles of international law, it has signally failed to respect the division of functions outlined above.[2] The theme of this chapter is therefore the usurpation and abuse of judicial functions by the executive, particularly in the form of extra-judicial punishments, be they violent and indiscriminate methods of arrest, the use of torture in interrogation, or the punishment of administrative detainees through the maintenance of cruel and inhumane conditions in the detention centres.

However, the military government is not solely to blame since the judges who hold themselves out as administrators of justice are in our view equally guilty of a dereliction of duty. Thus the excessive remanding in custody of arrestees, the acceptance of confessions extracted under duress, the trial of detainees *en masse* in so called "quick trials" and the failure to apply international law are all examples of unacceptably low standards.

Our interpretation of the policy behind this system of "law and order" is that it has served Israel's political ambitions in the Occupied Territories. The jurisdiction of local courts has been illegally curtailed (see Appendix 6-A), and that of Israeli courts extended, thus further entrenching the Israeli settler presence in the Territories. At the same time, the local Palestinian population has been subjected to the use of arrest, interrogation and detention as intimidatory and punitive measures in pursuit of the Israeli military government's apparent goal of control through repression.

These themes will be discussed in the following steps:

(1) the administration of justice, including the procedures and practice of arrest, interrogation and trial as a means of punishing individuals and controlling the population at large;

(2) the penal system as a means of repression and intimidation;

(3) the dual judicial system (i.e. Israeli and local court structure) which is discussed in Appendix 6-A.

B. The Administration of Justice

1. Arrest: A Policy of Punishment and Repression

Arrest in the Occupied Territories takes on the form of punishment and intimidation either (1) as a prelude to often brutal beatings, or (2) in the form of mass arrests of sometimes hundreds of people, as part of a range of collective punishments employed by the Israeli authorities.

a. Arrest as prelude to beatings

Arrest in the Occupied Territories appears to be used not only to apprehend suspects with a view to questioning and possible prosecution, but also as a form of punishment or intimidation in itself. Any discussion of arrests in the Occupied Territories thus has to confront the problem of definition, since arrest is often simply an excuse for army brutality.

This chapter examines those cases where an individual is taken into custody and transported either to a formal place of detention or to an informal holding site such as a school yard, a bus, etc. The seizure of persons for the sole purpose of physically assaulting them (for example the many cases where people have been "arrested," taken to a remote spot, beaten and "dumped") are dealt with in Chapter 1 above.

The rules governing the procedures of arrest and initial detention are contained in Military Order Concerning Security Instructions no. 378 (1970) (hereinafter M.O. 378). Article 78 (A) of the order states:

> Any soldier may arrest without a warrant any person contravening the provisions of this order or in respect of whom there is reason to suspect that he has committed an offence under this order.[3]

Offences specified in the order include "any act likely to disturb the peace or public order" (Article 68), any "insulting behaviour" towards any member of the security forces (Article 65), and negligently (in Arabic *ihmal*) causing damage to any property belonging to any member of the security forces (Article 76).

These provisions in themselves permit the arrest of persons without a warrant in a broad range of circumstances; in practice, however, they have long been treated as licensing the arrest of persons not because they are genuinely suspected of any offence, but rather in order to further the ends of punishment and control.

Most of those arrested are either picked up off the streets, taken from home at night, or arrested after answering a summons to the military headquarters. Arrests from the home are often carried out in such a way as to cause maximum fear not only to the arrestee but to his or her family as well. Typically, a large number of soldiers come to the house during the night, kick and sometimes break down the door, conduct a search of the house, in the process often causing damage and breakages and beating other members of the family, and then take away the arrestee.

According to M.O. 378 (as amended), once an arrest is completed the arresting soldier has a duty to take the arrestee "as early as possible to a police station or a place of detention." However, al-Haq has documented literally dozens of examples of arrests which have led to beatings and ill-treatment at the time of arrest and on the way to "a police station or a place of detention," both before and during the current uprising. The following extracts from al-Haq's affidavits are therefore illustrative of practices that are both widespread and common:

Riyad 'Abd-al-Rahman Kamel, 21, a Bir Zeit University student and a resident of Qabatia, described his arrest in the following terms:

> At around twelve noon on 10 January 1988, while I was watching a women's march in town from the veranda, I heard sounds of shooting and saw soldiers chasing young men. Then I saw a soldier pointing his finger at me and moments later they stormed the house, about twenty in number. One came towards me, followed

by others, grabbed my hair and shoulders and began to beat me and drag me. My family tried to save me but the soldiers beat them as well, especially my father.

We left the house and the soldiers dragged me towards an Egged bus about fifty meters from the house. They took me inside and for more than five minutes the soldiers beat me severely with their gun butts. The bus started moving in a southerly direction when I lost consciousness and fell on the floor.

I regained consciousness and found one of the soldiers trying to drag me down the bus steps. Aided by another soldier, he got me down by the wall of Salah al-Din mosque inside the town. There one of them tied my hands behind my back with his belt and threw me on the ground. While I was lying there, one of them brought a large stone weighing 30-40 kg. and put it on my stomach, saying in broken Arabic: "If this rock is too small I'll bring a bigger one." I stayed in this condition for approximately an hour, during which time the soldiers brought two young men and placed stones on them in a similar fashion but on their legs. Every time the soldiers brought a young man one soldier would dance and say: "'Od achad!" or "another one!"

The rock was removed and I remained lying near the wall until about 4:30 p.m. During this period some soldiers would approach me and the other young men and beat us at their whim. They sometimes beat me with clubs and other times kicked me or punched me in the face and head.

By 4:30 p.m. there were more than twelve young men. They loaded us into the bus which drove south and stopped inside a military camp I know well, near Zababda village. We got out and were ordered to sit between the trees inside the camp. They blindfolded us and one of them started calling our names from our personal identification cards which they had taken from us near the mosque in Qabatia.

We stayed like this until about 8:00 p.m. approximately; then they ordered us into the bus. We got in blindfolded, and the bus started moving. After about twenty minutes the bus stopped inside the military headquarters in Jenin. There they took us, hitting us all the while, into a building which I later found out was the barracks. There they removed the blindfolds and a soldier came, who, from his dress, appeared to be an officer. He asked in broken Arabic: "Where are the Qabatia boys?" Then he examined us and asked about the reason for our presence there and what caused the beating marks on our bodies and faces. Indeed, some of us were bleeding from the face and legs and others were barefoot and in pyjamas. He ordered us to be released at about 8:30 p.m.

After the incident I went to medical doctors for treatment of the swelling of my face and body and the many painful bruises caused by the beating.[4]

On 1 May 1988, Ziyad 'Abd-al-Karim al-Roum, a 26-year old electrician from Qaddoura Refugee Camp in Ramallah, was arrested. He describes the procedure in the following manner:

> ...I was ordered to climb into the vehicle. After we had travelled for only 20 meters the vehicle stopped near a group of soldiers. One of them hit me more than five times on my left knee with his metal helmet. He stopped after I started screaming. The vehicle continued and took me to Ramallah Police Station. About 30 soldiers were standing there. Three of them began kicking me on my chest and stomach with their boots. One of them grabbed me by the hair and kneed me in the face. I was taken to the yard of the police station and on my way the soldiers who were there hit me when I passed in front of them...After a while a soldier came running and he jumped in the air and landed on my left leg with his boots; he repeated this seven times...After an hour of harsh beating, especially on my leg, I was taken by two soldiers to a room on the second floor...

The affiant was then interrogated, signed a confession in Hebrew to the effect that he had been throwing stones and participating in demonstrations, and was told that he would be transferred to the Dhahriya Military Detention Centre.

> 15 minutes later a soldier took me to an army bus which was parked near the station and made me climb into the bus, where I saw a number of Arab youths—about seven—sitting in the back seats. I sat near the back door of the bus. There were six soldiers in the bus. While it was travelling in the direction of al-Bireh, I was looking downwards [when] the said soldier kicked me in the face, hit me with his club five times on my head and then kicked me twice on my forehead. I started bleeding, and blood continued flowing onto my clothes. I did not try to wipe it off because I was protecting my head with my hands. After driving around al-Bireh and Ramallah for about half an hour, the bus stopped at Ramallah Central prison...After that the said soldier came another time and he stood on my leg. I felt great pain and began screaming as loud as I could, and he stepped down. Some time later they took the rest of the youths into the tent. I stayed outside for I could not stand up...

The affiant was taken to a clinic where an army doctor treated the wounds on his head; he was then driven to Hadassah Mount Scopus Hospital in West Jerusalem.

> When I was dropped off and my eyes were uncovered, I could see that I was in Hadassah Mount Scopus Hospital. I knew this because I had been there before. A doctor who may have been an Arab, as he spoke Arabic, X-rayed my leg. When I asked him about the result, he told me that my leg was broken near the knee-joint, that the muscles of my leg were swollen and that I needed a surgical operation. I was taken back to the emergency room where I was injected with an anaesthetic and had my leg put in a cast. The doctor told the soldiers to bring me back on Wednesday 4 May for the operation. The soldiers handcuffed me again and covered my eyes and took me to Ramallah prison. They put me in a tent after they removed the handcuffs and eye cover. The Arabs in the tent put a blanket underneath me and covered me with another one. That night I could not sleep from the pain I was suffering.
>
> The next day, 2 May, breakfast was brought to me but I could not eat and remained in pain until 10 o'clock. Then a soldier came and ordered two persons to carry me and follow him. He ordered them to put me in an army car. The car travelled for a distance of 100 meters outside the prison. Then the soldier gave me my identity card and a medical report and told me to go to any hospital or doctor and left me in the street. I walked on one leg, then a passing Arab car stopped and gave me a lift to my house. On the second day at 5 o'clock I went to Dr. Husseini's clinic in [East] Jerusalem. After he examined my leg and saw the X-ray photographs he decided to operate on my leg on Saturday 3 May 1988.[5]

On 20 April 1988 'Abd-al-Nasser Khalil Hussein Abou-'Ein, 27, from Qaddoura Refugee Camp was arrested:

> I sat in the back of the jeep, on the floor, and the jeep began to move in the direction of the main road to Jerusalem. On the way I saw a number of soldiers, whom I estimated to be eight in number, attacking someone I know well—his name is Yousef Hassan Ghaban—beating him with their fists and dragging him. The jeep stopped near them and they put him inside. Blood was flowing from his head and his face. The jeep then went to the Ramallah Police Station...
>
> When we got there one of the soldiers took Yousef out and pushed him into the police station. I saw [the soldier] beat him with the butt of his gun and with his fist. One of the soldiers pulled me out roughly but I tripped and the upper part of my body was hanging

out of the jeep. A soldier standing there hit me with the muzzle of his gun in my right eye and I immediately felt the blood coming out. He then pushed me to make me sit in the station's yard but I refused and said: "Why do you hit me and push me like this?" and he said "I'll kill you" and forced me to sit. The soldiers present began to curse me and the other young men sitting nearby, including Yousef. These curses included "sons of whores" and "we want to kill you" and "we want to cut your throats," said in both Arabic and Hebrew.[6]

On 1 June 1988 one of al-Haq's fieldworkers, 'Abd-al-Karim Ahmad Kana'an, swore an affidavit part of which is reprinted here:

> I was arrested on 16 March 1988 at my home by three soldiers and one man in plain clothes. They refused to show me any arrest warrant whatsoever. In front of my wife and children, I was handcuffed and blindfolded and pushed into a jeep. In the jeep, I was punched on the head to shouts of "stone thrower"...
>
> After two days we were taken by bus to Atlit [a prison near Haifa]. On the way, we were beaten, humiliated, and forced to curse Arafat. They would call "Wahad, Tnain, Talata" and we had to reply "Listen!" They asked "Who is a *manyac?*" [Arabic for "butt-fucker"] and we had to reply "Arafat."[7]

b. Mass arrest

A second rationale behind the policy of arrests in the Occupied Territories appears to be collective punishment of the population through mass and indiscriminate arrests. If people know that the result of disturbances is the likelihood of arrest, even if there is no reasonable suspicion that they were personally involved, there is a chance that this will discourage disobedience. However, this can be counterproductive, since if people know that they are likely to be arrested whether or not they have committed an offence, the incentive to respect the law is removed.

Mass arrests have been carried out since late December 1987, with round-ups of several hundreds in the space of one week reported on numerous occasions. Such measures provoked Amnesty International to issue a statement on 5 January 1988 that:

> it was concerned that soldiers had carried out arbitrary arrests without warrants and without telling detainees why they were being arrested.
>
> It had reports...that soldiers had been visiting homes at night and arresting all teenagers present.[8]

Mass and indiscriminate arrests have continued. A few examples will serve to illustrate this. In April 1988 following the "Beita incident" in which 2 Palestinians and an Israeli died, 60 villagers were arrested and all other males rounded up and put in the village school for questioning for a period of 5 days.[9] On 8 June 1988, following the injury of 2 soldiers in a jeep by a "molotov cocktail" in al-Janiya near Ramallah, troops gathered all males over the age of 14 in the village into the local schoolyard for questioning.[10] Other mass arrests have occurred during curfews placed on towns, villages and refugee camps. For example, during the extended curfew placed on the town of Qalqiliya from 6-14 September 1988, at least 200 people were reported arrested.[11] Following the killing of 4 Israeli citizens in Jericho on 30 October 1988, hundreds of males between the ages of 16 and 60 were arrested and detained in the local school.[12] And recently, prior to the announcement of a Palestinian state on 15 November 1988, dozens of arrests were made throughout the Territories as part of the IDF's moves to stifle anticipated Palestinian celebration of the announcement.[13]

As a result of the policy of mass and indiscriminate arrests in the wake of an individual incident, the whole male population in the vicinity of such an incident, in particular between the ages of 14 and 30, can expect to be arrested. The fear of arrest (and its consequences) lay behind the following tragic incident as related by the victim, Hazem Jaser Mutlaq Jaber, 14, a student and resident of Hebron:

> At about twelve noon on 9 October 1988, I was in the yard of my house which lies opposite the Traffic Department in Hebron. I noticed a military vehicle stopping on the main road near the Department; I went into the house, but on hearing about ten gunshots, came out to see what had happened. I saw some youths running away. They went down one of the alleyways near my house. I was afraid that the soldiers would raid my house and arrest me, so I started running away with the youths. About two hundred meters away from the house, I felt pain in my right side, at the back. I had heard shots, and when I looked at the place that was hurting I saw a lot of blood and realised I'd been hit. After about five meters I was unable to keep running and fell to the ground. I looked up and saw five soldiers surrounding me. Two of them proceeded to drag me along the ground, one of them holding my right hand and the other my right foot. After they had dragged me about a hundred meters, some women attacked the soldiers and managed to get me away from them. I was taken to 'Aliya government hospital about four kilometers away. About ten soldiers came there and one of them came forward and asked the doctor, Isma'il Bdayr, if they could take me away. The soldier said in Arabic: "I want to take him." The doctor, however, refused, saying "there is heavy bleeding and

he needs an urgent operation." The soldier was obliged to leave along with the others he had come with. An operation was immediately performed on my intestines. The next day I was moved to al-Maqassed Hospital [in East Jerusalem] and stayed there for treatment; I can't move my right leg now; the medical report confirmed that the nerves of my right leg have been affected.[14]

2. Interrogation
a. The first 18 days
Article 78 of M.O. 378 provides that immediately following arrest, a person may be detained for up to 18 days without coming before a court—as compared with 48 hours under Israeli law. The 18-day period is composed of an initial period of 96 hours (4 days) during which any soldier can issue an arrest warrant which may be extended for two additional periods of 7 days each by an officer. In the past, al-Haq lawyers have argued, unsuccessfully, that the common practice of authorising the full initial 18-day period in one decision on the first day of detention, rather than in three separate stages, was illegal. However, in a recent case the President of the Military Courts expressed the view (albeit in closed judge's chambers) that M.O. 378 required that 3 separate decisions be made relating to the 96 hours, 7 days and the further 7 days respectively.[15]

At the end of the 18-day period, the detainee must be released if he/she has not been charged, unless a judge extends the period. The hearing is generally held in the place of detention itself or in closed judge's chambers. According to al-Haq lawyers, the police generally ask for a further period of 60 or 45 days and are usually granted a lesser period. The police may show the judge some evidence but are under no obligation to show this to the defence. At this hearing the judge may ask the defendant for his response, and will record any indication of partial confession. Any such submission is treated as a judicial admission for the purposes of any trial that may follow. If the period initially granted by the judge proves to be insufficient, it can be extended for up to six months until a charge sheet has been drawn up (usually after a confession has been obtained), unless a lawyer is present, in which case the judge may require the charge sheet to be prepared within a certain period. If the detainee is charged, the judge will almost always extend the detention "until the end of legal proceedings."

During the uprising, arrestees awaiting trial have almost automatically been remanded in custody. The Legal Director of the Association for Civil Rights in Israel, Joshua Schoffman, stated in an interview in January that:

It seems there is virtually automatic detention until trial regardless of the age, the personal circumstances and even the severity of the allegations against the suspects. The judges are only giving consideration to the *prima facie* evidence and not giving any weight to the circumstances of the individual. There is an assumption that anyone arrested is dangerous and those few cases in which people have been released until their trial have all involved very young defendants.[16]

b. Incommunicado detention

M.O. 1220 (issued in March 1988) gives the families of detainees the right to be informed "without delay" about the reason for arrest and the place of detention unless the detainee himself requests otherwise. However, the same order, which amends Article 78 (d) of M.O. 378, allows the military authorities to keep the detention secret for 8 days provided that they obtain a court order. This provision means that the order in fact offers little improvement to the detainee.

Under M.O. 29 (in the West Bank) and M.O. 410 (in the Gaza Strip) the right to consult a lawyer was dependent on the Prison Commander being convinced that the request to see a lawyer was made for the purpose of dealing with the legal affairs of the detainee and that it would not impede the course of the investigation: thus there is no absolute right to see a lawyer.[17]

M.O. 1220 contains new provisions on the detainee/lawyer relationship, granting the detainee the right to consult a lawyer of his choice immediately after the arrest. The police, however, have the authority to suspend this right for a period of up to 15 days on "security grounds." As in the case of family notification, this new provision does not alter the fact that Palestinian detainees have no absolute right to consult a lawyer on arrest or in the crucial early days of detention.[18]

In theory various safeguards exist to ensure that detainees' families and lawyers are informed of their whereabouts after the initial period of interrogation has been completed. According to an agreement with the International Committee of the Red Cross (ICRC) dating from 1979, the authorities are supposed to inform the ICRC of the whereabouts of all detainees within twelve days of arrest and to allow the ICRC to visit after fourteen days. Thus, even when this system is working, a family will usually have to wait at least 12 days before it knows if a relative has been arrested or has perhaps disappeared for some other reason.

In May 1988 Paul Grossrieder, at the time head of the ICRC Delegation to Israel and the Occupied Territories, complained in an interview that the ICRC was:

unable to give proper and accurate information to the families of detainees...We sometimes receive notification before [the twelve days], sometimes afterwards or not at all.[19]

Eventually the ICRC was forced to carry out a census of prisoners and to establish its own tracing system in order to keep tabs on them but it appears that the practice of frequent transfers of detainees from prison to prison makes it difficult to keep information up to date.

Military orders provide that each detainee must be registered upon entering a detention centre or police station. However, in past practice, the effect of these requirements has frequently been nullified either because prison personnel refuse to say whether or not a particular detainee is registered or not, or give false information, or because the detainee is being questioned in a section of the detention centre (usually by the Shin Bet) without the knowledge of the detention centre personnel.

In practice, a common means of locating a detainee prior to the uprising was through information gained from visiting other prisoners. That this should be so is itself a condemnation of the prison system, which is clearly chaotic. During the uprising there has been a considerable deterioration even in this situation. Lawyers who could formerly ask the Legal Advisor of the Military Government to locate their clients have found responses from his office entirely inadequate, and indeed it has become rare to obtain any response at all. Al-Haq's most recent experience of this concerns the arrest of one of its researchers, Riziq Shuqeir, and the re-arrest of a field worker, 'Abd-al-Karim Kana'an, on 19 November 1988. Despite inquiries by his lawyer and family, Riziq Shuqair's whereabouts were unknown until the ICRC established his location at Dhahriya detention centre on the 27 November 1988; 'Abd-al-Karim Kana'an has been placed under administrative detention for six months even though he was released from Ansar III on 19 September 1988 after serving an identical order. Al-Haq was only able to ascertain the status of 'Abd-al-Karim Kana'an through the independent inquiries of the Lawyers Committee for Human Rights (LCHR).

In a letter sent by the LCHR to the Israeli Prime Minister Yitzhak Shamir on 10 March 1988, the Committee requested an end to the practice of *incommunicado* detention. The letter concluded that:

> no reform of detention procedures would be more valuable than a modification of Israel's agreement with the Red Cross that would allow the ICRC to visit detainees within 24 hours of their arrest, and on an unrestricted basis thereafter. We believe that nothing will effectively restrain the Shin Bet—and in turn ensure a modicum of

due process—save guaranteed immediate access to detainees by the International Committee of the Red Cross.[20]

Moreover, prison administrators themselves have admitted that they have had problems keeping track of detainees. Various statements have been made by the authorities concerning technological advances in their record-keeping systems. For example, on 24 July 1988 the IDF Central Command unveiled a computerised command and information centre which was intended to provide up-to-date information on the whereabouts and status of every person held in army camps in the West Bank. Each prison (except Ofer detention centre) now reportedly holds a computerised list of inmates which is transferred every 48 hours to the information centre in the Central Command.[21]

Al-Haq has as yet noticed no improvement in this chaotic system. We continue to be regularly visited by people whose family members have been arrested, perhaps in the middle of the night, and then disappeared for days or weeks. The inhumanity of this state of affairs of course lies in not knowing the whereabouts of an individual. In addition the practice of holding accused detainees in circumstances where they are without access to a lawyer runs contrary to Article 72 of the Fourth Geneva Convention, which states:

> Accused persons shall have the right to present evidence necessary to their defence...They shall have the right to be assisted by a qualified advocate or counsel of their choice, who shall be able to visit them freely and shall enjoy the necessary facilities for preparing the defence.

It will be seen below that it is precisely during the period of *incommunicado* detention that detainees frequently undergo some form of physical ill-treatment or torture, thus reinforcing the concern felt by relatives and friends for the safety of detainees.

c. Treatment of detainees under interrogation
During the initial period of detention following arrest, the detainee may be interrogated either by military personnel, security personnel (Shin Bet) or the police. During this period, when the detainee typically has access to neither lawyer nor family, he/she is most vulnerable.

Human rights bodies have for many years documented and published complaints about the prevalence of torture and ill-treatment of Palestinians in Israeli places of detention.[22] After years of denial by the Israeli authorities that prisoners and detainees were subjected to torture as well as cruel, inhuman and degrading treatment, it was revealed last year by an official Israeli Commission of Inquiry (the Landau Commission) that the constant denial in court by Shin Bet of methods used to extract information from suspects amounted to systematic perjury. The Commission found that Shin Bet agents had committed criminal assault, and used blackmail and threats as part of a repertoire of interrogation techniques. However they stopped short of using the word "torture" to describe any of these techniques, preferring instead the euphemistic term "physical pressure."

Having made its dramatic findings (published in November 1987), the Commission concluded that the most serious aspect of the inquiry was that of perjury by Shin Bet witnesses over a number of years, and further stated that the future use of "moderate physical and psychological pressure" was permissible on the basis of legal arguments of "necessity" and "justification."[23]

The International Covenant of Civil and Political Rights absolutely prohibits torture and cruel, inhuman or degrading treatment. The Convention Against Torture likewise outlaws such treatment. Given the documentation collected not only by al-Haq but by many other organisations of the prevalence of torture and ill-treatment, the conclusions of the Landau Commission give rise to serious concern. The Commission distinguished information extracted by Shin Bet using "physical pressure" solely for the investigative purposes of Shin Bet from information so extracted and used as the basis for a confession in criminal proceedings. The former, they said, might be acceptable in certain circumstances, even though information so obtained could not be used for the purposes of the latter. However, not only is it unacceptable that detainees be subjected to authorised physical ill-treatment (often amounting to torture, according to al-Haq's information) for purposes of investigation alone, but there is a grave danger inherent in the official stamp of approval of physical force that this will serve to encourage the further extraction of coerced confessions.[24]

The LCHR in their letter quoted above further recommended (*inter alia*) that the Commission's findings be re-evaluated at cabinet level, that a system be developed to ensure that Shin Bet did not violate international law through sleep deprivation, hooding or blindfolding and beatings, and that procedures be developed for the discipline of Shin Bet officers responsible for abuses against detainees.

During the uprising there has been a sharp increase of deaths in prisons, detention centres and police stations. The virtual impossibility of conducting independent autopsies or investigations into the causes and circumstances of these deaths is discussed below. However, in addition, al-Haq has continued to document other instances where

The Administration of Justice   213

detainees have complained of treatment prohibited under international law:

Taha Mousa 'Abd-al-'Aziz Nassar, 38, an English teacher from Halhoul near Hebron, was arrested on 26 May 1988 and taken to Hebron police station. The account he gives is from an al-Haq sworn affidavit:

> The first session was with Gabi. He was the person who accused me of escaping from the Intelligence officer. He cursed me, calling me a bastard..., threatening that he would break my nose. He was humiliating me. The session lasted about one quarter of an hour, without beating. Then he led me to the cupboard where I was handcuffed with a hood covering my head. I tried to stand but I couldn't, and I couldn't stretch my legs in a normal way. I sat squatting and stayed like that for about five hours until I was led by someone to the interrogation room. The guard had taken the hood off my head but the handcuffs were left on. There I saw Gabi, the interrogator who interviewed me the first time. He said: "We know that you are a member of a teachers' committee, but what we want to know is which political faction you serve and who directs you." I told him that I was a member of the West Bank Teachers' Committee and a member of the Workers' Union in the West Bank and the Gaza Strip, that I wasn't affiliated to any political faction, and that my work was confined to defending the teachers' union rights.
>
> He then started using his hands to beat and box my chest and face and then kicked my genitals, causing me great pain. Immediately after that he ordered the guard to escort me to cell number 11. On 16 June 1988 I was transferred to Atlit Detention Camp. We were transferred in an Egged bus which took about 36 detainees, each pair cuffed together. When we arrived at Atlit and after descending from the bus a soldier led a group of three detainees, of whom I was one, to Section C.
>
> On the morning of 14 July 1988, about 150 detainees, of whom I was one, were transferred to the Beitunia [Ofer] Detention Camp. In the bus our hands were bound in front of us with plastic straps. The soldiers forced us to bend over while seated in the bus until our heads touched our knees. About 100 meters outside of Atlit prison, five soldiers got into the bus and started beating us on our heads and backs with the butts of their rifles. One of the soldiers also beat me on the shoulder with the butt of his rifle and kicked my knees and feet with his heavy boots. I suffered great pain in my shoulders. When we arrived at Beitunia prison near Ramallah, my left shoulder was bleeding. The pain got worse, especially in the top parts of my spine. After my release I was X-rayed at the

Maqassed Hospital and it appeared that my spine was badly damaged; I am being treated now.[25]

3. Trial

The prisoners of the uprising, with the notable exception of the large number of those who have been put under administrative detention or released without trial, are subjected to military trials. (See also Appendix 6-A).

During the uprising most detainees have been tried *en masse* in so-called "quick trials." On 1 January 1988 it was reported that in one week in Gaza 187 people appeared before the Gaza Central Court, of whom 153 were convicted and sentenced.[26] This form of trial, in which dozens of people are bussed to court and tried in rapid succession, is not a novelty in the Occupied Territories. Rather it is one of the ways in which the efficiency of the military court system has been used to the advantage of the authorities at times of mass unrest.

The most common charge faced by the prisoners of the uprising is that of "disturbing public order." Most of those who are accused of "disturbing public order" are brought to trial without having been subjected to the lengthy and intensive interrogations routinely conducted by the Shin Bet. Instead, the military authorities obtain statements from the detainee and the arresting soldier at the police station immediately after the arrest. In most cases, the detainee will deny the accusation, while the soldier's statement will incriminate the suspected person.

The authorities apparently rely on the fact that the soldier's incriminating statement, together with his testimony before the court, are invariably considered by the military courts as sufficient evidence to convict Palestinian detainees. The evidence of the Israeli soldier in the military court is almost always believed in preference to the detainee's.

One problem that Palestinian detainees face is that in many cases soldiers do not come to court to testify, so the court adjourns the case to a future date for the purpose of hearing the soldier's evidence. In other cases it is the detainee who is not brought to the court from prison, and again the case is adjourned. Meanwhile, the detainee remains in custody. Bail requests are granted only after the detainee has been in custody for a period of time close to the expected sentence.

C. The Penal System

1. Estimated Number of Detainees During the Uprising

Six months after the beginning of the current uprising in the Occupied

Territories, al-Haq estimated that more than 17,000 Palestinians had been arrested and detained in jails, of which over 10,000 were being held on 9 June. This figure included over 2,000 administrative detainees in al-Haq's estimation, although the official figure released by the armed forces in May 1988 was 1,770 (as compared with 73 administrative detainees in June 1987).[27]

Al-Haq estimates that there are currently at least 9-10,000 Palestinians in detention. This figure combines the totals for: 1) those held in military detention centres (4,950 as of 31 October 1988); 2) those held in conventional prisons who were arrested since December 1987 and have yet to be charged (2,060); and 3) the large proportion of the 4,850 individuals who were in prison on the eve of the uprising and have not since been released.

We believe our estimate to be conservative, since it does not include detainees held in tents at conventional prisons nor those detained in police stations, and consider that the figures issued from time to time by the Israeli authorities are underestimated. This may reflect the difficulties they themselves have been having in keeping accurate records of prisoners. Clearly it is also in their interest to issue figures that underestimate the numbers of detainees. Thus, Rabin announced on 30 August 1988 that 18,000 had been arrested since the beginning of the uprising, and that 5,600 were then in detention of whom 2,600 were administrative detainees.[28] For reasons which will become clear, there is no means of arriving at an exact number of detainees. However, given an estimated renewal rate of 40 percent of detention orders from the first 6 months of the uprising it is our estimate that the current number of administrative detainees is at least 3,000.

2. Conventional and Military Centres of Detention in the Occupied Territories and Israel

There are several types of detention centres in which Palestinians from the Occupied Territories are detained (apart from informal, makeshift ones like schools): conventional prisons, army detention centres, Israeli military government buildings and police stations, and prisons and detention centres inside Israel. Women prisoners are generally held in Israeli jails (see below). Figures in brackets relate to the number of persons held in each centre as of 31 October 1988 unless otherwise stated:

a. Conventional Prisons in the Occupied Territories
Jenin (100), Nablus (200), Ramallah (160), Hebron (200) and Jnaid (600), in the West Bank, and the Central Prison in Gaza (350). These prisons

fall under the authority of the General Administration of Prisons, a department of the Israeli Ministry of Police.

These prisons, with the exception of Jnaid and Gaza, have two sections: one which holds sentenced prisoners, and another which holds those who are under interrogation or who are awaiting trial. Jnaid and the Central Prison in Gaza have separate sections for administrative detainees. Tulkarem prison, which was closed in 1983 because of unhealthy living conditions, was re-opened during the uprising.

b. Military Detention Centres

The figures in brackets here relate to numbers of inmates in May and October 1988 respectively.

West Bank: al-Fara'a (600; 440), Tulkarem (100; 151), Dhahriya (650; 455), Hebron 2 (200: May), Ofer (183: October).

Gaza: Katiba (Ansar II), (800, 633).

All these centres are run by the Israeli army and hold unsentenced prisoners. Dhahriya, Hebron 2 and Ofer were opened during the uprising. According to our information Hebron 2 is no longer in use.

Al-Haq's information indicates that these centres are often the scene of brutal treatment of detainees: one death has already occurred in the Russian Compound in Jerusalem since the beginning of the uprising (see below), and allegations have been made of cruel, inhuman and degrading treatment (see for example Appendix 6-B below).

c. Israeli Military Government Buildings and Police Stations in the Occupied Territories

Police stations in the West Bank exist in Hebron, Bethlehem, Ramallah, Nablus, Tulkarem, Jenin and Jericho.[29]

Because of the short duration of detention in these centres it is not possible as a rule to estimate the number of detainees held there; however, both the Ramallah prison and Jericho are also believed to contain several hundred detainees. These have not been included in the overall totals given in section (a) above.

d. Prisons and Detention Centres in Israel

Detention centres in Israel have been made use of more frequently than prisons during the uprising. These include Ketsyot or Ansar III (1726); Atlit Detention Centre near Haifa (686); Ramla prison (used to keep administrative detainees from Jerusalem); and Megiddo (679), which opened on 31 May 1988. The number of detainees in the Russian Compound (Moskobiya) in West Jerusalem is estimated by al-Haq at 100.

3. Conditions in Detention Centres

Al-Haq has prepared reports on the conditions of detention in many of the centres existing prior to the uprising and, subject to minor changes, the conditions remain much as they were.[30] Since 9 December 1987 the large class of detainees who are kept at al-Fara'a, Dhahriya and Ketsyot but who are not interrogated have experienced severe conditions as well. They suffer from deliberately harsh prison conditions, both physical and psychological. In Appendix 6-B we discuss in some detail two of the new army detention centres, Dhahriya and Ketsyot (Ansar III), and therefore confine ourselves here to a few general comments.

Several individuals and groups have found cause to visit centres of detention during the uprising, including the Association for Civil Rights in Israel, the Lawyers Committee for Human Rights (on 18 August 1988 two detainees were shot to death) and 3 Israeli judges (see Appendix 6-B). Another visit by a group of Israeli parliamentarians to Dhahriya detention centre resulted in a verdict by one of them that conditions were "reasonable."[31] But on 21 July 1988 the *Jerusalem Post* stated that:

> military sources confirmed that five soldiers, including an officer and a woman soldier, are being courtmartialled on charges of beating prisoners on 22 occasions at the Dhahriya detention centre. In one case according to the charges, an officer beat prisoners who refused to mimic animal calls. In other instances prisoners were clubbed, kicked and smashed into the walls, according to the charge sheet.

To the best of al-Haq's knowledge, no findings have yet been published by the authorities.

It is true that the period under review is exceptional. In periods of unrest it is expected that prisons could become overcrowded and that conditions consequently worsen. But this cannot excuse the deliberate harshness of the treatment in this period—the detention of many who have not been tried, who are not serving sentence for offences that they have been informed of and have been able to challenge. Neither can it excuse the denial of access to lawyers and families, nor the physical ill-treatment of prisoners.

These circumstances cause particular concern for the treatment of minors in detention, since under Israeli military orders minors between the ages of 12 and 14 may be detained for up to 6 months. In a visit to Ofer detention centre in Beitunia near Ramallah during the uprising, MK Dedi Zucker found a total of 17 detainees under the age of 16. The total number of detainees under the age of 16 was put between 300 and 400 by the Israeli Ombudsman for children, Dr Horowitz.[32] According to the charity Save the Children in East Jerusalem, the number of minors under 16 imprisoned between 9 December 1987 and 8 August 1988 was 307. However in contrast to the Israeli authorities' response to mass protestation in 1982 when hundreds of young people were rounded up and imprisoned without trial, the punishment centres presently operating are full of Palestinians ranging in age from 13 to 80 years.

4. Deaths in Detention and Autopsies

Along with a marked increase in the other human rights abuses described in this report, al-Haq has noted an alarming rise in deaths in detention since the beginning of the uprising. Compared with 1987, when one Palestinian died in prison, by the end of October 1988 at least eight Palestinians died while in the custody of the military authorities: five in the West Bank, who are alleged by the authorities to have committed suicide, two shooting deaths in Ansar III, and one beating death in the Gaza Strip, although because of al-Haq's focus on the West Bank the latter three cases were not documented by the organisation. Independent investigation into the cause of these deaths has been made impossible by the authorities' refusal in many cases to make public the results of the official investigations (including autopsy reports), and by their refusal to allow independent forensic experts either to be present at the official autopsies or to conduct second autopsies on behalf of the families of the deceased.

Six of the deaths that occurred in detention in 1987 and 1988 include the following:
- 'Awad Hamdan of Rummana (Tulkarem), who died from "asphyxiation" in the Jenin prison on 21 July 1987, two days after his arrest.
- Ibrahim al-Ray, who died in Ayalon prison on 11 April 1988, an alleged suicide.
- Nasser Suleiman Dweidar of Jericho, who died while in custody on 20 June 1988, an alleged suicide.
- 'Atta 'Ayyad of Qalandiya Refugee Camp, who died in the Dhahriya detention centre on 14 August 1988, an alleged suicide.
- Nabil Ibdah of Beit Hanina, a suburb of East Jerusalem, who died in the Moskobiya detention centre on 16 August 1988, an alleged suicide.
- Ibrahim al-Umtour of Sa'ir (Hebron), who died in the Dhahriya detention centre on 21 October 1988, an alleged suicide.

Ascertaining the cause of death of a Palestinian detainee is impeded by a number of factors which include the following:

a. Denying the family access to the results of the official investigation
Although an official investigation, including an autopsy, is carried out by the authorities in each case of death in detention as a matter of routine procedure, the findings of such an investigation are not automatically made available to the family and lawyer of the deceased, and in any case these findings cannot necessarily be trusted. In addition, if the report is made available, this usually occurs after a considerable delay, making a second autopsy, even if it were permitted, a nearly impossible task due to the passage of time.

For example, in the case of 'Awad Hamdan, who died in Jenin prison before the uprising on 21 July 1987, the family's lawyer, Felicia Langer, was unable to obtain the results of the official investigation until more than a year after the death, and then only after repeated requests. His family was informed on different occasions that he had died of (1) a heart attack (message of the prison authorities relayed by the ICRC), (2) a snake bite (the Military Governor of Tulkarem), (3) pneumonia (the first—unpublished—autopsy report of the Abu Kbir Institute for Forensic Medicine in Tel Aviv), and (4) asphyxiation (the second Abu Kbir report). The first Abu Kbir report, which was not made available to the lawyer, turned out to be false; the second Abu Kbir report was made available to Ms. Langer more than a year after the death. At the time of writing, Advocate Langer is still pressing the authorities to state in detail how Hamdan had died from asphyxiation. Meanwhile, proceedings have been initiated against the (anonymous) agent of the Israeli internal intelligence service, the Shin Bet, who had been responsible for Mr. Hamdan in Jenin prison; the agent was reportedly charged with "causing death through negligence." At the time of writing, these proceedings, which are being held in secret, have not yet been completed.[33]

b. Preventing the family from examining the body before burial
The families of the deceased are routinely prevented from taking a close look at the body of their relative. In most cases where a Palestinian dies in the custody of the Israeli authorities, the families are not permitted to organise a funeral and are forced to bury the corpse in great haste and in the middle of the night, in the presence of only a handful of immediate relatives and a large contingent of soldiers, and without having the chance to examine the body in detail. It should be noted here that there is no Palestinian expertise in forensic medicine in Israel or the Occupied Territories, so an expert would have to be brought in from abroad.

In the case of 'Atta 'Ayyad, for example, who died in the Dhahriya detention centre on 14 August 1988, the family reported that the army clamped a curfew on Qalandiya Camp on the evening of Sunday, August

14, and delivered the body to the family around 1:30 the next morning. The family was given about twenty minutes to bury the body; only the closest relatives were allowed to be present. Soldiers told the family that they should not look at the body but hurry up, and warned them not to talk about it with others. As a result of the family's request for specialist advice, an American pathologist sponsored by the Boston-based Physicians for Human Rights flew from the United States to carry out an investigation into the circumstances of the death. However, as a result of having to bury the body at such short notice, the family was unable to give more than a few details about the condition of the body.

c. Refusing the presence of a family representative during autopsy
Attempts to allow a doctor commissioned by the families of the deceased to be present during the official autopsy have so far failed. Generally, the official autopsy is carried out before the relatives are aware of the death or before they have been able to contact a lawyer, who in turn must contact a doctor.

This is illustrated by the case of Ibrahim al-Ray, who died in Ramla prison on 11 April 1988. The authorities claimed that his death was a suicide. On the day of his death his lawyer, Leah Tsemel, made a request to a military court to have a doctor be allowed to attend the official autopsy for the family, but her request was denied. Ms Tsemel then directed a similar request to the director of the Abu Kbir Institute, who initially granted the request. But the next day, when the autopsy was to take place, the doctor commissioned by the family was prevented from being present during the autopsy. The family did manage to obtain a copy of the official autopsy report, which stated that Mr al-Ray had died of choking. Yet the official findings were put in doubt by reports by the family that they had observed traces of violence on their relative's body at the time of burial.[34]

d. Refusal to allow the family to exhume the body in order to perform a second autopsy
Requests for permission to exhume the body of a Palestinian who died in detention and to have a second autopsy performed by a forensic expert independently commissioned by the family of the deceased—a universally accepted right also enshrined in Israeli law—have not been granted by the Israeli authorities.

This is illustrated by the case of 'Awad Hamdan, cited above. In that case, al-Haq, with the consent of the family, submitted a request for exhumation to the health official in charge of the Tulkarem district, as per procedure. This official, who has legal authority to grant or deny the request, instead forwarded it to the Legal Advisor to the Military Government in Bet El, who failed to respond to the request.[35]

The existing practice of keeping detainees incommunicado, sometimes for protracted periods of time, in sections of prisons under the exclusive authority of Shin Bet encourages abuse. In addition, the failure to publish findings of official investigations encourages attempts to cover up the truth. Frequent reports about abuse in prisons received by al-Haq, leading in some cases to death, underline the need for proper supervision in prisons and thorough investigations when abuse is reported to have occurred, and publication of the findings of such investigations. In addition, independent investigations must be encouraged, as they offer an added protection to detainees by raising the cost of attempts at a cover-up.

At present, supervision of detention facilities by the authorities is insufficient, and recommendations resulting from investigations carried out by official bodies, including the Israeli High Court of Justice, if adequate, are not sufficiently acted upon. Al-Haq has pointed out this problem in previous reports.[36]

Supervision by independent agencies like the ICRC is severely circumscribed. The ICRC, as noted earlier in this chapter, is not allowed access to a detainee until the 14th day after arrest, and lawyers are routinely denied access to a client until after the latter has signed a confession. Through agreement between the ICRC and the authorities, ICRC findings cannot be made public.

The need for supervision is highlighted in a case like that of 'Atta 'Ayyad, who died in the Dhahriya Military Detention Centre on 14 August 1988. Sworn affidavits obtained by lawyers from detainees who were in Dhahriya at the time of his death state that the victim had been heard screaming for two nights prior to his death while in isolation, and that he had been in excellent health previous to being placed in isolation.

The detainee's lawyer, 'Abed 'Assali, was prevented from visiting from the date of arrest, 23 June 1988, until the date of Mr 'Ayyad's death almost two months later. The young man's family also made an attempt to visit him, since his name had appeared on the ICRC list of detainees who could be visited, but when they arrived in Dhahriya on visitors' day they were turned back by prison officials. Also, in the case of Ibrahim al-Umtour, who died in Dhahriya on 21 October 1988, supervision might have saved a life. Testimonies submitted by Palestinians detained in Dhahriya at the time of death indicate that Mr Al-Umtour had been severely beaten and had kept other detainees awake with his screams for two days prior to his death. Proper supervision might have led to steps being taken to ensure that the victim was removed from his interrogators in time and given the necessary medical care.

The need for independent investigations is underlined by the apparent attempts of some officials to cover up the truth. In the case of Naser Dweidar of Jericho, who died shortly after his arrest on 20 June 1988, army officers came to the home of the director of the Jericho government hospital on the evening of the death, requesting a signed death certificate that was otherwise left blank. The doctor refused the request in the absence of the corpse and on the grounds that he did not keep death certificates at his home.[37] The existence of two contradictory official autopsy reports in the case of 'Awad Hamdan, too, suggests a deliberate attempt at cover-up as well.

The causing of death in detention through torture or "negligence" (and including aggravated suicide as a result of torture) is one of the gravest violations of human rights that can occur.[38] However, although theoretically protected by international law, few effective means of enforcing these international legal provisions are currently available. At a 1986 meeting of the UN Commission of Human Rights, the Special Rapporteur stated, *inter alia*:

> One of the ways in which governments can show that they want this abhorrent phenomenon of arbitrary or summary executions eliminated is by investigating, holding inquests, prosecuting and punishing those found guilty. There is, therefore, a need to develop international standards designed to ensure that investigations are conducted into all cases of suspicious death and, in particular, those at the hands of the law enforcement agencies in all situations. *A death in any type of custody should be regarded, prima facie, as summary or arbitrary execution*, and appropriate investigation should immediately be made to confirm or rebut the presumption. The results of investigations should be made public. [Emphasis added][39]

It is clear that Israel is not complying with these standards and procedures and the result has been at least eight deaths since December 1987, as well as the others prior to the uprising. The refusal by the Israeli authorities to accept any of the requests of Palestinians or outside international bodies to break this vicious and cruel circle of secrecy is thus a clear invitation to murder.

5. *Detention of Palestinian Women*
During the uprising thirteen Palestinian women have been administratively detained for six months, although many more have been arrested

and detained for shorter periods of time.

Until the end of July 1988, the Neve Tertsa women's prison in Ramla was the only conventional women's prison. However, the capacity of this prison was between between 35-40 only; most women were therefore in three detention centres:
- "Kishon" or Jalameh detention centre near Haifa.
- "Abu-Kbir" detention centre in Tel-Aviv.
- "Moskobiya"police station (Russian Compound)in Jerusalem.

In July 1988 a new women's prison known as "Hasharon" or Telmond prison was opened after Palestinian prisoners went on strike at Neve Tertsa during May, June and July 1988 (see below). All political prisoners at Abu-Kbir and Jalameh detention centres and most of the detainees at Neve Tertsa (except 4 from the Gaza Strip and 1 from the West Bank) were transferred to Telmond prison. The Moscobiya detention centre continued to be used as a women's prison.[40]

While virtually every administrative detainee has suffered arbitrary and punitive conditions of imprisonment during the uprising, women detainees have faced additional problems stemming from the fact that until the opening of the Telmond prison facility, conditions for women detainees were wholly inadequate. As a result, women political prisoners were subject to a regime of inadequate health care and harassment from criminal prisoners.

Tahani Abou-Daqqa, from 'Abasan in Gaza, was in her second month of pregnancy when detained in Neve Tertsa prison. She was suffering from health problems related to her pregnancy, and had asked to be checked by a gynaecologist on a number of occasions. The Israeli group "Women for Women Political Prisoners" intervened in her case and asked the prison administration to allow a gynaecologist to examine Tahani, but their demand was refused. Tahani's health situation deteriorated and she had a miscarriage in prison on 5 July 1988, when she was in her fourth month of pregnancy.

Mariam Isma'il who was administratively detained for six months on 24 March 1988, suffered from stomach and kidney problems before her imprisonment. She was severely ill-treated and kept in solitary confinement for 33 days in the Russian Compound prior to her administrative detention. She started to suffer from pains in her back but although she asked for medical treatment several times, it was denied.

Even political prisoners who have been severely beaten by the Israeli criminal prisoners with whom they have been confined, e.g. Muna Sarasra and Jinan al-Bitar, were denied medical treatment.

Among the major problems facing Palestinian women prisoners is that they are held in the same sections as Israeli criminal prisoners, from whom they are liable to suffer abuse and physical threat. Although in most cases they are held in separate rooms, Palestinian women prisoners are still subjected to constant harassment by these Israeli criminal detainees. In the Abu-Kbir detention centre, for example, women prisoners have asked on several occasions for their transfer to Neve Tertsa due to harassment from criminal detainees who were kept in rooms close to those of the Palestinian women.

On 26 May 1988, Palestinian political prisoners at Jalameh prison were attacked by criminal prisoners. After a 24-hour hunger strike, the prison administration promised to improve their conditions. According to a released detainee Palestinian political prisoners at Jalameh had to take turns sleeping, in order to protect themselves from physical abuse. In another incident Jinan al-Bitar, who had been issued with a six-month administrative detention order on 17 August 1988, was badly bruised and cut in an attack on her at Jalameh prison.

On 24 July 1988, Muna Sarasra from Jerusalem was attacked by 15 Israeli criminal prisoners at Neve Tertsa prison in the presence of male guards, who made no attempt to intervene to stop the attack until she had been injured. On the same day, 'Itaf 'Alian and Im'an Sirhan were kicked and beaten by four male and several female warders in the presence of a prison officer.[41]

Continuous intimidation caused political prisoners at Neve Tertsa prison go on strike at the end of May 1988. Political prisoners refused to go out of their rooms for meals or for their breaks unless the administration of the prison met their demands, including:

- Different times for political prisoners' and Israeli criminal prisoners' meals and breaks
- The elimination of opportunities for Israeli criminal prisoners to mix with or harass political prisoners.
- Provision for Palestinian political prisoners to mix with Palestinian administrative detainees. Until late July, the administration of the prison was preventing the five administrative detainees held at Neve Tertsa prison from mixing with political prisoners. To the first women administratively detained, this has meant near-solitary confinement.

Forty days later the administration of the prison continued to refuse these demands. On 27 June 1988, political prisoners announced a four-day hunger strike—without result. It was only after an attack on a prison guard by two political prisoners that a decision was made by the prison administration to open a new women's prison for Palestinian political prisoners. By 1 August 1988, almost all Palestinian political prisoners except those held at Moskobiya were lodged at Telmond prison, in a new compound separated from the rest of the prison where Israeli criminal prisoners are held. (Those held at Moskobiya are still subject to harassment by Israeli criminal prisoners).

A number of prisoners who are currently held at Telmond have been awaiting trial for unacceptably long periods of time. Since May 1988 only one political prisoner, Amira Isma'il Shamrouh, aged 44, from Deheisha Refugee Camp, has been tried. Most of the political prisoners who are awaiting trial were arrested during June and July 1988. However, Marwa Qatmera, aged 23, from al-'Izaria, was arrested in December 1987 and is still awaiting trial. Among the 32 political prisoners that were held at Telmond prison on 15 August 1988, 21 were awaiting trial, 7 were under administrative detention and only 4 had been sentenced.

D. Conclusion

For many years it has been apparent to al-Haq that the administration of justice in the Occupied Territories is effectively an executive branch of the Israeli Military Government, which pursues its policy goals through ever-increasing control over the legal infrastructure and population of the Territories. During the uprising the numbers of those indiscriminately arrested and detained have risen dramatically; the army has intensified its practice of beating and ill-treating those under interrogation and detention; new detention centres have been opened; and the number of unexplained deaths in detention rose as well.

It is evident that in the Occupied Territories arrest and interrogation are not the necessary prelude to "normal" criminal investigations but rather serve as a means of intimidating the Palestinian population with a view to controlling expressions of protest against the occupation. Likewise, centres of detention contribute to this goal by virtue of their punitively harsh conditions. Those who are tried rather than administratively detained have often not been granted the benefit of a fair trial, but have rather been subjected to cursory and inadequate hearings.

These measures, from the removal of the right of local inhabitants to bring actions in the local courts (see Appendix 6-A) to human rights abuses committed in the name of justice by the various authorities responsible for trying individuals in the courts, are clearly prohibited under international humanitarian and human rights law. Unfortunately, mere illegality has not deterred Israel's highest judicial officers from sanctioning Shin Bet methods of interrogation, nor from approving the location of the detention centre Ansar III outside of the Occupied Territories (see Appendix 6-A). Rather, it is clear that the uprising is to be put down, whatever the means.

FOOTNOTES TO CHAPTER 6

1. The fact that Israel does not recognise the applicability of the most important of these, namely the Fourth Geneva Convention, to the Occupied Territories does not affect al-Haq's view that the Convention represents the correct minimum standard nor does it affect the legal duty of world states to ensure its observance (see Article 1 of the Fourth Geneva Convention).
2. See, for example, Law in the Service of Man (LSM)/Al Haq, *Jnaid: The New Israeli Prison in Nablus, an Appraisal* (1984); International Commission of Jurists (ICJ) and LSM/Al Haq, *Torture and Intimidation in the West Bank: The Case of al-Fara'a Prison* (1985); Emma Playfair, *Administrative Detention in the Occupied West Bank* (LSM/Al-Haq, 1986); ICJ, LSM/Al-Haq and Gaza Centre for Law and Rights, *Justice? The Military Court System in the Israeli-Occupied Territories* (1987); LSM/Al-Haq, *Dhahriya: Centre for Punishment* (1988); LSM/Al-Haq, *Ansar 3: A Case for Closure*, (1988).
3. Al-Haq translation.
4. Al-Haq Affidavit No. 1286.
5. Al-Haq Affidavit No. 1260.
6. Al-Haq Affidavit No. 1254.
7. Affidavit taken by Advocate Tamar Peleg.
8. Amnesty International News Release, (AI Index: MDE 15\01\88).
9. Al-Haq report.
10. Al-Haq report.
11. *Jerusalem Post*, 8 September 1988.
12. Al-Haq report.
13. *Jerusalem Post*, 11 November 1988.
14. This statement does not constitute a formal al-Haq affidavit since the victim was under 16 years of age.
15. Case no. 4712/88.
16. *Jerusalem Post*, 8 January 1988.
17. See al-Haq publication *Justice*, p. 21.
18. See al-Haq Briefing Paper no. 3, *The Military Court System* (1987).
19. *Jerusalem Post*, 27 May 1987.
20. Copy of letter available at al-Haq.
21. *Jerusalem Post*, 25 July 1988.
22. See for example *Report of the Special Committee to Investigate Israeli Practices Affecting Human Rights of the Population of the Occupied Territories* (26 October 1970 and 5 October 1971); Amnesty International, *Report on the Treatment of Certain Prisoners under Interrogation in Israel* (1970); *Memorandum to the United Nations Security Council* (8 June 1970); annual *Amnesty International Report* (1977-1980, 1982-1986 and 1988 inclusive); Amnesty International, *Torture in the Eighties* (1984), pp. 233-6; ICJ and LSM/Al-Haq, *The Case of al-Fara'a Prison* (1985).
23. See *Report of the Comission of Enquiry into the Methods of Interrogation of the General Security Service in Regard to Hostile Terrorist Activity*, Part 4, "Conclusions."
24. Article 7 of the International Covenant on Civil and Political Rights and Article 5 of the Universal Declaration of Human Rights state (in so far as is

relevant):

No one shall be subjected to torture or to cruel, inhuman or degrading treatment or punishment.

Torture is defined in the first article of the Convention against Torture and other Cruel, Inhuman or Degrading Treatment or Punishment (adopted by the General Assembly of the United Nations on 10 December 1984):

For the purposes of this Convention, torture means any act by which severe pain or suffering, whether physical or mental, is intentionally inflicted on a person for such purposes as obtaining from him or a third person information or a confession, punishing him for an act he or a third person has committed or is suspected of having committed, or intimidating or coercing him or a third person, or for any reason based on discrimination of any kind, when such pain or suffering is inflicted by or at the instigation of or with the consent or acquiesence of a public official or other person acting in an official capacity. It does not include pain or suffering arising only from, inherent in or incidental to lawful sanctions.

25. Al-Haq Affidavit No. 1431.
26. *Jerusalem Post*, 1 January 1988.
27. *Jerusalem Post*, 20 May 1988. Our calculations are based on the capacity of Israeli detention centres, the length of prison sentences handed down by military courts for "disturbing public order" (the most common charge) findings from our own fieldwork and interviews with detainees.
28. *Al Quds* newspaper, 31 August 1988.
29. Order amending M.O. 378, issued 11 August 1988.
30. See note 3 *supra*.
31. *Jerusalem Post*, 14 January 1988.
32. *Jerusalem Post*, 27 May 1988.
33. Conversations with Advocate Felicia Langer.
34. Conversations with Advocate Lea Tsemel.
35. Correspondence in al-Haq records.
36. ICJ and LSM/Al-Haq, *The Case of al-Fara'a Prison*, note 2 *supra*.
37. A doctor who examined the body later, Dr. Nazih Muslih, the Director of Health Services in the Jericho area, found irregular marks on the left ear and face of Mr. Dweidar's body, and asked for an official autopsy to be performed at the Abu Kbir Institute. On 21 June, Mr. Dweidar's family was informed by the army that their relative had committed suicide in prison. Al-Haq does not know the results, if any, of the official investigation into the causes of death.
38. See Article 6 of the International Covenant of Civil and Political Rights which states: "No one shall be arbitrarily deprived of life."
39. UN Doc. E/CN.4/1986/21, p. 99.
40. It was reported by *Al-Sha'ab* newspaper on 25 October 1988 that the Israeli authorities are planning to open a new women's prison in Nablus.
41. Women's Organization for Political Prisoners, *A Report on Harassment of Political Prisoners*, 28 July 1988.

Appendix 6-A

THE JUDICIAL SYSTEM

A more insidious, less visible use of the system of law and order than the executive's usurpation of judicial functions of punishment, as described in the pages above, has been the creeping annexation of the legal infrastructure of the Occupied Territories. This has taken the form of enlarging the jurisdiction of Israeli courts over both Palestinians and Israeli settlers while allowing the local courts to wither for lack of reform. The following few paragraphs describe the outlines of the two systems of law that have emerged as a result.

1. Court Structure and Jurisdiction: As Applicable to Palestinians Resident in the West Bank and Gaza Strip

So far as criminal matters are concerned Palestinians are subject to the jurisdiction of either the local courts (i.e. non-Israeli) or military courts (see M.O. 378). A criminal matter will come before a military court if the Area Commander decides that a "security" element is involved. So far as civil matters are concerned, local courts retain exclusive jurisdiction, with the exception of certain matters dealt with by a military "Objections Committee." This committee, established in 1967, has jurisdiction to hear certain matters previously within the jurisdiction of local courts, for example appeals at first instance against assessments of tax and customs duties.

Numerous problems of effectiveness have beset this legal system. Among these may be included the following: the quality of court services in local courts (standard of judges, court officials and general services); access to the courts (often expensive and in cases involving the armed forces or the State of Israel requiring a permit from the military); and lack of inspection of the courts. In 1985 a number of judges were tried for corruption and bribery; the majority of appeal and district court judges were removed and replaced. At the same time a court inspector was appointed but was dismissed one year after and has not been replaced. These problems are merely compounded by the fact that all judges are appointed by the Area Commander.

Nor is there an independent legal profession as a result of M.O. 1164 which restricts the formation of independent associations. On 16 September 1987 the Israeli High Court decision unanimously found that the restriction on the formation of a Bar Association should be reconsidered, there being no valid reasons of security for the restriction. However the

Civil Administration has yet to act on the decision. [See R. Shehadeh, *Occupier's Law: Israel and the West Bank* (Institute for Palestine Studies, 2nd ed. 1988), p. 224.]

So far as the military courts are concerned these are relatively efficient; however this efficiency has degenerated into "quick trials" at times of unrest, i.e. trials where groups of individuals charged separately are tried *en masse*. Nor is there any possibility of appeal from the military courts; the only recourse is an appeal for mercy to the military governor of the area in which the convicted person resides although this will not suspend execution of the sentence.

2. Court Structure and Jurisdiction: As applicable to Israeli Settlers in the West Bank and Gaza Strip

Settlers who are involved in criminal matters may be tried in criminal courts in Israel or military courts; in practice settlers never come before a local court.

In civil matters settlers may be subject either to local courts, Israeli courts or settlement courts (established in March 1981 and now called "courts for local affairs"). This may be pre-determined by the terms of a contract. In practice it is virtually impossible for a Palestinian to serve papers on a settler since settlements are usually well guarded and entry restricted. In matters concerning personal status (marriage, divorce, inheritance, custody) Rabbinical courts have sole jurisdiction.

Increasingly the Israeli High Court has held itself out as competent to judicially review decisions of military courts and local courts. However with the abolition in 1967 of the Court of Cassation (the highest court of appeal in the Jordanian system) and the reduction of the jurisdiction of local courts there remains a large gap in the system of appeal. In addition the Israeli High Court has increasingly accepted arguments by respondents of "security imperatives" and "effective deterrence" (see also the conclusions of the Landau Report).

Many of the qualified lawyers in the West Bank have been on strike since the Israeli occupation began in 1967. At the time when the strike began in 1967 they felt that aspects of the Israeli treatment of the legal system demanded that they boycott the system in order not to lend it legitimacy by continuing to practise within it. (These included the failure of the Israeli courts to recognise the applicability of the Fourth Geneva Convention to the occupation, the annexation of East Jerusalem and the removal of the Court of Appeal from Jerusalem to Ramallah.)

Practising lawyers in Gaza themselves went on strike on 27 December 1987 in an unprecedented move. The Gaza Bar Association sent a letter to the Israeli military authorities stating the reasons for the strike. These included:

(1). the mass and arbitrary arrest of Palestinians conducted by the Israeli military authorities in Gaza;

(2). the severely sub-standard conditions under which the detainees in military detention centres, especially in "Ansar II," were living, and the systematic beatings and humiliation from which they suffer;

(3). the unjust practices and procedures before the military courts.

The strike was followed by lawyers in West Bank military courts but suspended after a period of 3 weeks at the request of their clients.

The development of a dual system of law is contrary to the terms of the Hague Regulations, Article 23 (h) of which states that:

> ...it is especially forbidden to declare abolished, suspended or inadmissible in a court of law the rights and actions of the nationals of the hostile party.

(Other international law governing the judicial and penal systems is principally contained in Articles 64-78 of the Fourth Geneva Convention.)

Appendix 6-B

ARMY DETENTION CENTRES

1. Dhahriya Detention Centre

The following summary of conditions at Dhahriya detention centre is based on a report published by al-Haq in May 1988, since when some improvements have been noticed by detainees, although the report's conclusions remain broadly correct. (The report includes a survey of the relevant local and international law governing conditions of prisons).

Dhahriya detention centre, the first to be opened especially for the prisoners of the uprising, is situated at the north entrance to the village of Dhahriya, some miles south of the West Bank city of Hebron.

The detention centre was built by the British as an army camp for their soldiers, and it continues to serve the same purpose for the Israeli army. On 21 December 1987, at the beginning of the current uprising, the military authorities turned over parts of the buildings of the camp for a detention centre for the prisoners of the uprising.

On 1 May 1988, around 650 detainees were being held at Dhahriya, but more than 3,000 have had passed through the centre in the six months since its establishment. On 31 October 1988 there were 450 detainees. Those held there include members of all sectors of Palestinian society: journalists, students, merchants, university lecturers, intellectuals, workers, farmers.

Some of the worst complaints of beating and ill-treatment received by al-Haq relate to treatment during transport to or from prison, particularly of those bound for Dhahriya detention centre. They are pushed onto a bus, blindfolded and handcuffed. Each detainee has to sit with his head bowed below the level of the back of the chair in front, regardless of the length of the journey, and is forbidden to make any move. During the journey, soldiers beat the prisoners, shout at them and insult them and generally create an atmosphere of terror by beating their clubs against the seats.

Once they have arrived, detainees at Dhahriya are beaten, humiliated and subjected to a list of rules aimed at degrading the person. They suffer from gross overcrowding in rooms, cells and tents, absence of sanitary installations and deprivation of facilities to maintain personal hygiene. Such conditions serve as a constant reinforcement of the physical humiliation of the detainee; the dirt and discomfort deny the detainee any degree of personal dignity.

In addition, detainees complain of deprivation of sleep; the poor level of medical care; forced labour; deprivation of exercise; insufficient food; isolation from the outside world; and restrictions on family and lawyers' visits. It is such practices and conditions that make Dhahriya a centre for illegal punishment rather than merely for detention.

- Overcrowding in the prison has been chronic from the start. Al-Haq's information indicates that initially there were six rooms at the prison, three of which measured as much as 100 square meters each. In some cases, as many as 170 detainees were placed in one of these rooms; thus each person had considerably less than one square meter to himself. Later, the prisoners were themselves ordered to reconstruct these rooms to create more rooms and cells. By the beginning of May there were 20 rooms, measuring from 12 to 40 square meters each, and an additional 10 small cells. The cells in Dhahriya are used for solitary confinement; they are small and have no windows. Tents of some 10m x 4m and holding 23 to 28 detainees each are also in use.

  Overcrowding in the rooms, and the inadequate size and number of windows, and the fact that these are either covered with metal shields or look over a closed area, prevent the detainees from getting

enough light or fresh air, nor is there adequate space for all to lie down to sleep.
- Detainees report that they have no proper toilet facilities in their rooms, cells or tents. Instead, they are provided with a bucket to be used by all prisoners in the room. The bucket stays in the room all the time, and is emptied only when it is full, upon the permission of the guard on duty. At times the bucket overflows onto the floor. When taken out to be emptied, the bucket is sometimes left outside for some hours, until the guard decides to give it back to the prisoners.
- Maintenance of personal hygiene for a detainee in Dhahriya is a practical impossibility. The military authorities do not provide an adequate supply of basic facilities for the detainees to keep themselves clean. Prisoners do not have a water source in their rooms or cells, and the water that is provided is often insufficient even for each person in the room to wash his face once in the morning. Permission to bathe is granted only once every 10 days. An affidavit given by a prisoner at Dhahriya states:

> Within a period of 17 days, I was allowed to bathe only once. No hot water was provided. We had to shower in cold water...They took us out to a small nearby room, which had two water pipes...We were ten prisoners and they had given us only 8 minutes to shower. They provided us with two bars of soap, and one dirty towel for each pair of us...

- Deprivation of sleep appears to be a deliberate part of the daily ritual of soldiers at Dhahriya. The process of counting detainees takes place at least twice a day, and is timed to occur at times when detainees are sleeping, late at night or very early in the morning. During this process, detainees have to stand up against the wall with their heads down. Detainees who are kept outside in the yard at night are forced by soldiers to make all kinds of loud noises so as to disturb the sleeping detainees.
- Medical treatment in Dhahriya is dealt with in Chapter 2 under the section "Medical Treatment in Prisons and Detention Centres."
- Unlike other prisons and detention centres, prisoners at Dhahriya are not granted an exercise break outside their rooms. They are thus locked up in their unhealthy rooms for 24 hours a day, except when being punished outside the rooms or forced to work. Newspapers and radios are not permitted for detainees, and contact between prisoners in different rooms is also prohibited.
- Food is served on the floor of the rooms, with one serving being

shared between several prisoners. Detainees complain that the quality and quantity of food is poor, even by prison standards. Hot drinks such as tea are frequently cold on arrival, and each glass has to be shared by two prisoners or more. One or two jars of water are given to each room a day. This water is to be used for all purposes, including drinking and washing.

In addition to the conditions mentioned above, prisoners are subjected to maltreatment by their army guards. The following are among the most common practices:

- Newcomers are spread-eagled against the wall, and forced to repeat after the guard whatever he says. This is known as the process of learning the "rules of behaviour." "Ken, Captain" (Hebrew for "Yes, Captain") is the password for survival that all detainees must use whenever they have to respond to any soldier. Each time a soldier passes, detainees must stand up, face the wall with heads down and hands behind their backs. Any detainee that fails to do so is subjected to harsh beatings. When a soldier enters the room at day or night, every detainee has to stand with his hands behind his back and face to the wall. A former detainee at Dhahriya reported that they had to stand in the manner described above an average of 17 times per day.
- Severe and arbitrary beating in an individual or collective manner is often reported in Dhahriya. One detainee describes his experience on the day he went to court:

Yesterday, 22 March 1988, I was taken to court. During my absence, my room-mates were apparently ordered to stand up for the evening meal, but they refused. At that moment I was brought back from the court. As I was being admitted to the room, soldiers came and asked for the detainee in charge of the room. [The prison authorities place a detainee in charge of each room to facilitate communication with the administration.] It was me. I was ordered out of the room into the corridor. Four soldiers were there. Immediately, they started beating me all over my body. Then I was taken to see the commander of the prison. I told him that I was in court when the prisoners refused to stand up, but he would not listen, and said: "If you do not stand up we will break your bones." I was then ordered back to my room. The same soldiers who beat me first also took me back to the room. I was beaten again in the corridor, then they ordered me into the room and started to beat everybody. Until now I have a horrible pain in my back and I cannot stand up on my legs normally.

The lawyer who took the statement saw injuries on the affiant's left eye and leg, and noticed that he could not walk properly.
* Tear gas is reported to have been been used against detainees within their closed rooms at least once, on 27 December 1987, when one detainee allegedly tried to cut his wrists as a protest against conditions in the prison. Guards soon afterwards sprayed tear gas inside the rooms.

Al-Haq concludes that such treatment and conditions are clearly intended to be punitive irrespective of guilt or innocence. The conditions of detention in Dhahriya, and the systematic and deliberate maltreatment appear to be deliberately aimed at creating a permanent state of despair and at instilling fear. It seems that the Israeli authorities believe that by so treating detainees it can break their spirit. The prison is thus one of the means used in an attempt to force the Palestinians into submission.

2. Ketsyot Detention Centre (Ansar III)
(Like the above discussion of conditions in Dhahriya detention centre, the following summary of conditions in Ansar III is based on a detailed report, published by al-Haq in August 1988.)

Opened on 18 March 1988, Ketsyot (popularly known as Ansar III) is one of a number of new military detention centres established during the current uprising in the West Bank and Gaza, including Dhahriya, Hebron 2 and Beitunia. Capable of holding at least 4,000 detainees (and of being expanded virtually without limit), it is the largest of all the centres now being used. The vast majority of prisoners being held there are administrative detainees.

[Al-Haq issued two Press Releases, one on 2 April 1988, and another on 31 May 1988, expressing concern about conditions there, and in the latter, calling for its immediate closure. Four of al-Haq's field-workers have been administratively detained there; one, 'Abd-al-Karim Kana'an, was released after the expiration of his six-month order; however on 19 November 1988 he was re-arrested with another al-Haq employee, Riziq Husein Shuqeir Maraba. Both were being held in Dhahriya detention centre at press time, Mr. Kana'an on an administrative detention order. The other three, Ghazi Shashtari, Sha'wan Jabarin, and Zahi Jaradat, all had their detention orders renewed for a further six months when their release date came up. Ghazi Shashtari and Zahi Jaradat have been adopted as Prisoners of Conscience by Amnesty International and all are the subject of a forthcoming report by the Lawyers Committee for Human Rights based (*inter alia*) on a visit to Ansar III in August 1988.]

Ansar III quickly gained notoriety for the harshness of living conditions there. These are a result partly of the desert location, and partly of the restrictions and rules laid down by the prison authorities:

- The camp is situated in the Negev desert, about 68 km south of Beersheba, near the Egyptian border. The desert location, with very hot temperatures in daytime combined with bitterly cold nights, causes considerable hardship to detainees, especially since they are accommodated in tents. (Holding detainees in prisons outside the Occupied Territories violates Article 76 of the 1949 IV Geneva Convention.)
- Isolation from the outside world is one of the major problems, largely because of the location of the prison, and because of restrictions placed by the authorities on family and other visits. For example, persons wishing to visit relatives must prove that they have paid all their taxes before they can be issued a visitor's permit for a fee of 20 JD, and the authorities insist on transporting visitors to the prison in military vehicles. Prisoners have asked their families not to visit them under these conditions, and visits do not take place. (Such restrictions are not imposed on family visits to other detention centres, even those outside the Territories such as Megiddo. The ICRC have refused to arrange family visits to Ansar III, because of the conditions imposed).

  Lawyers' visits, although not permitted for the first month, are now allowed, but difficulties remain. Lawyers are not always granted permission to see all their clients at one time, and in some cases the prison authorities deny that someone is being held in the prison. When visits do take place, time is severely restricted by the prison authorities and there is no confidentiality between lawyer and client as guards are always present. Aside from those visits, and those of the ICRC delegates, detainees in Ansar III have no direct contact with the outside world. In addition, letters and newspapers have been seriously restricted.
- Daily living conditions are poor. Inadequate water supply was one of the most serious complaints of detainees when the prison was first opened. Now detainees have enough for drinking water and to have a quick shower about once a week. The sanitary installations are inadequately ventilated and are not emptied often enough, attracting flies and other insects. Neither are detainees given sufficient changes of clothes, including underwear. In addition, medical care is seriously deficient; there is only one medical officer for all detainees, and the treatment offered is superficial and inadequate, unless someone is seriously ill when they will be transferred to the

Beersheba hospital.

Daily, each prisoner is "counted" three to four times. This involves all detainees leaving their tents, sitting cross-legged on the ground, hands behind their backs and heads bowed, while the guards call out the number of each prisoner. In summer, this procees is extremely wearing, and the midday count in the heat of the noon sun often causes detainees to faint.

- Punishment—both individual and collective—is severe. Individuals are often placed in solitary confinement for extended periods of time, as punishment for such things as laughing during the count, attempting to talk to detainees from a different compound, and failing to obey camp regulations. They may be beaten, tied in the "banana" position and left for many hours. Collective punishments are also commonplace, including turning off the water supplies for hours at a time, depriving detainees of food and cigarettes, and compelling detainees to get down on their knees, lower their heads and stay in the same position for long periods of time. On occasions, tear gas has been thrown into the tents.
- Until early June, detainees were not allowed to receive letters from their family; since then, due largely to efforts of the ICRC, mail has been allowed to pass back and forth. For about five months detainees had access only to some press clippings from the Hebrew and Arabic press prepared by the prison authorities. Now they are allowed one copy of three major newspapers for each tent every day. Radios and books are forbidden.

Frustration and anger at the inhumane conditions in Ansar III undoubtedly contributed to the appalling incident on August 16 when two prisoners were shot dead by members of the prison staff, during a disturbance by prisoners in which stones, beds, and other articles were hurled by the prisoners. An investigation into the incident has appparently not yet been completed.

All of the features described above contravene international humanitarian law, as laid down in the Fourth Geneva Convention of 1949. The isolation of detainees from the outside world apart from visits by the ICRC and lawyers, means detainees are extremely vulnerable, and may encourage abuses by the camp authorities of the humanitarian codes prescribed by international law. It also contributes to the demoralisation of detainees who are often told neither the length of time they are to spend in detention, nor the reason for their being there. The sense that there are no standards which detainees can rely on and that there is no one to turn to is one of the most serious and reprehensible aspects of

Ansar III.

In these circumstances of enforced physical isolation it is all the more important that basic living conditions conform to the minimum standards required by international law. The effects are cumulative; viewed in isolation, not all the deprivation suffered is of the most severe type, but ill-treatment does not need to consist of physical torture to be immensely serious. Put in the context of the other daily abuses and the physical isolation, there can be little doubt that conditions at Ansar III constitute inhumane and degrading treatment.

As a result of a suit filed by lawyer Lea Tsemel and Avigdor Feldman in the High Court (date of hearing 14 August 1988) protesting conditions in Ansar III, and complaining of its illegality under the IV Geneva Convention by virtue of its location, three judges (Meir Shamgar, Chief Justice; Menahem Alon, Deputy Chief Justice; and Gavriel Bach, Justice) visited the detention centre to inspect for themselves what conditions were like.

In its decision handed down on 8 September 1988, the Court held that the "central and most significant problem" was that of over-crowding. Concerning allegations of "violent and humiliating treatment" during transportation to Ansar III the court found that the claims were insufficiently concrete, but commented that "the hurting of a bound, helpless person is shameful and brutal and necessitates a response appropriate to the severity of the act." The Court rejected claims of ill-treatment by the centre's staff of detainees, but held that the disciplinary measures at the centre including making inmates stand in corners for up to 2 hours were unacceptable. Medical treatment was found to be adequate. Finally the court recommended that a permanent advisory committee be set up to report on conditions within the camp.

The fact that Ansar III has been the subject of a review by the Israeli High Court is in itself welcome. Moreover the Court made certain findings and recommendations which, if carried out, would considerably improve the lot of detainees. However, the court's findings on medical treatment and beatings in the camp itself fly in the face of the evidence which al-Haq has documented. In addition, al-Haq strongly disagrees with the Court's ruling that detaining Palestinian prisoners from the Occupied Territories in Ansar III, inside Israel, is not a violation of international law. Article 76 of the IV Geneva Convention is explicit on this matter. In the meantime, thousands of Palestinian political prisoners continue to suffer in the harsh climate, summer and winter, of the Negev Desert.

Part III
REPRESSION OF PALESTINIAN INFRASTRUCTURE

Part III

Chapter 7

ECONOMIC SANCTIONS

On 1 September 1988, the Israeli military authorities in the West Bank issued a new military order, which imposed a complete ban on the export of several products from the West Bank to both Israel and Jordan.[1] The list of banned exports included olive oil, one of the mainstays of the West Bank economy. The order, which at press time had not (yet) been enforced, capped a year in which the military authorities increasingly resorted to economic punishments in order to quell the popular uprising. If and when the authorities begin to strictly enforce the order, this could have grave consequences for West Bank farmers and entrepreneurs, and especially olive growers, since olives are for many Palestinians the main if not sole source of income during the year.[2]

Measures taken against olive growers were only the latest in a series of economic moves designed by the military authorities to bring the Palestinian community in the Occupied Territories to its knees. Even before the uprising, the authorities had instituted economic restrictions against individuals, communities, and even entire areas, to (1) advance Israel's own agenda of colonisation, and (2) punish those who actively opposed the occupier's policy and break their resistance by making their continued opposition prohibitively expensive.[3]

A. Historical Background

From the beginning of the occupation, Israel has sought to deploy Palestinian resources to its own economic advantage, while at the same time attempting to "normalise" life in the Territories. According to a report issued by the Ministry of Defence, the authorities pursued a policy after June 1967 whose key elements were "normalization, based on economic prosperity and social stability," and a "guarantee of personal and civic freedoms." The effect, the report claimed, was that the "Green Line" dividing Israel from the Territories "actually disappeared, 'de facto' if not 'de jure'." [4] The aim of the policy of "normalisation," whose main architect was then Minister of Defence Moshe Dayan, was to integrate Israel economically into the Middle East, and to tie the West Bank and

Gaza inextricably to Israel by making the Territories fully dependent on the Israeli economy. In the process, the authorities changed the infrastructure of the Territories, using the military occupation as a guise, in clear contravention of international law, especially Article 43 of the Regulations appended to the IV Hague Convention 1907. Article 43 states:

> The authority of the legitimate power having in fact passed into the hands of the occupant, the latter shall take all the measures in his power to restore, and ensure, as far as possible, public order and safety, while respecting, unless absolutely prevented, the laws in force in the country.

The cornerstones of the policy of "normalisation" were a policy of "open bridges" with Jordan and a free flow of goods and labour across the Green Line. Thus, workers from the Occupied Territories were encouraged to work in Israel, while markets in the Territories were opened up to Israeli products, which also found their way, under West Bank labels, into Jordan and the Arab world as a whole. In the years leading up to the uprising, an average of 120,000 Palestinians from the Territories were employed in various locations in Israel, and the West Bank and Gaza had come to constitute the second largest export market for Israeli products after the United States.

The Occupied Territories have also been progressively integrated into the Israeli system on the level of infrastructure, including roads and electricity, and social services, like health and welfare. Most of their budget is derived internally through the taxation of the local population. In 1976, the authorities introduced a value-added tax (VAT). This is in contravention of international law, which stipulates that an occupier may not institute new taxes in the territory under its control.[5] Palestinians have had no influence in decisions concerning the allocation of budget funds, and in fact al-Haq has been unable to obtain a copy of the annual budget from the military authorities. According to Meron Benvenisti, the Occupied Territories are likely to have become "a net source of revenue to the Israeli Treasury."[6]

In short, in the enforced "common market" that has come to exist between Israel and the Territories since 1967, the Israeli economy has been the main beneficiary, while Palestinians have borne a disproportionate share of the burden: in the Territories military orders were issued making the cultivation, harvesting, processing, manufacturing, marketing and exporting of any crop or product contingent on the acquisition of a permit from the military authorities. To protect Israeli growers and manufacturers, permits would be withheld from those who wished to engage in economic activities that might compete with Israeli products. Generally speaking, any form of independent economic activity was obstructed if not made impossible. All banks which were in operation in the West Bank before 1967 were closed at the start of the occupation. In addition, the types of standards and quality criteria that apply in Israel were not made to apply in the Territories, which thus became a dumping ground for a number of shoddy products, or outdated food products, from Israel or abroad.[7]

In 1982, under Minister of Defence Ariel Sharon, new restrictions were clamped on economic life in the Occupied Territories, reflecting the political agenda of the Likud which considers the West Bank and Gaza as an integral part of "Greater Israel." New military orders were issued concerning the entry of money into the area, the acceptance of loans for public institutions, and the imposition of new taxes (for example Military Orders 952, 974, 998 and 1118, among many).[8] As recently as January 1985, Defence Minister Yitzhak Rabin was quoted as saying that "there will be no development [in the Territories] initiated by the Israeli government, and no permits will be given for expanding agriculture or industry [there], which may compete with the State of Israel." [9]

Given the growing dependence of the Territories' economy on that of Israel, economic punishments have become an increasingly powerful tool in the hands of the military authorities for asserting control. Such punishments have almost invariably been of a collective nature. For example, for several months in 1983-4, all applications for permits (drivers' licences, travel permits, building permits, permits to open a shop, etc.) submitted by residents of Deheisha Refugee Camp near Bethlehem were turned down, apparently in response to continued stone throwing from the camp at Israeli vehicles driving on the Bethlehem-Hebron road. One practice that has been consistently popular with the authorities throughout the occupation is the uprooting of fruit trees, especially olive trees. This punishment has been applied usually but by no means exclusively to areas from which stones are alleged to have been thrown at Israeli vehicles.[10]

On 7 December 1987, the European Community (EC) reached an agreement with the Israeli government making it possible for Palestinian agricultural and industrial producers in the Territories to export directly (i.e. circumventing Israeli marketing organisations) to EC member states. The EC Council of Ministers had issued a Regulation in October 1986 rectifying an anomaly in its otherwise consistent trade policy in the Mediterranean basin. Until the 1986 Regulation the Occupied Territories were the only geographical area excluded from the trade benefits extended by the EC to Mediterranean countries. The agreement of the Israeli government and the implementation of the Regulation was a long time coming, and even since it has been obtained, those Palestinian producers who have attempted to avail themselves of the new option of exporting directly to EC countries have faced obstruction from the side of the Israeli authorities, while prospective exporters have been deterred by continuing bureaucratic harassments.[11] This may reflect the reluctance on Israel's part to consent to economic actions which stand in direct contradiction to its own long-term economic and political interests in the Territories.

The popular uprising that began in December 1987 has sought to reverse the political and economic patterns of the previous twenty years, and to re-assert Palestinian interests. Palestinians have made a concerted effort to extract themselves from the structures set up by the occupier. The Israeli response to this attempt has been the stepped-up use of economic sanctions, a logical extension of a well-proven practice. The scope of the uprising, which has mobilised residents of towns, villages and camps throughout the Territories, simply gave the authorities an excuse to use such sanctions on a much wider, indeed unprecedented scale. During the first year of the uprising, economic sanctions were either carried out directly by the military authorities against specific targets, or were the result of other punishments of a collective nature, like extended curfews.

Although the first official report that the authorities were considering punitive economic measures appeared in the Israeli press in mid-January 1988,[12] economic sanctions played a part in the Israeli response to the uprising from the start. Initially these measures were aimed primarily at shopkeepers, who were in the forefront of non-violent protest from the early days of the uprising through an extended commercial strike. But later, as the uprising continued unabated, the authorities began striking at entire communities, using fuel bans, monetary restrictions and marketing prohibitions collectively, while enforcing tax laws individually. On 20 January, Yehuda Litani, the Middle East Editor of the *Jerusalem Post*, stated in an article that

> the defence minister and the military establishment are convinced that...economic measures along with the policy of "force, power and blows" will bring the riots and the strikes in the territories to an early end.

B. Economic Measures Against Commerce and Traders

Merchants and traders were among the first to suffer financially in the uprising. The actions taken against them, and later against suppliers and carriers of goods and even against individual purchasers, were of a crude, strongarm character, involving wanton destruction of foodstuffs and other goods and damage to shops.

From the beginning of the uprising, the army sought to break the commercial strike which was observed intermittently and locally in December but had become general by mid-January.[13] The army's initial response in December was an extension of the pattern followed prior to the uprising: shops that were closed were forced to open, either through intimidation and threats of sealing, or by being broken open with mallets and crowbars. Shopkeepers who failed to obey orders had their shops welded shut. In March and April, the army stepped up the practice by forcing stores to open during strike hours and to close during shopping hours.[14]

In many cases in the West Bank documented by al-Haq, soldiers entered shops and spoiled the goods, mixing bleach with flour, trampling on bread, smashing eggs, breaking a refrigerator full of meat, and upturning fruit stalls. Al-Haq has also documented cases where store owners were beaten by soldiers, as in the case of Nidhal Muhammad al-'Ataba, a shopkeeper in al-Bireh, on 23 April 1988.[15] And on at least one occasion, in the Qaddoura Refugee Camp on 20 January 1988, a tear gas canister was thrown into a shop by an army officer, who then locked the shopkeeper, Hasan Isma'il Saleh, inside the shop, causing serious injuries requiring the man's hospitalisation.[16] In Am'ari Refugee Camp, on 21 January, soldiers pulled two burning tires into the butcher's shop of Mustafa Khamis Dhib, with the result that it burned down.[17]

These activities were not confined to shopkeepers, but were also applied against traders in markets, barrowmen, and persons selling their own produce, including villagers marketing their crops in town. In the Ramallah/al-Bireh market on 2 April, for example, the army wreaked havoc among the vegetable stalls and, after having forcibly evicted fruit and vegetable merchants from the area, closed the outside gates.[18] Some individual examples of these pervasive practices documented by al-Haq during the winter and spring of 1988 include:

(a) Palestinians (buyers and sellers) were intermittently prevented from entering the central market in Bethlehem in this period; on 26 March, soldiers spoiled vegetables and other foodstuffs in the town's main street; on 22 March, twenty stores were ordered closed without reason being stated; on 2 April, 42 more were ordered closed; on 28 April, an additional number of shops were welded shut.

(b) On 29 March, soldiers broke into a bakery in Ramallah, mixed foodstuffs together and trampled on bread.

(c) On 2 April, soldiers broke into a number of shops in Ramallah and al-Bireh, breaking wares and throwing gas canisters inside.

(d) On 2 and 6 April, soldiers rampaged through the streets of Ramallah and Nablus, attacking vendors and destroying vegetables; similar events took place in Hebron on 6 and 9 April, and again in Ramallah on 7 April.

(e) On 3 April, the army ordered pharmacies in Hebron to close. Pharmacies (as well as bakeries) have been exempted on a rotating basis from observing the strikes called by the Palestinian leadership.

(f) On 6 April, soldiers raided the brick factory owned by Ahmad Dhib 'Atta in the al-Bireh industrial area, and destroyed many of the bricks.

(g) On 24 April, the army confiscated the identity cards of street vendors in Jenin, and ordered them to stop selling their merchandise; several shops in Jenin were ordered closed from 5 until 8 May.

The authorities have also applied administrative means to break the commercial strike. Legal procedures concerning the right to open commercial establishments were amended, forcing those applying for a permit to open a shop to sign an undertaking to keep their store open all day.[19]

The authorities have also acted against striking shopkeepers in East Jerusalem. Having been illegally annexed in 1967 and put under Israeli law, East Jerusalem is generally treated differently from the West Bank. Jerusalem police have not resorted to the degree of brutality that characterises the army units operating in the Territories, but shopkeepers have nonetheless been subjected to a number of punitive measures and to continuing harassment. On 23 April, for example, the Central Area Commander, General Amram Mitzna, used the Defence Regulations of 1945 to order 25 shops located on Prophets Street in East Jerusalem, which had been observing a complete commercial strike except for the hours between 2 and 5 p.m., to remain open from 8:30 a.m. until 7 p.m. as of 24 April, in the "interest of public order." The order was defied by the store owners on 24 April. That same day, General Mitzna issued a new order, advising shopkeepers to close between 2 and 7 p.m. When they refused to comply, fourteen of the merchants were arrested on 25 April and taken to court, charged with disobeying a military order, and then released on bail on 27 April. The merchants were found guilty on 8 November and were sentenced to pay a fine or spend a month in jail.[20] In addition, the main shopping street in East Jerusalem, Salah al-Din Street, has been closed to traffic during the morning shopping hours since the spring.

On 5 May, the military authorities announced a three-day ban on commercial activity in the West Bank as punishment for the general commercial strike carried out by merchants on 4 May. The *Jerusalem Post* reported:

> The IDF order was announced on loudspeakers yesterday morning in the centres of the main towns and was immediately enforced by soldiers. Arab sources in Nablus said that immediately after the announcement, troops prevented Arab residents carrying any merchandise from leaving the casbah. The sources added that passengers were dragged out of taxis by soldiers after being asked if the ride had been paid for. In Kalkilya, according to local sources, troops used tear gas to force merchants to comply with the order and close their shops. Trucks loaded with vegetables were prevented from entering West Bank towns. In Ramallah troops reportedly used force to stop activity in the main market.[21]

C. An Economic "War of Attrition": Restrictions on Money, Bans on Fuel, Water and Electricity, and Destruction of Property

Having failed to put down the uprising, the Israeli authorities expanded the use of punitive economic measures in February and March. Restrictions were imposed on the amount of money that could be brought into the area from abroad, the supply of fuel to Palestinian gas stations in the West Bank was halted for a month, international telecommunications links with the Territories were cut, and selected communities were isolated for prolonged periods during which they were subjected to a policy of economic strangulation, and sometimes had their water, telephones and electricity disconnected as well. (Examples of some of these practices are given in Chapter 5, and in the section on agriculture below.) By mid-March, the totality of these practices was referred to as a "semi-economic war of attrition" or "economic warfare" by some Israeli commentators.[22] This war, it was explained, was fought alongside the more violent struggle between the army and youngsters in the streets. Use of the term "war of attrition" ignores the reality of the conflict, however: the attempts made by Palestinians to "disengage" from more than twenty years of Israeli economic constriction have had little more than a ripple effect on the Israeli economy. The Israeli response of stepped-up economic sanctions in order to reassert control and proceed with the original economic plan has therefore been disproportionate, in addition to being illegal for its punitive and collective character.

One of the most important new measures has been a restriction on the amount of money that could be brought into the area from abroad. On 14 February, the Coordinator of Affairs in the Territories, Shmuel Goren, announced that moves had been made to prevent the transfer of "PLO funds" to the Territories from abroad. He specified that drivers coming over one of the bridges from Jordan, who had previously been permitted to carry unlimited amounts of money, were now allowed to bring in no more than JD 200 (about $600) each per occasion.[23]

A month later, additional restrictions were placed on all Palestinian travellers. In mid-March, the authorities announced a reduction in the limit of undeclared money that could be brought into the area from abroad, from JD 2,000 to JD 400.[24] Those who applied for a permit to bring in larger sums report that their applications were refused, with no reason being given. In addition, the authorities said they would monitor funds brought in by the various relief organizations active in the Territories. Official money-changers were subjected to new restrictions as well: in mid-March, they were prohibited from travelling to or from Jordan.[25] West Bank residents wishing to withdraw money from their bank accounts at the Cairo-Amman Bank faced a limit of JD 400 per month. Al-Haq has documented several cases of individuals whose money was confiscated upon arrival in the country at Ben-Gurion Airport, apparently because they were carrying more than JD 400 each.

In an interview with the *Jerusalem Post*, published on 30 May, Goren explained Israeli policy as follows:

> Because of concern that money to finance the uprising will come from Palestinian organizations abroad, we have reinstituted restrictions on bringing in funds... There are a few cases involving several hundreds of thousands of dollars, where dozens of residents of the territories arrived at Ben-Gurion with sums of money larger than permitted. Residents of the territories need advance approval to bring in more than 400 Jordanian dinars ([then] about $1,200), as is the case at the Jordan River bridges.

The Jordanian dinar is legal tender in the West Bank, and as a currency is much stabler than the Israeli shekel. Most institutions in the West Bank keep their liquid assets in dinars, and indeed most transactions are carried out in dinars. West Bankers' bank accounts are usually kept in Jordan, however. Until the opening in 1987 of a branch of the Cairo-Amman Bank, which itself is subject to a number of restrictions, no Arab banks had been allowed to operate in the area. West Bank residents were therefore forced to open bank accounts in Jordan, where they could get an interest on their deposits.

The effective prevention of the transfer of funds from Jordanian banks therefore means that the Israeli authorities have crippled the operations of these institutions, which include not only businesses, but also charitable and educational bodies. There has been no suggestion that such funds are being used for illegal or improper purposes. In addition, it cannot be argued by the authorities that the receipt of funds for payment of salaries of hundreds of employees constitutes a security threat. In many cases, these institutions, as is argued in chapter 9, provide much needed services such as welfare, medical services and education, which are not provided by the authorities themselves. By blocking access to these funds, the Israeli authorities are therefore exacerbating problems concerning the provision of basic services in the Territories.

Furthermore, a large proportion of the population of the Territories is dependent for its livelihood on remittances sent by their relatives living abroad. The blocking of transmission of such funds on the claim that they are from illegal sources, rather than determining which funds are from illegal sources and blocking only those, is an arbitrary and indiscriminate measure causing hardship to many families.

A second measure introduced as part of the authorities' response to the uprising in the Territories was a ban on the supply of fuel, including gasoline as well as kerosene for heating, to all Palestinian-operated gas stations in the West Bank, except for vital installations such as hospitals, pumping stations and power plants. The ban was put into effect on 13 March for one week, was then renewed for five days and again for one month, finally to end on 24 April. The ban was at first explained as a security measure on the grounds that stones and petrol bombs had been thrown at delivery trucks. This argument was belied, however, by the fact that deliveries continued to be made to gas stations on Jewish settlements in the West Bank. Additionally, it was clear from the fact that Palestinians continued to be able to purchase gas at these settlement gas stations throughout the ban that the measure was a form of harassment and could not be justified by security considerations.

Representative examples of other economic measures of a punitive nature include:

(a) the closure of three Palestinian bus companies (in Bethlehem, 'Izariya and Ramallah) for one week in June 1988, allegedly for having participated in a commercial strike.[26]

(b) forcing residents of first Gaza and later the West Bank to renew their car licence plates and identity cards at high cost.[27]

(c) placing bans on workers travelling to their jobs in Israel, such as all Gaza workers on 13 May.[28]

(d) forcing pre-payment of utility bills, for example in al-Bureij Refugee Camp in the Gaza Strip in June.[29]

(e) failure to repair the broken water pump in the Jenin area, which led to a shortage of piped water in the Jenin area for six months, from the end of March until the end of September 1988.[30]

(f) the wanton destruction of property during army raids on population centres, as in the Balata Refugee Camp on 11 December 1987, the village of Beit Lid near Tulkarem on 24 February 1988, the village of Battir near Bethlehem on 9 March, Jalazon Refugee Camp on 16 March, the village of Beit Ummar in the Hebron area on 8 April, the village of 'Aroura on 8 July, the town of Qalqiliya during a prolonged curfew from 6 until 14 September, and Qalandiya Refugee Camp on 20 November.[31]

(g) prevention of entry of food into towns and villages, as in the case of the village of Beni Na'im in the Hebron area, which was punished in this way for 16 days from 16 March; a similar restriction was imposed on the town of Ya'bad in the Jenin area during the same period.[32]

(h) disconnection of electricity, water and telephone lines for prolonged periods during army sieges of population centres (see Chapter 5 on isolation).

D. The Forced Payment of Taxes

One of the toughest economic sanctions, militarily and administratively enforced tax payments, came in response to a spreading tax revolt as Palestinians increasingly began to refuse payment of value-added tax (VAT) and other taxes as part of a mass campaign of civil disobedience called for by the local leadership. Merchants and entrepreneurs have generally resented the VAT since its illegal imposition in 1976, and have on previous occasions refused payment. In response, tax authorities accompanied by the army would routinely carry out raids on shops in order to enforce payment of the VAT as well as other taxes.

Since February, revenues accruing to the Israeli authorities from tax collection in the Territories have dropped sharply. In the absence of a public budget it is impossible to state precisely the extent to which revenues have fallen since the beginning of the uprising. It is clear, however, that the tax strike forced the authorities to revise their expenditure plans for the present fiscal year (April 1988-April 1989). On 14 April, Civil Administration officials threatened that services would be reduced as a result of a decline in tax collection.[33] In July, the authorities announced that 1,000 Civil Administration employees would be laid off, including a number who worked in government hospitals. Nine thousand government schoolteachers were on half salary for a month between 15 April and 15 May, and on 6 October, the authorities announced that salaries would not be paid at all for the duration of the (forced) school closure.

The fall in revenues accruing to the Israeli authorities is due to three factors: a widespread refusal to pay (mostly indirect) taxes, a fall in taxable income due to reduced incomes in the context of a slackening economy, and disruption of the authorities' tax collection capabilities following the resignation of most Palestinian civil servants employed in the tax department of the West Bank and Gaza Civil Administrations in March.

As before the uprising, when short tax strikes did occur, the response of the authorities to the tax revolt was two-pronged: in the first place, the granting of permits and licences of any kind was made contingent on payment of taxes, among other required criteria (including obtaining a certificate of "good conduct" from the internal intelligence service, the Shin Bet). Such permits include, among others, drivers' licences, travel permits, identity cards, birth certificates, permits to visit relatives detained in the Ketsyot detention centre (Ansar III), construction permits, and import and export licences. In addition, in a number of cases in October 1988, the use of olive presses was prohibited until advance, and unprecedently high, sums of VAT had been paid to the authorities. In the Gaza Strip, the authorities decided to invalidate the identity cards of all adult residents as part of a campaign "to retake and retain the initiative" in May. The *Jerusalem Post* reported:

> Residents affected by the step are to be prohibited from leaving the confines of the Gaza Strip until they have submitted proof that they have paid all Israeli and local taxes, utility bills, and traffic tickets, and are wanted neither by the police nor security forces investigators, whereupon they will be granted new identity cards.[34]

Secondly, tax collectors accompanied by the army have carried out raids in towns and villages, seizing private property pending payment of taxes. Typically, a curfew would be imposed, and the army would enter homes impounding property or summon property owners to makeshift tax offices (usually schools) to present proof of payment of taxes. Al-Haq has documented confiscations of jewelry, vehicles and (occasionally exorbitant) sums of money, for example in the town of Beit Sahour at the beginning of July 1988. In addition, Palestinians have been stopped at roadblocks by police or army carrying lists; if their name appeared on the list, their car would be seized and returned only after the person had paid all outstanding taxes, as estimated by the authorities. In other instances, identity cards were confiscated and returned only after taxes had been paid.[35]

Representative examples of forced payment of taxes, documented by al-Haq, include:

(a) On 4 June 1988, residents of Jenin were ordered to go to the area of the municipality and pay outstanding taxes. Those who did not or could not do so had their cars confiscated.

(b) On 9 June, Ramallah and al-Bireh traders were ordered by the head of the local Chamber of Commerce to go to the Civil Administration. There, officials confiscated the ID cards of some of the merchants.

(c) On 19 July, soldiers surrounded the town of Ya'bad in the Jenin area from 3.00 a.m. until the evening of the same day. All car owners were ordered to go to a local school. Owners' ID cards were confiscated and they were ordered to pay their taxes.

(d) On 25 July, the army raided the village of Silat al-Harithiya in the Jenin area to collect taxes. Two residents were injured during the raid, and several suffered after-effects from tear-gas inhalation.

(e) On 26 July, cars and ID cards belonging to residents of the town of Qabatiya in the Jenin area were confiscated in an attempt to force payment of taxes.

Al-Haq intervened with the military authorities on the subject of militarily enforced tax collection in Ramallah and al-Bireh on 6 July 1988 and in Beit Sahour on 7 July. (See Appendix 7-A.) The Legal Advisor of the Military Government responded in a letter on 24 October, arguing that tax collectors are authorised to place a lien on vehicles and other private property in order to enforce payment of taxes, and may be accompanied by soldiers "for security reasons." (See Appendix 7-B.) The authorities have in fact assumed blanket powers to unleash the army on population centres to collect taxes, impounding private property, especially cars, at will. They have failed, however, to break the tax boycott.

E. Punitive Measures Against the Agricultural Sector

Because the West Bank economy is an essentially agrarian one, punitive measures taken against the agricultural sector have had the largest impact of all collective punishments on the economic well-being of the

Palestinian community. Farmers in West Bank villages have perhaps suffered more than others from specific sanctions as well as prolonged curfews and sieges. If a farmer is not permitted access to his fields in order to irrigate the crop, spray it, or harvest it, the entire crop may be lost.

Freedom of movement during a curfew appears to be at the discretion of each individual military "curfew commander": while some allow those under curfew to leave their homes for an hour or two each day, others lift the curfew only once every five days and make no special concessions to farmers. (See also the section on curfews in chapter 5.) As a result, farmers have in many cases lost all or part of their crops. During a 25-day curfew in Qalqiliya from 26 March until 10 April, for example, no work in the fields was possible at all, and many crops were lost in their entirety. Al-Haq also has documentation on a number of villages in the northern West Bank where fruit and vegetables were allowed to rot as a result of prolonged curfews. These villages include: Deir al-Hatab, Salem, Beit Dajan and Beit Furik.[36] During the olive-picking season, as will be shown below, curfews also led to economic losses.

In addition, individual farmers and communities have been subject to acts of wanton destruction and vandalism, especially of crops, fruit trees, wells and equipment. The following are a few examples of such practices, documented by al-Haq:

(a) On 19 December 1987, and again on 15 March 1988, plastic greenhouses and crops were destroyed by the army in the village of Deir al-Ghussoun in the Tulkarem area.

(b) On 7 March, soldiers with bulldozers uprooted a hundred fruit-bearing olive trees in the village of Silat al-Harithiya near Jenin on the pretext that they were too close to the main road and that people could hide behind them and throw stones at passing Israeli cars.

(c) On 22 March, the army uprooted eighty fruit-bearing olive trees belonging to twelve farmers in the village of Bidiya in the Tulkarem area, without stating a reason.

(d) On 8 April, army vehicles demolished four tractors and smashed up shop windows and private cars in the village of Beit Ummar in the Hebron area.

(e) On 9 April, 160 olive trees were uprooted by the army in the village of Kufel Harith in the Nablus area.

(f) On 10 April, the army uprooted olive trees on 30 dunums of land in the village of Beita near Nablus following the killing by an Israeli settler of two Palestinians and an Israeli girl, and the killing of another Palestinian by the army.[37]

(g) On 14 April, 57 beehives were destroyed by the army in the village of Jiftlik in the Jordan Valley.

Finally, certain villages or areas have been subject to blanket bans on the marketing and exporting of their produce. In the case of the town of Qabatiya in the Jenin area, for example, residents were blocked from exporting their crops and quarry stone, the town's mainstay, to Jordan following the killing of a collaborator in the town on 24 February. Qabatiya has 18 quarries, employing approximately 500 workers. The ban was lifted on 15 August.[38] For a period in the middle of March, farmers from the Jericho area were prevented on a daily basis from bringing produce into town until after the three hours of shopping in the morning set by the Palestinian leadership.[39] On 29 April, Fathi al-Halayka, the owner of the Palestinian Ceramics Factory in the town of Halhoul near Hebron, was prohibited from exporting ceramics to Jordan. Farmers in Yamoun in the Jenin district have been banned from exporting their crops to Jordan during the uprising.[40]

In a speech on 22 June, Minister of Defence Yitzhak Rabin set down Israeli policy regarding collective punishments of an economic nature, stating, according to a report in the *Jerusalem Post*, that economic and administrative punishments were designed to show that civil disobedience and the boycott of the Israeli administrative institutions were "an unattainable dream." Rabin added:

> We try to limit [punitive] administrative and economic measures to definable centres of civil disobedience, but it is not always possible to localize the effect of such measures.[41]

In the following months, additional measures were taken to prevent entire villages from harvesting, processing, marketing and exporting their crops.

At the beginning of July, for example, the Civil Administration in the West Bank clamped a ban on the shipping of plums from the village of Beit Ummar in the Hebron area to Israel and Jordan.[42] A similar ban was imposed on the village of Idhna near Hebron at the same time. In the middle of August, after an extended curfew on the village of Til near Nablus, all marketing of figs and yoghurt was prohibited to village residents.[43] At the beginning of September, the authorities blocked the export of grapes from the town of Halhoul and the villages of Sa'ir and Shuyoukh in the Hebron district. Community leaders from Halhoul, according to the *Jerusalem Post*, "were summoned to military government headquarters and told that the ban would be lifted if they maintained quiet [in the town]."[44]

In October, toward the end of the first year of the uprising, the authorities' policy of economic sanctions climaxed with the blocking of the harvesting and processing of olives, and the marketing and exporting of olive oil, one of the cornerstones of the Palestinian economy in the Territories. Already in September, the authorities had issued threats against "villages active in the uprising." On 22 September, for example, the *Jerusalem Post* quoted Israeli military sources as stating that "the authorities are planning to use the forthcoming olive-picking season in the West Bank to hit back at villages that are centres of unrest, by banning their exports of olives and olive-oil." General Amram Mitzna, the Central Area Commander, was quoted as saying on 22 September:

> We will not accept a situation in which villages or areas riot...and then be able to act as though nothing had happened. This was the policy during the plum harvest and during the grape harvest. It will also be in effect during the olive harvest.[45]

During the first week of October, the olive harvest began in several villages in the Territories. On 11 October, the *Jerusalem Post* reported that:

> Bidiya, southeast of Kalkilya, remained under curfew for the fifth day after masked assailants gunned down the local mukhtar. Palestinian sources said electricity had been cut off, and villagers were warned that they would not be allowed to market their olives and oil during the forthcoming olive-picking season.

And on 12 October, the *Jerusalem Post* reported that on 11 October, people in the village of Bal'a near Tulkarem defied a curfew imposed on the village earlier in order to start picking olives. Following a clash with the Israeli army,

> [t]roops announced that the curfew remained in force and that olive picking was banned until further notice, confiscating keys to five olive presses.[46]

According to al-Haq's information, sums of up to 8,000 JD ($ 16,000) were demanded as "back taxes" from owners of the three presses in the village. The owners came to an agreement with the authorities, paying amounts ranging from 800 to 1,200 Jordanian dinars, which are unprecedented amounts for olive presses. The owners were not given back their keys, however. They started operating their presses nevertheless, but they were told by the army that if any demonstrations were to occur in the village, the presses would be closed down.[47]

Similar problems were reported in other villages. In the village of

Burqin in the Jenin area, for example, the olive picking season began on 15 October 1988. According to al-Haq's information, the army began to carry out raids on Burqin regularly after 15 October. On several such occasions, residents who were in the fields picking olives were ordered to return to the village to remove slogans painted on village walls.

On 19 October, an olive press owned by the al-Jarar family in Burqin was raided by soldiers who were accompanied by Israelis in civilian dress. The apparent reason for the raid was that one of the owner's sons was on the army's "wanted" list. The press was closed down and vital parts were dismantled and confiscated. In addition, the door to the olive press was welded shut. Soldiers damaged the press motor, and made holes in a number of sacks filled with olives. While leaving the press, the soldiers tried to tow away a tractor, but failed in their attempt.

On 20 October, a curfew was imposed on Burqin, making it impossible for villagers to go out and harvest their olives. During the curfew, wage-workers from surrounding villages began picking olives for Burqin villagers, but on 26 October, the army issued an order forbidding them to do so. In one incident reported to al-Haq, the army took away a number of full sacks of olives. The curfew was finally lifted after 22 days, on 11 November.

In another example, the army carried out a raid on the village of 'Aboud in the Ramallah area on 24 October. Soldiers verbally ordered the owners of two olive presses to shut down their presses. Keys to the two presses were confiscated. The army gave no reason for its action. Clashes broke out between villagers and the army that day.

One day later, on 25 October, at five o'clock in the morning, the army announced through a loudspeaker: "Residents of 'Aboud! You are forbidden to pick olives until further notice!" Soldiers turned back a number of villagers who were already on their way to the fields. A curfew was then imposed on the village. Later that day, an army bulldozer uprooted ten olive trees, nine of which belonged to the Greek Orthodox Church. The reason given for the action was that stones had been thrown from the area of the trees.

The next day, 26 October, a delegation of press owners accompanied by the mukhtar (village head) of 'Aboud visited the offices of the Civil Administration at Beit El, requesting that the keys to the presses be returned to them. Instead, an official (said by the press owners to be the military governor) demanded from each of the press owners the sum of 10,000 shekels (approximately $5,500) in (unspecified) taxes because, in his words, "you throw stones." In addition, he demanded that each worker at the two presses pay 100 dinars (approximately $250) in (unspecified) taxes. He added: "But since you cannot pay these taxes, I am not giving you the keys back."

On 27 October, the owners made a second request to get their keys returned to them, this time from the commander of the army unit patrolling 'Aboud. The commander told them: "Since today the village is quiet, I will give you the keys back."

In mid-October, a new military order, known as the "General Announcement Concerning the Export of Goods (Judea and Samaria), 1988," became public in the West Bank. The order was issued by the Head of the Civil Administration in the West Bank, Shaike Erez, pursuant to Military Order 1252, the "Order Concerning the Transportation of Goods (Judea and Samaria)(Order No. 1252) 1988," and was dated 1 September 1988.

Under the new order, which took effect on 1 September 1988, all previous export permits granted under Military Order 49 of 1967, ("Prohibition on the Transportation of Goods") were cancelled. Instead, general permission was given to export goods to Israel and Jordan (provided all outstanding taxes were paid) with the exception of those goods listed in schedules 1 (for Israel) and 2 (for Jordan) of the order.

Included in the two schedules were a number of products and materials, including quarry stone, saplings, sage, thyme, eggs, antiques, medicine, petrol, and others. Most prominent among these products, however, was olive oil, which was listed in both schedules 1 and 2. The new military order thus effectively prohibited the export of olive oil from the West Bank to both Israel and Jordan. At press time, it was not clear whether the order was being implemented or not. However, the fact remains that if the authorities decide to stop exports of olive oil to Jordan, they have created the legal basis to do so.

It is also not yet clear whether the order as well as rendering the traditional external markets inaccessible, also effectively prevents the direct export of olive oil and other goods to countries of the EC by blocking their transport through Israel. At press time, Israel's good faith in agreeing to implementation of the EC Regulation referred to above has yet to be tested. This latest military order cannot be seen as demonstrating any such good faith with regard to Palestinian agricultural exports.

Although the data for 1988 are not yet in, the disruption of the picking, processing, marketing and exporting of olives and olive oil is bound to have grave consequences for the West Bank economy. Over the period 1967-1985 the value of olives in the West Bank and Gaza constituted an average 14.52 percent of the total value of agricultural production, most of this deriving from the West Bank. However the percentage fluctuated between 3.8 and 37.9 percent. The proportion of West Bank GNP derived from agriculture as a whole is about a third. On average therefore about 5 percent of West Bank GNP derives from olives (including olive oil), although this has been as high as 12 percent in good years.

The 1988 olive harvest was widely expected to be a particularly good one for olives, worth as much as US$ 150 million according to local sources. The total value of olive oil that was expected to be available for export from the West Bank this year was approximately US$ 50-60 million. Already at the beginning of November, the price of a container of oil (17 kilograms) had, taking into account the devaluation of the dinar in October, fallen to more than 50 percent below the 1986 and 1987 prices.

The interference with the harvesting and marketing of agricultural crops and other products through military orders and the imposition of prolonged curfews violates several principles of international law:

(1) the absolute prohibition of collective punishment and reprisals, under Article 33 of the IV Geneva Convention 1949 and Article 50 of the Regulations appended to the 1907 Hague Convention; and

(2) the obligation to restore and ensure "l'ordre et la vie publics," under Article 43 of the Regulations appended to the 1907 Hague Convention: Israel as an Occupier is under a clear duty to maintain civil and economic life in the West Bank and Gaza Strip while retaining the right to take measures in the interest of security. However, through the use of collective penalties, Palestinian trade and the livelihood of whole communities are being held hostage to Israel's own political agenda. Rather than discharging its obligation to uphold and protect "la vie publique," Israel is employing sanctions that wilfully damage commercial life in the Occupied Territories, and threaten the livelihood of hundreds of thousands of people.

FOOTNOTES TO CHAPTER 7

1. The "General Announcement Concerning the Export of Goods (Judea and Samaria), 1988." For more detail, see the section on olives at the end of this chapter.
2. See section at the end of this chapter on the economic importance of olives and olive oil in the Occupied Territories.
3. See Jonathan Kuttab, "The Acquisition of Property in the West Bank," *Le Monde Diplomatique*, August 1983; Raja Shehadeh, "The Changing Juridical Status of Palestinian Areas under Occupation: Land Holdings and Settlements," in Naseer H. Aruri, editor, *Occupation: Israel Over Palestine*, AAUG, 1983; Mona Rishmawi, *Planning in Whose Interest? Land Use Planning as a Strategy for Judaization*, Al-Haq/Law in the Service of Man, 1986; and Raja Shehadeh, *Occupier's Law: Israel and the West Bank*, Washington, D.C.: Institute for Palestine Studies, 1985.
4. The State of Israel–Ministry of Defence, Coordinator of Government Operations in Judaea and Samaria, Gaza District, Sinai, Golan Heights, *A Thirteen-Year Survey (1967-1980)* Jerusalem, 1981, p. 2.
5. See, for example, Gerhard von Glahn, "Taxation under Belligerent Occupation," a paper presented at a conference organised by al-Haq in East Jerusalem, 22-25 January 1988.
6. Meron Benvenisti, *The West Bank Data Project: A Survey of Israel's Policies*. Washington, D.C.: The American Enterprise Institute, 1984, p. 10.
7. There is no regulation in the Territories which says that descriptions on products imported into the area should be written in Arabic. Medical drugs produced in Israel, for example, often include instructions written in Hebrew only. At the same time, any item produced in the Territories marketed in Israel must have Hebrew labelling.
8. See Raja Shehadeh, *Occupier's Law, op. cit.*, pp. 117-23.
9. *Jerusalem Post*, 15 February 1985.
10. Al-Haq has ample documentation about this practice in its files.
11. Al-Haq has ample documentation on this subject in its files.
12. The *Jerusalem Post* reported on 13 January that economic measures were under consideration by the Israeli cabinet. The measures remained unspecified, except for the "complete closure of the West Bank and Gaza to bar workers from coming to their jobs in Israel during widespread disturbances."
13. The Palestinian leadership has organised regular days of general strike, while setting limited opening hours for the remaining days of the week.
14. On 17 March, the army went around in jeeps equipped with loudspeakers in all areas of the West Bank, announcing that shops, contrary to the instructions of the Palestinian leadership, were to remain closed in the morning, and should open after the noon hour. *Al-Quds*, 18 March 1988.
15. Al-Haq Affidavit No. 1255.
16. Al-Haq Affidavit No. 1227.
17. Al-Haq Affidavit No. 1163.
18. Al-Haq documentation.
19. Reported in *al-Quds*, 24 March 1988.
20. *Jerusalem Post*, 24, 25, 28 April, and 9 November 1988.

21. *Jerusalem Post*, 6 May 1988.
22. For example, Middle East editor Yehuda Litani in the *Jerusalem Post*, 20 January 1988, and Defence correspondent Ze'ev Schiff in *Ha'aretz*, 20 March 1988.
23. *Jerusalem Post*, 15 February 1988.
24. *Al-Quds*, 18 March 1988, and quoting Rabin on 24 March 1988.
25. *Al-Quds*, 18 March 1988, quoting Ma'ariv.
26. Al-Haq has copies of the military orders in its files.
27. See, for example, *Jerusalem Post*, 8 May 1988.
28. *Jerusalem Post*, 13 May 1988.
29. *Jerusalem Post*, 15 June 1988.
30. Initially, the authorities informed the Jenin municipality that the pump would be repaired in 15 days. This did not happen. Al-Haq wrote a letter to the authorities on 8 August, requesting clarification as to why it took so long to repair the pump. The pump was eventually put back into operation on 28 September. According to al-Haq's calculations, more than 40,000 people were affected by the water shortage.
31. Al-Haq documentation.
32. Al-Haq documentation.
33. *Jerusalem Post*, 15 April 1988.
34. *Jerusalem Post*, 8 May 1988.
35. Al-Haq Affidavits Nos. 1257, 1368 and 1407.
36. Member of Knesset Dedi Zucker claimed at the end of June that he had similar information. *Jerusalem Post*, 29 June 1988.
37. See also, *Jerusalem Post*, 11 April 1988.
38. Al-Haq documentation.
39. *Al-Fajr* (English Weekly), 30 March 1988.
40. Al-Haq documentation.
41. *Jerusalem Post*, 23 June 1988.
42. *Jerusalem Post*, 3 July 1988.
43. *Jerusalem Post*, 23 September 1988.
44. *Jerusalem Post*, 9 September 1988.
45. Quoted by George Moffett in the *Christian Science Monitor*, 27 September 1988.
46. The reporter erred in the number of presses in Bal'a: there are only three.
47. Al-Haq Affidavits Nos. 1465 and 1466.

Appendix 7-A

AL-HAQ LETTER TO THE MILITARY AUTHORITIES CONCERNING TAX RAIDS

[Al-Haq letterhead]

28 July 1988
Our Ref: 2677

Mr. David Yahav
The Legal Advisor of the Military Government
Beit El

Dear Mr. Yahav,

Al-Haq would like to bring to your attention its account of the actions taken by the army in the El-Bireh/Ramallah area on 6 July 1988 to collect taxes from local residents and businesses.

At approximately 6:30 a.m. on Wednesday 6 July, a detachment of soldiers entered the towns of Ramallah and El-Bireh, erected a number of roadblocks, and began randomly confiscating identification cards and private cars. Residents were ordered to go the military governor's office, prove that they had paid all taxes imposed upon them and their buinesses, and only then would their property be returned.

In our view such measures are completely arbitrary and do not adhere to any form of legal procedure. The Jordanian Income Tax Law No. 25 of 1964 as amended by Israeli military orders, the "Regulation for Customs on Local Products" (vol. 72) and the "Regulation for the Organization of Account Books" (vol. 73), both appearing in *Proclamations, Orders, and Appointments Published by the Israeli Military Government in the West Bank* (1985), give the authorities wide-ranging powers to collect delinquent payments. Specifically, section 15 of the "Regulation for Customs on Local products" allows for a variety of measures to be taken, and has in fact been widely contested for the excessive powers it gives the authorities. It does not, however, under any circumstances grant powers for the confiscation of private property by extra-judicial measures. The procedures provided for in the regulations include prior written notification of delinquent payment and the right of appeal, both of which were rendered inoperative by the actions of the military on 6/7/88.

Most disturbing to al-Haq, however, is that the Ramallah events appear to be part of a larger pattern of such violations. The day after the incidents described above, for instance, on Thusday 7 July, staffmembers from al-Haq visited the town of Beit Sahour and reported that similar actions had taken place. In this case, however, soldiers also entered private homes, confiscating gold and monies, and imposed a prolonged curfew on the entire town which lasted until 17 July.

Al-Haq requests to know what the legal justifications are for such actions. If none exist we request the immediate cessation of such incidents.

We look forward to hearing from you.

Sincerely,

Mona Rishmawi, Advocate
Al-Haq

Appendix 7-B

LETTER FROM THE MILITARY AUTHORITIES CONCERNING TAX COLLECTION

[Military Government letterhead]

Judea & Samaria Region
Dept: of the Legal Advisor

To Adv. Mona Rishmawi Date: 24.10.1988
P.O. Box 1413 Ref: 6650 (411)
Ramallah

Subject: Letter dated 28/7/88 Regarding the levying of taxes

After receiving the responses of officials regarding this subject we would like to state as follows:

The levying of taxes is implemented through the use of legal means of levying [taxes]. The payment of taxes has recently decreased. It has therefore become necessary to apply tax collection measures to a larger number of tax payers. Only legitimate methods [of collection] have been adopted against these tax payers.

One of the methods used by tax collectors is to attach a lien on property and vehicles that belong to tax payers. [They do so] under the authority provided to them by the law concerning collection of public taxes, once the debt of the tax payers has become final.

It should be pointed out that due to the security situation prevailing in the region, soldiers accompany tax collectors. This, however, is done only for security reasons: Tax collection by the imposition of a curfew on a certain region has never been carried out. The drastic measure of imposing a curfew has been adopted only for security reasons.

Regarding the incidents that took place in Beit Sahour on 7 July 1988: Tax collection was carried out *without a curfew*. A curfew was imposed only after a riot by the residents took place, for security reasons and to safeguard public order. We will be ready in the future to deal with any application forwarded to us that includes accurate details of an incident (place and date of incident, and names of the people concerned). Other than this, we will not deal with general applications that are baseless and do not include aforementioned details.

Respectfully Yours,

Aluf-Mishne David Yahav, Legal Advisor

Chapter 8

REPRESSION OF EDUCATION*

A. Introduction

Educational institutions, educational activities, teachers and students in the West Bank have been subject to a series of repressive measures imposed by the military authorities since the beginning of the uprising in December 1987. These measures include: the long-term closure of schools; the prohibition of homestudy and make-up classes in alternative locations; the use of schools as military outposts and the destruction of school property; and military raids on primary and secondary schools.[1]

Most of these measures are not new. The Israeli authorities have limited academic freedom throughout the past 21 years of military occupation. The Israeli military shut Bir Zeit University, for instance, 14 times between 1973 (one year before it was upgraded to a university) and 1987.[2] Secondary and primary schools have also been closed in the past. In 1982, two governmental schools in Ramallah—the Secondary Girls' School and the Secondary Boys' School—were shut by military order for two months.

Measures which disrupt the education of individual students have also been utilised. Between 1983 and 1987, al-Haq documented numerous cases of short-term detention without charge of high school seniors during their matriculation exams. (There were 34 such cases in 1983 alone.)

In addition, in at least 5 separate incidents in 1984, threatening slogans or bombs were found in West Bank schools. In one case on 10 March 1984, two unexploded bombs were found at the United Nations Relief and Works Agency's elementary school for girls in Ramallah.

While historically students, teachers and educational institutions have been targetted by the Israeli army, the scope of the military

---

* An earlier version of this chapter was published in November 1988 as an al-Haq report under the title "Israel's War against Education in the Occupied West Bank: A Penalty for the Future."

restrictions on education during the last year has been unprecedented. These restrictions have had enormous impact on the population because of the traditional importance of education in Palestinian society.[3]

This chapter focuses on the closure of schools and argues that such closure is illegal. Three related topics are also considered: the prohibition of make-up classes, the military occupation of school buildings and subsequent destruction of school property, and military raids on schools.

In examining these areas, this chapter first presents the official Israeli position on various military actions and then explores the measures actually adopted. In the last section the actions of the Israeli military are analysed in light of local and international laws pertaining to education.

B. Israeli Justifications for Limiting Academic Activity

The Israeli military authorities have justified school closures on security grounds. As early as 24 December 1987, Defence Minister Yitzhak Rabin warned: "We will close schools which have ceased to fulfill their function as educational institutions and which have been consistent in allowing their children out into the street." Since the closure of all schools on 3 February 1988 the Israeli military authorities have offered similar explanations. For example, according to the *Jerusalem Post*, the Israeli Civil Administration of the West Bank described secondary and primary schools as "centres of unrest" and "centres of violent protest."[4]

Security is given as an explanation for the closure of universities as well. These institutions have been described by a military spokesman as "traditionally a hot-bed of anti-Israeli protest."[5] While no detailed rationale has been forwarded for the prohibition of make-up classes for students, the authorities have stated that such classes are "in violation of a military order," presumably a reference to the order closing educational institutions.[6]

C. Closure of Educational Institutions

The Israeli authorities' conduct towards academic activity during the last year does not indicate a concern for security. Rather, due to their breadth, the procedures used appear to be designed to penalise the community as a whole. Closure orders, for example, have not been issued solely to schools where "violent demonstrations" were alleged to have occurred. Instead, all 1,194 West Bank schools were closed simultaneously without regard for activities at any specific location.

At press time, during the last week of November 1988, all schools—public, private, those run by UNRWA, vocational training centres and universities—in all areas of the West Bank except East Jerusalem had been shut down by the military authorities.[7] Secondary and primary schools have not been permitted to operate for 8 of the last 12 months.[8] The four major universities and all institutes of higher education have now been closed for over 11 months.[9] The closure of every school, community college, and university in the West Bank affects approximately 300,000 school-age children, as well as 18,000 university and community college students. (Students of all ages constitute roughly 40 percent of the population of the West Bank.)

A closure order issued on 3 February 1988 simultaneously shut all primary and secondary schools "until further notice" just as they were resuming classes after their mid-year break.[10] It is clear from the timing of this order that it was not issued in response to sustained activities taking place on school grounds.

Moreover, no distinctions were made on the basis of grade level. Thus, even if the Israeli justifications for school closures were made in good faith, there is no explanation for preventing first and second graders (who obviously cannot be considered a threat to security) from attending school.

On 23 May 1988, West Bank schools that were not in areas under curfew were permitted to reopen. Some schools remained open until shut by a general closure order issued by the military on 21 July 1988.[11] Others were closed before 21 July, following what military spokesmen described as "disturbances." Not all of these disturbances were violent. Some consisted of sit-down demonstrations or the displaying of national symbols, such as the Palestinian flag. For instance, an UNRWA school at Nur al-Shams Refugee Camp was closed on 17 July 1988 because a Palestinian flag was raised on the building.[12] The displaying of such symbols and non-violent demonstrations do not in themselves threaten public order. They certainly do not merit so harsh a response as the closure of a school for a prolonged period.

Furthermore, in Gaza during the past year there have been at least as many clashes between school-aged children and the Israeli army as there have been in the West Bank. Yet primary and secondary schools in Gaza were permitted to open in the autumn.[13] This distinction highlights the logical inconsistencies in the justification offered for school closures.

D. Suppression of Alternative Education

The suppression of alternative classes most clearly discredits the security rationale offered for the closure of schools. Over the last twelve months, some teachers have given classes to small groups of students (five students at a time, for example) at off-campus locations in an attempt to off-set the consequences of long-term school closures. There has been no allegation that the participants in these classes are involved in anything other than purely academic activities. Nevertheless, these classes have been declared illegal and have repeatedly been raided by the Israeli military. These raids generally result in the arrest of students and teachers. To give one example, on 6 September 1988 the Society of Friends of Al-Najah University in Nablus (a community organization providing support to the University) was closed down "indefinitely" after soldiers raided the Society during a small make-up class for high school students. Two students and two teachers were arrested.[14] In this case the director of the Society was told he would be charged and prosecuted for permitting make-up classes to take place on the premises.

In October al-Haq learned that the Israeli military also informed schools that actions such as passing out workbooks to primary and secondary school chidren for home study would not be tolerated.

E. The Effects of the Closure of Educational Institutions

The closure of schools has had no noticeable effect on the level of protest. In fact, in many cases school closures have prompted demonstrations by school children and by the civilian population as a whole. In July, for instance, school children in Qalqiliya held a sit-down demonstration on school property to protest the closure of two of their schools. According to the *Jerusalem Post*, "[s]oldiers firing tear gas and rubber bullets entered the buildings and dozens of schoolgirls were injured..."[15] On 3 October 1988 a general strike was observed throughout the West Bank and Gaza to protest the closure of educational institutions. These and other examples demonstrate that school closures have not contributed to the "restoration" of public order.

The extended closure of educational institutions has had a number of serious consequences for the local community. For public government schools, continued school closures will result in an enormous strain on the educational infrastructure for the coming year. Approximately 30,000 children reached school-age this year. If the schools remain shut during the 1988-89 academic year, then next year's first-grade class will be twice as large. Public school teachers warn that the school system does not have the resources—human or physical—to absorb a 100 percent increase in the number of first-grade students. Public schools are already over-crowded. Class sizes range from 45 to 65 pupils per class. For instance, in 1987 teachers reported that in Bethany Elementary School in 'Izariya, there were 55 pupils in one second-grade class. Five of these students had to stand during classes because there was simply no space in the room for extra chairs. Thus, continued closures pose serious long-term problems for the entire system of public education.

Prolonged school closures may further exacerbate this problem by reducing the number of available public school teachers. On 15 April 1988 the military authorities announced that the approximately 9,000 public school teachers would receive only one half of their salaries for that month, and thereafter were on "unpaid leave" as long as schools remained closed. This policy was continued until 23 May when schools re-opened.[16] On 6 October 1988 the military again ordered that salaries not be paid while schools were closed. As a result many teachers have faced extreme economic hardship.

Primary school teachers point out that while closures retard the academic development of all children, they are particularly damaging for young children who have yet to learn to read or are in the process of becoming literate. The longer a child waits to learn to read, the more difficult it becomes.

The closure of schools during the spring term also created specific problems for high school seniors. Because schools were only allowed to open for two months in the spring of 1988, students were not able to cover sufficient materials to take the second half of their matriculation exams. As a result the exams were cancelled. Jordanian education authorities (who administer matriculation exams) agreed to double the scores from the first semester to allow these students to graduate. The resulting scores were less than sound. The questionable validity of the test results is an important issue because these scores form the basis for admission to universities in the West Bank and throughout the Middle East.

For private primary and secondary schools prolonged closure creates serious financial problems. Many such schools are on the brink of bankruptcy, because their major expenses, such as teachers' salaries and rent, have continued while income in the form of tuition payments has ceased. Private school administrators explain that they must continue to pay their teachers if they wish to have a staff when the schools are permitted to reopen. Moreover, private school enrollment for the 1988-

89 academic year has dropped dramatically. With continuing school closures, some parents prefer to send their children to schools in East Jerusalem or abroad. Consequently, even when schools reopen, tuition income will be less than before.

Extended closure has created similar problems for universities. No academic pursuits of any kind are permitted on university campuses while the closure orders are in force. As part of this policy, faculty and researchers are denied access to their laboratories and offices. Other university facilities such as libraries are closed to use. As a result the education and research of over 17,000 college students and 2,500 faculty and researchers has been halted.

Graduating seniors are especially affected by the closure of universities. Many have post-graduation plans for employment or graduate school that are contingent upon their attainment of a degree.

The institutions themselves have also suffered. Not having received tuition fees for almost a year, many universities and institutes of higher education (most of which are private) are currently facing a financial crisis.

F. Military Raids on Educational Institutions

In the two months schools were open (from 23 May through 21 July 1988), al-Haq received numerous reports concerning Israeli military harassment of school children and attacks on primary and elementary schools by soldiers armed with tear gas, rubber bullets and live ammunition.

These actions were not necessary for the maintenance of public order. In some instances schools were quiet before the arrival of the military. Educators report that in many instances the disturbances were provoked by an army presence in front of the school. In other cases, the Israeli army raided schools in response to demonstrations taking place on school grounds.

The amount of force used in these instances is excessive in proportion to the activities taking place. For example, on 27 June 1988 at approximately 8:45 a.m. a demonstration was held in al-Hussein Secondary School in the Hebron district. Students were sitting in the playground chanting slogans against the occupation. Soldiers surrounded the school and began shooting tear gas and rubber and alluminum bullets at the students. According to eye-witnesses, more than 30 students fainted from tear gas, and at least 15 were wounded by rubber or alluminum bullets.

G. Military Occupation of Schools and Destruction of School Property

The occupation of schools by Israeli military units has been a common occurrence during the uprising. The armed forces have used schools both as make-shift detention centres and as temporary military bases. For instance, the military turned the Bissan Elementary School in Nablus into a military base from 3 February to 4 May 1988, while the Beit 'Our Preparatory Girls School in the village of Beit 'Our al-Tahta in the Ramallah district was used as a detention centre for almost one-and-a-half months between 21 March and 6 May 1988.

A more recent example is the occupation of the Beit Sahour Secondary Boys' School in the Bethlehem district on 18 October 1988. On 27 October, the school administration was asked to pass on telephone, electricity and water bills to the military government.[17] This request suggested plans for a lengthy occupation, raising questions concerning the reopening of schools in the near future.

Evidence of army vandalism was found in more than 31 schools when they reopened in May 1988.[18] Journalists who visited Khalduniya School in Nablus (which was used as a military base from 3 February until the beginning of May 1988) said that they saw anti-Arab graffiti and Israeli army insignias painted and carved into the school walls; broken windows, desks, chairs, closets and laboratory equipment; and excrement both in the bathrooms and in adjacent rooms.[19] In addition, al-Haq has received numerous reports of the destruction of school equipment, particularly desks, chairs, books, and schoolroom windows in various parts of the West Bank.

H. Legal Analysis

1. The Illegality of the Use of Schools as Temporary Military Posts and of Military Raids on Schools

The occupation of schools and the destruction of school property are clear violations of international humanitarian law. Article 56 of the Hague Regulations addendum to the IV Hague Convention of 1907 (hereinafter Hague Regulations) expressly prohibits "all seizure of, destruction or willful damage [of] institutions dedicated to...education."[20] The international community developed the Hague Regulations to apply to the exigencies of war and belligerent occupation. They provide the minimum standards which must be accommodated irrespective of the circumstances. Therefore, security needs do not excuse the breach of this provision.

Military raids on schools are regulated by general principles of international humanitarian law which restrict the use of force against civilian objects. At the heart of these principles is the rule that the amount of force used should be in proportion to the incidents taking place. The indiscriminate use of rubber bullets and tear gas against school children who were not engaged in any activity or who were participating in a peaceful demonstration cannot be justified on the basis of this rule. Similarly, live ammunition—deadly force—cannot be used to repel force which is non-life threatening such as the throwing of stones.

2. *The Closing of Schools Violates Both Local and International Laws in Force in the West Bank*

Even if the security rationale put forward by the Israeli military were legitimate, the long-term closure of all schools would still be impermissible because it violates local and international laws in force in the West Bank. The West Bank is governed by Jordanian Law (the local law which was in force before the Israeli occupation of the West Bank in 1967) and Israeli military orders amending those laws. Also applicable are the Hague Regulations,[21] the IV Geneva Convention of 1949 Relative to the Protection of Civilian Persons in Time of War,[22] the Universal Declaration of Human Rights of 1948 and other basic human rights instruments. Virtually all of these treaties are breached by extended school closure. The following discussion analyses these violations, beginning with an examination of local law.

(a) *School closure orders violate local education laws*

Education in the West Bank is chiefly regulated by Jordanian Education Law #16 of 1964 (hereinafter Education Law #16) and amendments to it published by the Israeli military authorities.[23] According to Education Law #16, the Minister of Education's powers to close schools are very limited. He is also under an obligation to enforce compulsory education. Prolonged closures are therefore illegal.

Education Law #16 mandates compulsory education for children from the first through the ninth grades.[24] In addition, children under the age of 16 who wish to attend school cannot be denied access to education except for medical reasons.[25]

Moreover, primary and secondary school closures are explicitly prohibited by Article 112 of Education Law #16, which regulates school attendance at both the compulsory and voluntary levels of education. Article 112 states:

[T]he number of school days in each of the compulsory and secondary stages in each scholastic year shall be between 205-210 days for schools which have one vacation day per week and between 170-175 days for schools which have two days off per week...*It is not possible to end the school year except after this number of days has been completed.* [Emphasis added.][26]

As far as government schools are concerned, there are no exceptions to this rule.

As for private schools, there are clauses which allow their closure under specific circumstances. For example, Article 75 of Law #16 provides that a private school may be shut if the owner of such an institution contravenes a specific provision of the education law. However, there are strict procedural safeguards. The director of a private school must be given 10 days to correct the violation, and if the violation continues beyond that point the Minister of Education must recommend closure to the Council of Ministers who decide whether a school should be closed.

Article 97 provides that a private school may be shut for a short period if there are poor health conditions in a particular school building and if school administrators were instructed to rectify the situation but failed to do so during a three-month warning period. These are the only exceptions under the law and they clearly were not invoked and cannot be used as a legal basis for the orders closing schools for 9 of the last 12 months.

Military Order #854 of 1980, which amends Education Law #16, contains provisions relating to the licensing of private educational institutions. Paragraph (c) of Article 59, as amended, permits the Chief of Police and the Military Governor to "take into account considerations of public order among other considerations" when granting licences to educational institutions.[27] This amendment is also inapplicable here since private schools retained their licences during their closure by the armed forces. Furthermore, there are no licensing provisions for government schools. Therefore, the blanket closure of schools cannot be based on this regulation.

The legal basis for shutting a school should normally be contained in the order declaring the closure. However, the closure orders issued in the last 12 months fail to refer to any legal authority. In the majority of West Bank districts on 3 February 1988, for instance, the local district director (who is appointed by the Israeli Civil Administration) informed school administrators that the military had ordered schools to shut on 4 February 1988 and remain closed for an indefinite period of time. In the Ramallah school district, this directive was issued in written form. The order (consisting of one sentence) was distributed to administrators of Ramallah schools. It read as follows:

> The schools of this district will close until further notice as of the morning of Thursday, 4 February 1988.[28]

The Israeli military issued similar orders (verbally) to all West Bank school districts on 3 February 1988. Since no legal authority is referred to here or in subsequent orders, these are illegal directives.

Moreover, the closure of educational institutions "until further notice" was overturned by the Israeli High Court in 1981. That year, the court considered a case involving the shutting of Bir Zeit University for an indeterminate length of time. The court instructed the military authorities to replace the phrase "until further notice" with a specific period of time. The order issued on 3 February 1988 thus violates this directive.

There are no other provisions of local law which could possibly provide a legal basis for the shutting of educational institutions. Thus, neither Jordanian Education Law #16 of 1964 nor subsequent Israeli amendments grant the officer who replaces the Ministry of Education or any other officer appointed by him the power to shut educational institutions for prolonged periods of time. Therefore, school closure orders are clearly illegal under local law.

(b) *The protracted closure of schools and universities denies students of all ages the right to education as codified by international law*

The right to education is well established in international law. This right is articulated in the IV Geneva Convention, the International Covenant on Economic, Social and Cultural Rights, and the Universal Declaration of Human Rights, as well as in regional human rights treaties in force throughout Europe, the Americas and Africa. Article 26(1) of the Universal Declaration of Human Rights provides that:

> [e]veryone has the right to education...Technical and professional education shall be made generally available and higher education shall be equally accessible to all on the basis of merit.

The closure of all educational institutions for almost an entire school year and the arrest of students in alternative classes is an extreme violation of this right. Academic freedom has also been effectively terminated since teachers can be arrested for instructing even two students, and faculty, researchers and students are denied access to university libraries and laboratories.

Moreover, as an occupying power Israel has a duty under international law to provide education to primary and secondary school children. Article 50 of the IV Geneva Convention, for example, states that an occupier must "...facilitate the proper working of all institutions devoted to the care and education of children." The Universal Declaration of Human Rights[29] and the International Covenant on Economic, Social and Cultural Rights[30] also mandate compulsory education for children. Therefore, by preventing Palestinian children from attending school for seven of the last ten months, Israel has been in violation of international law.

(c) *The measures adopted by Israel ignore its obligation to protect public life*

The right to education is also generally protected by Israel's obligation to ensure "public order and safety" of the occupied population. This principle is often referred to as "la vie publique" or the general right to public life. It stems in part from Article 43 of the Hague Regulations. Article 43 states that the occupier:

> shall take all measures in his power to restore, and ensure, as far as possible, public order and safety, *while respecting, unless absolutely prevented, the laws in force in the country*. [Emphasis added.][31]

The logical application of this principle would place the occupier under an obligation to enable the local population to acquire education. An exception could arguably be made, however, if in extreme circumstances of public disorder the "safety" of the population could only be secured by short and temporary closures of schools in specific localities. The extended general closure of all schools cannot be justified on the basis of the above principle.

This becomes clearer when it is remembered that the orders closing all schools have also been interpreted by the military authorities as prohibiting the continuation of the educational process in any form—including make-up classes outside of school premises and even the distribution of homework to students.

Education is a basic right which the population must be allowed to enjoy. Therefore, even if schools were in fact "centres of unrest," as the Israeli authorities have often claimed without providing proof, the long-term closure of educational institutions is illegal.

In other parts of the world where law enforcement authorities have been faced with student protest, schools and universities have been closed for short periods of time. But the prolonged closure of *all* educational institutions appears to be without international precedent.[32]

I. Conclusion

As the above review of the local and international laws in force in the West Bank makes clear, the Israeli authorities' closure of all schools and universities for a prolonged period of time is blatantly illegal and constitutes an illegitimate exercise of power by the Israeli military.

The security rationale put forward by the government to justify school closure is supported by neither the facts nor the law. The Israeli government's actions force the conclusion that it is education itself that is targetted and that it is intended as another means of penalising the civilians living under occupation. It appears to al-Haq that the goal of this collective punishment is to raise the cost of the current uprising in the hope that the will of the local population will be broken.

The military are well aware of the high value which the Palestinian population has traditionally placed on education, and perhaps this has informed their decisions. It is undisputed amongst educators that denial of instruction to students at certain stages in their education leaves serious gaps in their cognitive development which will be very difficult to correct at a later stage. By preventing Palestinian students of all ages from receiving an education, the Israeli authorities are therefore punishing present and future generations.

FOOTNOTES TO CHAPTER 8

1. Educators and students have also been arrested, detained and in some instances deported. For example, Bir Zeit University reported that between 9 December 1987 and 15 October 1988 at least 123 students and 20 faculty or employees were detained. (University administrators pointed out that this figure may be incomplete due to the difficulty of compiling information while the University is closed.) On 1 August 1988, Ahmad Muhammad Jaber, a 35-year old field worker in Bir Zeit University's Adult Rural Education Programme, was deported to Lebanon along with seven other Palestinians. According to the *Jerusalem Post* of 2 August, Jaber is "accused of organizing riots and strikes." In addition, of the 25 Palestinians issued deportation orders on 17 August 1988, two were members of Bir Zeit University. One, Taysir 'Arouri, is a 42-year old lecturer in physics. The second, 'Abd-al-Hamid al-Baba, is a 25-year old student of chemistry. Both were alleged to have participated in popular committees set up during the uprising.
2. These closures were for various durations. See Bir Zeit University Public Relations Office, *A Report on the Status of Academic Freedom and Human Rights at Bir Zeit University in the Twentieth Year of the Israeli Military Occupation*, March 1988, page 21.
3. The long-term closure of all educational institutions has met with public opposition from the West Bank Palestinian community. Student groups, parents and teachers have all issued statements and protests demanding the re-opening of schools. For instance, the Union of Employees of the Educational Sectors of the West Bank (which includes employees of government, private and U.N. Relief and Works Agency [UNRWA] schools) published an open letter entitled "An Urgent Call To UNESCO" in October 1988 requesting that UNESCO guarantee formal education in the West Bank.
4. Joel Greenberg and Bradley Burston, "West Bank Schools to Reopen," *Jerusalem Post*, 18 May 1988. Also see Joel Greenberg, "Alternative Classes Blocked in West Bank," *Jerusalem Post*, 9 September 1988.
5. *Ibid.*
6. *Jerusalem Post*, 9 September 1988, *supra* note 4.
7. East Jerusalem, annexed by Israel in 1967, is not under military jurisdiction but governed by Israeli law. However, Palestinian schools in East Jerusalem have also been ordered shut for various periods of time during the last twelve months. For details of these closures see Appendix 8-B. Some facts regarding the repression of academic activity in Gaza are presented in Appendix 8-C. However, a full discussion of the situation in Gaza is not detailed in this report since al-Haq has not conducted fieldwork in Gaza.
8. See Appendix 8-A for full details of school closures.
9. University closures are detailed in Appendix 8-A.
10. Schools were to resume classes on 1 February 1988 after a six-week vacation in private schools, and an approximately one-month long break in public schools. It is important to note that by 3 February, all universities were also closed.
11. Due to the closure of all schools during the four months which normally constitute the spring semester, schools were to have operated until the end

of August, and to have begun the next school year in September 1988, forgoing the usual summer vacation.
12. See Joel Greenberg and Ben Lynfield, "Palestinians to Hold Solidarity Strike With Prisoners in Negev," *Jerusalem Post*, 18 July 1988.
13. This is not to suggest that education in Gaza has not been disrupted by military action. Curfews and short-term closures [for two or three days] have regularly obstructed the education process. However, classes have not been banned as a matter of policy.
14. See Joel Greenberg, "Alternative Classes Blocked in West Bank," *Jerusalem Post*, 9 September 1988.
15. Joel Greenberg and Joshua Brilliant, "Teenager Killed as Areas Unrest Continues," *Jerusalem Post*, 3 July 1988.
16. Teachers were paid between May and September 1988.
17. *Al-Tali'a*, 27 October 1988, page 8.
18. See Joel Greenberg, "School Kids Flock Back to Class in West Bank," *Jerusalem Post*, 24 May 1988.
19. *Ibid*.
20. The Hague Regulations are accepted by Israel as part of the body of customary international law.
21. *Ibid*.
22. Israel signed the IV Geneva Convention on 8 December 1949 and ratified it on 6 July 1951. However, Israel rejects the notion that the West Bank is an occupied territory. It maintains that the Territories were not part of any sovereign state and that therefore, legally, they are not occupied. As a consequence, the Israeli government does not view specific provisions of the Geneva Conventions which pertain to the duties of an occupier as applicable to the West Bank on a *de jure* basis. However, the Israeli government states that, *de facto*, it applies the "humanitarian" provisions of the Fourth Convention, without having ever specified what these are. It is important to note that Israel is alone in this interpretation of international law. The rest of the international community agrees that the West Bank and Gaza are under belligerent occupation, and that therefore the IV Geneva Convention is one of the laws in force in the Territories.
23. See the "Order Concerning Education Law Number 16, 1964, (Amendment for the West Bank), (Order Number 854), 5740-1980," issued by General Benjamin Eli'ezer, then Military Commander of the Central Area (which includes the entire West Bank). It is important to note that this order violates explicit restrictions contained in the IV Geneva Convention and the Hague Regulations pertaining to an occupier's powers to alter local laws. For an in-depth discussion of Military Order #854 see: Jonathan Kuttab, Esq., "Analysis of Military Order #854 and Related Orders Concerning Educational Institutions in the Occupied West Bank," al-Haq/Law in the Service of Man, 1981.
24. See Articles 10-12, Jordanian Education Law #16 of 1964.
25. *Ibid.*, Article 13.
26. Article 112 as amended by Jordanian Law #7; published in the *Official Gazette*, 16 January 1967, Gazette number 1978, page 21.
27. Amendment to Article 59 #5 (b. and c.) of Military Order #854; *supra* note 23.
28. See the copy of this order and al-Haq's legal opinion issued on 13 February

1988 in Appendices 8-D and 8-E.
29. Article 26(1) of the Universal Declaration states that "...Education should be free, at least in the elementary stages. Elementary education shall be compulsory." (Emphasis added.)
30. Signed by Israel on 19 December 1966. Entered into force in January 1976. Article 13(2) (a) provides that "[p]rimary education shall be compulsory and available free to all." (Emphasis added.)
31. Article 43 of the Hague Regulations, *supra* note 20. The term "vie publique" appears in the original French version. This provision of the Hague Regulations also restricts the ability of the occupier to change local laws. That aspect of Article 43 is inapplicable here since closure orders are simply directives issued by the military which have no legislative effect.
32. To the best of al-Haq's knowledge, the closest similar incident occurred in South Africa, during the uprising of 1985-86. In September of 1985 South African authorities closed down 20 schools in the Eastern Cape for three months in a reported response to student unrest and boycott of schools. (Various schools in other locations were closed for different time periods during that year.) However, that and subsequent school closures did not involve the shutting of all educational institutions for black students in South Africa for 9 months.

Appendix 8-A

THE CLOSURE OF WEST BANK EDUCATIONAL INSTITUTIONS (EXCEPT EAST JERUSALEM)

Schools

Primary and secondary schools were ordered to stop classes "until further notice" on 3 February 1988 and closed on 4 February. The order was renewed on a monthly basis until May. On 3 May the authorities announced that elementary and high schools could resume instruction of students in grades 1 through 6 on 21 May 1988. Classes were allowed to open for grades 7 to 9 on 28 May and on 7 June grades 10 to 12 were allowed to resume. Thus, by the first week in June elementary and high school students were back in school. It is important to note that some schools did not reopen at this time because they were located in areas which were under curfew.

When schools reopened, the military authorities stated that they could function until the end of August and begin the new school year in September. In mid-June, however, the army shut all schools for two days after, according to an army spokesman, "pupils in several schools had taken part in strikes and disturbances." (Joel Greenberg, "IDF Officer Hospitalized After Incident in Tulkarm; West Bank Schools Closed For Two Days," *Jerusalem Post*, 15 June 1988.) On 12 July 1988 six schools (in different locations) were ordered closed; on 15 July, 23 more schools were closed. On 21 July all the schools which were still open were ordered shut. The authorities gave 18 September as the new reopening date.

Kindergarten classes at private elementary schools were allowed to open in September 1988. Primary and secondary schools from first grade upward, on the other hand, were not allowed to open at that time. Instead, the authorities announced on 1 September that these schools must remain closed until 1 October 1988. On 30 September 1988 the closure order was extended; the new opening date was set for 15 November 1988, and then extended again until 1 December 1988, by which time this report had gone to press.

Institutes of Higher Education

Palestinian colleges and universities were not all closed on the same date. Bethlehem University, for example, received a three-month closure order on 29 October 1987 following demonstrations on campus during which a student was shot dead by the Israeli army. The University reopened on 1 February 1988 for one day. At the end of the day, school administrators were told that the University was "closed indefinitely." Bethlehem University has now been closed for over one year, the longest university closure in the West Bank since the beginning of the occupation. The four remaining major universities in the West Bank, Bir Zeit University, Hebron University, Al-Najah University and Jerusalem (Al-Quds) University, were closed in January 1988.

Several colleges and training institutes were closed during the first weeks of the uprising. For example, the Modern Community College and the Tira Community College for Women, both in Ramallah, were served with closure orders in December 1987.

By early February 1988, all Palestinian institutions of higher learning had been closed "until further notice." Individual closure orders were renewed on a monthly basis until August 1988. In August, all colleges and universities were informed—via the newspapers—of an extension of their monthly closure orders until 1 October 1988 and thereafter "until further notice." This order was then extended to 15 November on 30 September 1988. When the military government announced that it would begin reopening schools on 1 December 1988, it specifically excluded universities, stating that they would remain closed for the forseeable future.

Appendix 8-B

SCHOOL CLOSURES IN EAST JERUSALEM

The 31 government primary and secondary schools in East Jerusalem were closed for four months between 7 February and 22 May 1988. (The original closure order was for an indefinite period of time.) These schools service approximately 16,000 children. During that time, private East Jerusalem schools were on strike in protest at the closure of all other schools in the West Bank.

Schools were supposed to reopen at the beginning of September. However, only kindergarten and first-grade students were allowed back in classes on schedule. Two weeks later, on 14 September, second and third graders were permitted back to school. By 6 October 1988 all primary and secondary school children were able to attend classes. But one week later four East Jerusalem schools were re-closed by the Israeli military.

The Abou Dis College of Science and Technology in Jerusalem has been closed since December 1987.

Appendix 8-C

SCHOOL CLOSURES IN THE GAZA STRIP

The Islamic University in Gaza has been closed since December 1987. Primary and secondary schools, with the exception of those in areas under curfew, remained open during the winter and spring of 1988. However, according to educators 35 percent to 50 percent of the school days were lost (due, for example, to curfews); as a result the school year was extended for three weeks. The school year ended in June and exams were given in July 1988.

The re-opening of secondary schools this fall was delayed from September to 11 October 1988. Primary schools were permitted to open in September. The first six weeks of the 1988-1989 school year were used to review the previous year's work, again due to time lost during the 1987-1988 school year.

Appendix 8-D

ORDER CLOSING DISTRICT SCHOOLS ISSUED IN FEBRUARY 1988 BY THE MILITARY AUTHORITIES

In the name of God, the Merciful, the Compassionate

The Civil Administration for the Areas of Judea and Samaria
Office of the Director of the Education Department, Ramallah District

Number: 49/91/118
Date: 3 February 1988

To the Respected Principals of the governmental, UNRWA, and private schools.
Subject: Closure of Schools.

Greetings,
The schools of this district will close until further notice as of the morning of Thursday, 4 February 1988.

With respect,

(Signature)

The Director of Education
CC: The Officer of the Civil Administration for Educational Affairs.
The Director of Educational Planning, Curricula, and Supervision.
The UNRWA Director of Education
The UNRWA Educational Observer
File No. 14/90
File No. 71/100

Appendix 8-E

LEGAL OPINION ON THE CLOSURE OF SCHOOLS ISSUED BY AL-HAQ

[Al-Haq letterhead]

13 February 1988

The Directors of the Education Departments in the districts of the West Bank recently issued an order to all governmental, UNRWA, and private schools to close until further notice. In the opinion of al-Haq/Law in the Service of Man this order is both illegal and non-binding.

The above-mentioned order contradicts Jordanian Education Law No. 16 of 1964, still in force in the West Bank. Law 16 does not in any of its articles give the Director of the Education Department or even the Minister of Education the authority to collectively close schools for an indefinite period of time as has been done.

According to Article 26 of the Universal Declaration of Human Rights, education is a fundamental human right, and it is therefore impermissible to issue any declaration which brings the educational process to a halt.

Because the order affects approximately 285,000 students and may cause them to lose the entire school year, al-Haq considers it important to provide the students and their guardians as well as the school authorities with its legal perspective on the matter.

Chapter 9

REPRESSION OF ORGANISATIONAL ACTIVITY

A. Background

During twenty-one years of military rule, the Israeli authorities have made few efforts to provide needed services to the population in the West Bank and Gaza. In keeping with their agenda of gradual *de facto* annexation, services were furnished only to the extent absolutely necessary to satisfy the population's most basic needs, not to assist in the development of an infrastructure of services in the Territories.[1] In response, Palestinians in the 1970s began expanding existing charitable organisations, reviving trade unions whose activities had been frozen in 1967, and building new institutions to close the gap between the demands of a growing and diversifying population and the few services provided by Israeli government installations.[2]

Charitable, medical, educational, workers', professional and research organisations have played a dual role in the Territories. On the one hand, they compensated for the government's unwillingness to satisfy social needs by offering relief, organising literacy and vocational training classes, setting up health insurance schemes, providing preventive medical care in villages and camps, expanding knowledge of local history and culture through research, and so forth. On the other hand, being the only organisational forms permitted under occupation, they cemented the base of Palestinian society in the Territories and contributed to its leadership.

Two types of organisations exist in the Territories: formally registered institutions which conduct research and other activities and may or may not be service-oriented; and grassroots organisations which seek to mobilise people while providing services, and which may or may not be registered. Formal institutions include educational, research, charitable and human rights institutions and others. Grassroots organisations include trade unions, women's committees, voluntary work committees, medical and agricultural relief committees, as well as youth and cultural clubs throughout the Territories.

Israeli policy since 1967 has been to divide the population under its control in order to dominate it more easily. Although the authorities could not prevent the emergence of this organisational infrastructure, they have consistently attempted to break it and prevent it from becoming an alternative to their own administration. They have done so through administrative restrictions, through intimidation of the membership—actual or potential—of such organisations, and through harassment including detention and deportation of the organisations' leadership. On occasion, institutions have been closed, either for definite periods or permanently. The authorities routinely use administrative procedures to carry out their punitive actions, citing "security concerns" as a justification. Al-Haq has documented such practices since the mid-1980s, especially with regard to trade unions.³

B. Repression of the Labour Movement

During the uprising, the authorities targetted the Palestinians' organisational infrastructure, especially after their initial response to civil resistance—violence, mass arrests, deportations—had failed to achieve the desired results. Trade unions were early victims of the authorities' response to the uprising. According to al-Haq's documentation, during the entire period under review after December 1987:

(1) at least 24 trade union offices in the West Bank were closed down for periods ranging from one to two years. The authorities claim that trade unions are front organisations for factions in the PLO, but have not provided evidence for such charges.⁴

(2) the General Federation of Trade Unions in Nablus, one of three such labor federations in the West Bank, was closed down for two years for "security" reasons on 23 August. The closure also affected the work of six unions active in the Nablus area which have offices in the Federation's building.

(3) on 20 January, the army raided the compound housing the only seven labour unions in the Gaza Strip, confiscating documents present on the premises. Unionists reported, and a visiting al-Haq researcher verified, that soldiers smashed plumbing fixtures during the raid, which caused flooding in several of the offices.

(4) union activists have been detained, often administratively, i.e. for renewable periods of six months without charges or trial. On 26 August, at least 38 labour activists, many of whom are leaders of local unions or members of the executive committees of the labour federations, were in administrative detention.

(5) one labour leader was deported, and five more were ordered deported, without charges or trial:
- 'Adnan Dagher, former head of the Construction Workers Union in Ramallah and a member of the executive committee of one of the three labour federations, deported on 1 August;
- Radwan Ziyada, the Secretary-General of the Quarry Workers and Stonecutters Union in Hebron and a member of the executive committee of one of the three labour federations, ordered deported on 8 July;
- Muhammad al-Labadi, Deputy Secretary-General of the Workers Union Bloc (one of the four main union blocs in the West Bank), ordered deported on 8 July;
- Majed al-Labadi, brother of Muhammad, the Treasurer of the Printing Press Workers Union in East Jerusalem, ordered deported on 17 August;
- 'Oda Yousef Ma'ali, a member of the executive committee of the Hotel and Restaurant Workers Union in East Jerusalem, ordered deported on 17 August;
- Jamal Faraj, a member of the executive committee of the Construction and General Institutions Workers Union in Bethlehem, ordered deported on 17 August.

The new wave of repression against the union movement during the uprising has had a chilling effect on labour organising. Many unions not under formal closure orders have closed their offices voluntarily because workers and staff were staying away for fear of being arrested. The combined effect of the formal and voluntary closures has been a minimum of union activity in the Territories, despite continuing exploitation of workers,[5] both in the Territories and in Israel, which renders the work of trade unions crucial. According to labour organisers, a large number of workers from the Territories employed in Israel have lost their jobs due to frequent absences caused either by general strikes or army curfews on population centers in the Territories. In the West Bank and Gaza, workers face lay-offs as their employers are hit by the economic downturn during the uprising. Repression of the labour movement therefore exacerbates existing labour problems, while undermining one of the largest organisational infrastructures in the Occupied Territories.

C. Repression of Other Institutions

It was not until the summer of 1988 that the authorities began a concerted attack against other organisations, after earlier policies of brutal violence (see chapter 1 on the use of force) and mass arrests (see chapter 6 on the judicial system) had failed to put an end to the uprising. On 20 June 1988, some seven months after the beginning of the uprising, the army raided and partially closed the offices of the Society of In'ash al-Usra (Family Rehabilitation Society) in al-Bireh for a period of two years, claiming that materials of an inciting nature were kept in the Society. In'ash al-Usra is the largest charitable association in the Occupied Territories, servicing thousands of women and their families in the West Bank. Its closure affects especially the underprivileged population groups in the West Bank: village women, orphans and others.

The Society's president, Samiha Khalil, took the case of the closure of In'ash al-Usra to the High Court, where the military authorities have been asked to show cause why the society has been closed for two years, and the case is still pending. Shortly before appealing to the High Court, Mrs Khalil was charged before a military court with ten counts of incitement and one count of possession and distribution of "hostile materials." (See Appendix 9-A for a case study on In'ash al-Usra.)

The closure order against In'ash al-Usra turned out to be the first of a series of such orders against similar institutions in the Occupied Territories. In August, the authorities stepped up their repression of organisational activity in the wake of the announcement by King Hussein of Jordan on 31 July that Jordan would disengage legally and administratively from the West Bank, giving Palestinians a free hand to administer themselves. The Israeli authorities issued several warnings that they would prevent any organisational activity "linked to the PLO," and several of the institutions closed during August and September were in fact closed on the pretext that they served as covers for PLO activities. The institutions that were closed include, chronologically:

(1) *The Arab Studies Society* in East Jerusalem, the largest research organisation and resource center in the Occupied Territories employing a staff of 38, ordered (partially) closed for the period of one year on 30 July, for "security" reasons. According to the police, the Society was "controlled and financed by the Fatah organization and served as the organization's tool to promote its aims and attain the objectives of the uprising."[6] (See Appendix 9-B for a case study on the Society.)

(2) *The General Federation of Trade Unions* in Nablus, mentioned above, which was closed on 23 August.

(3) *The Society of the Friends of the Sick* in Tulkarem, a medical institution, closed for two years on 23 August, for "security" reasons. (See Appendix 9-C for a case study on the Society.)

(4) *The Organisation for the Care of Ecology and Society* in

Qalqiliya, a small charitable organisation, closed for a year on 23 August, for "security" reasons.

(5) *The Federation of Professional Associations* in the East Jerusalem suburb of Beit Hanina, which houses seven professional associations, closed for the period of one year on 26 August. The authorities claimed, according to the weekly *al-Fajr* (28 August), that "meetings inspired by the PLO were held at the building in order to establish alternative bodies to those of the Israeli 'civil administration.'" The compound comprises offices for the associations of doctors, dentists, engineers, agricultural engineers, lawyers, veterinarians and pharmacists.

(6) *The Federation of Charitable Associations* in East Jerusalem, which coordinates activities of some 106 member societies in the West Bank, closed down for a year on 28 August. According to Israeli police sources quoted by the *Jerusalem Post* (29 August), the Federation had served as a conduit for PLO funds to the Occupied Territories, "which are distributed under the cover of welfare and economic aid and are used to advance PLO objectives in the area."

(7) *The Society of Friends of Al-Najah University* in Nablus, an educational organisation, closed indefinitely on 5 September. Authorities told the Society's director that he had violated a military order by allowing (high school) classes to be held in the building.[7]

(8) *An additional fourteen educational centers* in Nablus, closed on 19 September, for the same reasons as in the case of the Society mentioned in (7) above.

Other Palestinian institutions have experienced other forms of obstruction. For example, the offices of the Economic Development Group, a Palestinian non-profit development organisation in East Jerusalem, were raided on 18 July 1988 by Israeli army and police, preventing a meeting with dairy producers that had been scheduled to take place on the premises that day. Members of the Group have been called in by the authorities for questioning as well. A meeting of the Palestinian Society for the Study of International Affairs on 20 August was canceled after the organisation's director, Dr. Mahdi 'Abd-al-Hadi, received a warning from the authorities not to proceed, and the army and members of the Israeli intelligence service cordoned off the neighbourhood in East Jerusalem where the meeting had been scheduled to take place.[8]

Steps have also been taken against individual members of such organisations. For example:

(1) Feisal al-Huseini, director of the Arab Studies Society, was placed in administrative detention (without charges or trial) for a period of six

months on 30 July. He had previously been in administrative detention from 13 April 1987 until 9 July 1987, and from 12 September 1987 until 9 June 1988. Amnesty International has adopted him as a Prisoner of Conscience;

(2) Amin al-Khatib, chairperson of the Federation of Charitable Associations, was placed in administrative detention for a period of three months (a period later reduced to two months) on 20 July 1988;

(3) Samiha Khalil, director of In'ash al-Usra, was formally charged with incitement and possession of illegal material and was awaiting trial at press time;

(4) Dr. Nabil al-Ja'bari, head of the Board of Trustees of Hebron University, spent just over two months in administrative detention, from 10 March until 13 May 1988.

D. Banning of Popular Organisations

The authorities have also targeted the informal mass organisations. The first to be affected was the Shabiba ("Youth") Movement in the Territories, an umbrella grassroots organisation that was active in a number of local committees in the Territories, including trade unions and student committees. The Shabiba movement was outlawed by the authorities under Article 84 (1)(b) of the British Defence (Emergency) Regulations 1945 on 19 March 1988 on the claim that it was "one of the front organizations of Fatah" in the Territories.[9] According to Joel Greenberg, writing in the *Jerusalem Post* of 20 March,

> The Shabiba, whose members include college students, pupils, and Palestinian youngsters not in school, has branches throughout the Territories and in East Jerusalem...Among its open activities were community projects such as home renovation, aid to the elderly and youth programmes. Security officials considered it to be in fact a recruiting mechanism for Fatah, through which young Palestinians are mobilized for anti-Israel attacks and nationalist political activity.

As a result of the legal ban, any member can now be arrested and tried, even for performing such innocuous activities as aiding the elderly. However, since arresting and detaining all members of the Shabiba movement is impossible, the outlawing of the movement means a relaxation of existing legislation on Palestinian organisations, making it possible for the authorities to make selective arrests of community activists who cannot otherwise be accused of any illegal activities. The Ministry of Defence reported on 19 March that several youth centers run by Shabiba had been closed down,[10] while lawyers report that hundreds of detainees have been charged with membership in the Shabiba movement.

On 18 August, the authorities went even further, outlawing the so-called "popular committees." These committees have been set up in villages, camps and neighbourhoods since the beginning of the uprising to provide vital services to the population living in an emergency situation, and to carry out the instructions of the Palestinian local leadership. The banning order was issued by a decree of the Minister of Defence under Article 84 (1)(b) of the British Defence Regulations.[11] A statement issued by the Ministry of Defence stated that "any person remaining a member of the popular committees, and any person assisting them faces imprisonment and prosecution."[12]

Defence Minister Rabin clarified that the banning order "provided a more convenient legal means to deal with the members and leaders of the popular committees" which, he claimed, had been responsible for the "institutionalization of the uprising."[13] On the day of the banning order, the authorities announced that between 200 and 300 activists of the popular committees were already being held in administrative detention in the Ansar III prison camp in the Negev, and that the 25 Palestinians ordered deported on 17 August were also committee activists.[14]

By its sweeping nature, the order banning popular committees affects the work of a large number of grassroots, service-oriented committees throughout the Territories. For example, any member of a committee providing preventive health care in a refugee camp now runs the risk of being prosecuted for membership in an illegal organisation. If carried out with full force, the banning of the popular committees will effectively thwart all grassroots activity in the Territories. At best, the banning will deter health professionals and others from participating in vital humanitarian activities on a mass level.

E. Rights Violated

The sweeping nature of the measures against popular organisations in the Territories in 1988, especially against organisations carrying out charitable activities, seems to indicate an intent to undermine the institutional infrastructure of the Palestinian population in the Occupied Territories.[15] However, the right of individuals to participate in the cultural and social development of their community is recognised in a variety of international human rights instruments, including the 1948

Universal Declaration of Human Rights. The importance of this right together with related rights such as freedom of expression and freedom of thought and conscience cannot be overstressed, constituting as they do basic requirements in democratic societies.

Despite Israel's obligation as an occupant under international law to restore and ensure public order and safety, the authorities have, during the last two decades, and especially since the beginning of the popular uprising in December 1987, harassed local charitable and other voluntary organisations, making their proper functioning difficult. As stated above, institutions have been shut down for varying periods of time, and members have been arrested. In the past, such organisations have been raided, and materials have been confiscated. At times, soldiers would be posted at the entrance of a building and force anyone wishing to enter to be photographed. Generally, funding of such organisations from abroad has been made difficult through military orders (e.g. M.O. 998 of 1982) and additional restrictions placed on entry of money during the uprising. Moreover, charitable organisations in the Territories are not exempt from paying value-added tax (VAT), unlike charitable organisations in Israel itself. (See Chapter 7, on economic sanctions.)

The standard accusations by the authorities justifying the closure of such organisations are that they are fronts for banned organisations (usually factions of the Palestine Liberation Organisation), as in the case of the trade unions, or that activities hostile to the State of Israel have taken place on the premises, as for example in the case of In'ash al-Usra. The order closing the building is usually based on the Defence (Emergency) Regulations 1945. Article 129 (1)(b) of these Regulations states:

(1) A Military Commander may by order...

(b) if it appears to him to be necessary or expedient so to do in the interests of public safety, the defence of Palestine or the maintenance of public order, require the occupiers of premises of any specified class or description or of any specified premises, throughout his area or in any specified town, village, quarter or street to close and keep the same closed for such period as may be specified, together with any gates or other openings leading thereto.

If in fact illegal activities took place on the premises of an organisation, the military authorities can bring those responsible to court and provide evidence of the alleged offences.[16] In the absence of concrete evidence concerning alleged illegal activities of organisations in the Territories, the authorities customarily resort to an administrative, extrajudicial measure, which allows them to close a building without bringing formal charges or presenting evidence. In addition, it is not the organisation's activities that are banned, but the building that is closed, so that no activities, of any nature, can take place within. If the authorities were legitimately concerned about the legality of certain activities taking place inside a building, the logical response would be to bring charges against those responsible or to ban the organisation, not to close the premises while permitting the organisation to reconstitute itself and continue its work elsewhere.

In al-Haq's view, closure orders against Palestinian institutions in the Occupied Territories and the banning of grassroots movements constitute a violation of the internationally-recognised right to freedom of assembly, as well as a violation of due process. The right to a fair trial is at the root of any civilised system of justice. (See Article 10 of the Universal Declaration of Human Rights, and Articles 71-73 of the IV Geneva Convention 1949.)

In none of the closures mentioned above did the authorities issue a prior warning against those in charge of the organisation; in no case were those in charge given the opportunity to see or hear any evidence against the organisation. Indeed the manner and timing of the closures seem designed to ensure the absence of any reasoned response. Continuing harassment of organisational activity in the Occupied Territories is a grave violation of the authorities' obligation under international law to restore and maintain public order.

FOOTNOTES TO CHAPTER 9

1. Budgets for schools and hospitals run by the government, for example, have been wholly inadequate. Government hospitals complain of insufficient and insufficiently trained staff, a shortage of equipment and medical supplies, and low salaries compared with the private sector. Health care is curative rather than preventive. Little is spent on the infrastructure: there are still many areas without piped water, with poor sanitation and sewage systems, and a high ratio of persons per house, especially in the refugee camps. As a result, common problems and diseases in the Territories are malnutrition and respiratory and gastro-intestinal infections. Low budgets for public schools have led to serious overcrowding, with an average of 35 students per class (as opposed to 27 per class in Jewish schools in Israel). Schools have been subject to frequent closures, and teachers have been arbitrarily dismissed or transferred to other areas.
2. See Joost R. Hiltermann, "Before the Uprising: The Organization and Mobilization of Palestinian Workers and Women in the Israeli-Occupied West Bank and Gaza Strip," PhD Dissertation, University of California, Santa Cruz, 1988.
3. See Joost R. Hiltermann, "Mass-Based Organizations in the West Bank and Gaza: Offering Services Because of and Despite the Military Occupation." Presented at a conference organised by al-Haq in Jerusalem, 22-25 January 1988.
4. For arguments concerning this issue, *ibid.*
5. See "Testimony of al-Haq/Law in the Service of Man Before the Generalized System of Preferences SubCommittee," 1988.
6. Quoted in the *Jerusalem Post*, 2 August 1988.
7. *Jerusalem Post*, 6 September 1988.
8. *Al-Fajr* weekly, 28 August 1988.
9. *Jerusalem Post*, 20 March 1988.
10. *Ibid.*
11. The military order that was issued to announce the banning was signed by the Military Commander of the Central Area, General Amram Mitzna.
12. *Jerusalem Post*, 19 August 1988.
13. *Ibid.*
14. *Ibid.*
15. The declaration of an independent Palestinian state on 15 November 1988 could do little in the short term to alter the status of the Occupied Territories, whose inhabitants for all practical purposes remain, at least for the time being, stateless.
16. They have done so in only one of the cases mentioned in this chapter, the case of Samiha Khalil, the director of In'ash al-Usra. If Mrs Khalil is in fact found guilty and convicted, closing the organisation would still be an extra-judicial punishment, affecting a large number of staff and an even larger number of West Bankers who benefit from the organisation's services.

Appendix 9-A

THE SOCIETY OF IN'ASH AL-USRA IN AL-BIREH

In'ash al-Usra, founded in 1965, is the largest charitable organisation in the West Bank. During the last 23 years it has provided basic social services to the Palestinian community.

The Society's work centers on the needs of Palestinian society. Its program has been adapted to local conditions over time. After the Israeli occupation of the West Bank in 1967 the activities of In'ash al-Usra focussed on offering short-term relief to Palestinian refugees and other victims of the war in charitable form. Soon thereafter, however, the Society changed its priorities and began providing work opportunities in order to allow people to fulfill a productive role in their communities. Income-generating projects in which many people, especially women, became involved were initiated. Until its closure in June 1988, the Society operated the following productive projects:

(1) Sewing: In'ash al-Usra workshops manufactured ready-made clothes which were sold in local markets and did not compete with Israeli products. Clothes were also sewn on order. Workers involved in this project were employed by the Society.

(2) Knitting: This project was divided into two sections. Hand-knitting was done by women in their own homes, and machine-knitting was carried out on the premises of the Society.

(3) Embroidery: Women in villages were paid by In'ash al-Usra to produce traditional Palestinian embroidery. The work was carried out by women in their homes, but finished items would then be marketed by the Society at its distribution centre. Besides being an income-generating project for women, this initiative also fulfilled one of the primary aims of the Society: the preservation and dissemination of Palestinian heritage and culture.

(4) Bakery: Biscuits and cakes were produced at the Society and sold in local Palestinian markets.

(5) Home products: Women prepared and preserved food products which were then sold locally by the Society.

Through these productive projects, the Society of In'ash al-Usra became increasingly self-sufficient, and was thus able to increase its charitable activities, which included the following:

(1) Financial aid to victims of war and needy families unable to support themselves.

(2) A sponsorship project by which friends of the Society inside the West Bank or abroad sponsored children whose parents had been killed during the 1967 war or were serving long periods of imprisonment in Israeli detention centers.

(3) Scholarships for children from poor families and scholarships and loans for university students.

(4) Medical assistance for the needy. This was done through agreements with Palestinian doctors who were ready to treat an avarage of ten cases annually free of charge. The Society also had an agreement with a Palestinian hospital to transfer any case for treatment free of charge.

As a women's organisation, In'ash al-Usra has offered vocational training in different occupations to women in order to increase their employment opportunities. Until its closure, the Society had five vocational centers which included training in the following occupations: sewing, machine-knitting, hair-dressing and beauty training, embroidery by machine, and business and secretarial training.

The Society of In'ash al-Usra also operates an orphanage, a nursery and a kindergarten. In cooperation with the Higher Committee for Adult Education in the Occupied Territories, it runs a literacy campaign for women. The Society has a library that is open to the public.

On 8 June 1988, prior to the closure order, the Society of In'ash al-Usra was raided by the army and a number of files and letters, a register of addresses, and video cassettes were confiscated. The raid took place when the town of al-Bireh was under curfew and at a time when the president of the Society, Samiha Khalil, was not present. After the raid Mrs Khalil was summoned several times to the Ramallah police station, where she was interrogated about the confiscated material. On the day of the closure, 20 June, the premises of the Society were searched again by the army, who confiscated more material. Mrs Khalil was summoned for interrogation and told that the authorities would press charges. No charge sheet was prepared, however, until after the Society appealed the closure order to the High Court.

The closure order against In'ash al-Usra, although excluding the nursery, orphanage, and kindergarten, has disrupted the functioning of the whole organisation and has deprived hundreds of Palestinian families from their only source of income and financial aid. 152 persons are employed in full-time jobs at In'ash al-Usra, while 4,800 women are employed in the village embroidery project. The closure order will also prevent 1,300 children from receiving aid through the sponsorship project and prevent approximately 200 women students trained at the vocational training centers from receiving their certificates, thus eliminating their employment opportunities outside the Society. Most importantly, however, both rural and urban inhabitants of the West Bank will be denied the much-needed services offered by the Society.

Appendix 9-B

THE ARAB STUDIES SOCIETY IN EAST JERUSALEM

The Arab Studies Society, founded in 1980, is a non-profit research organisation based in East Jerusalem. With a staff of 38, it has sought to conduct wide-ranging research into social, economic, political and cultural aspects of Palestinian society in Israel and the Occupied Territories, as well as Arab civilisation in general.

The Society was closed for the period of a year, by military order, on 30 July 1988. The following facilities were effectively terminated as a result of the closure order:

(1) the documentation and information center, including:
- a library containing over 5,000 books and periodicals in Arabic, English and Hebrew dealing with Middle East issues. The library includes encyclopedias and a collection of British government documents from the Mandate period.
- documentation and information archives comprising hundreds of documents (including originals) related to Palestinian and Israeli affairs from 1918 to the present day.
- newspaper archives consisting of indexed articles on over 1,000 topics from Palestinian daily newspapers and the *Jerusalem Post* from 1979 to the present day.
- collections of historical maps of Palestine and of photographs of Palestinians and significant sites.

(2) the research center, which has conducted in-house research and published a number of studies under the Society's name.

(3) the statistics center, which has produced statistical studies on the Occupied Territories.

(4) the Israeli affairs center, which has translated articles from Israeli Hebrew-language papers and magazines into Arabic and English, and has published selections of these articles in a periodical.

On 3 August, four days after the forced closure of the Society, the Society's premises were again raided by the army. Valuable property belonging to the Society was confiscated, including archive files, newspaper clippings, computers discs, a list of library books and the office personnel file.

Appendix 9-C

THE SOCIETY OF FRIENDS OF THE SICK IN TULKAREM

The Society of Friends of the Sick in Tulkarem, founded in April 1986, is a member of the General Association of Charitable Societies in East Jerusalem, whose offices were closed on 28 August 1988. The Society is unique in the Tulkarem area in providing medical services at low cost to hundreds of families in the town and in surrounding villages and camps, the majority of them low-income families.

The following facilities were closed as a result of the order issued by the Military Commander on 23 August:

(1) a physiotherapy unit, which treats an average of 200 patients each month. Handicapped patients from the Tulkarem area with mobility problems greatly benefited from the Society's proximity.

(2) laboratory facilities.

(3) an X-ray unit, which cost 50,000 Jordanian dinars (approximately $125,000) and had begun operations only shortly before the closure.

Patients now have to travel over 30 miles to the nearest medical facilities, in Nablus. For some, age or physical handicap has made this impossible. In addition, the closure effectively terminated the employment of the Society's 12 staff members.

Following the closure, the Society's director, Dr. Riyad Shalabi, fearing that the Society's equipment might suffer due to prolonged neglect, asked permission from the military authorities to remove the equipment, and especially the X-ray facility, from the Society's premises. When this request was denied, Dr. Shalabi asked the authorities for permission to donate the equipment to the government hospital in Tulkarem, again in vain.

CONCLUSION

When the Israeli occupation of the West Bank and Gaza began, the military commanders of the two regions issued military proclamations which concentrated all legislative, executive and judicial power in their hands. Since then, there has no longer been a real possibility of civil life in the Occupied Territories consistent with the principle of the rule of law.

Today, twenty-one years later, the situation speaks for itself. As the report demonstrates, the Israeli authorities' heavy-handed response to the Palestinian uprising has been out of all proportion to accepted norms. This response has taken the form not only of a brutal military repression but also far-reaching attacks on the Palestinian economic and social infrastructure—including the long-term closure of schools and universities. Furthermore, this year has marked the first time that ongoing flagrant violations of human rights have been publicly proclaimed and pursued as policy at the highest levels of the Israeli government.

When one looks at the totality of Israeli practices in the Occupied Territories, one conclusion is inescapable: that the current situation cannot be allowed to continue. Nor can there be any countenancing of the Israeli hope of a return to "order" or "normalcy." It is precisely the Israeli version of "order" that maintained an administrative and military system of control which has consistently violated the most basic human rights for twenty-one long years of occupation. The "normalcy" that Israel advocates is one where the military authorities legislate, execute and judge, and are free to pursue a mission consisting of the progressive alienation of Palestinian land and establishing illegal Jewish settlements on it. Israel is an occupier with an agenda in which the rights and aspirations of 1.5 million Palestinians under its rule have no place.

The Israeli measures of control described in this report and put to such brutal use in confronting the uprising were developed and refined throughout the two decades of occupation. During these twenty years, the world community of states did not succeed in securing Israel's compliance with its obligations under international law. In the twenty-first year, the Palestinians rose up in a clear expression of a population's assertion of its rights in the spirit of self-reliance; in response, the Israelis came down hard, setting new precedents of violations and abuses. At the high cost of hundreds dead, tens of thousands wounded and imprisoned, hundreds of homes demolished and a near-ruined economy, the international community is being served with an urgent notice: the absolute necessity for immediate change.

The urgency of the situation demands, at a minimum, a temporary interim measure to protect the Palestinian population. To this end al-Haq has recently directed its efforts towards the options available under international law. Article 1 of the Fourth Geneva Convention states:

> The High Contracting Parties undertake to respect and to ensure respect for the present Convention in all circumstances.

States thus have a legal obligation to *ensure respect* for the provisions of the Fourth Geneva Convention using such legal means as they have at their disposal. Until now, the instruments of international humanitarian law referred to in this report have been used only as yardsticks against which to assess violations, and in real terms have afforded the Palestinians of the Occupied Territories *none* of the protections enshrined in their provisions. Article 1 is a basis for the active international intervention to safeguard the lives and rights of the Palestinians as Protected Persons under the Convention that has been lacking in the past. Without an active commitment on the part of the international community of nations, the avenues of legal protection for Palestinians in the Occupied Territories from abuses, excesses, and systematic policies which violate their guaranteed rights are effectively non-existent.

However, enforcement of the law regulating occupation is not an end in itself since it is abundantly clear from the report that the Israeli military occupation is ultimately irreconcilable with the principle of the rule of law. Enforcement of the law is thus merely an interim measure for the safeguarding and preservation of those human and physical resources which form the basis of the Palestinian nation. Clearly, the most fundamental right of a people, recognised as such by the international community, enshrined in the body of international law, and proclaimed by the community of nations as binding, is the right to self-determination.

The attainment of this right has been the central and primary aim of the Palestinians within the Occupied Territories and without. This remains the main hope for permanently guaranteeing the Palestinians a life free of human rights abuses and unjustifiable regulations; a life in which one can write without censorship, travel without restrictions, associate without penalty, and pay taxes while fully cognizant of and in agreement with how one's money is spent. In other words, the demand is for a truly normal society under the rule of law, where due process is faithfully respected and conflicts are resolved peacefully through an independent judiciary. These principles were affirmed on 15 November 1988 by the Palestine National Council in its Declaration of Independence of the Palestinian State. The PNC also sounded a welcome note in its commitment to the Universal Declaration of Human Rights and to the principles of non-discrimination on grounds of race, religion, colour, creed, or sex.

The Palestinians' insistent call for the realisation of their right to self-determination, besides being a demand for a life of dignity and freedom, also embodies the hoped-for re-constitution of the Palestinian nation. Such a hope is inconsistent with Israel's aforementioned agenda, and therefore, any expression of it, in the occupier's view, must be punished. The occupier's attack on this nation is—no more and no less—a punishment for its desire to be.

About South End Press

South End Press is a nonprofit, collectively run book publisher with over 150 titles in print. Since our founding in 1977, we have tried to meet the needs of readers who are exploring or are already committed to the politics of radical social change. Our goal is to publish books that encourage critical thinking and constructive action on the key political, cultural, social, economic, and ecological issues shaping life in the United States and in the world. In this way, we hope to give expression to a wide diversity of democratic social movements and to provide an alternative to the products of corporate publishing.

If you would like to receive a free catalog of South End Press books or get information on our membership program—which offers two free books and a 40% discount on all titles—please write us at South End Press, 116 Saint Botolph Street, Boston, MA 02115.

Other Books of Interest Available from South End Press

The Battle of Beirut:
Why Israel Invaded Lebanon
Michael Jansen

The Fateful Triangle:
The United States, Israel, and the Palestinians
Noam Chomsky

Israeli Foreign Policy:
South Africa and Central America
Jane Hunter

My War Diary:
Lebanon, June 5—July 1, 1982
Dov Yermiya

Intifada:
The Palestinian Uprising Against Israeli Occupation
Zachary Lockman & Joel Beinin